**THE BOOK** ®

# Ford Ka
# Service and Repair Manual

A K Legg LAE MIMI

*(3570 - 1AM3 - 224)*

**Models covered**

All Ford Ka models

1299 cc petrol engine

© Haynes Publishing 2008

ABCDE
FGHIJ

A book in the **Haynes Service and Repair Manual Series**

ISBN **978 1 85960 928 6**

**British Library Cataloguing in Publication Data**
A catalogue record for this book is available from the British Library.

Printed in the USA

**Haynes Publishing**
Sparkford, Yeovil, Somerset BA22 7JJ, England

**Haynes North America, Inc**
861 Lawrence Drive, Newbury Park, California 91320, USA

**Haynes Publishing Nordiska AB**
Box 1504, 751 45 UPPSALA, Sverige

# Contents

## LIVING WITH YOUR FORD KA

## Roadside Repairs

## Weekly Checks

## Lubricants, fluids and tyre pressures

## MAINTENANCE

## Routine maintenance and servicing

# Contents

## REPAIRS & OVERHAUL

## REFERENCE

The Ford Ka model range was introduced into the UK in October 1996 as a radically-styled supermini car. It is available in three main variants - the basic Ka version, the Ka-2 model which has power steering as standard, and the Ka-3 model which has both power steering and air conditioning. Also there has been a number of Special Editions introduced throughout the years, which are available in different level of trims. In October 2000, the Ka 1.3 Luxury was introduced, which has extras including alloy wheels, chrome exhaust tailpipe, leather interior and radio/CD player.

The transversely-mounted engine is the well-proven 1.3 litre Endura-E push rod engine which has been fitted to Fiesta and Escort models for many years, although the Ka engine has been considerably updated and is fitted with sequential injection and Ford's EEC-V electronic engine management system.

A manual 5-speed transmission is fitted, being mounted at the left-hand side of the engine.

All models have front-wheel-drive with fully-independent front and semi-independent rear suspension. The front suspension is of conventional McPherson strut type, incorporating lower arms, and an anti-roll bar. The rear suspension comprises a rear 'twist-beam' axle with trailing arms and McPherson struts.

Rack and pinion steering is fitted to all models. Power-assisted steering is fitted as standard on Ka-2 and Ka-3 models, the pump being belt-driven from the engine crankshaft pulley.

The brakes are vacuum servo-assisted and split diagonally as a safety feature.

All models have a comprehensive trim level. A driver's air bag is fitted as standard, and a passenger's air bag is optional. On later models, side airbags are also available. Electric windows, anti-lock brakes, and air conditioning are all available.

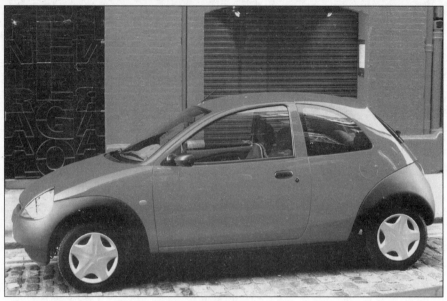

**Ford Ka**

For the home mechanic, the Ford Ka is a straightforward vehicle to maintain, although access to some components from the top of the engine is restricted. From beneath the engine, access to most components is easy. Running costs for the Ford Ka have been intentionally kept to a minimum.

## Your Ford Ka manual

The aim of this manual is to help you get the best value from your vehicle. It can do so in several ways. It can help you decide what work must be done (even should you choose to get it done by a garage). It will also provide information on routine maintenance and servicing, and give a logical course of action and diagnosis when random faults occur. However, it is hoped that you will use the manual by tackling the work yourself. On simpler jobs it may even be quicker than booking the car into a garage and going there twice, to leave and collect it. Perhaps most important, a lot of money can be saved by avoiding the costs a garage must charge to cover its labour and overheads.

The manual has drawings and descriptions to show the function of the various components so that their layout can be understood. Tasks are described and photographed in a clear step-by-step sequence. The illustrations are numbered by the Section number and paragraph number to which they relate - if there is more than one illustration per paragraph, the sequence is denoted alphabetically.

References to the 'left' or 'right' of the vehicle are in the sense of a person in the driver's seat, facing forwards.

## Acknowledgements

Thanks are due to Draper Tools Limited, who provided some of the workshop tools, and to all those people at Sparkford who helped in the production of this manual.

**We take great pride in the accuracy of information given in this manual, but vehicle manufacturers make alterations and design changes during the production run of a particular vehicle of which they do not inform us. No liability can be accepted by the authors or publishers for loss, damage or injury caused by any errors in, or omissions from, the information given.**

## The Ford Ka Team

Haynes manuals are produced by dedicated and enthusiastic people working in close co-operation. The team responsible for the creation of this book included:

| | |
|---|---|
| **Author** | A.K. Legg |
| **Sub-editor** | Sophie Yar |
| **Editor & Page Make-up** | Steve Churchill |
| **Workshop manager** | Paul Buckland |
| **Photo Scans** | Steve Tanswell |
| | John Martin |
| **Cover illustration & Line Art** | Roger Healing |
| **Wiring diagrams** | Matthew Marke |

**We hope the book will help you to get the maximum enjoyment from your car. By carrying out routine maintenance as described you will ensure your car's reliability and preserve its resale value.**

Working on your car can be dangerous. This page shows just some of the potential risks and hazards, with the aim of creating a safety-conscious attitude.

# General hazards

### Scalding

• Don't remove the radiator or expansion tank cap while the engine is hot.
• Engine oil, automatic transmission fluid or power steering fluid may also be dangerously hot if the engine has recently been running.

### Burning

• Beware of burns from the exhaust system and from any part of the engine. Brake discs and drums can also be extremely hot immediately after use.

### Crushing

• When working under or near a raised vehicle, always supplement the jack with axle stands, or use drive-on ramps. *Never venture under a car which is only supported by a jack.*

• Take care if loosening or tightening high-torque nuts when the vehicle is on stands. Initial loosening and final tightening should be done with the wheels on the ground.

### Fire

• Fuel is highly flammable; fuel vapour is explosive.
• Don't let fuel spill onto a hot engine.
• Do not smoke or allow naked lights (including pilot lights) anywhere near a vehicle being worked on. Also beware of creating sparks (electrically or by use of tools).
• Fuel vapour is heavier than air, so don't work on the fuel system with the vehicle over an inspection pit.
• Another cause of fire is an electrical overload or short-circuit. Take care when repairing or modifying the vehicle wiring.
• Keep a fire extinguisher handy, of a type suitable for use on fuel and electrical fires.

### Electric shock

• Ignition HT voltage can be dangerous, especially to people with heart problems or a pacemaker. Don't work on or near the ignition system with the engine running or the ignition switched on.

• Mains voltage is also dangerous. Make sure that any mains-operated equipment is correctly earthed. Mains power points should be protected by a residual current device (RCD) circuit breaker.

### Fume or gas intoxication

• Exhaust fumes are poisonous; they often contain carbon monoxide, which is rapidly fatal if inhaled. Never run the engine in a confined space such as a garage with the doors shut.

• Fuel vapour is also poisonous, as are the vapours from some cleaning solvents and paint thinners.

### Poisonous or irritant substances

• Avoid skin contact with battery acid and with any fuel, fluid or lubricant, especially antifreeze, brake hydraulic fluid and Diesel fuel. Don't syphon them by mouth. If such a substance is swallowed or gets into the eyes, seek medical advice.
• Prolonged contact with used engine oil can cause skin cancer. Wear gloves or use a barrier cream if necessary. Change out of oil-soaked clothes and do not keep oily rags in your pocket.
• Air conditioning refrigerant forms a poisonous gas if exposed to a naked flame (including a cigarette). It can also cause skin burns on contact.

### Asbestos

• Asbestos dust can cause cancer if inhaled or swallowed. Asbestos may be found in gaskets and in brake and clutch linings. When dealing with such components it is safest to assume that they contain asbestos.

# Special hazards

### Hydrofluoric acid

• This extremely corrosive acid is formed when certain types of synthetic rubber, found in some O-rings, oil seals, fuel hoses etc, are exposed to temperatures above 400°C. The rubber changes into a charred or sticky substance containing the acid. *Once formed, the acid remains dangerous for years. If it gets onto the skin, it may be necessary to amputate the limb concerned.*
• When dealing with a vehicle which has suffered a fire, or with components salvaged from such a vehicle, wear protective gloves and discard them after use.

### The battery

• Batteries contain sulphuric acid, which attacks clothing, eyes and skin. Take care when topping-up or carrying the battery.
• The hydrogen gas given off by the battery is highly explosive. Never cause a spark or allow a naked light nearby. Be careful when connecting and disconnecting battery chargers or jump leads.

### Air bags

• Air bags can cause injury if they go off accidentally. Take care when removing the steering wheel and/or facia. Special storage instructions may apply.

### Diesel injection equipment

• Diesel injection pumps supply fuel at very high pressure. Take care when working on the fuel injectors and fuel pipes.

⚠ *Warning: Never expose the hands, face or any other part of the body to injector spray; the fuel can penetrate the skin with potentially fatal results.*

# Remember...

## DO

• Do use eye protection when using power tools, and when working under the vehicle.

• Do wear gloves or use barrier cream to protect your hands when necessary.

• Do get someone to check periodically that all is well when working alone on the vehicle.

• Do keep loose clothing and long hair well out of the way of moving mechanical parts.

• Do remove rings, wristwatch etc, before working on the vehicle – especially the electrical system.

• Do ensure that any lifting or jacking equipment has a safe working load rating adequate for the job.

## DON'T

• Don't attempt to lift a heavy component which may be beyond your capability – get assistance.

• Don't rush to finish a job, or take unverified short cuts.

• Don't use ill-fitting tools which may slip and cause injury.

• Don't leave tools or parts lying around where someone can trip over them. Mop up oil and fuel spills at once.

• Don't allow children or pets to play in or near a vehicle being worked on.

The following pages are intended to help in dealing with common roadside emergencies and breakdowns. You will find more detailed fault finding information at the back of the manual, and repair information in the main chapters.

# If your car won't start and the starter motor doesn't turn

☐ Open the bonnet and make sure that the battery terminals are clean and tight.
☐ Switch on the headlights and try to start the engine. If the headlights go very dim when you're trying to start, the battery is probably flat. Get out of trouble by jump starting (see next page) using a friend's car.

# If your car won't start even though the starter motor turns as normal

☐ Is there fuel in the tank?
☐ Is there moisture on electrical components under the bonnet? Switch off the ignition, then wipe off any obvious dampness with a dry cloth. Spray a water-repellent aerosol product (WD-40 or equivalent) on ignition and fuel system electrical connectors like those shown in the photos. Pay special attention to the ignition coil wiring connector and HT leads.

A Check the security and condition of the battery connections.

B Check the engine wiring plug connection on the bulkhead.

C Check the HT lead connections at the ignition coil on the rear of the engine.

Check that electrical connections are secure (with the ignition switched off). Spray the connector plugs with a water-dispersant spray like WD40 if you suspect a problem due to damp.

D Check that the HT leads are securely connected to the spark plugs.

E Check that none of the engine-related fuses have blown.

# Jump starting

*Jump starting will get you out of trouble, but you must correct whatever made the battery go flat in the first place. There are three possibilities:*

**1** *The battery has been drained by repeated attempts to start, or by leaving the lights on.*

**2** *The charging system is not working properly (alternator drivebelt slack or broken, alternator wiring fault or alternator itself faulty).*

**3** *The battery itself is at fault (electrolyte low, or battery worn out).*

When jump-starting a car using a booster battery, observe the following precautions:

✔ Before connecting the booster battery, make sure that the ignition is switched off.

✔ Ensure that all electrical equipment (lights, heater, wipers, etc) is switched off.

✔ Take note of any special precautions printed on the battery case.

✔ Make sure that the booster battery is the same voltage as the discharged one in the vehicle.

✔ If the battery is being jump-started from the battery in another vehicle, the two vehicles MUST NOT TOUCH each other.

✔ Make sure that the transmission is in neutral (or PARK, in the case of automatic transmission).

**1** Connect one end of the red jump lead to the positive (+) terminal of the flat battery

**2** Connect the other end of the red lead to the positive (+) terminal of the booster battery.

**3** Connect one end of the black jump lead to the negative (-) terminal of the booster battery

**4** Connect the other end of the black jump lead to the right-hand engine mounting bracket

**5** Make sure that the jump leads will not come into contact with the fan, drive-belts or other moving parts of the engine.

**6** Start the engine using the booster battery and run it at idle speed. Switch on the lights, rear window demister and heater blower motor, then disconnect the jump leads in the reverse order of connection. Turn off the lights etc.

# Wheel changing

 **Warning: Do not change a wheel in a situation where you risk being hit by another vehicle. On busy roads, try to stop in a lay-by or a gateway. Be wary of passing traffic while changing the wheel - it is easy to become distracted by the job in hand.**

## Preparation

☐ When a puncture occurs, stop as soon as it is safe to do so.

☐ Park on firm level ground, if possible, and well out of the way of other traffic.

☐ Use hazard warning lights if necessary.

☐ If you have one, use a warning triangle to alert other drivers of your presence.

☐ Apply the handbrake and engage first or reverse gear.

☐ Chock the wheel diagonally opposite the one being removed – a couple of large stones will do for this.

☐ If the ground is soft, use a flat piece of wood to spread the load under the jack.

## Changing the wheel

**1** The jack and wheel brace are stored on the left-hand side of the luggage compartment. Remove the moulded cover, then unscrew the retaining bolt and remove the jack and wheel brace. Detach the wheel brace from the jack.

**2** The spare wheel is in a cradle under the rear of the vehicle. Pull up the cover in the luggage compartment for access to the spare wheel cradle securing screw. Using the wheel brace, loosen the screw by 6 to 8 turns then unhook the spare wheel cradle from the securing bracket under the back of the vehicle, and lower the cradle until it is resting on the floor.

**3** On models where the wheel nuts are not visible, use the blade end of the wheel brace to prise off the wheel trim. Using the wheel brace, loosen each wheel nut by half a turn. Where a locking wheel nut is fitted, it will be necessary to use the special adapter supplied in the tool kit to remove the nut.

**4** Locate the jack head below the reinforced jacking point nearest the wheel to be changed, and on firm ground. Ensure that the lug on the jack head engages with the cut-out in the jacking point.

**5** Turn the jack handle clockwise until the wheel is raised clear of the ground. At this stage, slide the spare wheel under the vehicle next to the jack as a precaution.

**6** Unscrew the wheel nuts, noting which way round they fit (tapered side inwards), and remove the wheel. Remove the spare wheel from under the car and locate the removed wheel in its place.

**7** Locate the spare wheel on the studs and tighten the nuts moderately with the wheel brace. Lower the vehicle to the ground, then securely tighten the wheel nuts progressively in diagonal sequence.

## Finally...

☐ Have the wheel nuts tightened to the specified torque (see Chapter 10) at the earliest possible opportunity.

☐ Remove the wheel chocks.

☐ Stow the jack and tools in the luggage compartment, and refit the removed wheel in the cradle. Raise the cradle before driving the vehicle.

☐ Check the tyre pressure on the wheel just fitted. If it is low, or if you don't have a pressure gauge with you, drive slowly to the nearest garage and inflate the tyre to the right pressure.

☐ Have the punctured wheel repaired at the earliest opportunity, or another puncture will leave you stranded.

# Identifying leaks

Puddles on the garage floor or drive, or obvious wetness under the bonnet or underneath the car, suggest a leak that needs investigating. It can sometimes be difficult to decide where the leak is coming from, especially if the engine bay is very dirty already. Leaking oil or fluid can also be blown rearwards by the passage of air under the car, giving a false impression of where the problem lies.

 *Warning: Most automotive oils and fluids are poisonous. Wash them off skin, and change out of contaminated clothing, without delay.*

 **HAYNES HINT** *The smell of a fluid leaking from the car may provide a clue to what's leaking. Some fluids are distinctively coloured.*
*It may help to clean the car carefully and to park it over some clean paper overnight as an aid to locating the source of the leak.*
*Remember that some leaks may only occur while the engine is running.*

## Sump oil

Engine oil may leak from the drain plug...

## Oil from filter

...or from the base of the oil filter.

## Gearbox oil

Gearbox oil can leak from the seals at the inboard ends of the driveshafts.

## Antifreeze

Leaking antifreeze often leaves a crystalline deposit like this.

## Brake fluid

A leak occurring at a wheel is almost certainly brake fluid.

## Power steering fluid

Power steering fluid may leak from the pipe connectors on the steering rack.

# Towing

When all else fails, you may find yourself having to get a tow home – or of course you may be helping somebody else. Long-distance recovery should only be done by a garage or breakdown service. For shorter distances, DIY towing using another car is easy enough, but observe the following points:
☐ Use a proper tow-rope – they are not expensive. The vehicle being towed must display an 'ON TOW' sign in its rear window.
☐ Always turn the ignition key to the 'on' position when the vehicle is being towed, so that the steering lock is released, and that the direction indicator and brake lights will work.
☐ The front towing eye is of the screw-in type, and is located on the right-hand side of the luggage compartment. The towing eye screws into the threaded hole below the right-

hand headlight, accessible after prising out a cover in the bumper, and has a **left-hand thread** - ie it screws in anti-clockwise **(see illustration)**. The same eye is used for the rear towing eye, the threaded hole being below the right-hand rear light cluster. Use the wheel brace to tighten the eye into its thread.
☐ Before being towed, release the handbrake and make sure the transmission is in neutral.
☐ Note that greater-than-usual pedal pressure will be required to operate the brakes, since the vacuum servo unit is only operational with the engine running.
☐ The driver of the car being towed must keep the tow-rope taut at all times to avoid snatching.
☐ Make sure that both drivers know the route before setting off.

☐ Only drive at moderate speeds and keep the distance towed to a minimum. Drive smoothly and allow plenty of time for slowing down at junctions.

**The towing eye is screwed into a *left-hand thread* hole**

# Introduction

There are some very simple checks which need only take a few minutes to carry out, but which could save you a lot of inconvenience and expense.

These "Weekly checks" require no great skill or special tools, and the small amount of time they take to perform could prove to be very well spent, for example;

☐ Keeping an eye on tyre condition and pressures, will not only help to stop them wearing out prematurely, but could also save your life.

☐ Many breakdowns are caused by electrical problems. Battery-related faults are particularly common, and a quick check on a regular basis will often prevent the majority of these.

☐ If your car develops a brake fluid leak, the first time you might know about it is when your brakes don't work properly. Checking the level regularly will give advance warning of this kind of problem.

☐ If the oil or coolant levels run low, the cost of repairing any engine damage will be far greater than fixing the leak, for example.

# Underbonnet check points

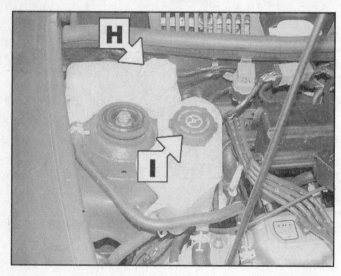

## 1.3 litre Endura engine

**A** *Engine oil level dipstick*

**B** *Engine oil filler cap*

**C** *Coolant expansion tank (up to model year 1999)*

**D** *Brake (and clutch) fluid reservoir*

**E** *Power steering fluid reservoir (up to model year 1999)*

**F** *Screen washer fluid reservoir*

**G** *Battery*

**H** *Coolant expansion tank (from model year 1999)*

**I** *Power steering fluid reservoir (from model year 1999)*

# Engine oil level

## Before you start

✔ Make sure that your car is on level ground.
✔ Check the oil level before the car is driven, or at least 5 minutes after the engine has been switched off.

## The correct oil

*Modern engines place great demands on their oil. It is very important that the correct oil for your car is used (See "Lubricants, fluids and tyre pressures on page 0•16").*

## Car Care

● If you have to add oil frequently, you should check whether you have any oil leaks. Place some clean paper under the car overnight, and check for stains in the morning. If there are no leaks, the engine may be burning oil.

● Always maintain the level between the upper and lower dipstick marks (see photo 3). If the level is too low severe engine damage may occur. Oil seal failure may result if the engine is overfilled by adding too much oil.

**1** The dipstick top is brightly coloured for easy identification (see "*Underbonnet check points*" on page 0•10 for exact location). Withdraw the dipstick.

**3** Note the oil level on the end of the dipstick, which should be between the upper 'MAX' mark and lower 'MIN' mark. If the oil level is only just above, or below, the 'MIN' mark, topping-up is required.

**2** Using a clean rag or paper towel wipe all oil from the dipstick. Insert the clean dipstick into the tube as far as it will go, then withdraw it again.

**4** Oil is added through the filler cap aperture. Lift off the cap using a twisting motion. Top-up the level taking care not to spill the oil. A funnel may be useful in reducing spillage. Add the oil slowly, checking the level on the dipstick often, and allowing time for the oil to flow to the sump. Add oil until the level is just up to the 'MAX' mark on the dipstick - don't overfill (see "*Car care*" left).

---

# Coolant level

 *Warning: DO NOT attempt to remove the expansion tank pressure cap when the engine is hot, as there is a very great risk of scalding. Do not leave open containers of coolant about, as it is poisonous.*

## Car Care

● With a sealed-type cooling system, adding coolant should not be necessary on a regular basis. If frequent topping-up is required, it is likely there is a leak. Check the radiator, all hoses and joint faces for signs of staining or wetness, and rectify as necessary.

● It is important that antifreeze is used in the cooling system all year round, not just during the winter months. Don't top-up with water alone, as the antifreeze will become too diluted.

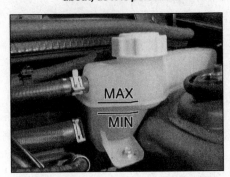

**1** The coolant level varies with the temperature of the engine. 'MIN' and 'MAX' marks are shown on the side of the tank. When the engine is cold, the coolant level should be between the two marks, but ideally on the 'MAX' mark. When the engine is hot, the level will rise above the 'MAX' mark slightly.

**2** If topping up is necessary, **wait until the engine is cold**. Slowly unscrew the expansion tank cap, to release any pressure present in the cooling system, and remove it.

**3** Add a mixture of water and antifreeze to the expansion tank until the coolant level is on the 'MAX' mark. Refit the cap and tighten it securely. **Note:** *On vehicles from model year 1999, the expansion tank has been moved to the right-hand rear corner of the engine compartment (see Underbonnet check points on page 0.10).*

# Brake (and clutch) fluid level

**Warning:**
● Brake fluid can harm your eyes and damage painted surfaces, so use extreme caution when handling and pouring it.

● Do not use fluid that has been standing open for some time, as it absorbs moisture from the air, which can cause a dangerous loss of braking effectiveness.

 ● Make sure that your car is on level ground.
● The fluid level in the reservoir will drop slightly as the brake pads wear down, but the fluid level must never be allowed to drop below the "MIN" mark.

## Safety First!

● If the reservoir requires repeated topping-up this is an indication of a fluid leak somewhere in the system, which should be investigated immediately.

● If a leak is suspected, the car should not be driven until the braking system has been checked. Never take any risks where brakes are concerned.

**1** The "MAX" and "MIN" marks are indicated on the side of the reservoir, which is located at the rear left-hand side of the engine compartment. The fluid level must be kept between these two marks.

**3** Carefully add fluid, avoiding spilling it on surrounding paintwork. Use only the specified hydraulic fluid; mixing different types of fluid can cause damage to the system and/or a loss of braking effectiveness. Bear in mind that the level in the reservoir will rise slightly when the cap/float assembly is refitted. After filling to the correct level, refit the cap securely. Wipe off any spilt fluid.

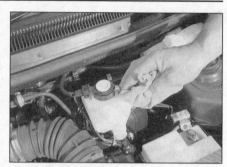
**2** If topping-up is necessary, first wipe the area around the filler cap with a clean rag, then hold the fluid level sensor wiring plug as the cap is unscrewed. When adding fluid, it's a good idea to inspect the reservoir. The fluid should be changed if dirt is visible.

**4** Check the operation of the low fluid level warning light. Switch on the ignition and ask an assistant to press the button on top of the reservoir cap. The brake fluid level/ handbrake "on" warning light should come on - if not, the level switch, wiring or bulb may be faulty. If the warning light comes on and the fluid level is not low, check that the handbrake is not on. Switch off the ignition after testing.

# Power steering fluid level

## Before you start:
✔ Park the vehicle on level ground.
✔ Set the steering wheel straight-ahead.
✔ The engine should be turned off.

 For the check to be accurate, the steering must not be turned once the engine has been stopped.

## Safety First!
● The need for frequent topping-up indicates a leak, which should be investigated immediately.

**1** The reservoir is located at the right-hand rear corner of the engine compartment. The fluid level is visible through the reservoir body; when the system is at operating temperature, the level should be up to the 'MAX' mark on the side of the reservoir.

**2** If topping-up is required, wipe clean the area around the reservoir filler neck and unscrew the filler cap from the reservoir.

**3** When topping-up, use the specified type of fluid and do not overfill the reservoir. When the level is correct, securely refit the cap. **Note:** On vehicles from model year 1999, the reservoir has been moved around the side of the suspension top mounting (see Underbonnet check points on page 0.10).

## Screen washer fluid level*

*The underbonnet reservoir also serves the tailgate washer.*

Screenwash additives not only keep the winscreen clean during foul weather, they also prevent the washer system freezing in cold weather - which is when you are likely to need it most. Don't top up using plain water as the screenwash will become too diluted, and will freeze during cold weather. *On no account use coolant antifreeze in the washer system - this could discolour or damage paintwork.*

1 The screen/tailgate washer fluid reservoir filler neck is located in the centre of the engine compartment rear bulkhead, and the filler cap is brightly coloured. The screen washer level cannot easily be seen. Remove the filler cap, and look down the filler neck - if fluid is not visible, topping-up is required.

2 When topping-up the reservoir, add a screenwash additive in the quantities recommended on the bottle.

## Wiper blades

1 Check the condition of the wiper blades; if they are cracked or show any signs of deterioration, or if the glass swept area is smeared, renew them. For maximum clarity of vision, wiper blades should be renewed annually, as a matter of course.

**HAYNES HiNT** *If smearing is still a problem despite fitting new wiper blades, try cleaning the windscreen with neat screen-wash additive or methylated spirit.*

2 To remove a windscreen wiper blade, pull the arm fully away from the screen until it locks. Swivel the blade through 90°, then depress the locking clip at the base of the mounting block, and slide the blade out of the hooked end of the arm. Where applicable, don't forget to check the tailgate wiper blade as well. The blade can be removed by swivelling the blade through 90°, then sliding the blade from the arm. Fit the new blade using a reversal of the removal procedure.

3 To remove the tailgate wiper blade, pull the arm away from the window until it locks. Carefully prise the blade from the arm using the fingers only until it is released. Fit the new blade using a reversal of removal procedure.

# Tyre condition and pressure

It is very important that tyres are in good condition, and at the correct pressure - having a tyre failure at any speed is highly dangerous. Tyre wear is influenced by driving style - harsh braking and acceleration, or fast cornering, will all produce more rapid tyre wear. As a general rule, the front tyres wear out faster than the rears. Interchanging the tyres from front to rear ("rotating" the tyres) may result in more even wear. However, if this is completely effective, you may have the expense of replacing all four tyres at once! Remove any nails or stones embedded in the tread before they penetrate the tyre to cause deflation. If removal of a nail does reveal that the tyre has been punctured, refit the nail so that its point of penetration is marked. Then immediately change the wheel, and have the tyre repaired by a tyre dealer.

Regularly check the tyres for damage in the form of cuts or bulges, especially in the sidewalls. Periodically remove the wheels, and clean any dirt or mud from the inside and outside surfaces. Examine the wheel rims for signs of rusting, corrosion or other damage. Light alloy wheels are easily damaged by "kerbing" whilst parking; steel wheels may also become dented or buckled. A new wheel is very often the only way to overcome severe damage.

New tyres should be balanced when they are fitted, but it may become necessary to re-balance them as they wear, or if the balance weights fitted to the wheel rim should fall off. Unbalanced tyres will wear more quickly, as will the steering and suspension components. Wheel imbalance is normally signified by vibration, particularly at a certain speed (typically around 50 mph). If this vibration is felt only through the steering, then it is likely that just the front wheels need balancing. If, however, the vibration is felt through the whole car, the rear wheels could be out of balance. Wheel balancing should be carried out by a tyre dealer or garage.

**1 Tread Depth - visual check**
The original tyres have tread wear safety bands (B), which will appear when the tread depth reaches approximately 1.6 mm. The band positions are indicated by a triangular mark on the tyre sidewall (A).

**2 Tread Depth - manual check**
Alternatively, tread wear can be monitored with a simple, inexpensive device known as a tread depth indicator gauge.

**3 Tyre Pressure Check**
Check the tyre pressures regularly with the tyres cold. Do not adjust the tyre pressures immediately after the vehicle has been used, or an inaccurate setting will result. Tyre pressures are shown on page 0•16.

# Tyre tread wear patterns

### Shoulder Wear

**Underinflation (wear on both sides)**
Under-inflation will cause overheating of the tyre, because the tyre will flex too much, and the tread will not sit correctly on the road surface. This will cause a loss of grip and excessive wear, not to mention the danger of sudden tyre failure due to heat build-up.
*Check and adjust pressures*
**Incorrect wheel camber (wear on one side)**
*Repair or renew suspension parts*
**Hard cornering**
*Reduce speed!*

### Centre Wear

**Overinflation**
Over-inflation will cause rapid wear of the centre part of the tyre tread, coupled with reduced grip, harsher ride, and the danger of shock damage occurring in the tyre casing.
*Check and adjust pressures*

*If you sometimes have to inflate your car's tyres to the higher pressures specified for maximum load or sustained high speed, don't forget to reduce the pressures to normal afterwards.*

### Uneven Wear

Front tyres may wear unevenly as a result of wheel misalignment. Most tyre dealers and garages can check and adjust the wheel alignment (or "tracking") for a modest charge.
**Incorrect camber or castor**
*Repair or renew suspension parts*
**Malfunctioning suspension**
*Repair or renew suspension parts*
**Unbalanced wheel**
*Balance tyres*
**Incorrect toe setting**
*Adjust front wheel alignment*
**Note:** *The feathered edge of the tread which typifies toe wear is best checked by feel.*

# Battery

*Caution: Before carrying out any work on the vehicle battery, read the precautions given in "Safety first" at the start of this manual.*

✔ Make sure that the battery tray is in good condition, and that the clamp is tight. Corrosion on the tray, retaining clamp and the battery itself can be removed with a solution of water and baking soda. Thoroughly rinse all cleaned areas with water. Any metal parts damaged by corrosion should be covered with a zinc-based primer, then painted.

✔ Periodically (approximately every three months), check the charge condition of the battery as described in Chapter 1.

✔ On batteries which are not of the maintenance-free type, periodically check the electrolyte level in the battery - see Chapter 1.

✔ If the battery is flat, and you need to jump start your vehicle, see **Roadside Repairs**.

*Battery corrosion can be kept to a minimum by applying a layer of petroleum jelly to the clamps and terminals after they are reconnected.*

**1** The battery is located in the left-hand front corner of the engine compartment. The exterior of the battery should be inspected periodically for damage such as a cracked case or cover.

**3** If corrosion (white, fluffy deposits) is evident, remove the cables from the battery terminals, clean them with a small wire brush, then refit them. Automotive stores sell a tool for cleaning the battery post . . .

**2** Check the tightness of battery clamps to ensure good electrical connections. You should not be able to move them. Also check each cable for cracks and frayed conductors.

**4** . . . as well as the battery cable clamps

# Bulbs and fuses

✔ Check all external lights and the horn. Refer to the appropriate Sections of Chapter 12 for details if any of the circuits are found to be inoperative.

✔ Visually check all accessible wiring connectors, harnesses and retaining clips for security, and for signs of chafing or damage.

 *If you need to check your brake lights and indicators unaided, back up to a wall or garage door and operate the lights. The reflected light should show if they are working properly.*

**1** If a single indicator light, stop-light or headlight has failed, it is likely that a bulb has blown and will need to be replaced. Refer to Chapter 12 for details. If both stop-lights have failed, it is possible that the switch has failed (see Chapter 9).

**2** If more than one indicator light or tail light has failed, it is likely that either a fuse has blown or that there is a fault in the circuit (see Chapter 12). The fuses are located in the fusebox, below the driver's side of the facia. For access to the fuses, pull out the bottom of the fusebox cover and unhook it.

**3** To replace a blown fuse, use the plastic tool provided on the fusebox cover to pull the fuse from its location then fit the new one. If the fuse blows again, it is important that you find out why - a complete checking procedure is given in Chapter 12.

## Lubricants and fluids

Engine . . . . . . . . . . . . . . . . . . . . . . . . . . . . . . . . . . Multigrade engine oil, viscosity SAE 10W/30 or 10W/40, to API SH or ACEA A1-96, A2-96, or A3-96

Cooling system . . . . . . . . . . . . . . . . . . . . . . . . . . . . Motorcraft Super Plus 4 antifreeze (blue/green) to Ford specification ESD-M97 B49-A, or Motorcraft Super Plus 2000 antifreeze (orange) to Ford specification WSS-M97 B44-D*

Manual transmission . . . . . . . . . . . . . . . . . . . . . . . SAE 75W/90 synthetic oil, to Ford specification WSD-M2C200-C

Brake (and clutch) hydraulic system . . . . . . . . . . . . . . . . . Hydraulic fluid to Ford specification SAM-6C9103-A, DOT 4

Power steering . . . . . . . . . . . . . . . . . . . . . . . . . . . . Automatic transmission fluid to Ford specification ESP-M2C 166-H

*\* Do not mix the two types of coolant listed with each other, nor top-up with any other type of coolant.*

## Choosing your engine oil

Engines need oil, not only to lubricate moving parts and minimise wear, but also to maximise power output and to improve fuel economy.

### HOW ENGINE OIL WORKS

#### • Beating friction

Without oil, the moving surfaces inside your engine will rub together, heat up and melt, quickly causing the engine to seize. Engine oil creates a film which separates these moving parts, preventing wear and heat build-up.

#### • Cooling hot-spots

Temperatures inside the engine can exceed 1000° C. The engine oil circulates and acts as a coolant, transferring heat from the hot-spots to the sump.

#### • Cleaning the engine internally

Good quality engine oils clean the inside of your engine, collecting and dispersing combustion deposits and controlling them until they are trapped by the oil filter or flushed out at oil change.

### OIL CARE - FOLLOW THE CODE

To handle and dispose of used engine oil safely, always:

OIL BANK LINE
**0800 66 33 66**
www.oilbankline.org.uk

• *Avoid skin contact with used engine oil. Repeated or prolonged contact can be harmful.*
• *Dispose of used oil and empty packs in a responsible manner in an authorised disposal site. Call 0800 663366 to find the one nearest to you. Never tip oil down drains or onto the ground.*

## Tyre pressures

| Tyre pressures (tyres cold): | Front | Rear |
| --- | --- | --- |
| Normally-laden (up to 3 people): | | |
| 155/70R13T tyres . . . . . . . . . . . . . . . . . . . . . . . | 2.2 bars (32 psi) | 1.8 bars (26 psi) |
| 165/65R13T tyres . . . . . . . . . . . . . . . . . . . . . . . | 2.1 bars (31 psi) | 1.8 bars (26 psi) |
| 165/60R14T . . . . . . . . . . . . . . . . . . . . . . . . . . | 2.1 bars (31 psi) | 1.8 bars (26 psi) |
| Fully-laden: | | |
| All tyre sizes . . . . . . . . . . . . . . . . . . . . . . . . . | 2.5 bars (37 psi) | 2.5 bars (37 psi) |

**Note:** *Pressures apply to original-equipment tyres, and may vary if any other make of tyre is fitted; check with the tyre manufacturer or supplier for the correct pressures if necessary.*

# Chapter 1
# Routine maintenance and servicing

## Contents

## Degrees of difficulty

 **Easy,** suitable for novice with little experience

**Fairly easy,** suitable for beginner with some experience

**Fairly difficult,** suitable for competent DIY mechanic

**Difficult,** suitable for experienced DIY mechanic

**Very difficult,** suitable for expert DIY or professional

**Lubricants and fluids** ..................................... Refer to end of "Weekly checks" on page 0•16

## Capacities

**Engine oil**
Including oil filter (approximate) ............................. 3.25 litres
Excluding oil filter (approximate) ........................... 2.75 litres
Difference between dipstick minimum and maximum level notches ... 0.75 litre

**Cooling system**
Total (approximate) ........................................ 5.25 litres

**Transmission**
Manual transmission (approximate) ......................... 2.8 litres

**Washer fluid reservoir**
Total ..................................................... 4.0 litres

**Fuel tank**
All models ................................................ 42 litres

## Engine

Valve clearance (cold):
  Inlet ................................................ 0.20 mm
  Exhaust:
    Engines built up to 20/11/96 ...................... 0.30 mm
    Engines built from 20/11/96* ...................... 0.50 mm
*These engines are marked with a valve clearance sticker on the cylinder head cover*

## Cooling system

Antifreeze mixture:
  50% antifreeze ....................................... Protection down to -37°C
  55% antifreeze ....................................... Protection down to -45°C
**Note:** *Refer to antifreeze manufacturer for latest recommendations.*

## Ignition system

Spark plugs:
  Type/electrode gap ................................... Bosch HR 78 X/Not adjustable
    Motorcraft AGRF 22 CD1/1.0 mm

## Brakes

Friction material minimum thickness:
  Front brake pads ..................................... 1.5 mm
  Rear brake shoes ..................................... 1.0 mm

## Torque wrench settings

| | Nm | lbf ft |
| --- | --- | --- |
| Engine sump drain plug | 25 | 18 |
| Manual transmission filler/level plug | 35 | 26 |
| Roadwheel nuts | 85 | 63 |
| Spark plugs | 17 | 13 |

The maintenance intervals in this manual are provided with the assumption that you, not the dealer, will be carrying out the work. These are the minimum maintenance intervals recommended by us for vehicles driven daily, but subjected only to 'normal' use. If you wish to keep your vehicle in peak condition at all times, you may wish to perform some of these procedures more often. Because frequent maintenance enhances the efficiency, performance and resale value of your vehicle,

we encourage you to do so. If your usage is not 'normal', shorter intervals are also recommended - the most important examples of these are noted in the schedule. These shorter intervals apply particularly if you drive in dusty areas, tow a caravan or trailer, sit with the engine idling or drive at low speeds for extended periods (ie, in heavy traffic), or drive for short distances (less than four miles) in below-freezing temperatures.

When your vehicle is new, it should be

serviced by an approved manufacturer's dealer service department to protect the factory warranty. In many cases, the initial maintenance check is done at no cost to the owner. Note that this first free service (carried out by the selling dealer 1500 miles or 3 months after delivery), although an important check for a new vehicle, is not part of the regular maintenance schedule, and is therefore not mentioned here.

## Every 5000 miles or 6 months, whichever comes first
☐ Renew the engine oil and filter (Section 3)

**Note:** *Ford recommend that the engine oil and filter are changed every 10 000 miles or 12 months. However, oil and filter changes are good for the engine and we recommend that the oil and filter are renewed more frequently, especially if the vehicle is used on a lot of short journeys.*

## Every 10 000 miles or 12 months, whichever comes first
☐ Check and, if necessary, adjust the valve clearances (Section 4)
☐ Check the condition of the auxiliary drivebelt(s) (Section 5)
☐ Check all components, pipes and hoses for fluid leaks (Section 6)
☐ Check the front brake pads and discs for wear (Section 7)
☐ Check the rear brake shoes and drums for wear (Section 8)
☐ Check the steering and suspension components for condition and security (Section 9)
☐ Check the condition of the driveshaft gaiters (Section 10)
☐ Check the condition of all seat belts (Section 11)
☐ Lubricate all hinges and locks (Section 12)
☐ Check the roadwheel nuts are tightened to the specified torque (Section 13)
☐ Carry out a road test (Section 14)

## Every 20 000 miles
☐ Renew the pollen filter (Section 15)*
☐ Check battery electrolyte level (Section 16)

***Note:** If the vehicle is used in dusty conditions, the pollen filter should be renewed more frequently.*

## Every 30 000 miles
☐ Renew the spark plugs and check the ignition system (Section 17)
☐ Renew the air filter (Section 18)
☐ Check the oil filler cap and crankcase ventilation system (Section 19)
☐ Check the manual transmission oil level (Section 20)

## Every 60 000 miles
☐ Renew the fuel filter (Section 21)

## Every 3 years, regardless of mileage
☐ Renew the brake fluid (Section 22)

## Every 4 years, regardless of mileage
**Note:** *Models using Motorcraft Super Plus 4 antifreeze (blue/green) to Ford specification ESD-M97 B49-A*
☐ Renew the coolant and check the condition of the expansion tank pressure cap (Section 23)

## Every 10 years, regardless of mileage
**Note:** *Models using Motorcraft Super Plus 2000 antifreeze (orange) to Ford specification WSS-M97 B44-D*
☐ Renew the coolant and check the condition of the expansion tank pressure cap (Section 23)

## Every 15 years, regardless of mileage
☐ Renew the air bag(s) (Section 24)

## Underbonnet view of a Ka-3 model

1  Engine oil filler cap
2  Engine oil level dipstick
3  Idle air control valve
4  Inlet manifold
5  Air conditioning refrigerant charge outlets
6  Front suspension top mounting
7  Power steering hydraulic fluid reservoir (up to model year 1999)
8  Windscreen/tailgate washer fluid reservoir
9  Throttle body housing
10  Brake vacuum servo unit
11  Brake hydraulic fluid reservoir
12  Coolant expansion tank (up to model year 1999)
13  Circuit breaker fuses
14  Mass air flow meter (up to model year 1999)
15  Battery
16  Air cleaner cover
17  VIN plate
18  Oxygen sensor
19  Spark plugs and HT leads
20  Thermostat housing

**Note:** *See "Weekly checks" for the locations (from model year 1999) for the power steering reservoir and the coolant expansion tank*

## Front underbody view of a Ka-3 model

1  Air conditioning compressor
2  Catalytic converter and exhaust manifold
3  Radiator
4  Power steering hydraulic lines
5  Left-hand engine/ transmission mounting
6  Manual transmission
7  Rear engine/transmission mounting
8  Gearchange linkage
9  Stabiliser bar
10  Front suspension lower mounting bracket
11  Steering gear
12  Air conditioning dehydrator
13  Driveshaft
14  Engine oil drain plug
15  Steering track rod
16  Front suspension lower arm
17  Front suspension lower balljoint
18  Front brake caliper
19  Oil filter
20  Exhaust front section

## Rear underbody view of a Ka-3 model

1   Rear suspension strut
    lower mounting
2   Spare wheel
3   Fuel evaporative system
    charcoal canister
4   Exhaust rear silencer and
    tailpipe
5   Rear brake backplate
6   Handbrake cable
7   Fuel tank
8   Rear axle assembly front
    mounting
9   Rear axle 'twist' beam

## 1  General information

This Chapter is designed to help the home mechanic maintain his/her vehicle for safety, economy, long life and peak performance.

The Chapter contains a master maintenance schedule, followed by Sections dealing specifically with each task in the schedule. Visual checks, adjustments, component renewal and other helpful items are included. Refer to the accompanying illustrations of the engine compartment and the underside of the vehicle for the locations of the various components.

Servicing your vehicle in accordance with the mileage/time maintenance schedule and the following Sections will provide a planned maintenance programme, which should result in a long and reliable service life. This is a comprehensive plan, so maintaining some items but not others at the specified service intervals, will not produce the same results.

As you service your vehicle, you will discover that many of the procedures can - and should - be grouped together, because of the particular procedure being performed, or because of the proximity of two otherwise-unrelated components to one another. For example, if the vehicle is raised for any reason, the exhaust can be inspected at the same time as the suspension and steering components.

The first step in this maintenance programme is to prepare yourself before the actual work begins. Read through all the Sections relevant to the work to be carried out, then make a list and gather all the parts and tools required. If a problem is encountered, seek advice from a parts specialist, or a dealer service department.

## 2  Regular maintenance

If, from the time the vehicle is new, the routine maintenance schedule is followed closely, and frequent checks are made of fluid levels and high-wear items, as suggested throughout this manual, the engine will be kept in relatively good running condition, and the need for additional work will be minimised.

It is possible that there will be times when the engine is running poorly due to the lack of regular maintenance. This is even more likely if a used vehicle, which has not received regular and frequent maintenance checks, is purchased. In such cases, additional work may need to be carried out, outside of the regular maintenance intervals.

If engine wear is suspected, a compression test (refer to Chapter 2A) will provide valuable information regarding the overall performance of the main internal components. Such a test can be used as a basis to decide on the extent of the work to be carried out. If, for example, a

compression test indicates serious internal engine wear, conventional maintenance as described in this Chapter will not greatly improve the performance of the engine, and may prove a waste of time and money, unless extensive overhaul work is carried out first.

The following series of operations are those most often required to improve the performance of a generally poor-running engine:

### Primary operations

a) Clean, inspect and test the battery (refer to "Weekly checks").
b) Check all the engine-related fluids (refer to "Weekly checks").
c) Check the condition and tension of the auxiliary drivebelt (Section 5).
d) Renew the spark plugs (Sections 17).
e) Check the condition of the air filter, and renew if necessary (Section 18).
f) Renew the fuel filter (Section 21).
g) Check the condition of all hoses, and check for fluid leaks (Section 6).

If the above operations do not prove fully effective, carry out the following secondary operations:

### Secondary operations

All items listed under "Primary operations", plus the following:

a) Check the charging system (refer to Chapter 5A).
b) Check the ignition system (refer to Chapter 5B).
c) Check the fuel system (refer to Chapter 4A).

3.4 Removing the oil filler cap

3.5 Loosening the engine sump drain plug

3.9 Using an oil filter removal tool to loosen the filter

# Every 5000 miles or 6 months, whichever comes first

### 3 Engine oil and filter renewal

1 Frequent oil and filter changes are the most important preventative maintenance procedures which can be undertaken by the DIY owner. As engine oil ages, it becomes diluted and contaminated, which leads to premature engine wear.

2 Before starting this procedure, gather together all the necessary tools and materials. Also make sure that you have plenty of clean rags and newspapers handy, to mop up any spills. Ideally, the engine oil should be warm, as it will drain more easily, and more built-up sludge will be removed with it. Take care not to touch the exhaust or any other hot parts of the engine when working under the vehicle. To avoid any possibility of scalding, and to

3.11 Apply a light coating of clean engine oil to the sealing ring on the new filter

protect yourself from possible skin irritants and other harmful contaminants in used engine oils, it is advisable to wear gloves when carrying out this work.

3 Firmly apply the handbrake then jack up the front of the vehicle and support it on axle stands (see "Jacking and Vehicle Support").

4 Remove the oil filler cap (see illustration).

5 Using a spanner, or preferably a socket and bar, slacken the drain plug about half a turn (see illustration). Position the draining container under the drain plug, then remove the plug completely.

 **HAYNES HiNT** *As the plug releases from the threads, move it away sharply, so that the stream of oil from the sump runs into the container, not up your sleeve!*

6 Allow some time for the oil to drain, noting that it may be necessary to reposition the container as the oil flow slows to a trickle.

7 After all the oil has drained, wipe the drain plug and the sealing washer with a clean rag. Examine the condition of the sealing washer, and renew it if it shows signs of scoring or other damage which may prevent an oil-tight seal. Clean the area around the drain plug opening, and refit the plug complete with the washer and tighten it securely.

8 Move the container into position under the oil filter which is located on the rear of the cylinder block.

9 Use an oil filter removal tool to slacken the filter initially, then unscrew it by hand the rest of the way (see illustration). Empty the oil from the old filter into the container.

10 Use a clean rag to remove all oil, dirt and sludge from the filter sealing area on the engine.

11 Apply a light coating of clean engine oil to the sealing ring on the new filter, then screw the filter into position on the engine (see illustration). Tighten the filter firmly by hand only - do not use any tools.

12 Remove the old oil and all tools from under the vehicle then lower the vehicle to the ground.

13 Fill the engine through the filler hole, using the correct grade and type of oil (refer to "Weekly Checks" for details of topping-up). Pour in half the specified quantity of oil first, then wait a few minutes for the oil to drain into the sump. Continue to add oil, a small quantity at a time, until the level is up to the lower mark on the dipstick. Adding approximately a further 0.75 litre will bring the level up to the upper mark on the dipstick.

14 Start the engine and run it for a few minutes, while checking for leaks around the oil filter seal and the sump drain plug. Note that there may be a delay of a few seconds before the low oil pressure warning light goes out when the engine is first started, as the oil circulates through the new oil filter and the engine oil galleries before the pressure builds up.

15 Stop the engine, and wait a few minutes for the oil to settle in the sump once more. With the new oil circulated and the filter now completely full, recheck the level on the dipstick, and add more oil as necessary.

16 Dispose of the used engine oil safely with reference to "General repair procedures".

# Every 10 000 miles or 12 months, whichever comes first

### 4 Valve clearance check and adjustment

This procedure is described in Chapter 2A.

### 5 Auxiliary drivebelt check and renewal

#### Checking

1 A single auxiliary drivebelt is fitted at the right-hand side of the engine. The length of the drivebelt varies according to whether air conditioning and/or power steering is fitted. An automatic adjuster is fitted so checking of the drivebelt tension is unnecessary.

2 Due to their function and material makeup, drivebelts can fail after a long period of time and should therefore be inspected regularly.

3 Since the drivebelt is located very close to the right-hand side of the engine compartment, the right-hand headlight must be removed (see Chapter 12, Section 7) for access to the tensioner and pulleys. If preferred, the front of the vehicle may also be raised and supported on axle stands (see *"Jacking and Vehicle Support"*) for access to the crankshaft pulley.

4 With the engine stopped, inspect the full length of the drivebelt for cracks and separation of the belt plies. It will be necessary to turn the engine (using a spanner or socket and bar on the crankshaft pulley bolt) in order to move the belt from the pulleys so that the belt can be inspected thoroughly. Twist the belt between the pulleys so that both sides can be viewed. Also check for fraying, and glazing which gives the belt a shiny appearance. Check the pulleys for nicks, cracks, distortion and corrosion.

### Renewal

5 To remove the drivebelt, first remove the right-hand headlight as described in Chapter 12, Section 7 and if necessary jack up the front of the vehicle and support it on axle stands (see *"Jacking and Vehicle Support"*) for access to the crankshaft pulley. Where necessary, unbolt and remove the crankshaft pulley cover.

6 Using a spanner on the tensioner centre bolt, turn the tensioner clockwise to release the drivebelt tension **(see illustration)**. Note how the drivebelt is routed, then remove the belt from the pulleys.

7 Fit the new drivebelt onto the crankshaft, alternator, power steering pump, and air conditioning compressor pulleys as applicable, then turn the tensioner clockwise and locate the drivebelt on the pulley. Make sure that the drivebelt is correctly seated in all of the pulley grooves, then release the tensioner.

8 Where necessary, lower the vehicle to the ground.

### 6  Hose and fluid leak check

1 Visually inspect the engine joint faces, gaskets and seals for any signs of water or oil leaks. Pay particular attention to the areas around the cylinder head cover, cylinder head, oil filter and sump joint faces. Bear in mind that, over a period of time, some very slight seepage from these areas is to be expected - what you are really looking for is any indication of a serious leak. Should a leak be found, renew the offending gasket or oil seal by referring to the appropriate Chapters in this manual.

2 Also check the security and condition of all the engine-related pipes and hoses, and all braking system pipes and hoses. Ensure that all cable ties or securing clips are in place,

**5.6  Turn the tensioner clockwise with a spanner, then remove the belt from the pulleys**

and in good condition. Clips which are broken or missing can lead to chafing of the hoses, pipes or wiring, which could cause more serious problems in the future.

3 Carefully check the radiator hoses and heater hoses along their entire length. Renew any hose which is cracked, swollen or deteriorated. Cracks will show up better if the hose is squeezed. Pay close attention to the hose clips that secure the hoses to the cooling system components. Hose clips can pinch and puncture hoses, resulting in cooling system leaks. If the crimped-type hose clips are used, it may be a good idea to replace them with standard worm-drive clips.

4 Inspect all the cooling system components (hoses, joint faces, etc) for leaks **(see Haynes Hint)**.

5 Where any problems are found on system components, renew the component or gasket with reference to Chapter 3.

6 With the vehicle raised, inspect the fuel tank and filler neck for punctures, cracks and other damage. The connection between the filler neck and tank is especially critical. Sometimes a rubber filler neck or connecting hose will leak due to loose retaining clamps or deteriorated rubber.

7 Carefully check all rubber hoses and metal fuel lines leading away from the fuel tank. Check for loose connections, deteriorated hoses, crimped lines, and other damage. Pay

**For a quick check, the thickness of friction material remaining on the inner brake pad can be measured through the aperture in the caliper body.**

*A leak in the cooling system will usually show up as white- or rust-coloured deposits on the area adjoining the leak.*

particular attention to the vent pipes and hoses, which often loop up around the filler neck and can become blocked or crimped. Follow the lines to the front of the vehicle, carefully inspecting them all the way. Renew damaged sections as necessary. Similarly, whilst the vehicle is raised, take the opportunity to inspect all underbody brake fluid pipes and hoses.

8 From within the engine compartment, check the security of all fuel, vacuum and brake hose attachments and pipe unions, and inspect all hoses for kinks, chafing and deterioration.

9 Where applicable, check the condition of the power steering fluid pipes and hoses.

### 7  Front brake pad and disc wear check

1 Apply the handbrake, then jack up the front of the car and support it securely on axle stands (see *"Jacking and Vehicle Support"*). Remove the front roadwheels.

2 For a comprehensive check, the brake pads should be removed and cleaned. The operation of the caliper can then also be checked, and the condition of the brake disc itself can be fully examined on both sides. Refer to Chapter 9 for further information **(see Haynes Hint)**.

3 On completion refit the roadwheels and lower the car to the ground.

### 8  Rear brake shoe and drum wear check

1 Remove the brake drum as described in Chapter 9, Section 7.

2 Taking the necessary precautions to avoid inhalation of dust, remove all traces of brake dust from the brake drum, backplate and shoes.

3 Measure the thickness of the friction material of each brake shoe at several points; if either shoe is worn at any point to the

**9.4 Check for wear in the hub bearings by grasping the wheel and trying to rock it**

minimum thickness or less (see Specifications), all four shoes must be renewed as a set. The shoes should also be renewed if any are fouled with oil or grease. There is no satisfactory way of degreasing friction material, once contaminated.

**4** If either of the brake shoes are worn unevenly, or fouled with oil or grease, trace and rectify the cause before reassembly.

## 9 Steering and suspension check

### Front suspension and steering check

**1** Raise the front of the vehicle, and securely support it on axle stands (see "*Jacking and Vehicle Support*").

**2** Visually inspect the balljoint dust covers and the steering rack-and-pinion gaiters for splits, chafing or deterioration. Any wear of these components will cause loss of lubricant, together with dirt and water entry, resulting in rapid deterioration of the balljoints or steering gear.

**3** On vehicles with power steering, check the fluid hoses for chafing or deterioration, and the pipe and hose unions for fluid leaks. Also check for signs of fluid leakage under pressure from the steering gear rubber gaiters, which would indicate failed fluid seals within the steering gear.

**4** Grasp the roadwheel at the 12 o'clock and 6 o'clock positions, and try to rock it **(see illustration)**. Very slight free play may be felt, but if the movement is appreciable, further investigation is necessary to determine the source. Continue rocking the wheel while an assistant depresses the footbrake. If the movement is now eliminated or significantly reduced, it is likely that the hub bearings are at fault. If the free play is still evident with the footbrake depressed, then there is wear in the suspension joints or mountings.

**5** Now grasp the wheel at the 9 o'clock and 3 o'clock positions, and try to rock it as before. Any movement felt now may again be caused by wear in the hub bearings or the steering track-rod balljoints. If the outer balljoint is worn, the visual movement will be obvious. If the inner joint is suspect, it can be felt by placing a hand over the rack-and-pinion rubber gaiter and gripping the track-rod. If the wheel is now rocked, movement will be felt at the inner joint if wear has taken place.

**6** Using a large screwdriver or flat bar, check for wear in the suspension mounting bushes by levering between the relevant suspension component and its attachment point. Some movement is to be expected, as the mountings are made of rubber, but excessive wear should be obvious. Also check the condition of any visible rubber bushes, looking for splits, cracks or contamination of the rubber.

**7** With the car standing on its wheels, have an assistant turn the steering wheel back and forth, about an eighth of a turn each way. There should be very little, if any, lost movement between the steering wheel and roadwheels. If this is not the case, closely observe the joints and mountings previously described. In addition, check the steering column universal joints for wear, and also check the rack-and-pinion steering gear itself.

### Rear suspension check

**8** Chock the front wheels, then jack up the rear of the vehicle and support securely on axle stands (see "*Jacking and Vehicle Support*").

**9** Working as described previously for the front suspension, check the rear hub bearings, the suspension bushes and the strut mountings for wear.

**10** Check for any signs of fluid leakage around the shock absorber, or from the rubber gaiter around the piston rod. Should any fluid be noticed, the shock absorber/strut is defective internally, and should be renewed. **Note:** *Shock absorbers should always be renewed in pairs on the same axle.*

**11** The efficiency of the shock absorber may be checked by bouncing the vehicle at each corner. Generally speaking, the body will return to its normal position and stop after being depressed. If it rises and returns on a rebound, the shock absorber is probably suspect. Also examine the shock absorber upper and lower mountings for any signs of wear.

## 10 Driveshaft gaiter check

**1** With the vehicle raised and securely supported on stands (see "*Jacking and vehicle support*"), turn the steering onto full lock then slowly rotate the roadwheel. Inspect the condition of the outer constant velocity (CV) joint rubber gaiters while squeezing the gaiters to open out the folds **(see illustration)**. Check for signs of cracking, splits or deterioration of the rubber which may allow the grease to escape and lead to water and grit entry into the joint. Also check the security and condition of the retaining clips. Repeat these checks on the inner CV joints. If any damage or deterioration is found, the gaiters should be renewed as described in Chapter 8.

**2** At the same time check the general condition of the CV joints themselves by first holding the driveshaft and attempting to rotate the wheel. Repeat this check by holding the inner joint and attempting to rotate the driveshaft. Any appreciable movement indicates wear in the joints, wear in the driveshaft splines or loose driveshaft retaining nut.

## 11 Seat belt check

**1** Check the seat belts for satisfactory operation and condition. Inspect the webbing for fraying and cuts. Check that they retract smoothly and without binding into their reels.

**2** Check that the seat belt mounting bolts are tight, and if necessary tighten them to the specified torque wrench setting with reference to Chapter 11.

## 12 Hinge and lock lubrication

**1** Work around the vehicle and lubricate the hinges of the bonnet, doors and tailgate with a light machine oil.

**2** Lightly lubricate the bonnet release mechanism and exposed section of the inner cable with a smear of grease **(see illustration)**.

**3** Check carefully the security and operation

**10.1 Check the condition of the driveshaft gaiters**

**12.2 Lightly lubricate the bonnet release mechanism and exposed section of inner cable with a smear of grease**

of all hinges, latches and locks, adjusting them where required. Check the operation of the central locking system.

**4** Check the condition and operation of the tailgate struts, renewing them if either is leaking or no longer able to support the tailgate securely when raised.

### 13 Roadwheel nut tightness check

**1** Where applicable, remove the wheel trims, and slacken the roadwheel nuts slightly.
**2** Tighten the nuts to the specified torque, using a torque wrench.

### 14 Road test

### Instruments and electrical equipment

**1** Check the operation of all instruments and electrical equipment.
**2** Make sure that all instruments read correctly, and switch on all electrical equipment in turn, to check that it functions properly.

### Steering and suspension

**3** Check for any abnormalities in the steering, suspension, handling or road "feel".
**4** Drive the vehicle, and check that there are no unusual vibrations or noises.
**5** Check that the steering feels positive, with no excessive "sloppiness", or roughness, and check for any suspension noises when cornering and driving over bumps.

### Drivetrain

**6** Check the performance of the engine, clutch, transmission and driveshafts.
**7** Listen for any unusual noises from the engine, clutch and transmission.
**8** Make sure that the engine runs smoothly when idling, and that there is no hesitation when accelerating.
**9** Check that, where applicable, the clutch action is smooth and progressive, that the drive is taken up smoothly, and that the pedal travel is not excessive. Also listen for any noises when the clutch pedal is depressed.
**10** Check that all gears can be engaged smoothly without noise, and that the gear lever action is not abnormally vague or "notchy".
**11** Listen for a metallic clicking sound from the front of the vehicle, as the vehicle is driven slowly in a circle with the steering on full-lock.

Carry out this check in both directions. If a clicking noise is heard, this indicates wear in a driveshaft joint (see Chapter 8).

### Check the operation and performance of the braking system

**12** Make sure that the vehicle does not pull to one side when braking, and that the wheels do not lock prematurely when braking hard.
**13** Check that there is no vibration through the steering when braking.
**14** Check that the handbrake operates correctly, without excessive movement of the lever, and that it holds the vehicle stationary on a slope.
**15** Test the operation of the brake servo unit as follows. Depress the footbrake four or five times to exhaust the vacuum, then start the engine. As the engine starts, there should be a noticeable "give" in the brake pedal as vacuum builds up. Allow the engine to run for at least two minutes, and then switch it off. If the brake pedal is now depressed again, it should be possible to detect a hiss from the servo as the pedal is depressed. After about four or five applications, no further hissing should be heard, and the pedal should feel considerably harder.

# Every 20 000 miles

### 15 Pollen filter renewal

**1** To access the pollen filter, the passenger-side half of the windscreen cowl panel must be removed. Open the bonnet and pull up the rubber seal along the edge of the cowl panel. Prise out the screw covers, then remove the cowl panel screws and slide out the half-panel on the passenger side. **Note:** *Refer to photos 17.2a to 17.2d in Chapter 12, Section 17 – the wiper arms do not have to be removed.*
**2** Release the two clips, and open the pollen filter cover **(see illustration)**.
**3** Pull the filter from the housing.

**15.2 Pollen filter cover clip**

**4** Fit the new filter using a reversal of the removal procedure. Make sure that the filter is fitted with the removal tab and the "TOP/OBEN" marking visible.

### 16 Battery electrolyte level check

**1** Where a "sealed for life" maintenance-free battery is fitted, topping-up of the electrolyte in each cell is not possible. On other batteries the level of the electrolyte can be checked through the translucent sides - make sure that the level in each cell is up to the marking on the outside of the battery.
**2** If any cell requires topping up, obtain some distilled or de-ionised battery water, then remove the cell covers. Pour in the water until the cell plates are covered by just 2 or 3 mm. Refit and tighten the cover(s) on completion.

# Every 30 000 miles

### 17 Spark plug renewal and ignition system check

### Spark plug renewal

**1** The correct functioning of the spark plugs is vital for the correct running and efficiency of the engine. It is essential that the plugs fitted are appropriate for the engine; suitable types are specified at the beginning of this Chapter,

on the Vehicle Emissions Control Information (VECI) label located on the underside of the bonnet (only on models sold in some areas) or in the vehicle's Owner's Handbook. If the correct type is used and the engine is in good condition, the spark plugs should not need attention between scheduled replacement intervals. Spark plug cleaning is rarely necessary, and should not be attempted unless specialised equipment is available, as damage can easily be caused to the firing ends.

**2** If the marks on the original-equipment spark plug (HT) leads cannot be seen, mark the leads to correspond to the cylinder the lead serves. Twist the plug caps slightly to break the seal, then pull the leads from the plugs by gripping the end fitting, not the lead, otherwise the lead connection may be fractured.
**3** It is advisable to remove the dirt from the spark plug recesses using a clean brush, vacuum cleaner or compressed air before removing the plugs, to prevent dirt dropping into the cylinders.

**17.4 Tools required for changing spark plugs**

**17.9a Using a wire-type gauge when checking the gap**

**17.9b Measuring a spark plug gap with a feeler blade**

**4** Unscrew the plugs from the front of the cylinder head using a spark plug spanner, suitable box spanner or a deep socket and extension bar **(see illustration)**. Keep the socket aligned with the spark plug - if it is forcibly moved to one side, the ceramic insulator may be broken off. As each plug is removed, examine it as follows.

**5** Examination of the spark plugs will give a good indication of the condition of the engine. If the insulator nose of the spark plug is clean and white, with no deposits, this is indicative of a weak mixture or too hot a plug (a hot plug transfers heat away from the electrode slowly, a cold plug transfers heat away quickly).

**6** If the tip and insulator nose are covered with hard black-looking deposits, then this is indicative that the mixture is too rich. Should the plug be black and oily, then it is likely that the engine is fairly worn, as well as the mixture being too rich.

**7** If the insulator nose is covered with light tan to greyish-brown deposits, then the mixture is correct and it is likely that the engine is in good condition.

**8** The spark plug electrode gap is of considerable importance as, if it is too large or too small, the size of the spark and its efficiency will be seriously impaired. The gap should be set to the value given in the Specifications at the beginning of this Chapter.

**9** To set the gap, measure it with a feeler blade and then bend open, or closed, the outer plug electrode until the correct gap is achieved. The centre electrode should never

be bent, as this may crack the insulator and cause plug failure, if nothing worse. If using feeler blades, the gap is correct when the appropriate-size blade is a firm sliding fit **(see illustrations)**.

**10** Special spark plug electrode gap adjusting tools are available from most motor accessory shops, or from some spark plug manufacturers **(see illustration)**.

**11** Before fitting the spark plugs, check that the threaded connector sleeves are tight, and that the plug exterior surfaces and threads are clean **(see Haynes Hint)**. Apply a little copper grease to the threads before inserting the spark plugs.

**12** Remove the rubber hose (if used), and tighten the plug to the specified torque using the spark plug socket and a torque wrench. Refit the remaining spark plugs in the same manner.

**13** Connect the HT leads in their correct order. Ford recommends that the insides of the HT connectors are coated with silicone grease to a depth of 5 to 10 mm.

**17.10 To change the gap, bend the outer electrode only**

![HAYNES HINT]

*It is often difficult to insert spark plugs into their holes without cross-threading them. To avoid this possibility, fit a short length of rubber or plastic hose over the end of the spark plug. The flexible hose acts as a universal joint, to help align the plug with the plug hole. Should the plug begin to cross thread, the hose will slip on the spark plug, preventing thread damage to the cylinder head.*

### Ignition system check

⚠️ *Warning: Voltages produced by an electronic ignition system are considerably higher than those produced by conventional ignition systems. Extreme care must be taken when working on the system with the ignition switched on. Persons with surgically-implanted cardiac pacemaker devices should keep well clear of the ignition circuits, components and test equipment.*

**14** The spark plug (HT) leads should be checked whenever new spark plugs are fitted.

**15** Ensure that the leads are numbered before removing them, to avoid confusion when refitting. Pull the leads from the plugs by gripping the end fitting, not the lead, otherwise the lead connection may be fractured.

**16** Check inside the end fitting for signs of corrosion, which will look like a white crusty powder. Push the end fitting back onto the spark plug, ensuring that it is a tight fit on the plug. If not, remove the lead again and use pliers to carefully crimp the metal connector inside the end fitting until it fits securely on the end of the spark plug.

**17** Using a clean rag, wipe the entire length of the lead to remove any built-up dirt and grease. Once the lead is clean, check for burns, cracks and other damage. Do not bend the lead excessively, nor pull the lead lengthwise - the conductor inside might break.

**18** Disconnect the other end of the lead from the ignition coil by squeezing the clips. Check for corrosion and a tight fit in the same manner as the spark plug end. If an ohmmeter is available, check the resistance of the lead by connecting the meter between each end of the lead. Refit the lead securely on completion.

**19** Check the remaining leads one at a time, in the same way.

**20** If new spark plug (HT) leads are required, purchase a set for your specific engine.

**21** Even with the ignition system in first-class condition, some engines may still occasionally experience poor starting attributable to damp ignition components. To disperse moisture, a water-dispersant aerosol can be very effective.

**18.1 Unscrew the retaining screws . . .**

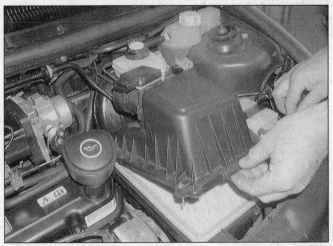

**18.2a . . . lift the cover . . .**

## 18 Air filter element renewal

1 The air cleaner is located in the left-hand front corner of the engine compartment, next to the battery. Unscrew and remove the screws securing the cover to the air cleaner body **(see illustration)**.
2 Lift the cover and remove the filter element

**18.2b . . . and remove the filter element**

from the base **(see illustrations)**. Note which way round it is fitted.
3 Wipe clean the interior surfaces of the cover and base. Also remove the foam filter from the crankcase ventilation inlet and clean it **(see illustration)**.
4 Refit the foam filter, then insert the new element making sure that it is seated correctly in the base.
5 Refit the cover and tighten the retaining screws.

## 19 Oil filler cap and crankcase ventilation system check

1 Remove and inspect the oil filler cap to ensure that it is in good condition, and not blocked up with sludge.
2 Disconnect the hoses at the cap, and clean the cap if necessary by brushing the inner mesh filter with petrol, and blowing through with an air line. Renew the cap if it is badly congested.
3 Refit the hoses and cap.

## 20 Manual transmission oil level check

1 Position the vehicle over an inspection pit, on vehicle ramps, or jack it up, but make sure that it is level (see "*Jacking and vehicle support*").
2 Remove all traces of dirt then unscrew the filler/level plug from the front face of the transmission. Note it is the plug furthest from the engine - do not confuse it with the blanking plug near the bellhousing **(see illustration)**.
3 The level must be between 5 mm and 10 mm below the bottom edge of the filler/level plug hole (use a cranked tool such as an Allen key to check the level). If necessary, top up the level with the specified grade of oil (see "*Lubricants and fluids*") **(see illustration)**.
4 When the level is correct, clean and refit the filler level plug and tighten it to the specified torque.
5 Where applicable, lower the car to the ground.

**18.3 Removing the foam filter from the crankcase ventilation inlet**

**20.2 Unscrewing the manual transmission oil filler/level plug**

**20.3 Topping-up the manual transmission with oil**

# Every 60 000 miles

**21.1 The fuel filter is located on the front left-hand corner of the fuel tank**

## 21 Fuel filter renewal

1 The fuel filter is located on the front left-hand corner of the fuel tank **(see illustration)**. First chock the front wheels, then jack up the rear of the vehicle and support it on axle stands (see *"Jacking and Vehicle Support"*).
2 Squeeze the tabs and disconnect the quick-release fittings from each end of the filter. Plug the fuel lines to prevent loss of fuel.
3 Note the fuel flow arrow on the filter, then unscrew and remove the clamp bolt and remove the filter from the mounting bracket which is riveted to the fuel tank flange.
4 Fit the new filter using a reversal of the removal procedure. Make sure the quick-release fittings are pushed fully onto the inlet and outlet stubs, and tighten the clamp bolt securely. Also make sure the filter is fitted the correct way around with the directional arrow pointing towards the fuel line leading to the engine compartment.

# Every 3 years, regardless of mileage

## 22 Brake fluid renewal

⚠️ *Warning: Brake hydraulic fluid can harm your eyes and damage painted surfaces, so use extreme caution when handling and pouring it. Do not use fluid that has been standing open for some time, as it absorbs moisture from the air. Excess moisture can cause a dangerous loss of braking effectiveness.*

1 The procedure is similar to that for the bleeding of the hydraulic system as described in Chapter 9 except that, on models with a conventional braking system, the brake fluid reservoir should be emptied by siphoning, using a clean poultry baster or similar before

starting, and allowance should be made for the old fluid to be expelled when bleeding a section of the circuit. On models fitted with ABS, reduce the fluid level in the reservoir (by siphoning or using a poultry baster), but do not allow the fluid level to drop far enough to allow air into the system - if air enters the ABS hydraulic unit, the unit must be bled using special Ford test equipment (see Chapter 9).
2 Working as described in Chapter 9, open the first bleed screw in the sequence, and pump the brake pedal gently until nearly all the old fluid has been emptied from the master cylinder reservoir. Top-up to the "MAX" level with new fluid, and continue pumping until only the new fluid remains in the reservoir, and new fluid can be seen emerging from the bleed screw. Tighten the screw, and top-up the reservoir level to the "MAX" level line.

> **HAYNES HiNT** *Old hydraulic fluid is invariably much darker in colour than the new, making it easy to distinguish the two.*

3 Work through all the remaining bleed screws in the sequence until new fluid can be seen at all of them. Be careful to keep the master cylinder reservoir topped-up to above the "MIN" level at all times, or air may enter the system and greatly increase the length of the task.
4 When the operation is complete, check that all bleed screws are securely tightened, and that their dust caps are refitted. Wash off all traces of spilt fluid, and recheck the master cylinder reservoir fluid level.
5 Check the operation of the brakes before taking the car on the road.

# Every 4 or 10 years, regardless of mileage (see note)

**Note:** *If the antifreeze used is Ford's own, or of similar quality, Ford state that the coolant need not be renewed for 4 years (blue/green coolant) or for 10 years (orange coolant). If the vehicle's history is unknown, if antifreeze of lesser quality is known to be in the system, or simply if you prefer to follow conventional servicing intervals, the coolant should be changed periodically (typically, every 3 years) as described here.*

## 23 Coolant renewal and pressure cap check

### Cooling system draining

⚠️ *Warning: Wait until the engine is cold before starting this procedure. Do not allow antifreeze to come in contact with your skin, or with the painted surfaces of the vehicle. Rinse off spills immediately with plenty of*

*water. Never leave antifreeze lying around in an open container, or in a puddle in the driveway or on the garage floor. Children and pets are attracted by its sweet smell, but antifreeze can be fatal if ingested.*

1 With the engine completely cold, remove the expansion tank filler cap. Turn the cap anti-clockwise, wait until any pressure

**23.3 Drain screw on the bottom left-hand corner of the radiator**

remaining in the system is released, then unscrew it and lift it off.
2 Position a suitable container beneath the radiator drain screw, at the bottom left-hand corner of the radiator.
3 Slacken the drain screw, and allow the coolant to drain into the container **(see illustration)**.
4 When the flow of coolant stops, tighten the radiator drain screw.
5 If the coolant has been drained for a reason other than renewal, then provided it is clean and less than two years old, it can be re-used, though this is not recommended.

### Cooling system flushing

6 If coolant renewal has been neglected, or if the antifreeze mixture has become diluted, then in time, the cooling system may gradually lose efficiency, as the coolant passages become restricted due to rust, scale deposits, and other sediment. The cooling system efficiency can be restored by flushing the system clean.

**7** The radiator should be flushed independently of the engine, to avoid unnecessary contamination.

### Radiator flushing

**8** Disconnect the top and bottom hoses with reference to Chapter 3.

**9** Insert a garden hose into the radiator top inlet. Direct a flow of clean water through the radiator, and continue flushing until clean water emerges from the radiator bottom outlet.

**10** If after a reasonable period, the water still does not run clear, the radiator can be flushed with a good proprietary cleaning agent. It is important that the manufacturer's instructions are followed carefully. If the contamination is particularly bad, remove the radiator then insert the hose in the bottom outlet and reverse-flush the radiator.

### Engine flushing

**11** Remove the thermostat as described in Chapter 3 then, if the radiator top hose has been disconnected from the engine, temporarily reconnect the hose.

**12** With the top and bottom hoses disconnected from the radiator, insert a garden hose into the radiator top hose. Direct a clean flow of water through the engine, and continue flushing until clean water emerges from the radiator bottom hose.

**13** On completion of flushing, refit the thermostat and reconnect the hoses with reference to Chapter 3.

### Cooling system filling

**14** Before attempting to fill the cooling system, make sure that all hoses and clips are in good condition, and that the clips are tight. Note that an antifreeze mixture must be used all year round, to prevent corrosion of the engine components. Also check that the cylinder block drain plug is in place and tight.

**15** Remove the expansion tank filler cap **(see illustration)**.

**23.15 Removing the expansion tank filler cap**

**16** Place a wad of rags around the expansion tank.

**17** Slowly fill the system until the coolant level reaches the "MAX" mark on the side of the expansion tank.

**18** Start the engine and allow it to run for only two minutes, while increasing the engine speed to a fast idle several times. Switch off the engine and top-up the coolant level.

**19** Refit and tighten the expansion tank filler cap.

**20** Start the engine, and allow it to run until it reaches normal operating temperature (until the cooling fan cuts in and out).

**21** Stop the engine, and allow it to cool, then re-check the coolant level with reference to *"Weekly checks"*. Top-up the level if necessary and refit the expansion tank filler cap.

### Antifreeze mixture

**22** The antifreeze should always be renewed at the specified intervals. This is necessary not only to maintain the antifreeze properties, but also to prevent corrosion which would otherwise occur as the corrosion inhibitors become progressively less effective.

**23** Always use an ethylene-glycol based antifreeze which is suitable for use in mixed-

**23.27 Inspecting the expansion tank pressure cap seal**

metal cooling systems. The quantity of antifreeze and levels of protection are given in the Specifications.

**24** Before adding antifreeze, the cooling system should be completely drained, preferably flushed, and all hoses checked for condition and security.

**25** After filling with antifreeze, a label should be attached to the expansion tank, stating the type and concentration of antifreeze used, and the date installed. Any subsequent topping-up should be made with the same type and concentration of antifreeze.

**26** Do not use engine antifreeze in the windscreen/tailgate washer system, as it will cause damage to the vehicle paintwork. A screenwash additive should be added to the washer system in the quantities stated on the bottle.

### Pressure (expansion tank) cap check

**27** With the engine cold, remove and clean the pressure cap, and inspect the seal for damage and/or deterioration. If there is any sign of damage or deterioration to the seal, fit a new pressure cap **(see illustration)**.

# Every 15 years, regardless of mileage

**24  Air bag renewal**

**1** The air bag must be renewed every 15 years since the efficiency of the propellant may deteriorate over this time. Removal and refitting procedures are given in Chapter 12.

**2** The old air bag should be disposed of

safely by a Ford dealer.

⚠ *Warning: Do not dispose of it with household rubbish as it contains explosives and is potentially* **dangerous in unqualified hands.**

# Chapter 2 Part A:
# Engine in-car repair procedures

## Contents

## Degrees of difficulty

| | | | | |
|---|---|---|---|---|
| **Easy,** suitable for novice with little experience  | **Fairly easy,** suitable for beginner with some experience  | **Fairly difficult,** suitable for competent DIY mechanic 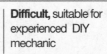 | **Difficult,** suitable for experienced DIY mechanic | **Very difficult,** suitable for expert DIY or professional |

## Specifications

### General

| | |
|---|---|
| Engine type . . . . . . . . . . . . . . . . . . . . . . . . . . . . . . . . . . . . . . . . . | Four-cylinder, in-line overhead valve |
| Designation . . . . . . . . . . . . . . . . . . . . . . . . . . . . . . . . . . . . . . . . | Endura-E |

Engine code*:
Up to 1999 model year (Emission level Stage II/Europe
    and D3/Germany . . . . . . . . . . . . . . . . . . . . . . . . . . . . . . . . . . JJB (37 kW/50 PS), J4D (44 kW/60 PS)
Mid 1999 model year on (Emission level Stage II/Europe
    except Germany) . . . . . . . . . . . . . . . . . . . . . . . . . . . . . . . . . . JJF (37 kW/50 PS), J4M (44 kW/60 PS)
Since 1999 model year (Emission level Stage II/Europe
    and D4/Germany) . . . . . . . . . . . . . . . . . . . . . . . . . . . . . . . . . JJD (37 kW/50 PS), J4K (44 kW/60 PS)
*Note that the 37 kW engine is only marketed in Germany and Austria.

| | |
|---|---|
| Capacity . . . . . . . . . . . . . . . . . . . . . . . . . . . . . . . . . . . . . . . . . . . | 1299 cc |
| Bore . . . . . . . . . . . . . . . . . . . . . . . . . . . . . . . . . . . . . . . . . . . . . . | 73.96 mm |
| Stroke . . . . . . . . . . . . . . . . . . . . . . . . . . . . . . . . . . . . . . . . . . . . | 75.48 mm |
| Compression ratio . . . . . . . . . . . . . . . . . . . . . . . . . . . . . . . . . . . | 9.5:1 |
| Firing order . . . . . . . . . . . . . . . . . . . . . . . . . . . . . . . . . . . . . . . . | 1-2-4-3 (No 1 cylinder at timing chain end) |
| Direction of crankshaft rotation . . . . . . . . . . . . . . . . . . . . . . . . . | Clockwise (seen from right-hand side of vehicle) |

### Valves

Valve clearance (cold):

| | |
|---|---|
| Inlet . . . . . . . . . . . . . . . . . . . . . . . . . . . . . . . . . . . . . . . . . . . . . | 0.20 mm |
| Exhaust: | |
|     Engines built up to 20/11/96 . . . . . . . . . . . . . . . . . . . . . . . . . | 0.30 mm |
|     Engines built from 20/11/96* . . . . . . . . . . . . . . . . . . . . . . . . | 0.50 mm |

*These engines are marked with a valve clearance sticker on the cylinder head cover

| | Inlet | Exhaust |
|---|---|---|
| Valve head diameter . . . . . . . . . . . . . . . . . . . . . . . . . . . . . . . . . . | 34.40 to 34.60 mm | 28.90 to 29.10 mm |
| Valve stem diameter: | | |
|     Standard . . . . . . . . . . . . . . . . . . . . . . . . . . . . . . . . . . . . . . | 7.025 to 7.043 mm | 6.999 to 7.017 mm |
|     Oversize 0.2 mm . . . . . . . . . . . . . . . . . . . . . . . . . . . . . . . . | 7.225 to 7.243 mm | 7.199 to 7.217 mm |
|     Oversize 0.4 mm . . . . . . . . . . . . . . . . . . . . . . . . . . . . . . . . | 7.425 to 7.443 mm | 7.399 to 7.417 mm |
| Valve stem-to-guide clearance . . . . . . . . . . . . . . . . . . . . . . . . . . | 0.020 to 0.069 mm | 0.046 to 0.095 mm |

### Valve springs

| | |
|---|---|
| Free length . . . . . . . . . . . . . . . . . . . . . . . . . . . . . . . . . . . . . . . . | 41.0 mm |

## Cylinder head

| | |
|---|---|
| Maximum permissible gasket surface distortion (measured over full length) . | 0.25 mm |
| Valve seat angle (inlet and exhaust) . . . . . . . . . . . . . . . . . . . . . . . . . . . . | 45° |
| Valve seat width (inlet and exhaust) . . . . . . . . . . . . . . . . . . . . . . . . . . . . | 1.18 to 1.75 mm* |

*The inlet and exhaust valves have special inserts which cannot be recut using conventional tools.*

## Camshaft

| | |
|---|---|
| Camshaft bearing diameter . . . . . . . . . . . . . . . . . . . . . . . . . . . . . . . . . . . | 39.615 to 39.635 mm |
| Bearing bush inside diameter: | |
|   Standard . . . . . . . . . . . . . . . . . . . . . . . . . . . . . . . . . . . . . . . . . . . . | 39.662 to 39.682 mm |
|   Oversize . . . . . . . . . . . . . . . . . . . . . . . . . . . . . . . . . . . . . . . . . . . . . | 39.662 to 39.713 mm |
| Camshaft thrust plate thickness . . . . . . . . . . . . . . . . . . . . . . . . . . . . . . . | 4.457 to 4.508 mm |
| Endfloat . . . . . . . . . . . . . . . . . . . . . . . . . . . . . . . . . . . . . . . . . . . . . . . . . | 0.02 to 0.19 mm |

## Cylinder block

| | |
|---|---|
| Cylinder bore diameter: | |
|   Standard 1 . . . . . . . . . . . . . . . . . . . . . . . . . . . . . . . . . . . . . . . . . . . | 73.94 to 73.95 mm |
|   Standard 2 . . . . . . . . . . . . . . . . . . . . . . . . . . . . . . . . . . . . . . . . . . . | 73.95 to 73.96 mm |
|   Standard 3 . . . . . . . . . . . . . . . . . . . . . . . . . . . . . . . . . . . . . . . . . . . | 73.96 to 73.97 mm |
|   Oversize 0.5 mm . . . . . . . . . . . . . . . . . . . . . . . . . . . . . . . . . . . . . . | 75.00 to 75.01 mm |
| Valve tappet diameter . . . . . . . . . . . . . . . . . . . . . . . . . . . . . . . . . . . . . . | 13.081 to 13.094 mm |
| Valve tappet clearance in cylinder block . . . . . . . . . . . . . . . . . . . . . . . . | 0.016 to 0.062 mm |

## Pistons and piston rings

| | |
|---|---|
| Piston diameter: | |
|   Standard 1 . . . . . . . . . . . . . . . . . . . . . . . . . . . . . . . . . . . . . . . . . . . | 73.91 to 73.92 mm |
|   Standard 2 . . . . . . . . . . . . . . . . . . . . . . . . . . . . . . . . . . . . . . . . . . . | 73.92 to 73.93 mm |
|   Standard 3 . . . . . . . . . . . . . . . . . . . . . . . . . . . . . . . . . . . . . . . . . . . | 73.93 to 73.94 mm |
|   Oversize 0.5 mm . . . . . . . . . . . . . . . . . . . . . . . . . . . . . . . . . . . . . . | 74.46 to 74.49 mm |
|   Oversize 1.0 mm . . . . . . . . . . . . . . . . . . . . . . . . . . . . . . . . . . . . . . | 74.96 to 74.99 mm |
| Piston-to-cylinder bore clearance . . . . . . . . . . . . . . . . . . . . . . . . . . . . . | 0.015 to 0.050 mm |
| Piston ring end gap - installed: | |
|   Top compression ring . . . . . . . . . . . . . . . . . . . . . . . . . . . . . . . . . . | 0.25 to 0.45 mm |
|   Second compression ring . . . . . . . . . . . . . . . . . . . . . . . . . . . . . . . | 0.45 to 0.75 mm |
|   Oil control ring . . . . . . . . . . . . . . . . . . . . . . . . . . . . . . . . . . . . . . . | 0.20 to 0.50 mm |
| Piston ring-to-groove clearance: | |
|   Compression rings . . . . . . . . . . . . . . . . . . . . . . . . . . . . . . . . . . . . | 0.20 mm (maximum) |
|   Oil control ring . . . . . . . . . . . . . . . . . . . . . . . . . . . . . . . . . . . . . . . | 0.10 mm (maximum) |
| Ring gap position: | |
|   Top compression ring . . . . . . . . . . . . . . . . . . . . . . . . . . . . . . . . . . | Offset 180° from oil control ring gap |
|   Second compression ring . . . . . . . . . . . . . . . . . . . . . . . . . . . . . . . | Offset 90° from oil control ring gap |
|   Oil control ring . . . . . . . . . . . . . . . . . . . . . . . . . . . . . . . . . . . . . . . | Aligned with gudgeon pin |

## Gudgeon pin

| | |
|---|---|
| Length . . . . . . . . . . . . . . . . . . . . . . . . . . . . . . . . . . . . . . . . . . . . . . . . . | 63.6 to 64.4 mm |
| Diameter: | |
|   White colour code . . . . . . . . . . . . . . . . . . . . . . . . . . . . . . . . . . . . . | 18.026 to 18.029 mm |
|   Red colour code . . . . . . . . . . . . . . . . . . . . . . . . . . . . . . . . . . . . . . | 18.029 to 18.032 mm |
|   Blue colour code . . . . . . . . . . . . . . . . . . . . . . . . . . . . . . . . . . . . . | 18.032 to 18.035 mm |
|   Yellow colour code . . . . . . . . . . . . . . . . . . . . . . . . . . . . . . . . . . . . | 18.035 to 18.038 mm |
| Clearance in piston . . . . . . . . . . . . . . . . . . . . . . . . . . . . . . . . . . . . . . . | 0.008 to 0.014 mm |
| Interference fit in connecting rod . . . . . . . . . . . . . . . . . . . . . . . . . . . . . | 0.016 to 0.048 mm |

## Crankshaft and bearings

| | |
|---|---|
| Main bearings . . . . . . . . . . . . . . . . . . . . . . . . . . . . . . . . . . . . . . . . . . . | 5 |
| Main bearing journal diameter: | |
|   Standard . . . . . . . . . . . . . . . . . . . . . . . . . . . . . . . . . . . . . . . . . . . . | 56.980 to 57.000 mm |
|   0.254 mm undersize (green) . . . . . . . . . . . . . . . . . . . . . . . . . . . . . | 56.726 to 56.746 mm |
| Main bearing journal-to-shell running clearance . . . . . . . . . . . . . . . . . | 0.009 to 0.056 mm |
| Crankpin (big-end) bearing journal diameter: | |
|   Standard . . . . . . . . . . . . . . . . . . . . . . . . . . . . . . . . . . . . . . . . . . . . | 40.99 to 41.01 mm |
|   0.254 mm undersize (green) . . . . . . . . . . . . . . . . . . . . . . . . . . . . . | 40.74 to 40.76 mm |
|   0.508 mm undersize . . . . . . . . . . . . . . . . . . . . . . . . . . . . . . . . . . . | 40.49 to 40.51 mm |
|   0.762 mm undersize . . . . . . . . . . . . . . . . . . . . . . . . . . . . . . . . . . . | 40.24 to 40.26 mm |
| Crankpin (big-end) bearing journal-to-shell running clearance . . . . . . . | 0.006 to 0.060 mm |
| Crankpin (big-end) bearing side clearance . . . . . . . . . . . . . . . . . . . . . . | 0.100 to 0.25 mm |
| Crankshaft endfloat . . . . . . . . . . . . . . . . . . . . . . . . . . . . . . . . . . . . . . . | 0.05 to 0.26 mm |
| Thrustwasher thickness: | |
|   Standard . . . . . . . . . . . . . . . . . . . . . . . . . . . . . . . . . . . . . . . . . . . . | 2.80 to 2.85 mm |
|   Oversize . . . . . . . . . . . . . . . . . . . . . . . . . . . . . . . . . . . . . . . . . . . . | 2.99 to 3.04 mm |

## Lubrication

| | |
|---|---|
| Engine oil type/specification . . . . . . . . . . . . . . . . . . . . . . . . . . . . . . . | See "*Lubricants, fluids and tyre pressures*" on page 0•16 |
| Engine oil capacity . . . . . . . . . . . . . . . . . . . . . . . . . . . . . . . . . . . . . . | See Chapter 1 Specifications on page 1•2 |

Oil pressure:
| | |
|---|---|
| At idle speed . . . . . . . . . . . . . . . . . . . . . . . . . . . . . . . . . . . . . . . . | 0.60 bars |
| At 2000 rpm . . . . . . . . . . . . . . . . . . . . . . . . . . . . . . . . . . . . . . . . | 1.50 bars |

Oil pump clearances:
| | |
|---|---|
| Outer rotor-to-body . . . . . . . . . . . . . . . . . . . . . . . . . . . . . . . . . . | 0.14 to 0.26 mm |
| Inner rotor-to-outer rotor . . . . . . . . . . . . . . . . . . . . . . . . . . . . . . | 0.051 to 0.127 mm |
| Rotor endfloat . . . . . . . . . . . . . . . . . . . . . . . . . . . . . . . . . . . . . . . | 0.025 to 0.06 mm |

## Torque wrench settings

| | Nm | lbf ft |
|---|---|---|
| Main bearing cap . . . . . . . . . . . . . . . . . . . . . . . . . . . . . . . . . . . . . | 95 | 70 |
| Crankpin (big-end) bearing cap bolts*: | | |
| Stage 1 . . . . . . . . . . . . . . . . . . . . . . . . . . . . . . . . . . . . . . . . . . . | 4 | 3 |
| Stage 2 . . . . . . . . . . . . . . . . . . . . . . . . . . . . . . . . . . . . . . . . . . . | Angle-tighten a further 90° | |
| Engine-to-transmission bolts . . . . . . . . . . . . . . . . . . . . . . . . . . . . | 44 | 32 |
| Crankshaft rear oil seal housing . . . . . . . . . . . . . . . . . . . . . . . . . . | 18 | 13 |
| Flywheel bolts . . . . . . . . . . . . . . . . . . . . . . . . . . . . . . . . . . . . . . . | 67 | 49 |
| Timing chain tensioner . . . . . . . . . . . . . . . . . . . . . . . . . . . . . . . . | 8 | 6 |
| Camshaft thrust plate bolts . . . . . . . . . . . . . . . . . . . . . . . . . . . . . | 11 | 8 |
| Camshaft sprocket bolt . . . . . . . . . . . . . . . . . . . . . . . . . . . . . . . . | 28 | 21 |
| Timing chain cover . . . . . . . . . . . . . . . . . . . . . . . . . . . . . . . . . . . | 10 | 7 |
| Crankshaft pulley bolt . . . . . . . . . . . . . . . . . . . . . . . . . . . . . . . . . | 115 | 85 |
| Oil pump . . . . . . . . . . . . . . . . . . . . . . . . . . . . . . . . . . . . . . . . . . | 18 | 13 |
| Oil pump cover . . . . . . . . . . . . . . . . . . . . . . . . . . . . . . . . . . . . . . | 10 | 7 |
| Sump: | | |
| Stage 1 . . . . . . . . . . . . . . . . . . . . . . . . . . . . . . . . . . . . . . . . . . . | 7 | 5 |
| Stage 2 . . . . . . . . . . . . . . . . . . . . . . . . . . . . . . . . . . . . . . . . . . . | 10 | 7 |
| Stage 3 (with engine warm) . . . . . . . . . . . . . . . . . . . . . . . . . . . . . | 10 | 7 |
| Oil pressure warning light switch . . . . . . . . . . . . . . . . . . . . . . . . . | 14 | 10 |
| Oil dipstick tube to inlet manifold . . . . . . . . . . . . . . . . . . . . . . . . | 2 | 1 |
| Rocker gear pedestal bolts . . . . . . . . . . . . . . . . . . . . . . . . . . . . . | 43 | 32 |
| Cylinder head bolts (may be re-used once only): | | |
| Stage 1 . . . . . . . . . . . . . . . . . . . . . . . . . . . . . . . . . . . . . . . . . . . | 30 | 22 |
| Stage 2 . . . . . . . . . . . . . . . . . . . . . . . . . . . . . . . . . . . . . . . . . . . | Angle-tighten a further 90° | |
| Stage 3 . . . . . . . . . . . . . . . . . . . . . . . . . . . . . . . . . . . . . . . . . . . | Angle-tighten a further 90° | |
| Rocker cover bolts . . . . . . . . . . . . . . . . . . . . . . . . . . . . . . . . . . . | 6 | 4 |
| Engine/transmission mountings: | | |
| Right-hand engine mounting bracket to body . . . . . . . . . . . . . . . | 50 | 37 |
| Right-hand engine mounting bracket to engine . . . . . . . . . . . . . . | 68 | 50 |
| Left-hand engine mounting . . . . . . . . . . . . . . . . . . . . . . . . . . . . . | 68 | 50 |
| Rear engine roll restrictor centre bolt . . . . . . . . . . . . . . . . . . . . . | 120 | 89 |

*New bolts must be used

---

## 1  General information

### How to use this Chapter

This Part of Chapter 2 is devoted to repair procedures possible while the engine is still installed in the vehicle. If the work is being carried out with the engine removed from the vehicle, some of the preliminary dismantling steps outlined will not apply.

Information concerning engine/transmission removal and refitting, and engine overhaul, can be found in Part B of this Chapter.

### Engine description

The engine is an overhead valve, water-cooled, four cylinder in-line design, designated Endura-E. This engine is very similar to the previous HCS-type engine fitted to Fiesta and Escort models, and apart from an aluminium sump fitted to certain models, and modifications to the inlet manifold and inlet system, is virtually identical. The engine is mounted transversely at the front of the vehicle together with the transmission to form a combined power unit.

The crankshaft is supported in five shell-type main bearings. The connecting rod big-end bearings are split shell-type, and are attached to the pistons by interference-fit gudgeon pins. Each piston is fitted with two compression rings and one oil control ring.

The camshaft, which runs on bearings within the cylinder block, is chain-driven from the crankshaft, and operates the valves via pushrods and rocker arms. The valves are each closed by a single valve spring, and operate in guides integral in the cylinder head.

The oil pump is mounted externally on the crankcase, incorporates a full-flow oil filter, and is driven by a skew gear on the camshaft.

### Repair operations possible with the engine in the car

The following work can be carried out with the engine in the car:

a) Rocker shaft assembly - removal, inspection and refitting.
b) Cylinder head - removal and refitting
c) Crankshaft pulley - removal and refitting.
d) Crankshaft oil seals - renewal.
e) Timing chain, sprockets and tensioner - removal, inspection and refitting.
f) Oil pump - removal and refitting.
g) Sump - removal and refitting.
h) Connecting rods and pistons - removal and refitting*.
i) Flywheel - removal, inspection and refitting.
j) Engine/transmission mountings - inspection and renewal.

*Although the operation marked with an asterisk can be carried out with the engine in the car after removal of the sump, it is better for the engine to be removed in the interests of cleanliness and improved access. For this reason, the procedure is described in Part B of this Chapter.

### Battery disconnection and reconnection

**Note:** *After the battery has been disconnected, the engine management system requires approximately 5 miles of driving to relearn its optimum settings. During this period, the engine may not perform normally. Refer to Chapter 5B.*

## 2 Compression test - description and interpretation

1 When engine performance is down, or if misfiring occurs which cannot be attributed to the ignition or fuel systems, a compression test can provide diagnostic clues as to the engine's condition. If the test is performed regularly, it can give warning of trouble before any other symptoms become apparent.

2 The engine must be fully warmed-up to operating temperature, the oil level must be correct, the battery must be fully charged and the valve clearances must be correct. The aid of an assistant will be required.

3 **Note:** *The following action will cause a fault code to be stored in the engine management ECU. Removal of the code is only possible using the Ford test equipment FDS2000, therefore the car will have to be taken to a Ford dealer after completing the compression test.* Refer to Chapters 4A and 12 and remove the fuel pump relay - it is located beneath the central junction box (CJB) behind the cover on the facia. Now start the engine and allow it to run until it stalls.

4 Disable the ignition system by disconnecting the 3-pin multi-plug from the ignition coil (right-hand rear of the engine). Remove all the spark plugs with reference to Chapter 1.

5 Fit a compression tester to the No 1 cylinder spark plug hole - the type of tester which screws into the plug thread is to be preferred.

6 Arrange for an assistant to hold the accelerator pedal fully depressed to the floor, while at the same time cranking the engine over for several seconds on the starter motor. Observe the compression gauge reading. The compression will build up fairly quickly in a healthy engine. Low compression on the first stroke, followed by gradually-increasing pressure on successive strokes, indicates worn piston rings. A low compression on the first stroke which does not rise on successive strokes, indicates leaking valves or a blown head gasket (a cracked cylinder head could also be the cause). Deposits on the underside of the valve heads can also cause low

compression. Record the highest gauge reading obtained, then repeat the procedure on the remaining cylinders.

7 Due to the variety of testers available, and the fluctuation in starter motor speed when cranking the engine, different readings are often obtained when carrying out the compression test. For this reason, actual compression pressure figures are not quoted by Ford. However, the most important factor is that the compression pressures are uniform in all cylinders, and that is what this test is mainly concerned with.

8 Add some engine oil (about three squirts from a plunger type oil can) to each cylinder through the spark plug holes, and then repeat the test.

9 If the compression increases after the oil is added, it is indicative that the piston rings are worn. If the compression does not increase significantly, the leakage is occurring at the valves or the head gasket. Leakage past the valves may be caused by burned valve seats and/or faces, or warped, cracked or bent valves.

10 If two adjacent cylinders have equally low compressions, it is most likely that the head gasket has blown between them. The appearance of coolant in the combustion chambers or on the engine oil dipstick would verify this condition.

11 If one cylinder is about 20 percent lower than the other, and the engine has a slightly rough idle, a worn lobe on the camshaft could be the cause.

12 On completion of the checks, refit the spark plugs and reconnect the HT leads and the ignition coil plug. Refit the fuel pump relay.

13 Have the fault code cleared from the ECU by a Ford dealer.

## 3 Top Dead Centre (TDC) for No 1 piston - locating

1 Top dead centre (TDC) is the highest point of the cylinder that each piston reaches as the crankshaft turns. Each piston reaches its TDC position at the end of its compression stroke, and then again at the end of its exhaust stroke. For the purpose of engine timing, TDC at the end of the compression stroke for No 1 piston is used. No 1 cylinder is at the crankshaft pulley/timing chain end of the engine. Proceed as follows.

2 Ensure that the ignition is switched off. Disconnect the HT leads from the spark plugs, then unscrew and remove the plugs as described in Chapter 1.

3 Turn the engine over by hand (using a spanner on the crankshaft pulley) to the point where the timing mark on the crankshaft pulley aligns with the TDC (0) mark on the timing cover **(see illustration)**. As the pulley mark nears the timing mark, the No 1 piston is simultaneously approaching the top of its cylinder. To ensure that it is on its

compression stroke, place a finger over the No 1 cylinder plug hole, and feel to ensure that air pressure exits from the cylinder as the piston reaches the top of its stroke. Note that some later models may not have a TDC mark on the pulley, in which case it will be necessary to feel for pressure as just described.

4 A further check to ensure that the piston is on its compression stroke can be made by removing the rocker cover (see Section 4), so that the movement of the valves and rockers can be observed.

5 With the TDC timing marks on the crankshaft pulley and timing cover in alignment, rock the crankshaft back and forth a few degrees each side of this position, and observe the action of the valves and rockers for No 1 cylinder. When No 1 piston is at the TDC firing position, the inlet and exhaust valve of No 1 cylinder will be fully closed, but the corresponding valves of No 4 cylinder will be seen to rock open and closed.

6 If the inlet and exhaust valves of No 1 cylinder are seen to rock whilst those of No 4 cylinder are shut, the crankshaft will need to be turned one full rotation to bring No 1 piston up to the top of its cylinder on the compression stroke.

7 Once No 1 cylinder has been positioned at TDC on the compression stroke, TDC for any of the other cylinders can then be located by rotating the crankshaft clockwise (in its normal direction of rotation), 180° at a time, and following the firing order (see *Specifications*).

8 On completion, refit the spark plugs and reconnect the HT leads.

## 4 Cylinder head rocker cover - removal and refitting

### Removal

1 Detach the HT leads from the spark plugs. Pull on the connector of each lead (not the lead itself), and note the order of fitting. Place the leads to one side.

2 Remove the engine oil filler cap and breather hose and place to one side.

**3.3 Timing mark on the crankshaft pulley aligned with the TDC (0) mark on the timing cover**

4.5a Engage tags of rocker cover gasket into the cut-outs in the cover

4.5b Refitting the rocker cover

5.6 Adjusting the valve clearances

3 Unscrew the four retaining bolts, and lift the rocker cover clear of the cylinder head. Recover the special extended washers, and remove the gasket.

### Refitting

4 Thoroughly clean the rocker cover, and scrape away any traces of old gasket remaining on the cover and cylinder head mating surfaces.
5 Fit a new gasket to the rocker cover, then refit the rocker cover (see illustrations). Insert the cover retaining bolts together with the extended washers, and tighten them to the specified torque wrench setting in a diagonal sequence.
6 Refit the engine oil filler cap and breather hose.
7 Reconnect the HT leads to their correct spark plugs.

### 5 Valve clearances - checking and adjustment

Note: The valve clearances must be checked and adjusted only when the engine is cold.
1 The importance of having the valve clearances correctly adjusted cannot be overstressed, as they vitally affect the performance of the engine. If the clearances are too big, the engine will be noisy (characteristic rattling or tapping noises) and engine efficiency will be reduced, as the valves open too late and close too early. A more serious problem arises if the clearances are too small, however. If this is the case, the valves may not close fully when the engine is hot, resulting in serious damage to the engine (eg. burnt valve seats and/or cylinder head warping/cracking). The clearances are checked and adjusted as follows.

2 Set the engine to TDC for No 1 piston, as described in Section 3. It is not essential to remove the spark plugs, although if they are removed the engine will be easier to turn when adjusting the valve clearances.
3 Remove the rocker cover as described in Section 4.
4 Starting from the thermostat end (right-hand from driver's seat) of the cylinder head, the valves are numbered as follows:

| Valve No | Cylinder No |
| --- | --- |
| 1 - Exhaust | 1 |
| 2 - Inlet | 1 |
| 3 - Exhaust | 2 |
| 4 - Inlet | 2 |
| 5 - Inlet | 3 |
| 6 - Exhaust | 3 |
| 7 - Inlet | 4 |
| 8 - Exhaust | 4 |

5 Adjust the valve clearances following the sequence given in the table below. Turn the crankshaft pulley 180° (half a turn) after adjusting each pair of valve clearances.

**HAYNES HiNT**
*Turning the engine will be easier if the spark plugs are removed first - see Chapter 1.*

6 The clearances for the inlet and exhaust valves differ (refer to the *Specifications*). Use a feeler blade of the appropriate thickness to check each clearance between the end of the valve stem and the rocker arm (see illustration). The gauge should be a firm sliding fit between the valve and rocker arm. Where adjustment is necessary, turn the adjuster bolt as required with a ring spanner to set the clearance to that specified. The adjuster bolts are of stiff-thread type, and require no locking nut.
7 On completion, refit the rocker cover as described in Section 4.

### 6 Cylinder head rocker gear - removal, inspection and refitting

#### Removal

1 Remove the rocker cover as described in Section 4.
2 Unscrew the four retaining bolts, and lift the rocker gear assembly from the cylinder head. As the assembly is withdrawn, ensure that the pushrods remain seated in their positions in the engine (see Haynes Hint).

#### Inspection

3 To dismantle the rocker shaft assembly, extract the split pin from one end of the shaft, then withdraw the spring washers and plain washers from the shaft.
4 Slide off the rocker arms, the support pedestals and coil springs from the shaft, but take care to keep them in their original order of fitting (see illustration).
5 Clean the respective components, and inspect them for signs of excessive wear or damage. Check that the oil lubrication holes in the shaft are clear.
6 Check the rocker shaft and arm pads which bear on the valve stem end faces for wear and scoring, and check each rocker arm on the shaft for excessive wear. Renew any components as necessary.

**HAYNES HiNT**

*If the pushrods are to be removed, keep them in the correct order of fitting by labelling them 1 to 8, starting from the thermostat end of the cylinder head, or locate them in a card.*

### Valve clearance adjustment sequence

| Valves "rocking" | Valves to adjust |
| --- | --- |
| 7 (inlet) and 8 (exhaust) - cylinder No 4 valves | 1 (exhaust), 2 (inlet) - cylinder No 1 valves |
| 5 (inlet) and 6 (exhaust) - cylinder No 3 valves | 3 (exhaust), 4 (inlet) - cylinder No 2 valves |
| 1 (exhaust) and 2 (inlet) - cylinder No 1 valves | 8 (exhaust), 7 (inlet) - cylinder No 4 valves |
| 3 (exhaust) and 4 (inlet) - cylinder No 2 valves | 6 (exhaust), 5 (inlet) - cylinder No 3 valves |

6.4 Rocker shaft partially dismantled for inspection

6.8 Flat on the rocker shaft (arrowed) to same side as rocker arm adjusting screws

### Refitting

**7** Apply clean engine oil to the rocker shaft prior to reassembling.

**8** Reassemble in the reverse order of dismantling. Make sure that the "flat" on the rear end of the rocker shaft is to the same side as the rocker arm adjusting screws (closest to the thermostat end of the cylinder head when fitted) **(see illustration)**. This is essential for the correct lubrication of the cylinder head components.

**9** Refit the rocker shaft assembly. As it is fitted, ensure that the rocker adjuster screws engage with their corresponding pushrods.

**10** Refit the rocker shaft retaining bolts, hand-tighten them and then tighten them to the specified torque wrench setting. As they are tightened, some of the rocker arms will apply pressure to the ends of the valve stems, and some of the rocker pedestals will not initially be in contact with the cylinder head - these should pull down as the bolts are tightened to their specified torque. If for any reason they do not, avoid the temptation to overtighten in order to pull them into position; loosen off the bolts, and check the cause of the problem. It may be that the rocker adjuster screws require loosening off in order to allow the assembly to be tightened down as required.

**11** Adjust the valve clearances as described in Section 5.

### 7 Cylinder head - removal and refitting

### Removal

**1** Depressurise the fuel system as described in Chapter 4A.

**2** Disconnect the battery negative (earth) lead (see Chapter 5A).

**3** On models with a mass air flow (MAF) sensor (models to mid 1999), release the clip and disconnect the air inlet duct from the throttle housing, then disconnect the wiring from the intake air temperature sensor and mass air flow sensor. Pull the air cleaner directly up from its mounting, disconnect the crankcase ventilation hose and remove the MAF sensor and air duct from the engine compartment.

> **HAYNES HiNT** *Whenever you disconnect any vacuum lines, coolant or emissions hoses, wiring connectors and fuel lines, always label them clearly, so that they can be correctly reassembled. Masking tape and/or a touch-up paint applicator work well for marking items. Take instant photos, or sketch the locations of components and brackets.*

**4** On models with a temperature manifold absolute pressure (TMAP) sensor (models from mid 1999), loosen the clip and disconnect the air inlet duct from the throttle housing, then remove the air cleaner (see Chapter 4A) and remove it, and disconnect the crankcase ventilation hose.

**5** Chock the rear wheels then jack up the front of the car and support it on axle stands (see *"Jacking and vehicle support"*).

**6** Disconnect the wiring from the camshaft position sensor (CMP).

**7** Refer to Chapter 1 and drain the cooling system.

**8** Unscrew the exhaust flange bolts securing the catalytic converter to the exhaust system, and also unscrew the mounting bolt securing the catalytic converter to the transmission.

**9** Disconnect the accelerator cable from the throttle housing with reference to Chapter 4A.

**10** Release the clips and disconnect the top hose and bypass hose from the thermostat housing. Use a pair of grips to release the clips.

**11** Release the alternator wiring from the clips next to the thermostat housing.

**12** Unscrew the bolts and remove the thermostat housing, then remove the thermostat and recover the gasket.

**13** On models with a mass air flow (MAF) sensor (models to mid 1999), unclip the engine wiring harness at the right-hand rear of the engine, then disconnect the brake vacuum line from the inlet manifold. Disconnect the vacuum line from the evaporative emission control canister purge solenoid valve (CANP), then remove the wiring connector casings from the bulkhead, prise them open and separate the wiring connectors.

**14** On models with a temperature manifold absolute pressure (TMAP) sensor (models from mid 1999), release the wiring harness at the right-hand rear of the engine and disconnect it, then disconnect the brake vacuum line from the inlet manifold. At the left-hand side of the bulkhead, disconnect the TMAP sensor wiring, then disconnect the vacuum line from the evaporative emission control canister purge solenoid valve (CANP).

**15** Unscrew and remove the oxygen sensor (see Chapter 4B), then unbolt and remove the heat shield from the exhaust manifold.

**16** Disconnect the HT leads from the spark plugs and from the ignition coil. The leads are marked with the corresponding cylinder numbers. Unscrew and remove the spark plugs.

**17** Unscrew the nuts and remove the exhaust manifold and catalytic converter from the studs on the cylinder head. Tie the manifold to one side, away from the head.

**18** Disconnect the coolant hose from the heater matrix exchanger by releasing the quick release coupling.

**19** Unscrew the bolt and move the engine oil dipstick tube away from the cylinder head.

**20** Disconnect the fuel supply and return lines at the quick release fittings. Place some rags beneath the fittings to catch any spilt fuel. Note that the fittings are modified on models built from mid 1999.

**21** Unbolt and remove the inlet manifold with reference to Chapter 4A.

7.33 Cylinder head gasket top-face marking ("OBEN - TOP")

7.35a Cylinder head bolt tightening sequence

**22** Position a trolley jack and block of wood beneath the sump and raise the engine slightly until the right-hand engine mounting is free of pressure. Disconnect the wiring then unscrew the single bolt and two nuts from the mounting.
**23** Lower the engine until the studs are free of the mounting.
**24** Refer to Section 4 and remove the rocker cover.
**25** Undo the four retaining bolts and lift clear the rocker gear assembly from the cylinder head.
**26** Lift out the pushrods. Keep them in order of fitting by labelling them 1 to 8, starting from the thermostat end of the cylinder head. Alternatively, push them through a piece of card in their fitted sequence.
**27** Progressively unscrew and loosen off the cylinder head retaining bolts in the reverse sequence to that shown for tightening (see illustration 7.35a). When they are all loosened off, remove the bolts, then lift the cylinder head clear and remove the gasket. The gasket must always be renewed; note that the cylinder head retaining bolts may be re-used, but only once. They should be marked accordingly with a punch or paint mark. If there is any doubt as to how many times the bolts have been used, they must be renewed.
**28** To dismantle/overhaul the cylinder head, refer to Part B of this Chapter. It is normal for the cylinder head to be decarbonised and the valves to be reground whenever the head is removed.

### Preparation for refitting

**29** The mating faces of the cylinder head and cylinder block must be perfectly clean before refitting the head. Use a hard plastic or wood scraper to remove all traces of gasket and carbon; also clean the piston crowns. Take particular care during the cleaning operations, as aluminium alloy is easily damaged. Also, make sure that the carbon is not allowed to enter the oil and water passages - this is

particularly important for the lubrication system, as carbon could block the oil supply to the engine's components. Using adhesive tape and paper, seal the water, oil and bolt holes in the cylinder block.

> **HAYNES HiNT** *To prevent carbon entering the gap between the pistons and bores, smear a little grease in the gap. After cleaning each piston, use a small brush to remove all traces of grease and carbon from the gap, then wipe away the remainder with a clean rag.*

**30** Check the mating surfaces of the cylinder block and the cylinder head for nicks, deep scratches and other damage. If slight, they may be removed carefully with a file, but if excessive, machining may be the only alternative to renewal.
**31** If warpage of the cylinder head gasket surface is suspected, use a straight-edge to check it for distortion. Refer to Part B of this Chapter if necessary.
**32** Clean the threads of the cylinder head bolts or fit new ones (as applicable) and clean out the bolt holes in the block. Screwing a bolt into an oil-filled hole can (in extreme cases) cause the block to fracture, due to the hydraulic pressure.

### Refitting

**33** Check that the new cylinder head gasket is the same type as the original, and that the "TOP" (or "OBEN") marking is facing upwards. Locate the new cylinder head gasket onto the top face of the cylinder block and over the dowels. Ensure that it is correctly aligned with the coolant passages and oilways **(see illustration)**.
**34** Lower the cylinder head carefully into position, then insert the retaining bolts and hand-tighten them.
**35** Tightening of the cylinder head bolts must be done in three stages, and in the correct sequence **(see illustration)**. First tighten all of the bolts in the sequence shown to the Stage 1 torque setting. When all of the bolts are tightened to the Stage 1 setting, further tighten each bolt (in sequence) through the Stage 2 specified angle of rotation. When the second stage tightening is completed on all of the bolts, further tighten them to the Stage 3 angle setting (in sequence) to complete. Where possible, use an angular torque setting gauge attachment tool for accurate tightening of stages two and three **(see illustrations)**.
**36** Lubricate the pushrods with clean engine oil, and then insert them into their original locations in the engine.

7.35b Tightening the cylinder head bolts (Stage 1)

7.35c Cylinder head bolt tightening (Stages 2 and 3) using an angle gauge

**37** Refit the rocker shaft assembly. As it is fitted, ensure that the rocker adjuster screws engage with their corresponding pushrods.
**38** Refit the rocker shaft retaining bolts, hand-tighten them and then tighten them to the specified torque wrench setting. As they are tightened, some of the rocker arms will apply pressure to the ends of the valve stems, and some of the rocker pedestals will not initially be in contact with the cylinder head - these should pull down as the bolts are tightened. If for any reason they do not, avoid the temptation to overtighten in order to pull them into position; loosen off the bolts, and check the cause of the problem. It may be that the rocker adjuster screws require loosening off in order to allow the assembly to be tightened down as required.
**39** Adjust the valve clearances as described in Section 5.
**40** Refit the rocker cover as described in Section 4.
**41** The remainder of the refitting procedure is a reversal of the removal process. Use new gaskets for the exhaust and inlet manifolds and for the thermostat housing. Tighten all fastenings to their specified torque setting (where given). Refer to Chapter 4A for details on reconnecting the fuel and exhaust system components. Ensure that all coolant, fuel, vacuum and electrical connections are securely made. When refitting the spark plugs, lightly coat their threads with copper grease before inserting them. Refer to Chapter 4B when refitting the oxygen sensor.
**42** On completion, refill the cooling system and top-up the engine oil (see Chapter 1 and *"Weekly Checks"*). When the engine is restarted, check for any sign of fuel, oil and/or coolant leakage from the various cylinder head joints. There is no requirement to retighten the cylinder head bolts after the engine has been started.

## 8  Crankshaft pulley - removal and refitting

### Removal

**1** Disconnect the battery negative (earth) lead (see Chapter 5A).
**2** Chock the rear wheels then jack up the front of the car and support it on axle stands (see *"Jacking and vehicle support"*). Remove the right-hand front roadwheel.
**3** Undo the fasteners and remove the right-hand front wheel arch liner. Release the coolant hose and power steering pipe from the clips.
**4** Remove the auxiliary drivebelt from the pulleys by turning the tensioner clockwise using a 15 mm spanner. Refer to Chapter 1 if necessary.
**5** Loosen off the crankshaft pulley retaining bolt. To prevent the crankshaft from turning, remove the starter motor (Chapter 5A) and

**10.2  Oil slinger removal from crankshaft**

lock the ring gear through the starter motor aperture.
**6** Fully unscrew the crankshaft pulley bolt, and withdraw the pulley from the front end of the crankshaft. If it does not pull off by hand, lever it free using a pair of suitable levers positioned diagonally opposite each other behind the pulley.
**7** If required, the crankshaft front oil seal can be renewed at this stage, as described in Section 15.

### Refitting

**8** Refitting is a reversal of the removal procedure ensuring that the pulley retaining bolt is tightened to the specified torque setting. Refit the auxiliary drivebelt with reference to Chapter 1.

## 9  Timing chain cover - removal and refitting

### Removal

**1** Remove the sump (see Section 11).
**2** Remove the crankshaft pulley as described in the previous Section.
**3** Disconnect the camshaft position sensor wiring multi-plug.
**4** Unscrew the retaining bolts, and carefully prise free the timing chain cover. Note that one of the bolt holes is split and the bolt also secures the water pump.
**5** A combined timing cover and water pump

**10.3  Chain tensioner arm removal from the pivot pin. Note tensioner retaining bolts (arrowed)**

gasket is fitted during production; if this is still in position, it will be necessary to cut away the old gasket using a sharp knife keeping as close as possible to the water pump. If the timing cover has been removed at any time, the single gasket used originally will have been replaced by an individual gasket.
**6** Clean the mating faces of the timing chain cover and cylinder block.
**7** If necessary, renew the crankshaft front oil seal in the timing cover prior to refitting the cover (see Section 15).

### Refitting

**8** Lightly lubricate the front end of the crankshaft and the radial lip of the timing chain cover oil seal (already installed in the cover). Using a new gasket, fit the timing chain cover, centring it with the aid of the crankshaft pulley - lubricate the seal contact surfaces beforehand. Refit and tighten the retaining bolts to the specified torque. Note that the sump mating faces of the cover and cylinder block must be level with each other.
**9** Refit the crankshaft pulley (see Section 8).
**10** Reconnect the camshaft position sensor multi-plug.
**11** Refit the sump as described in Section 11.

## 10  Timing chain, sprockets and tensioner - removal, inspection and refitting

### Removal

**1** Remove the timing chain cover as described in Section 9.
**2** Remove the oil slinger from the front face of the crankshaft, noting its orientation **(see illustration)**.
**3** Retract the chain tensioner cam back against its spring pressure, then slide the chain tensioner arm from its pivot pin on the front main bearing cap **(see illustration)**.
**4** Unbolt and remove the chain tensioner.
**5** Note the fitted position of the camshaft position sender plate, then unscrew and remove the camshaft sprocket bolts and remove the plate. Hold the sprocket stationary using a suitable tool engaged with the holes in the sprocket.
**6** Withdraw the camshaft sprocket and unhook the timing chain from the crankshaft sprocket.
**7** Slide the sprocket from the key on the nose of the crankshaft. If it is tight use a suitable puller. If necessary, remove the Woodruff key from the groove in the crankshaft.

### Inspection

**8** Examine the teeth on the timing sprockets for any signs of excessive wear or damage.
**9** The timing chain should always be renewed during a major engine overhaul. Slack links and pins are indicative of a worn chain. Unless the chain is known to be relatively new, it should be renewed.

**10** Examine the rubber cushion on the tensioner spring leaf. If grooved or deteriorated, it must be renewed.

### *Refitting*

**11** Commence reassembly by locating the Woodruff key in the crankshaft groove, making sure that it is parallel to the surface of the crankshaft.

**12** Slide on the crankshaft sprocket and engage it with the Woodruff key. If it is tight, use the pulley together with its bolt to press on the sprocket. Make sure the timing mark is on the outer face of the sprocket.

**13** Fit the timing chain tensioner and tighten the mounting bolts to the specified torque. Check that the face of the tensioner cam is parallel with the face of the cylinder block, ideally using a dial gauge. The maximum permissible error between two measuring points 20 mm apart is 0.16 mm. If necessary, loosen the mounting bolts, turn the tensioner as required, then tighten the bolts and recheck.

**14** Turn the crankshaft so that the timing mark on the crankshaft sprocket is directly in line with the centre of the camshaft sprocket mounting flange.

**15** Engage the camshaft sprocket with the timing chain, then engage the chain around the teeth of the crankshaft sprocket. Push the camshaft sprocket onto its mounting flange, and check that the sprocket retaining bolt holes are in alignment. Also check that the timing marks of both sprockets face each other. If required, turn the camshaft/sprocket as required to achieve this. It may also be necessary to remove the camshaft sprocket from the chain in order to reposition it in the required location in the chain to align the timing marks. This is a "trial and error" procedure, which must be continued until the exact alignment of the bolt holes and the timing marks is made **(see illustrations)**.

**16** Locate the camshaft position sender plate on the sprocket in its previously noted position, then insert the sprocket bolts and tighten them to the specified torque.

**17** Retract the timing chain tensioner cam, and then slide the tensioner arm onto its pivot pin. Release the cam so that it bears on the arm.

**18** Refit the oil slinger to the front of the crankshaft sprocket so that its convex side faces the sprocket.

**19** Refit the timing chain cover as described in Section 9.

## 11 Sump - removal and refitting

**Note:** *On engines with aluminium sumps, it will be necessary to remove the transmission and flywheel (see Chapter 7) to access the two sump bolts in the rear crankshaft oil seal housing.*

### *Removal*

**1** Disconnect the battery negative (earth) lead (see Chapter 5A).

**2** Refer Chapter 1 and drain the engine oil. Refit the sump drain plug.

**3** Unbolt the exhaust pipe from the catalytic converter flange beneath the front of the engine. Release the exhaust system mountings and position the exhaust to one side. On engines with aluminium sumps, it may be necessary to remove the exhaust manifold/catalytic converter as described in Chapter 4A.

**4** Remove the starter motor (see Chapter 5A).

**5** On engines with an aluminium sump (models with power steering and/or air conditioning), remove the gearbox/ transmission and flywheel as described in Chapter 7.

**6** On engines with air conditioning, remove the auxiliary drivebelt (Chapter 1), unbolt the compressor from the sump mounting and position the compressor to one side. Do not disconnect any refrigerant hoses.

**7** Undo the eighteen bolts securing the sump to the base of the engine crankcase, then prise free and lower the sump and remove the

gasket. If the sump is stuck tight to the engine, cut around the flange gasket with a sharp knife, then lightly tap and prise it free. Keep the sump upright as it is lowered, to prevent spillage of any remaining oil in it. Also be prepared for oil drips from the crankcase when the sump is removed.

**8** Remove any dirt and old gasket(s) from the contact faces of the sump, crankcase, timing chain cover and rear oil seal housing, then wash the sump out thoroughly before refitting. Check that the mating faces of the sump are not distorted. Check that the oil pick-up strainer is clear, cleaning it if necessary - refer to Chapter 2B, Section 10 for details of removing and refitting the pick-up tube.

### *Refitting*

**9** Thoroughly clean the sump and cylinder block mating faces.

**10** Apply sealing compound (available from Ford dealers) to the cylinder block mating face in the area of the joint between the timing chain cover and cylinder block, and the rear oil seal carrier and cylinder block. Also apply sealer into the corners of the semi-circular areas on the timing chain cover and rear oil seal housing.

**11** On engines with a steel sump, stick the new cork gaskets into position on the block face, using clean thick grease to retain them, then locate the new rubber gaskets into their slots in the timing chain cover and rear oil seal housing. The lugs of the cork gasket halves fit under the cut-outs in the rubber gaskets.

**12** On engines with an aluminium sump (models with power steering and/or air conditioning), locate the one-piece gasket on the sump ensuring that it is correctly seated in the semi-circular cut-outs.

**13** Locate the sump on the crankcase, then fit the retaining bolts and tighten them initially finger tight.

**14** On models with an aluminium sump, using a straight-edge, check that the sump flange is level with the surface of the cylinder block at the flywheel end of the engine. If necessary reposition the sump.

**10.15a  Fit the timing chain to the crankshaft and camshaft sprockets . . .**

**10.15b  . . . and check that the timing marks on the sprockets are in alignment**

**12.1 The oil pump is externally-mounted, on the rear-facing side of the crankcase**

**11.15 Sump bolt tightening sequence - arrow indicates front of car**

*Refer to Specifications for torque wrench settings*

*Stage 1 - Tighten in alphabetical order*
*Stage 2 - Tighten in numerical order*
*Stage 3 - Tighten in alphabetical order*

### Refitting

**6** If the original oil pump has been dismantled and reassembled and is to be re-used, or if a new pump is to be fitted, it must first be primed with engine oil prior to fitting. To do this, turn its driveshaft and simultaneously inject clean engine oil into it.
**7** Locate a new gasket on the pump mounting flange, then insert the pump, engaging the drivegear as it is fitted **(see illustration)**. Fit the retaining bolts, and tighten to the specified torque wrench setting.
**8** Fit a new oil filter on the oil pump body, as described in Chapter 1.
**9** Lower the vehicle to the ground, and top-up the engine oil as described in *"Weekly Checks"*.

**15** Tighten the bolts in the sequence shown through Stages 1 and 2, to the torques speci-fied **(see illustration)**. Note that different tight-ening sequences are specified for the tightening stages. Final (Stage 3) tightening is carried out after the engine has been started and warmed up.
**16** On models with an aluminium sump, refit the flywheel and transmission as described in Chapter 7.
**17** Where applicable, refit the air conditioning compressor (see Chapter 3), then refit the auxiliary drivebelt (see Chapter 1).
**18** Refit the starter motor (see Chapter 5A).
**19** Check that the flange mating faces are clean, then reconnect the exhaust pipe to the catalytic converter. Reconnect the exhaust system mountings. If removed, refit the exhaust manifold/catalytic converter as described in Chapter 4A.
**20** Check that the sump drain plug is fitted and tightened to the specified torque, then lower the vehicle to the ground.
**21** Refill the engine with oil (see Chapter 1).
**22** Reconnect the battery, then start the engine and run it up to its normal operating temperature. Check that no oil leaks are evident around the sump joint.
**23** After the engine has warmed up for

approximately 15 minutes, switch it off. Tighten the sump bolts to the Stage 3 torque wrench setting given in the *Specifications*, in the sequence shown (see illustration 11.15).

## 12 Oil pump - removal and refitting

### Removal

**1** The oil pump is externally-mounted, on the rear-facing side of the crankcase **(see illustration)**.
**2** Apply the handbrake and chock the rear wheels, then jack up the front of the car and support it on axle stands (see *"Jacking and vehicle support"*).
**3** Unscrew and remove the oil filter cartridge. It should unscrew by hand, but will probably be tight. Use a strap wrench to loosen it off, if required. Catch any oil spillage in a suitable container.
**4** Undo the three retaining bolts and withdraw the oil pump from the engine **(see illustration)**.
**5** Clean all traces of the old gasket from the mating surfaces of the pump and engine.

## 13 Oil pump - dismantling, inspection and reassembly

### Dismantling

**1** To inspect the oil pump components for excessive wear, undo the retaining bolts and remove the cover plate from the pump body. Remove the O-ring seal from the cover face **(see illustration)**.
**2** Wipe the exterior of the pump housing clean.

### Inspection

**3** Noting their orientation, extract and clean the rotors and the inner body of the pump

**12.4 Unscrewing the oil pump retaining bolts**

**12.7 Refitting the oil pump. Note the new gasket**

**13.1 Extract the O-ring from the groove in the oil pump**

**13.4a  Checking the outer body-to-rotor clearance**

**13.4b  Checking the inner rotor-to-outer rotor clearance**

**13.4c  Checking the rotor endfloat**

housing. Inspect them for signs of severe scoring or excessive wear, which if evident will necessitate renewal of the complete pump.

**4** Using feeler blades, check the clearances between the pump body and the outer rotor, the inner-to-outer rotor clearance, and the amount of rotor endfloat **(see illustrations)**.

**5** Check the drivegear for signs of excessive wear or damage.

**6** If the clearances measured are outside the specified maximum clearances and/or the drivegear is in poor condition, the complete pump unit must be renewed.

### Reassembly

**7** Refit the rotors into the pump (in their original orientation), lubricate the rotors and the new O-ring seal with clean engine oil, and refit the cover. Tighten the retaining bolts to the specified torque wrench setting.

## 14 Oil pressure warning light switch - removal and refitting

### Removal

**1** The oil pressure switch is located on the rear of the cylinder block, beneath the inlet manifold and above the oil pump **(see illustration)**. First apply the handbrake, then jack up the front of the vehicle and support it on axle stands (see *"Jacking and Vehicle Support"*).

**2** Disconnect the wiring from the oil pressure warning light switch.

**3** Unscrew the switch and remove it from the cylinder block. Be prepared for a little loss of oil.

### Refitting

**4** Clean the threads of the switch and the threads in the cylinder block. Also wipe away any oil which may have escaped from the switch hole.

**5** Apply suitable sealant to the threads, then insert the switch and tighten to the specified torque.

**6** Reconnect the wiring and lower the vehicle to the ground.

**7** Check and if necessary top-up the engine oil as described in *"Weekly checks"*.

## 15 Crankshaft oil seals - renewal

### Front oil seal

**1** Remove the crankshaft pulley as described in Section 8.

**2** Using a suitable claw tool, extract the oil seal from the timing chain cover, but take care not to damage the seal housing. As it is removed, note the fitted orientation of the seal in the cover.

**3** Clean the oil seal housing in the timing chain cover. Lubricate the sealing lips of the new seal and the crankshaft stub with clean engine oil.

**4** Locate the new seal into position so that it is squarely located on the crankshaft stub and in the housing, and is correctly orientated. Drift it into position using a large socket or other suitable tool, or the old seal, until the new seal is flush with the edge of the timing chain cover.

**5** Lightly lubricate the oil seal contact surface of the crankshaft pulley, then refit the pulley as described in Section 8.

### Rear oil seal

**6** Remove the flywheel as described in Section 16.

**7** Note the orientation and fitted depth of the oil seal to ensure correct fitting of the new seal.

**14.1  The oil pressure switch is located on the rear of the cylinder block**

**8** Using a suitable claw tool, lever the seal from the rear oil seal housing (taking care not to damage the housing).

**9** Clean the seal housing, the crankshaft rear flange face and the flywheel mating surface.

**10** Lubricate the crankshaft flange and the oil seal inner lip with clean engine oil.

**11** If Ford service tool No 21-102/01/02A/04 is available, position the seal on the service tool (ensuring correct orientation) and attach the tool to the rear of the crankshaft, then press the seal into its housing using the centre nut. Tighten the nut progressively to ensure that the oil seal enters its housing correctly. Remove the tool on completion.

**12** If the service tool is not available, start the oil seal in its housing using finger pressure initially then carefully tap it into the housing to its previously noted position making sure it is kept square. If a suitable length of metal tube is available, use this to drive in the seal.

**13** Check that the crankshaft rear flange and the flywheel mating faces are clean, then refit the flywheel as described in Section 16.

## 16 Flywheel - removal, inspection and refitting

### Removal

**1** Remove the transmission as described in Chapter 7, then remove the clutch as described in Chapter 6.

**2** Unscrew the six retaining bolts, and remove the flywheel from the rear flange of the crankshaft - take care not to drop the flywheel, as it is heavy. A tool similar to that shown (see illustration 16.5) can be fitted to prevent the flywheel/crankshaft from rotating as the bolts are loosened. If on removal, the retaining bolts are found to be in poor condition (stretched threads, etc) they must be renewed.

### Inspection

**3** Inspect the starter ring gear on the flywheel for any broken or excessively-worn teeth. If evident, the ring gear must be renewed; this is a task best entrusted to a Ford dealer or a competent garage. Alternatively, obtain a complete new flywheel.

**4** The clutch friction surface on the flywheel must be carefully inspected for grooving or hairline cracks (caused by overheating). If these conditions are evident, it may be possible to have the flywheel surface-ground to renovate it, providing that the balance is not upset. Regrinding is a task for an automotive engineer. If surface-grinding is not possible, the flywheel must be renewed.

### Refitting

**5** Check that the mating faces of the flywheel and the crankshaft are clean before refitting. Lubricate the threads of the retaining bolts with engine oil before they are screwed into position. Locate the flywheel on the crankshaft, and insert the bolts. Hand-tighten them initially, then tighten them in a progressive sequence to the specified torque wrench setting **(see illustration)**.
**6** Refit the clutch as described in Chapter 6 and the transmission as described in Chapter 7.

**17 Engine/transmission mountings -** inspection and renewal

### Inspection

**1** The engine/transmission mountings seldom require attention, but broken or deteriorated mountings should be renewed immediately, or the added strain placed on the driveline components may cause damage or wear.
**2** During the check, the engine/transmission must be raised slightly, to remove its weight from the mountings.
**3** Apply the handbrake and chock the rear wheels, then jack up the front of the car and support it on axle stands (see *"Jacking and vehicle support"*). Position a jack under the sump, with a large block of wood between the jack head and the sump, then carefully raise the engine/transmission just enough to take the weight off the mountings.

**16.5 Tightening the flywheel retaining bolts to the specified torque**

*Note the "peg" tool locking the ring gear teeth to prevent rotation as the bolts are tightened.*

**4** Check the mountings to see if the rubber is cracked, hardened or separated from the metal components. Sometimes, the rubber will split right down the centre.
**5** Check for relative movement between each mounting's brackets and the engine/transmission or body (use a large screwdriver or lever to attempt to move the mountings). If movement is noted, lower the engine and check the mounting nuts and bolts for tightness.

### Renewal

**6** The engine mountings can be removed if the weight of the engine/transmission is supported by one of the following alternative methods. First apply the handbrake, then jack up the front of the vehicle and support it on axle stands (see *"Jacking and Vehicle Support"*).
**7** Support the weight of the engine/transmission assembly from underneath using a jack and a suitable piece of wood between the jack and the sump, or between the jack and the transmission. Alternatively, attach a hoist to the lifting eyes on the engine. A third method is to use a suitable support bar with

end pieces which will engage in the water channel each side of the bonnet lid aperture. Using an adjustable hook and chain connected to the engine, the weight of the engine and transmission can then be taken from the mountings. Whichever method is used, make sure that the engine/transmission assembly is adequately supported.
**8** Once the weight of the engine and transmission is suitably supported, any of the mountings can be unbolted and removed as described in the following paragraphs.
**9** To remove the right-hand engine mounting, pull off the cable ties from the tops of the mounting studs, then unscrew the single bolt and two nuts. Lower the engine until the studs are free of the mounting. Remove the right-hand front wheel. Unbolt the support bracket from the body, then remove the mounting by unscrewing the two bolts located beneath the right-hand front wheel arch. If necessary, the remaining bracket can be unbolted from the engine cylinder block **(see illustration)**.
**10** The left-hand engine mounting is attached to the battery support bracket by two nuts. To remove the mounting, unscrew the nuts then unbolt the mounting from the transmission. If necessary, the battery support bracket may be unbolted from the body after removing the battery (see Chapter 5A).
**11** To remove the rear roll restrictor (engine mounting), first unscrew and remove the centre bolt **(see illustration)**. Hold the engine stationary since the restrictor will be under some tension. Unbolt the cover plate then unscrew the bolts securing the bracket to the body and recover the small plate. Unbolt the mounting from the front of the transmission.
**12** Refitting of all mountings is a reversal of the removal procedure. Do not fully tighten the mounting nuts/bolts until all of the mountings are in position. Check that the mounting rubbers do not twist or distort as the mounting bolts and nuts are tightened to their specified torques.

**17.9 Right-hand engine mounting bracket on the cylinder block**

**17.11 Removing the centre bolt from the rear roll restrictor**

# Chapter 2 Part B:
# Engine removal and overhaul procedures

## Contents

## Degrees of difficulty

**Easy,** suitable for novice with little experience

**Fairly easy,** suitable for beginner with some experience

**Fairly difficult,** suitable for competent DIY mechanic

**Difficult,** suitable for experienced DIY mechanic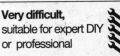

**Very difficult,** suitable for expert DIY or professional

## Specifications

**Torque wrench settings**
Refer to Specifications in Chapter 2A.

### 1 General information

Included in this Part of Chapter 2 are the general overhaul procedures for the cylinder head, cylinder block/crankcase and internal engine components.

The information ranges from advice concerning preparation for an overhaul and the purchase of replacement parts, to detailed step-by-step procedures covering removal, inspection, renovation and refitting of internal engine parts.

The following Sections have been compiled based on the assumption that the engine has been removed from the car. For information concerning in-car engine repair, as well as the removal and refitting of the external components necessary for the overhaul, refer to Part A, and to Section 5 of this Part.

### 2 Engine overhaul -
general information

It is not always easy to determine when, or if, an engine should be completely overhauled, as a number of factors must be considered.

High mileage is not necessarily an indication that an overhaul is needed, while low mileage does not preclude the need for an overhaul. Frequency of servicing is probably the most important consideration. An engine which has had regular and frequent oil and filter changes, as well as other required maintenance, will most likely give many thousands of miles of reliable service. Conversely, a neglected engine may require an overhaul very early in its life.

Excessive oil consumption is an indication that piston rings, valve stem oil seals and/or valves and valve guides are in need of attention. Make sure that oil leaks are not responsible before deciding that the rings and/or guides are bad. Perform a cylinder compression check to determine the extent of the work required.

Check the oil pressure with a gauge fitted in place of the oil pressure sender, and compare it with the value given in the Part A Specifications. If it is extremely low, the main and big-end bearings and/or the oil pump are probably worn out.

Loss of power, rough running, knocking or metallic engine noises, excessive valve gear noise and high fuel consumption may also point to the need for an overhaul, especially if they are all present at the same time. If a complete tune-up does not remedy the situation, major mechanical work is the only solution.

An engine overhaul involves restoring the internal parts to the specifications of a new engine. During an overhaul, the pistons and rings are renewed, and the cylinder bores are reconditioned. New main bearings, connecting rod bearings and camshaft bearings are generally fitted, and if necessary, the crankshaft may be reground to restore the journals. The valves are also serviced as well, since they are usually in less-than-perfect condition at this point. While the engine is being overhauled, other components, such as the starter and alternator, can be overhauled as well. The end result should be a like-new engine that will give many trouble-free miles. **Note:** *Critical cooling system components such as the hoses, auxiliary drivebelt, thermostat and water pump MUST be renewed when an engine is overhauled. The radiator should be checked carefully, to ensure that it is not clogged or leaking. Also, it is a good idea to renew the oil pump whenever the engine is overhauled.*

Before beginning the engine overhaul, read through the entire procedure to familiarise yourself with the scope and requirements of the job. Overhauling an engine is not difficult if you follow all of the instructions carefully, have the necessary tools and equipment, and pay close attention to all specifications; however, it can be time-consuming. Plan on the vehicle being tied up for a minimum of two weeks, especially if parts must be taken to an engineering works for repair or reconditioning. Check on the availability of parts, and make sure that any necessary special tools and equipment are obtained in advance. Most work can be done with typical hand tools, although a number of precision measuring tools are required for inspecting parts to

**4.5 Removing the cover from under the front of the engine compartment**

determine if they must be renewed. Often the engineering works will handle the inspection of parts, and offer advice concerning reconditioning and renewal. **Note:** *Always wait until the engine has been completely dismantled, and all components, especially the engine block, have been inspected before deciding what service and repair operations must be performed by an engineering works. Since the condition of the block will be the major factor to consider when determining whether to overhaul the original engine or buy a reconditioned unit, do not purchase parts or have overhaul work done on other components until the block has been thoroughly inspected.* As a general rule, time is the primary cost of an overhaul, so it does not pay to fit worn or substandard parts.

As a final note, to ensure maximum life and minimum trouble from a reconditioned engine, everything must be assembled with care, and in a spotlessly-clean environment.

## 3  Engine removal - methods and precautions

If you have decided that an engine must be removed for overhaul or major repair work, several preliminary steps should be taken.

Locating a suitable place to work is extremely important. Adequate work space, along with storage space for the vehicle, will be needed. If a garage is not available, at the very least a flat, level, clean work surface is required.

Cleaning the engine compartment and

**4.7 Disconnecting the crankcase ventilation hose from the engine oil filler cap**

engine before beginning the removal procedure will help keep tools clean and organised.

An engine hoist may be necessary, or alternatively two adequate trolley jacks and a length of wood may be used to lower the engine from the engine compartment. Make sure the equipment is rated in excess of the combined weight of the engine and transmission. Safety is of primary importance, considering the potential hazards involved in removing the engine from the vehicle.

If the engine is being removed by a novice, an assistant should be available. Advice and aid from someone more experienced would also be helpful. There are many instances when one person cannot simultaneously perform all of the operations required when removing the engine from the vehicle.

Plan the operation ahead of time. Arrange for, or obtain, all of the tools and equipment you will need, prior to beginning the job. Some of the additional equipment necessary to perform engine removal and installation safely and with relative ease are complete sets of spanners and sockets as described at the end of this manual, wooden blocks, and plenty of rags and cleaning solvent for mopping up spilled oil, coolant and fuel. If the hoist must be hired, make sure that you arrange for it in advance, and perform all of the operations possible without it beforehand. This will save you money and time.

Plan for the vehicle to be out of use for quite a while. An engineering works will be required to perform some of the work which the do-it-yourselfer cannot accomplish without special equipment. These places often have a busy schedule, so it would be a good idea to consult them before removing the engine, in order to accurately estimate the amount of time required to rebuild or repair components that may need work.

Always be extremely careful when removing and refitting the engine. Serious injury can result from careless actions. Plan ahead, take your time, and you will find that a job of this nature, although major, can be accomplished successfully.

## 4  Engine and manual transmission - removal, separation and refitting

**Note:** *The engine and manual transmission is lowered from the engine compartment, then separated on the bench.*

### Removal

**1** Apply the handbrake, then jack up the front of the vehicle and support it on axle stands (see *"Jacking and Vehicle Support"*). Remove both front roadwheels.
**2** On models fitted with air conditioning, have the refrigerant evacuated from the system by an air conditioning specialist, then remove the dehydrator and seal its ports as described in Chapter 3. While the system is disconnected,

make sure that it is sealed adequately to prevent entry of dust, dirt and foreign matter.

 *Warning: Do not attempt to remove the refrigerant yourself - this could result in personal injury.*

**3** Depressurise the fuel system by unscrewing the cap from the right-hand end of the fuel rail, and using a small screwdriver or similar tool to depress the Schrader valve. Cover the valve with cloth to catch the fuel. The alternative method, and the only method to use on 1999-on models, is simply to disconnect the fuel pump's electrical supply while the engine is running, by removing the fuel pump fuse (number 19), and to allow the engine to idle until it dies through lack of fuel. Turn the engine over once or twice on the starter to ensure that all pressure is released, then switch off the ignition. Do not forget to refit the fuse when work is complete. Refer to Chapter 4A if necessary.
**4** Disconnect the battery negative (earth) lead (see Chapter 5A).
**5** Unbolt the cover from under the front of the engine compartment, then drain the cooling system as described in Chapter 1 **(see illustration)**.
**6** If necessary, drain the engine oil with reference to Chapter 1.
**7** On models fitted with a mass air flow (MAF) sensor (models up to 1999), release the clip and disconnect the air duct from the throttle housing, then disconnect the wiring from the intake air temperature (IAT) sensor and mass air flow sensor. Pull the air cleaner directly up from its mounting, disconnect the crankcase ventilation hose from the engine oil filler cap and remove the MAF sensor and air duct from the engine compartment **(see illustration)**.

> **HAYNES HINT** *Whenever you disconnect any vacuum lines, coolant or emissions hoses, wiring connectors and fuel lines, always label them clearly, so that they can be correctly reassembled. Masking tape and/or a touch-up paint applicator work well for marking items. Take instant photos, or sketch the locations of components and brackets.*

**8** On models with a temperature manifold absolute pressure (TMAP) sensor (models from 1999), loosen the clip and disconnect the air inlet duct from the throttle housing, then undo the screws and disconnect the inlet duct from the air cleaner. Release the front of the air cleaner from the rubber grommet, then lift up the front of the air cleaner and pull forwards from the rear mounting rubbers. Disconnect the crankcase ventilation hose.
**9** Release the clips and disconnect the top hose and bypass hose from the thermostat housing. Use a pair of grips to release the clips **(see illustrations)**.
**10** Release the alternator wiring from the clips next to the thermostat housing **(see illustration)**.
**11** On models with a mass air flow (MAF)

4.9a Disconnecting the top hose . . .

4.9b . . . and bypass hose from the thermostat housing

4.10 Release the alternator wiring from the clips next to the thermostat housing

4.11a Disconnecting the engine wiring harness (on the bulkhead)

4.11b Use a screwdriver to pull back the collar to disconnect the brake vacuum line from the inlet manifold

4.13 Disconnecting the heater supply hose from the stub on the cylinder head

sensor (models up to 1999), unclip the engine wiring harness at the right-hand rear of the engine, then use a screwdriver to pull back the collar and disconnect the brake vacuum line from the inlet manifold. Disconnect the vacuum line from the evaporative emission control canister purge solenoid valve (CANP), then remove the wiring connector casings from the bulkhead, prise them open and separate the wiring connectors (see illustrations). Note that the connector housings should be renewed on refitting.

12 On models with a temperature manifold absolute pressure (TMAP) sensor (models from 1999), release the wiring harness at the right-hand rear of the engine and disconnect it, then disconnect the brake vacuum line from the inlet manifold. At the left-hand side of the bulkhead, disconnect the TMAP sensor wiring, then disconnect the vacuum line from the evaporative emission control canister purge solenoid valve (CANP).

13 Disconnect the heater supply hose from the

stub on the right-hand side of the cylinder head by releasing the quick release coupling (see illustration). Ford technicians use a special tool with two collars, which is inserted into the coupling in order to raise the plastic tabs over the shoulder on the stub. Without this tool it is very difficult to remove the coupling, although some success is possible if the outer housing is carefully levered over the plastic tabs - the locking tabs can then be removed from the stub and fitted to the outer housing for refitting.

14 On the bulkhead, disconnect the wiring from the vehicle speed sensor (VSS).

15 Release the accelerator outer cable from the clip on the throttle housing, then remove the adjustment ferrule from the support bracket and disengage the inner cable end fitting from the throttle segment. Position the accelerator cable to one side.

16 Unscrew both front suspension upper mounting locknuts five turns, while using an Allen key to hold the shock absorber piston rods stationary (see illustration). This is

necessary to prevent damage to the upper mountings when disconnecting the driveshafts.

17 Locate the oxygen sensor wiring plug on the engine compartment front crossmember, and disconnect it.

18 Disconnect the engine wiring harness plug located on the right-hand side of the bulkhead.

19 On models manufactured from 1999 onwards unbolt the alternator wiring cover.

20 Working beneath the car, unscrew the special nuts and remove the exhaust heat shield from the underbody (see illustration).

21 Unscrew the bolt and detach the gearchange stabiliser bar from the rear of the transmission (see illustration). At the same time, mark the position of the gearchange linkage/universal joint on the transmission selector rod, then unscrew and remove the clamp bolt and slide the linkage from the selector rod. Support the stabiliser bar and gearchange linkage to one side away from the area beneath the engine compartment.

4.16 Unscrew the upper mounting locknuts while using an Allen key to hold the shock absorber piston rods stationary

4.20 Removing the exhaust heat shield from the underbody

4.21 Unscrew the bolt and detach the gearchange stabiliser bar from the rear of the transmission

**4.23a  Use a Torx key to hold the front suspension clamp bolts while unscrewing the nuts . . .**

**4.23b  . . . then lever down the lower arms**

**4.24a  Disconnect the wiring from the multiple function switch . . .**

**22** Unscrew the exhaust flange bolts securing the catalytic converter to the exhaust system, then unhook the exhaust system mounting rubbers and lower the exhaust system to the ground. Recover the sealing ring from the flange joint. To prevent undue flexing of the braided section of the exhaust system, it is recommended that a temporary wooden or metal splint is wrapped around it and retained with cable ties.

**23** The right-hand and left-hand front suspension lower arms must now be disconnected from the hub carriers on each side. To do this, unscrew the nuts from the clamp bolts, drive out the bolts with a soft-metal drift, and carefully lever the lower arms down from the hub carriers. Note that the Torx heads of the clamp bolts are facing the front of the car **(see illustrations)**.

**24** On models fitted with a multiple function switch (pre-1999 models) on the front of the

transmission, disconnect the wiring from the switch, and also unbolt the earth lead from the transmission **(see illustrations)**.

**25** On models fitted with a reversing light switch (1999-on models) on the front of the transmission, disconnect the wiring from the switch, and also disconnect the transmission earth lead located at the rear of the transmission near the driveshaft.

**26** Cut free or release the clips securing the driveshaft inner gaiters to the inner joints on both sides **(see illustration)**.

**27** Carefully pull out the driveshaft tripodes from the inner joints on both sides and tie the driveshafts to one side away from the area beneath the engine compartment **(see illustration)**. The right-hand driveshaft should be swivelled forward and tied to the front of the engine compartment, but the shorter right-hand driveshaft should be swivelled to the rear and tied to the front suspension lower

arm bracket. If necessary, scoop out the grease from the joints and fill with new grease on refitting. Protect the joints and housings by tying plastic bags over them **(see illustrations)**.

*Caution: The inner driveshaft joints must not be bent more than 18° and the outer joints by more than 45°.*

**28** Unscrew the collar nut and disconnect the speedometer cable from the speed transmitter on the rear of the transmission **(see illustration)**.

**29** Disconnect the wiring from the starter motor by unscrewing the two nuts. Also unscrew the rear starter mounting bolt and release the earth lead.

**30** On models with power steering, clamp the hydraulic fluid reservoir supply hose near the pump (right-hand side of the engine). Position cloth beneath the pump to catch spilt fluid, then disconnect the hose. Unscrew the bolts

**4.24b  . . . then unbolt the earth lead from the transmission**

**4.26  Cut free the driveshaft inner gaiter clips**

**4.27a  Pull out the driveshaft tripodes from the inner joints on both sides**

**4.27b  Protect the driveshaft tripodes . . .**

**4.27c  . . . and housings by tying plastic bags over them**

**4.28  Unscrew the collar nut and disconnect the speedometer cable from the speed transmitter on the rear of the transmission**

4.30a On models with power steering, clamp the hydraulic fluid reservoir supply hose near the pump . . .

4.30b . . . unscrew the union . . .

4.30c . . . detach the power steering hydraulic pipes from the mountings . . .

4.30d . . . release the quick-release couplings at the left-hand side of the transmission . . .

4.30e . . . and right-hand end of the radiator . . .

4.30f . . . and remove the hydraulic pipes

and detach the power steering hydraulic pipes from the radiator lower crossmember. Position the container beneath the left-hand end of the pipes, then disconnect the unions. One of the unions has a hexagon nut and the other has a quick-release coupling which is released by prising up the plastic tabs. Also release the quick-release coupling at the right-hand end of the pipe. With the couplings released, the pressure pipe from the pump remains on the engine, and the remaining pipe can be removed completely **(see illustrations)**.

**31** On models with air conditioning, disconnect the refrigerant line from the top right-hand side of the condenser. To do this, reach through the aperture in the engine compartment front crossmember and unscrew the retaining nut.

**32** Undo the screw or nut, and detach the earth lead from the left-hand side of the engine compartment.

**33** Disconnect the fuel supply and return lines at the quick release couplings at the left-hand rear of the engine compartment by squeezing the release buttons. Tape over or plug the fuel lines to prevent entry of dust and dirt.

**34** To prevent damage to the camshaft position sensor when the engine is lowered, it is recommended that the sensor is removed from the timing cover with reference to Chapter 4A. Tape over the aperture to prevent entry of dust and dirt. It is also recommended that the stud be removed from the rear left-hand side of the transmission to provide clearance from the left-hand front suspension lower arm bracket.

**35** Support the weight of the engine and transmission. Either a suitable hoist or two trolley jacks and a length of wood may be used. The flat surfaces of the engine sump and transmission make the use of trolley jacks

particularly suitable. Make sure there is sufficient height beneath the front of the car to withdraw the assembly.

**36** Unscrew and remove the centre bolt from the engine rear roll restrictor (mounting). Unbolt the mounting bracket from the underbody and, if necessary, unbolt the bracket from the transmission **(see illustration)**.

**37** Pull the wiring cable supports from the top of the right-hand engine mounting, then unscrew the single bolt and two nuts securing the bracket to the engine **(see illustrations)**. The bracket remains attached to the body while the engine is being removed.

**38** Pull out the spring clip and disconnect the clutch hydraulic line from the support bracket. Refit the clip, then pull the hydraulic line out of the guide in the transmission casing - be prepared for some fluid loss by positioning a container beneath the hydraulic line. Also

4.36 Removing the rear roll restrictor bracket from the transmission

4.37a Pull off the wiring cable supports . . .

4.37b . . . then unscrew the single bolt . . .

4.37c . . . and two nuts from the right-hand engine mounting bracket

4.38 Disconnecting the breather hose from the rear of the transmission

4.39 Unscrew the nuts from the left-hand engine mounting to release the bracket from the bottom of the battery support bracket

disconnect the breather pipe from the rear of the transmission (see illustration).

39 Unscrew the nuts from the left-hand engine mounting to release the bracket from the bottom of the battery support bracket (see illustration).

40 With the help of an assistant, carefully lower the engine and transmission assembly from the engine compartment, making sure that it clears the surrounding components and bodywork. When access is possible after slightly lowering the assembly, loosen the clip and disconnect the coolant hose from the water pump. Further lower the assembly to the floor. If available, lower it onto a low trolley so that it can be withdrawn easily from under the car (see illustration). If the engine is to be overhauled, remove the wiring loom from the engine noting its location and routing.

4.40 Using a trolley jack to lower the engine/transmission assembly to the floor

## Separation

41 To separate the transmission from the engine, first remove the starter motor with reference to Chapter 5A.

42 Unscrew and remove the flange mounting bolts securing the transmission to the engine (see illustration). If the engine/transmission assembly is supported by the hoist and raised from the ground, leave one of the upper flange bolts finger-tight until you are ready to lift the transmission away from the engine.

43 With the help of an assistant withdraw the transmission directly from the engine making sure that its weight is not allowed to bear on the clutch friction disc (see illustration).

## Refitting

44 With the transmission separated from the engine, check that the clutch components (clutch cover, disc, release bearing and slave cylinder) are in good condition and still serviceable. The clutch friction disc linings can be checked by removing the clutch cover (refer to Chapter 6 if necessary).

45 Apply a smear of high-melting-point grease to the splines of the transmission input shaft. Do not apply too much, otherwise there is the possibility of the grease contaminating the clutch friction disc.

46 Check that the release bearing is correctly located in the slave cylinder inside the transmission bellhousing. Clean the mating surfaces and make sure that the adapter plate is correctly located on the dowels in the cylinder block.

47 With the help of an assistant, lift the transmission directly onto the engine making sure that the transmission input shaft enters the friction disc hub splines squarely. Insert the flange mounting bolts and tighten them to the specified torque.

48 Refit the starter motor with reference to Chapter 5A.

49 If removed, refit the wiring loom to the engine.

50 Position the engine/transmission assembly beneath the engine compartment (see illustration).

51 With the help of an assistant, carefully lift the assembly into position and refit the engine mountings but leave the nuts/bolts finger-tight at this stage. The rear roll restrictor should also be refitted loosely at this stage.

52 Obtain a metal plate, 10 mm thick, and insert this between the bracket on the right-hand end of the engine and the body. With the engine against the plate, tighten the two nuts and single bolt to the specified torque. Leave the plate in position at this stage.

53 Working beneath the left-hand side of the engine, position a 10 mm thick metal plate between the mounting bracket and the transmission housing. Position the engine so that the bracket is against the plate, then tighten the left-hand engine mounting nuts to the specified torque. Remove the plates.

54 Tighten the rear roll restrictor centre bolt to the specified torque. Check that the rubber mounting is central on the body bracket, then tighten the rear roll restrictor mounting bracket bolts.

4.42 The upper flange bolts securing the transmission to the engine

4.43 Separating the transmission from the rear of the engine

4.50 Engine/transmission assembly positioned beneath the engine compartment

**6.5a  Compress the valve spring to remove the collets . . .**

**6.5b  . . . then remove the valve spring retainer and spring . . .**

**6.5c  . . . followed by the valve**

**55** The remaining procedure is a reversal of removal, noting the following additional points.

a) Check and if necessary adjust the accelerator cable with reference to Chapter 4A.

b) Before inserting the driveshaft tripodes into the inner joints, pack each joint with 100 grams of constant velocity joint grease. Slide each joint fully in as far as the stop, then pull it out 20 mm before refitting the inner gaiters. Before tightening the clips, make sure any trapped air inside the gaiter is released by lifting the edge of the gaiter with a screwdriver.

c) Check and if necessary adjust the gearchange as described in Chapter 7.

d) Top up and bleed the clutch hydraulic system as described in Chapter 6.

e) Refill the cooling system as described in Chapter 1.

f) On models with air conditioning, have the system recharged with refrigerant by an air conditioning specialist.

g) Top up the power steering fluid reservoir with reference to "Weekly checks".

h) Tighten all nuts and bolts to the specified torque setting.

i) **Note:** After the battery has been reconnected, the engine management system requires approximately 5 miles of driving to relearn its optimum settings (refer to Chapter 5A). During this period, the engine may not perform normally.

## 5  Engine overhaul - dismantling sequence

**1** It is much easier to disassemble and work on the engine if it is mounted on a portable engine stand. These stands can often be hired from a tool hire shop. Before the engine is mounted on a stand, the flywheel must be removed from the engine, so that the engine stand bolts can be tightened into the end of the cylinder block.

**2** If a stand is not available, it is possible to disassemble the engine with it blocked up on a sturdy workbench or on the floor. Be extra-careful not to tip or drop the engine when working without a stand.

**3** If you are going to obtain a reconditioned

engine, all the external components must come off first, in order to be transferred to the replacement engine (just as they will if you are doing a complete engine overhaul yourself). Check with the engine supplier for details. Normally these components include:

a) Alternator and brackets.
b) Ignition coil, HT leads and spark plugs.
c) Thermostat and cover.
d) Fuel injection equipment.
e) Inlet and exhaust manifolds.
f) Oil filter.
g) Engine mountings and lifting brackets.
h) Ancillary (power steering pump, air conditioning compressor) brackets.
i) Oil filler tube and dipstick.
j) Coolant pipes and hoses.
k) Flywheel.

**Note:** When removing the external components from the engine, pay close attention to details that may be helpful or important during refitting. Note the fitted position of gaskets, seals, spacers, pins, washers, bolts and other small items.

**4** If you are obtaining a 'short' motor (which consists of the engine cylinder block, crankshaft, pistons and connecting rods all assembled), then the cylinder head, sump and oil pump will have to be removed also.

**5** If you are planning a complete overhaul, the engine can be disassembled and the internal components removed in the following order:

a) Engine external components (including inlet and exhaust manifolds).
b) Timing sprockets and chain.
c) Cylinder head.
d) Flywheel.

**6.6  Using pliers to pull the valve stem seals from the valve guides**

e) Oil pump.
f) Sump.
g) Pistons and connecting rods.
h) Crankshaft and main bearings.
i) Tappets and camshaft.

**6** Before beginning the disassembly and overhaul procedures, make sure that you have all of the correct tools necessary. Refer to the reference section at the end of this manual for further information.

## 6  Cylinder head - dismantling

**Note:** New and reconditioned cylinder heads are available from the manufacturers and from engine overhaul specialists. Due to the fact that some specialist tools are required for the dismantling and inspection procedures, and new components may not be readily available, it may be more practical and economical for the home mechanic to purchase a reconditioned head rather than dismantle, inspect and recondition the original head.

**1** Remove the cylinder head as described in Part A.

**2** If not already done, remove the inlet and exhaust manifolds with reference to Chapter 4A. Also remove all external brackets and elbows.

**3** Valve removal should commence with No 1 valve (nearest the timing chain end). Keep all components identified for location.

**4** To remove the valve springs and valves from the cylinder head, a standard valve spring compressor will be required. Fit the spring compressor to the first valve and spring to be removed. If, when the valve spring compressor is screwed down, the spring upper seat refuses to free and expose the split collets, gently tap the top of the tool, directly over the upper seat, with a light hammer. This will free the seat.

**5** With the valve spring compressed, remove the split collets, then loosen the compressor, and remove the retainer and spring. Withdraw the valve from the cylinder head **(see illustrations)**.

**6** Pull the valve stem seals from the valve guides using a pair of pliers **(see illustration)**.

**7** Repeat the removal procedure with each of the remaining seven valves in turn. As they are removed, keep the individual valves and their components together, and in their respective order of fitting, by placing them in a separate labelled bag **(see illustration)**.

### 7 Cylinder head and valves - cleaning, inspection and renovation

**1** Thorough cleaning of the cylinder head and valve components, followed by a detailed inspection, will enable you to decide how much valve service work must be carried out during the engine overhaul. If the head is extremely dirty, it should be steam cleaned, however, on completion make sure that all oil holes and oil galleries are cleaned.

### Cleaning

**2** Scrape away all traces of old gasket material and sealing compound from the cylinder head. Take care not to damage the cylinder head surfaces.
**3** Scrape away the carbon from the combustion chambers and ports, then wash the cylinder head thoroughly with paraffin or a suitable solvent.
**4** Scrape off any heavy carbon deposits that may have formed on the valves, then use a power-operated wire brush to remove deposits from the valve heads and stems.

### Inspection and renovation

**Note:** *Be sure to perform all the following inspection procedures before concluding that the services of an engine overhaul specialist are required. Make a list of all items that require attention.*

### Cylinder head

**5** Inspect the head very carefully for cracks, evidence of coolant leakage and other damage. If cracks are found, a new cylinder head should be obtained.
**6** Use a straight-edge and feeler blade to check that the cylinder head surface is not distorted. If the specified distortion limit is exceeded, machining of the gasket face is not

**6.7 Use a labelled plastic bag to store and identify valve components**

recommended by the manufacturers, so the only course of action is to renew the cylinder head.
**7** Examine the valve seats in each of the combustion chambers. If they are severely pitted, cracked or burned, then they will need to be renewed or recut by an engine overhaul specialist. If they are only slightly pitted, this can be removed by grinding the valve heads and seats together with coarse, then fine, grinding paste as described below.
**8** If the valve guides are worn, indicated by a side-to-side motion of the valve in the guide, new guides must be fitted. If necessary, insert a new valve in the guides to determine if the wear is on the guide or valve. If new guides are to be fitted, the valves must be renewed as a matter of course. Valve guides may be renewed using a press and a suitable mandrel, however, the work is best carried out by an engine overhaul specialist, since if it is not done skilfully, there is a risk of damaging the cylinder head.

### Valves

**9** Examine the head of each valve for pitting, burning, cracks and general wear, and check the valve stem for scoring and wear ridges. Rotate the valve, and check for any obvious indication that it is bent. Look for pits and excessive wear on the end of each valve stem. If the valve appears satisfactory at this stage, measure the valve stem diameter at several points using a micrometer **(see illustration)**. Any significant difference in the readings obtained indicates wear of the valve stem.

Should any of these conditions be apparent, the valve(s) must be renewed. If the valves are in satisfactory condition, or if new valves are being fitted, they should be ground (lapped) into their respective seats to ensure a smooth gas-tight seal.
**10** Valve grinding is carried out as follows. Place the cylinder head upside-down on a bench, with a block of wood at each end to give clearance for the valve stems.
**11** Smear a trace of coarse carborundum paste on the seat face, and press a suction grinding tool onto the valve head. With a semi-rotary action, grind the valve head to its seat, lifting the valve occasionally to redistribute the grinding paste **(see illustration)**. When a dull-matt even surface is produced on both the valve seat and the valve, wipe off the paste and repeat the process with fine carborundum paste. A light spring placed under the valve head will greatly ease this operation. When a smooth unbroken ring of light grey matt finish is produced on both the valve and seat, the grinding operation is complete. Be sure to remove all traces of grinding paste, using paraffin or a suitable solvent, before reassembly of the cylinder head.

### Valve components

**12** Examine the valve springs for signs of damage and discoloration, and also measure their free length using vernier calipers or a steel rule **(see illustration)** or by comparing the existing spring with a new component.
**13** Stand each spring on a flat surface, and check it for squareness. If any of the springs are damaged, distorted or have lost their tension, obtain a complete new set of springs. It is normal to renew the springs as a matter of course during a major overhaul.

### Rocker arm components

**14** Check the rocker arm contact surfaces for pits, wear, score marks or any indication that the surface-hardening has worn through. Dismantle the rocker shaft and check the components as described in Chapter 2A.

### Valve stem oil seals

**15** The valve stem oil seals should be renewed as a matter of course.

**7.9 Measuring the diameter of a valve stem**

**7.11 Grinding-in a valve seat**

**7.12 Checking the valve spring free length**

8.2a  Fitting a valve stem oil seal

8.2b  Using a special tool to fit the valve stem oil seals

8.3a  Oil the valve stems . . .

8.3b  . . . then insert the valves in their guides

8.5a  Apply a small dab of grease to each collet before installation - it will hold them in place on the valve stem

8.5b  A dab of grease on a screwdriver will help to fit the collets

## 8  Cylinder head - reassembly

1  Regardless of whether or not the head was sent away for repair work of any sort, make sure that it is clean before beginning reassembly. Be sure to remove any metal particles and abrasive grit that may still be present from operations such as valve grinding or head resurfacing. Use compressed air, if available to blow out all the oil holes and passages.

2  Lubricate the valve stem oil seals with clean engine oil, then fit them by pushing into position in the cylinder head using a suitable socket or special tool (see illustrations). Ensure that the seals are fully engaged with the valve guide.

3  Lubricate the valve stems then insert the valves into their original locations. If new valves are being fitted, insert them into the locations to which they have been ground. Take care not to damage the valve stem oil seal as each valve is fitted (see illustrations).

4  Locate the first spring and retainer over the valve stem.

5  Compress the valve spring and locate the split collets in the recess in the valve stem (see illustrations). Release the compressor, then repeat the procedure on the remaining valves.

6  With all the valves installed, place the cylinder head flat on the bench and, using a hammer and interposed block of wood, tap the end of each valve stem to settle the components.

7  The previously removed components can now be refitted with reference to Section 6.

## 9  Camshaft and tappets - removal, inspection and refitting

### Removal

1  Refer to the relevant Sections in Chapter 2A and remove the cylinder head, oil pump, timing chain and camshaft sprocket, and the sump.

2  Invert the engine so that it is supported on its cylinder head face (on a clean work area). This is necessary to make all of the tappets slide to the top of their stroke, thus allowing the camshaft to be withdrawn. Rotate the camshaft through a full turn, to ensure that all of the tappets slide up their bores, clear of the camshaft.

3  Before removing the camshaft, check its endfloat using a dial gauge mounted on the front face of the engine or feeler blades. Pull the camshaft fully towards the front (timing chain) end of the engine, then insert feeler blades between the camshaft sprocket flange and the camshaft thrust plate to assess the endfloat clearance (see illustration). The camshaft endfloat must be as specified (see Chapter 2A Specifications).

4  Undo the two retaining bolts, and remove the camshaft thrust plate (see illustration).

5  Carefully withdraw the camshaft from the front end of the engine (see illustration).

6  Extract each tappet in turn. Keep them in order of fitting by inserting them in a card with

9.3  Checking the camshaft endfloat

9.4  Removing the camshaft thrust plate

**9.5 Removing the camshaft from the front end of the engine**

**9.6 Removing the tappets, using a valve grinding tool suction cup**

the rings foul the ridge. However, it is reasonable to assume that a rebore and new pistons will be required in any case if the ridge is so pronounced.

6 Repeat the procedure for the remaining piston/connecting rod assemblies. Ensure that the caps and rods are marked before removal, as described previously, and keep all components in order.

eight holes in it, numbered 1 to 8 (from the timing chain end of the engine). A valve grinding suction tool will be found to be useful for the removal of tappets **(see illustration)**.

### Inspection

**7** Examine the camshaft bearing journals and lobes for damage or excessive wear. If evident, the camshaft must be renewed.

**8** Examine the camshaft bearing internal surfaces for signs of damage or excessive wear. If evident, the bearings must be renewed by a Ford dealer.

**9** If not carried out on removal, check the camshaft endfloat as described in paragraph 3. If the endfloat exceeds the specified tolerance, renew the thrust plate.

**10** It is seldom that the tappets wear excessively in their bores, but it is likely that after a high mileage, the cam lobe contact surfaces will show signs of wear. Where this condition is evident, renew the tappets.

### Refitting

**11** To refit the tappets and the camshaft, it is essential that the crankcase is inverted.

**12** Lubricate the tappets and their bores. Insert each tappet fully into its original bore in the cylinder block.

**13** Lubricate the camshaft bearings, camshaft and thrust plate, then insert the camshaft into the crankcase from the timing chain end.

**14** Fit the thrust plate and tighten the retaining bolts to the specified torque setting. Check that the camshaft is able to rotate freely, and that the endfloat is as specified (see Chapter 2A).

**15** Refer to the relevant Sections in Chapter 2A and refit the sump, camshaft sprocket, timing chain, oil pump and cylinder head.

## 10 Piston/connecting rod assemblies - removal

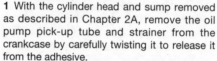

**1** With the cylinder head and sump removed as described in Chapter 2A, remove the oil pump pick-up tube and strainer from the crankcase by carefully twisting it to release it from the adhesive.

**2** Rotate the crankshaft so that No 1 big-end cap (timing end of the engine) is at the lowest point of its travel. If the big-end cap and rod are not already numbered, mark them with a marker pen or centre-punch **(see illustration)**. Mark both cap and rod to identify the cylinder they operate in.

**3** Unscrew and remove the big-end bearing cap bolts, and withdraw the cap complete with shell bearing from the connecting rod. Make sure that the shell remains in the cap and if necessary identify it for position.

**4** If only the bearing shells are being attended to, push the connecting rod up and off the crankpin, and remove the upper bearing shell. Keep the bearing shells and cap together in their correct sequence if they are to be refitted.

**5** If the piston is being removed, push the connecting rod up and remove the piston and rod from the top of the bore. Note that if there is a pronounced wear ridge at the top of the bore, there is a risk of damaging the piston as

## 11 Crankshaft - removal

**1** Remove the timing chain, crankshaft sprocket, sump, oil pick-up tube, flywheel and rear oil seal housing. The pistons/connecting rods must be free of the crankshaft journals, however it is not essential to remove them completely from the cylinder block.

**2** Before the crankshaft is removed, check the endfloat. Mount a dial gauge with the probe in line with the crankshaft and just touching the crankshaft **(see illustration)**.

**3** Push the crankshaft fully away from the gauge, and zero it. Next, lever the crankshaft towards the gauge as far as possible, and check the reading obtained. The distance that the crankshaft moved is its endfloat; if it is greater than specified (see Chapter 2A Specifications), new thrust washers will be required.

**4** If a dial gauge is not available, feeler blades can be used. Gently lever or push the crankshaft in one direction, then insert feeler blades between the crankshaft web and the main bearing incorporating the thrustwashers to determine the clearance.

**5** Check that the main bearing caps have marks to indicate their respective fitted positions in the block. They also have arrow marks pointing towards the timing end of the engine to indicate correct orientation **(see illustration)**.

**6** Unscrew the retaining bolts, and remove the main bearing caps. If the caps are reluctant to separate from the block face, lightly tap them free using a plastic- or copper-faced hammer. If the bearing shells are likely to be used again, keep them with their bearing caps for safekeeping. However,

**10.2 The big-end caps and connecting rods are normally marked with their relevant cylinder number**

**11.2 Checking the crankshaft endfloat with a dial gauge**

**11.5 Connecting rod big-end bearing cap and main bearing cap markings**

unless the engine is known to be of low mileage, it is recommended that they be renewed.

**7** Lift the crankshaft out from the crankcase, then extract the upper bearing shells from the crankcase, and the side thrustwashers from the centre main bearing. Keep them with their respective caps for correct repositioning if they are to be used again.

---

## 12 Cylinder block/ crankcase and bores - cleaning and inspection

### Cleaning

**1** For complete cleaning, the core plugs should be removed. Drill a small hole in them, then insert a self-tapping screw and pull out the plugs using a pair of grips or a slide-hammer. Also remove all external components and senders (if not already done), noting their locations (see illustration).
**2** Scrape all traces of gasket or sealant from the cylinder block, taking care not to damage the head and sump mating faces.
**3** If the block is extremely dirty, it should be steam-cleaned.
**4** After the block has been cleaned, clean all oil holes and oil galleries one more time. Flush all internal passages with warm water until the water runs clear, dry the block thoroughly and wipe all machined surfaces with a light rust-preventative oil. If you have access to compressed air, use it to speed up the drying process and to blow out all the oil holes and galleries.

 *Warning: Wear eye protection when using compressed air!*

**5** If the block is not very dirty, you can do an adequate cleaning job with hot soapy water and a stiff brush. Take plenty of time, and do a thorough job. Regardless of the cleaning method used, be sure to clean all oil holes and galleries very thoroughly, dry the block completely and coat all machined surfaces with light oil.
**6** The threaded holes in the block must be clean to ensure accurate torque wrench readings during reassembly. Run the proper-size tap into each of the holes to remove rust, corrosion, thread sealant or sludge, and to restore damaged threads (see illustration). If possible, use compressed air to clear the holes of debris produced by this operation. Now is a good time to clean the threads on the head bolts (if being re-used) and the main bearing cap bolts as well.
**7** At this stage, the main bearing caps can be refitted and their retaining bolts finger-tightened.
**8** After coating the mating surfaces of the new core plugs with suitable sealant, refit them in the cylinder block. Make sure that they are driven in straight and seated

**12.1 The core plugs should be removed with a puller - if they are driven into the block, they may be impossible to remove**

properly, or leakage could result. Special tools are available for this purpose, but a large socket, with an outside diameter that will just slip into the core plug, will work just as well.
**9** If the engine is not going to be reassembled right away, cover it with a large plastic bag to keep it clean and prevent it rusting.

### Inspection

**10** Visually check the block for cracks, rust and corrosion. Look for stripped threads in the threaded holes. If there has been any history of internal water leakage, it may be worthwhile having an engine overhaul specialist check the block with special equipment. If defects are found, have the block repaired, if possible, or renewed.
**11** Check the cylinder bores for scuffing and scoring. Normally, bore wear will be evident in the form of a wear ridge at the top of the bore. This ridge marks the limit of piston travel.
**12** Measure the diameter of each cylinder at the top (just under the ridge area), centre and bottom of the cylinder bore, parallel to the crankshaft axis (see illustration).
**13** Next measure each cylinder's diameter at the same three locations across the crankshaft axis. If the difference between any of the measurements is greater than 0.20 mm, indicating that the cylinder is excessively out-of-round or tapered, then remedial action must be considered.
**14** Repeat this procedure for the remaining cylinders, then measure the diameter of each piston at right-angles to the gudgeon pin axis, and compare the result with the information given in the Specifications (see illustration).

**12.6 All bolt holes in the block should be cleaned and restored with a tap**

By comparing the piston diameters with the bore diameters, an idea can be obtained of the clearances.
**15** If the cylinder walls are badly scuffed or scored, or if they are excessively out-of-round or tapered, have the cylinder block rebored (where possible) by an engine overhaul specialist. New pistons (oversize in the case of a rebore) will also be required.
**16** If the cylinders are in reasonably good condition, then it may only be necessary to renew the piston rings.
**17** If this is the case, the bores should be honed in order to allow the new rings to bed in correctly and provide the best possible seal. The conventional type of hone has spring-loaded stones, and is used with a power drill. You will also need some paraffin or honing oil and rags. The hone should be moved up and down the cylinder to produce a crosshatch pattern, and plenty of honing oil should be used. Ideally, the crosshatch lines should intersect at approximately a 60° angle. Do not take off more material than is necessary to produce the required finish. If new pistons are being fitted, the piston manufacturers may specify a finish with a different angle, so their instructions should be followed. Do not withdraw the hone from the cylinder while it is still being turned, but stop it first. After honing a cylinder, wipe out all traces of the honing oil. If equipment of this type is not available, or if you are not sure whether you are competent to undertake the task yourself, an engine overhaul specialist will carry out the work at a moderate cost.

**12.12 Measure the diameter of each cylinder just under the wear ridge (A), at the centre (B) and at the bottom (C)**

**12.14 Measure the piston skirt diameter at right-angles to the gudgeon pin axis, just above the base of the skirt**

**12.18a When refitting the oil pressure switch, apply suitable sealant to the threads . . .**

**18** Refit all external components and senders in their correct locations, as noted before removal **(see illustrations)**.

### 13 Piston/connecting rod assemblies - inspection and reassembly

## Inspection

**1** Before the inspection process can begin, the piston/connecting rod assemblies must be cleaned, and the original piston rings removed from the pistons.
**2** Carefully expand the old rings over the top of the pistons. The use of two or three old feeler blades will be helpful in preventing the rings dropping into empty grooves **(see illustration)**. Note that the oil control scraper ring is in two sections.
**3** Scrape away all traces of carbon from the top of the piston. A hand-held wire brush or a piece of fine emery cloth can be used once the majority of the deposits have been scraped away.
**4** Remove the carbon from the ring grooves in the piston by cleaning them using an old ring. Break the ring in half to do this. Be very careful to remove only the carbon deposits; do not remove any metal, or scratch the sides of the ring grooves. Protect your fingers - piston rings are sharp.
**5** Once the deposits have been removed, clean the piston/connecting rod assembly with paraffin or a suitable solvent, and dry thoroughly. Make sure the oil return holes in the ring grooves are clear.

**13.2 Using feeler blades to remove piston rings**

**12.18b . . . then insert it in the cylinder block and tighten to the specified torque**

**6** If the pistons and cylinder bores are not damaged or worn excessively, and if the cylinder block does not need to be rebored, the original pistons can be re-used. Normal piston wear appears as even vertical wear on the piston thrust surfaces, and slight looseness of the top ring in its groove. New piston rings, however, should always be used when the engine is reassembled.
**7** Carefully inspect each piston for cracks around the skirt, at the gudgeon pin bosses, and at the piston ring lands (between the piston ring grooves).
**8** Look for scoring and scuffing on the sides of the skirt, holes in the piston crown, and burned areas at the edge of the crown. If the skirt is scored or scuffed, the engine may have been suffering from overheating and/or abnormal combustion, which caused excessively-high operating temperatures. The cooling and lubricating systems should be checked thoroughly. Scorch marks on the sides of the pistons show that blow-by has occurred and the rings are not sealing correctly. A hole in the piston crown is an indication that abnormal combustion (pre-ignition, knocking or detonation) has been occurring. If any of the above problems exist, the causes must be corrected, or the damage will occur again. The causes may include inlet air leaks, incorrect fuel/air mixture or incorrect ignition timing.
**9** Corrosion of the piston, in the form of small pits, indicates that coolant is leaking into the combustion chamber and/or the crankcase. Again, the cause must be corrected, or the problem may persist in the rebuilt engine.
**10** If new rings are being fitted to old pistons, measure the piston ring-to-groove clearance by placing a new piston ring in each ring groove and measuring the clearance with a feeler blade. Check the clearance at three or four places around each groove, and compare with the maximum clearances given in the Specifications (see Chapter 2A). If a new ring is excessively tight, the most likely cause is dirt remaining in the groove.
**11** Check the piston-to-bore clearance by measuring the cylinder bore (see Section 12) and the piston diameter. Measure the piston across the skirt, at a 90° angle to the gudgeon pin, approximately half way down the skirt. Subtract the piston diameter from the bore diameter to obtain the clearance. If this is

greater than the figures given in the Specifications (see Chapter 2A), the block will have to be rebored and new pistons and rings fitted.
**12** Check the fit of the gudgeon pin by twisting the piston and connecting rod in opposite directions. Any noticeable play indicates excessive wear, which must be corrected. If the pistons or connecting rods are to be renewed, the work should be carried out by a Ford garage or engine overhaul specialist.
**13** Before refitting the rings to the pistons, check their end gaps by inserting each of them in their cylinder bores. Use the piston to make sure that they are square. Using feeler blades, check that the gaps are within the tolerances given in the Specifications (see Chapter 2A). Genuine rings are supplied pre-gapped; no attempt should be made to adjust the gaps by filing.

## Reassembly

**14** Install the new rings by fitting them over the top of the piston, starting with the oil control scraper ring sections. Use feeler blades in the same way as when removing the old rings. New rings generally have their top surfaces identified, and must be fitted the correct way round **(see illustration)**. Note that the first and second compression rings have different sections. Be careful when handling the compression rings; they will break if they are handled roughly or expanded too far. With all the rings in position, space the ring gaps at 120° to each other. The oil control scraper ring expander must also be positioned opposite to the actual ring.

### 14 Crankshaft - inspection

**1** Clean the crankshaft and dry it with compressed air if available.
> ⚠ **Warning: Wear eye protection when using compressed air! Be sure to clean the oil holes with a pipe cleaner or similar probe.**

**2** Check the main and big-end bearing journals for uneven wear, scoring, pitting and cracking.
**3** If the crankshaft has been reground, check

**13.14 Look for etched markings identifying the piston ring top surface**

for burrs around the crankshaft oil holes (the holes are usually chamfered, so burrs should not be a problem unless regrinding has been carried out carelessly). Remove any burrs with a fine file or scraper, and thoroughly clean the oil holes as described previously.

4 Using a micrometer, measure the diameter of the main bearing and connecting rod journals, and compare the results with the Specifications **(see illustration)**. By measuring the diameter at a number of points around each journal's circumference, you will be able to determine whether or not the journal is out-of-round. Take the measurement at each end of the journal, near the webs, to determine if the journal is tapered. If any of the measurements vary by more than 0.025 mm, the crankshaft will have to be reground, and undersize bearings fitted.

5 Check the oil seal contact surfaces at each end of the crankshaft for wear and damage. If an excessive groove is evident in the surface of the crankshaft, consult an engine overhaul specialist who will be able to advise whether a repair is possible or if a new crankshaft is necessary.

## 15 Main and big-end bearings - inspection

1 Even though the main and big-end bearings should be renewed during the engine overhaul, the old bearings should be retained for close examination, as they may reveal valuable information about the condition of the engine. The size of the bearing shells is stamped on the back metal, and this information should be given to the supplier of the new shells.

2 Bearing failure occurs because of lack of lubrication, the presence of dirt or other foreign particles, overloading the engine, and corrosion. Regardless of the cause of bearing failure, it must be corrected before the engine is reassembled, to prevent it from happening again **(see illustration)**.

3 When examining the bearings, remove them from the engine block, the main bearing caps, the connecting rods and the rod caps, and lay them out on a clean surface in the same general position as their location in the engine. This will enable you to match any bearing problems with the corresponding crankshaft journal.

4 Dirt and other foreign particles get into the engine in a variety of ways. Dirt may be left in the engine during assembly, or it may pass through filters or the crankcase ventilation system. It may get into the oil, and from there into the bearings. Metal chips from machining operations and normal engine wear are often present. Abrasives are sometimes left in engine components after reconditioning, especially when parts are not thoroughly cleaned using the proper cleaning methods. Whatever the source, these foreign objects

**14.4 Measure the diameter of each crankshaft journal at several points, to detect taper and out-of round conditions**

often end up embedded in the soft bearing material, and are easily recognised. Large particles will not embed in the bearing, and will score or gouge the bearing and journal. The best prevention for this cause of bearing failure is to clean all parts thoroughly, and keep everything spotlessly-clean during engine assembly. Frequent and regular engine oil and filter changes are also recommended.

5 Lack of lubrication (or lubrication break-down) has a number of interrelated causes. Excessive heat (which thins the oil), over-loading (which squeezes the oil from the bearing face) and oil leakage (from excessive bearing clearances, worn oil pump or high engine speeds) all contribute to lubrication breakdown. Blocked oil pass-ages, which usually are the result of misaligned oil holes in a bearing shell, will also oil-starve a bearing and destroy it. When lack of lubrication is the cause of bearing failure, the bearing material is wiped or extruded from the steel backing of the bearing. Temperatures may increase to the point where the steel backing turns blue from overheating.

6 Driving habits can have a definite effect on

**15.2 Typical bearing failures**

bearing life. Full-throttle, low-speed operation (labouring the engine) puts very high loads on bearings, which tends to squeeze out the oil film. These loads cause the bearings to flex, which produces fine cracks in the bearing face (fatigue failure). Eventually, the bearing material will loosen in pieces and tear away from the steel backing. Short-trip driving leads to corrosion of bearings, because insufficient engine heat is produced to drive off the condensed water and corrosive gases. These products collect in the engine oil, forming acid and sludge. As the oil is carried to the engine bearings, the acid attacks and corrodes the bearing material.

7 Incorrect bearing installation during engine assembly will lead to bearing failure as well. Tight-fitting bearings leave insufficient bearing oil clearance, and will result in oil starvation. Dirt or foreign particles trapped behind a bearing shell result in high spots on the bearing which lead to failure.

8 If new bearings are to be fitted, the bearing running clearances should be measured before the engine is finally reassembled, to ensure that the correct bearing shells have been obtained (see Sections 17 and 18). If the crankshaft has been reground, the engineering works which carried out the work will advise on the correct size bearing shells to suit the work carried out.

## 16 Engine overhaul - reassembly sequence

1 Before reassembly begins ensure that all new parts have been obtained and that all necessary tools are available. Read through the entire procedure to familiarise yourself with the work involved, and to ensure that all items necessary for reassembly of the engine are at hand. In addition to all normal tools and materials, jointing and thread locking compound will be needed during engine reassembly. *Do not* use any kind of silicone-based sealant on any part of the fuel system or inlet manifold, and *never* use exhaust sealants upstream of the catalytic converter.

2 In order to save time and avoid problems, engine reassembly can be carried out in the following order.
   a) Tappets and camshaft.
   b) Crankshaft and main bearings.
   c) Pistons and connecting rods.
   d) Sump.
   e) Oil pump.
   f) Flywheel.
   g) Cylinder head.
   h) Timing sprockets and chain.
   i) Engine external components (including inlet and exhaust manifolds).

3 Ensure that everything is clean prior to reassembly. As mentioned previously, dirt and metal particles can quickly destroy bearings and result in major engine damage. Use clean engine oil to lubricate during reassembly.

**17.4a Fit the bearing shells to their locations in the crankcase**

**17.4b The tab on each bearing shell must engage with the notch in the cylinder block or cap, and the oil holes in the upper shells must align with the block oilways**

**17.6 Place the crankshaft thrustwashers into position in the crankcase so that their oil grooves are facing outwards**

### 17 Crankshaft - main bearing running clearance check and refitting

**1** It is assumed at this point that the cylinder block/crankcase and crankshaft have been cleaned and repaired or reconditioned as necessary. Position the engine upside-down.
**2** Remove the main bearing cap bolts, and lift out the caps. Lay the caps out in the proper order, to ensure correct installation.
**3** If they're still in place, remove the old bearing shells from the block and the main bearing caps. Wipe the bearing recesses of the block and caps with a clean, lint-free cloth. They must be kept spotlessly-clean!

#### Main bearing clearance check

**4** Wipe clean the main bearing shell seats in the crankcase, and clean the backs of the bearing shells. Insert the respective upper shells (dry) into position in the crankcase. Note that the upper shells have grooves in them (the lower shells are plain, and have a wider location lug). Where the old main bearings are being refitted, ensure that they are located in their original positions. Make sure that the tab on each bearing shell fits into the notch in the block or cap **(see illustrations)**.
*Caution: Don't hammer the shells into place, and don't damage the bearing faces. No lubrication should be used at this time.*
**5** Before the crankshaft can be permanently installed, the main bearing running clearance

should be checked; this can be done in either of two ways. One method is to fit the main bearing caps to the cylinder block, with the bearing shells in place. With the cap retaining bolts tightened to the specified torque, measure the internal diameter of each assembled pair of bearing shells using a vernier dial indicator or internal micrometer. If the diameter of each corresponding crankshaft journal is measured and then subtracted from the bearing internal diameter, the result will be the main bearing running clearance. The second (and more accurate) method is to use a product known as 'Plastigauge'. This consists of a fine thread of perfectly-round plastic which is compressed between the bearing cap and the journal. When the cap is removed, the deformation of the plastic thread is measured with a special card gauge supplied with the kit. The running clearance is determined from this gauge. The procedure for using Plastigauge is as follows.
**6** Place the crankshaft thrustwashers into position in the crankcase, so that their oil grooves are facing outwards (away from the central web) **(see illustration)**. Hold them in position with a little grease. Clean the bearing surfaces of the shells in the block, and the crankshaft main bearing journals with a clean, lint-free cloth.
**7** With the crankshaft clean, carefully lay it in position in the main bearings **(see illustration)**. Do not use any lubricant; the crankshaft journals and bearing shells must be perfectly clean and dry.

**8** Cut several pieces of the appropriate-size Plastigauge (they should be slightly shorter than the width of the main bearings), and place one piece on each crankshaft journal axis **(see illustration)**.
**9** With the bearing shells in position in the caps, fit the caps to their numbered or previously-noted locations. Take care not to disturb the Plastigauge.
**10** Starting with the centre main bearing and working outward, tighten the main bearing cap bolts progressively to their specified torque setting. Don't rotate the crankshaft at any time during this operation.
**11** Remove the bolts and carefully lift off the main bearing caps, keeping them in order. Don't disturb the Plastigauge or rotate the crankshaft. If any of the bearing caps are difficult to remove, tap them from side-to-side with a soft-faced mallet.
**12** Compare the width of the crushed Plastigauge on each journal to the scale printed on the gauge to obtain the main bearing running clearance **(see illustration)**.
**13** If the clearance is not as specified, the bearing shells may be the wrong size (or excessively-worn if the original shells are being re-used). Before deciding that different size shells are needed, make sure that no dirt or oil was trapped between the bearing shells and the caps or block when the clearance was measured. If the Plastigauge was wider at one end than at the other, the journal may be tapered.

**17.7 Lowering the crankshaft in the main bearings**

**17.8 Lay the Plastigauge strips on the main bearing journals, parallel to the crankshaft centre-line**

**17.12 Compare the width of the crushed Plastigauge to the scale on the envelope to determine the main bearing running clearance**

**18.2 The location tab on each big-end bearing shell must engage with the notch in the connecting rod or cap**

**18.4a With the compressor fitted, use the handle of a hammer to gently drive the piston into the cylinder**

**18.4b Make sure that the arrow on the piston crown is facing the timing end of the engine**

14 Carefully scrape away all traces of the Plastigauge material from the crankshaft and bearing shells, using a fingernail or something similar which is unlikely to score the shells.

### Final crankshaft refitting

15 Carefully lift the crankshaft out of the engine. Clean the bearing surfaces of the shells in the block, then apply a thin layer of clean engine oil to each shell. Coat the thrustwasher bearing surfaces as well.

16 Make sure the crankshaft journals are clean, then lay the crankshaft back in place in the block. Clean the bearing surfaces of the shells in the caps, then lubricate them with oil. Install the caps in their respective positions, with the arrows pointing to the timing chain end of the engine.

17 Working on one cap at a time, from the centre main bearing outwards (and ensuring that each cap is tightened down squarely and evenly onto the block), tighten the main bearing cap bolts to the specified torque wrench setting.

18 Rotate the crankshaft a number of times by hand, to check for any obvious binding.

19 Check the crankshaft endfloat (refer to Section 11).

20 Refit the crankshaft rear oil seal housing together with a new oil seal as described in Chapter 2A.

21 Refit the components removed in Section 11.

### 18 Piston/connecting rod assemblies - big-end bearing running clearance check and refitting

1 Clean the backs of the big-end bearing shells and the recesses in the connecting rods and big-end caps. If new shells are being fitted, ensure that all traces of the protective grease are cleaned off using paraffin. Wipe the shells and connecting rods dry with a lint-free cloth.

2 Press the big-end bearing shells into the connecting rods and caps in their correct positions. Make sure that the location tabs are engaged with the cut-outs in the connecting rods **(see illustration)**.

### Big-end bearing running clearance check

3 Lubricate No 1 piston and piston rings, and check that the ring gaps are spaced at 120° intervals to each other.

4 Fit a ring compressor to No 1 piston, then insert the piston and connecting rod into No 1 cylinder. Make sure that the arrow on the piston crown is facing the timing end of the engine. With No 1 crankpin at its lowest point, drive the piston carefully into the cylinder with the wooden handle of a hammer, at the same time guiding the connecting rod onto the crankpin **(see illustrations)**.

5 To measure the big-end bearing running clearance, refer to the information contained in Section 17; the same general procedures apply. If the Plastigauge method is being used, ensure that the crankpin journal and the big-end bearing shells are clean and dry, then engage the connecting rod with the crankpin. Place the Plastigauge strip on the crankpin, fit the bearing cap in its previously-noted position, then tighten the bolts to the specified torque. Do not rotate the crankshaft during this operation. Remove the cap and check the running clearance by measuring the Plastigauge as previously described.

6 Repeat the above procedures on the remaining piston/connecting rod assemblies.

### Final refitting

7 Having checked the running clearance of all the crankpin journals and taken any corrective action necessary, clean off all traces of

**18.8 Angle-tightening the big-end bearing cap bolts**

Plastigauge from the bearing shells and crankpin.

8 Liberally lubricate the crankpin journals and big-end bearing shells. Refit the bearing caps once more, ensuring correct positioning as previously described. Tighten the bearing cap bolts to the specified torque and angles, and turn the crankshaft each time to make sure that it is free before moving on to the next assembly **(see illustration)**.

9 On completion, refit the oil pump pick-up tube as follows. First clean the joint area on the tube and the location hole in the crankcase. Coat the area indicated with the special adhesive activator available from Ford **(see illustration)**. Wait for a period of ten minutes, then smear the shaded area with the special adhesive (available from Ford) and immediately press the pick-up tube into position in the crankcase.

10 Refit the sump and cylinder head as described in Chapter 2A.

### 19 Engine - initial start-up after overhaul

1 With the engine refitted in the vehicle, double-check the engine oil and coolant levels (see "Weekly Checks"). Make a final

**18.9 Oil pick-up tube refitting details**

A  Area of sealant application - dimensions in mm
B  Edge must be parallel with engine longitudinal axis

check that everything has been reconnected, and that there are no tools or rags left in the engine compartment.

2 With the spark plugs removed, disable the ignition and fuel injection systems by disconnecting the low tension wires from the coil (see Chapter 5B) and depressurising the fuel system by removing the fuel pump relay on models up to 1999. On 1999-on models, disconnect the fuel pump's electrical supply while the engine is running, by removing the fuel pump fuse (number 19), and allow the engine to idle until it dies through lack of fuel. Turn the engine over once or twice on the starter to ensure that all pressure is released, then switch off the ignition. Do not forget to refit the fuse when work is complete. Refer to Chapter 4A if necessary. Crank the engine on the starter motor until the oil pressure light goes out.

3 Refit the spark plugs and connect the low tension wires. Refit the fuel pump relay or fuse.

4 Start the engine, noting that this may take a little longer than usual, due to the fuel pump being empty.

5 While the engine is idling, check for fuel, water and oil leaks. Where applicable, check the power steering pipe/hose unions for leakage. Do not be alarmed if there are some odd smells and smoke from parts getting hot and burning off oil deposits.

6 Keep the engine idling until hot water is felt circulating through the top hose, then switch it off.

7 After a few minutes, recheck the oil and coolant levels, and top-up as necessary (see "Weekly Checks").

8 There is no requirement to retighten the cylinder head bolts.

9 If new pistons, rings or crankshaft bearings have been fitted, the engine must be run-in for the first 500 miles (800 km). Do not operate the engine at full-throttle, nor allow it to labour in any gear during this period. It is recommended that the oil and filter be changed at the end of this period.

# Chapter 3
# Cooling, heating and air conditioning systems

## Contents

## Degrees of difficulty

| Easy, suitable for novice with little experience  | Fairly easy, suitable for beginner with some experience | Fairly difficult, suitable for competent DIY mechanic  | Difficult, suitable for experienced DIY mechanic | Very difficult, suitable for expert DIY or professional  |
|---|---|---|---|---|

## Specifications

| Torque wrench settings | Nm | lbf ft |
|---|---|---|
| A/C accumulator/dehydrator | 6 | 4 |
| A/C compressor driveplate to compressor | 13 | 10 |
| A/C compressor to sump | 25 | 18 |
| A/C high pressure control switch | 8 | 6 |
| A/C low pressure control switch | 5 | 4 |
| A/C refrigerant line to compressor | 20 | 15 |
| A/C refrigerant line to accumulator/dehydrator | 8 | 6 |
| A/C refrigerant line to condenser | 8 | 6 |
| Coolant temperature sensor to inlet manifold | 18 | 13 |
| Heater assembly to bulkhead | 9 | 7 |
| Pollen filter housing | 5 | 4 |
| Thermostat housing securing bolts | 27 | 20 |
| Water pump pulley securing bolts | 9 | 7 |
| Water pump securing bolts | 9 | 7 |

## 1 General information and precautions

### General information

The cooling system is of pressurised type, comprising a pump driven by the auxiliary drivebelt, an aluminium crossflow radiator, electric cooling fan, and a thermostat. The system functions as follows. Cold coolant from the radiator passes through the hose to the water pump, where it is pumped around the cylinder block and head passages. After cooling the cylinder bores, combustion surfaces and valve seats, the coolant reaches the underside of the thermostat, which is initially closed. The coolant passes through the heater, and is returned via the cylinder block to the water pump.

When the engine is cold, the coolant circulates only through the cylinder block, cylinder head and heater. When the coolant reaches a predetermined temperature, the thermostat opens and the coolant passes through to the radiator. As the coolant circulates through the radiator, it is cooled by the inrush of air when the car is in forward motion. Airflow is supplemented by the action of the electric cooling fan when necessary. Once the coolant has passed through the radiator, and has cooled, the cycle is repeated.

The electric cooling fan, mounted on the rear of the radiator, is controlled by a thermostatic switch. At a predetermined coolant temperature, the switch actuates the fan.

An expansion tank is fitted to allow for the expansion of the coolant when hot. The expansion tank is located in the left-hand rear corner of the engine compartment.

Refer to Section 10 for information on the air conditioning system.

### Precautions

**Warning: Do not attempt to remove the expansion tank filler cap, or disturb any part of the cooling system, while the engine is hot; there is a high risk of scalding. If the filler cap must be removed before the engine and radiator have fully cooled (even though this is not recommended) the pressure in the cooling system must first be relieved. Cover the cap with a thick layer of cloth, to avoid scalding, and slowly unscrew the filler cap until a hissing sound can be heard. When the hissing has stopped, indicating that the pressure has reduced, slowly unscrew the filler cap until it can be removed; if more hissing sounds are heard, wait until they have stopped before unscrewing the cap completely. At all times, keep well away from the filler cap opening.**

2.4 **Disconnecting the radiator top hose from the thermostat housing**

3.5 **Removing the radiator lower cover**

⚠️ *Warning: Do not allow antifreeze to come into contact with skin, or with the painted surfaces of the vehicle. Rinse off spills immediately, with plenty of water. Never leave antifreeze lying around in an open container, or in a puddle on the driveway or garage floor. Children and pets are attracted by its sweet smell, but antifreeze can be fatal if ingested.*

⚠️ *Warning: If the engine is hot, the electric cooling fan may start rotating with the ignition switched on, even if the engine is not running; be careful to keep hands, hair and loose clothing well clear when working in the engine compartment.*

⚠️ *Warning: Refer to Section 10 for precautions to be observed when working on models equipped with air conditioning.*

## 2 Cooling system hoses - disconnection and renewal

**Note:** *Refer to the warnings given in Section 1 of this Chapter before proceeding. Do not attempt to disconnect any hose while the system is still hot.*

**1** If the checks described in Chapter 1 reveal a faulty hose, it must be renewed as follows.
**2** First drain the cooling system (see Chapter 1). If the coolant is not due for renewal, it may be re-used if it is collected in a clean container.

**3** Before disconnecting a hose, first note its routing in the engine compartment, and whether it is secured by any clips or ties. Where the original spring clips are fitted, use a pair of grips to release them, otherwise use a screwdriver to release the clips. Move the clips along the hose, clear of the relevant inlet/outlet union. Carefully work the hose free.
**4** Note that the radiator inlet and outlet unions are fragile; do not use excessive force when attempting to remove the hoses **(see illustration)**. If a hose proves to be difficult to remove, try to release it by rotating the hose ends before attempting to free it.

> **HAYNES HINT** *If all else fails, cut the coolant hose with a sharp knife, then slit it so that it can be peeled off in two pieces. Although this may prove expensive if the hose is otherwise undamaged, it is preferable to buying a new radiator.*

**5** When fitting a hose, first slide the clips onto the hose, then work the hose into position. If clamp-type clips were originally fitted, you may wish to replace them with screw-type clips when refitting the hose. If the hose is stiff, use a little soapy water (washing-up liquid is ideal) as a lubricant, or soften the hose by soaking it in hot water.
**6** Work the hose into position, checking that it is correctly routed and secured. Slide each clip along the hose until it passes over the flared end of the relevant inlet/outlet union.

Tighten the clips securely where applicable.
**7** Refill the cooling system (see Chapter 1).
**8** Check thoroughly for leaks as soon as possible after disturbing any part of the cooling system.

## 3 Radiator - removal, inspection and refitting

### Removal

**1** Disconnect the battery negative lead with reference to Chapter 5A.
**2** Drain the cooling system as described in Chapter 1.
**3** Remove both front wheel arch liners as follows. Apply the handbrake, then jack up the front of the vehicle and support it on axle stands (see *"Jacking and Vehicle Support"*). Remove both front wheels. Undo the securing screws and remove both wheel arch liners from under the wings.
**4** Remove the front bumper with reference to Chapter 11.
**5** Undo the screws and remove the lower cover from under the radiator **(see illustration)**.
**6** Release the clips and remove the air intake ducting from the left-hand front corner of the engine compartment.
**7** Release the oxygen sensor wiring from the radiator fan shroud **(see illustration)**.
**8** Loosen the hose clip, and disconnect the top hose from the right-hand side of the radiator.
**9** On models with power steering, unbolt the PAS hydraulic line supports from the valance below the radiator **(see illustration)**.
**10** Loosen the hose clip, and disconnect the bottom hose from the right-hand side of the radiator. Alternatively, disconnect the hose from the thermostat housing cover.
**11** Disconnect the electric cooling fan wiring from the fan motor(s), and release from the clips **(see illustration)**.
**12** On models with air conditioning, undo the lower mounting bolts and detach the air conditioning condenser from the front of the radiator **(see illustration)**. Remove the flanged bolts from the front of the air conditioning condenser.

3.7 **Releasing the oxygen sensor wiring from the radiator fan shroud**

3.9 **On models with power steering, unbolt the PAS hydraulic line supports from the radiator**

3.11 **Disconnecting the electric cooling fan wiring**

**3.12 On models with air conditioning, detach the air conditioning condenser from the radiator**

**3.13a Undo the side mounting bolts . . .**

**3.13b . . . and release the mounting rubbers from the pegs**

**13** Unscrew the side mounting bolts and carefully lower the support panel from the radiator while supporting the radiator in its raised position. As the panel is lowered, release the mounting rubbers from the pegs on the bottom of the radiator **(see illustrations)**.

**14** Lower the radiator from the front of the engine compartment and withdraw it from under the car **(see illustration)**. Take care not to damage the cooling fins on the surrounding components as the radiator is lowered.

**15** If a new radiator is to be fitted, remove the electric fan assembly and transfer to the new radiator.

## Inspection

**16** If the radiator has been removed due to suspected blockage, reverse-flush it as described in Chapter 1. Clean dirt and debris from the radiator fins, using an air line (in which case, wear eye protection) or a soft brush. Be careful, as the fins are easily damaged, and are sharp.

**17** If necessary, a radiator specialist can perform a "flow test" on the radiator, to establish whether an internal blockage exists.

**18** A leaking radiator must be referred to a specialist for permanent repair. Do not attempt to weld or solder a leaking radiator, as damage may result.

**19** In an emergency, minor leaks from the radiator can be cured by using a suitable radiator sealant (in accordance with its manufacturer's instructions) with the radiator in the car.

**20** Inspect the radiator mounting rubbers, and renew them if necessary.

## Refitting

**21** Refitting is a reversal of removal, bearing in mind the following points.

  a) *Ensure that the mounting rubbers are correctly located in the engine compartment front crossmember and radiator lower support member* **(see illustration)**.

  b) *Ensure that all hoses are correctly reconnected, and their retaining clips correctly located, and where necessary securely tightened.*

  c) *On completion, refill the cooling system as described in Chapter 1.*

**3.14 Lowering the radiator from the engine compartment front crossmember**

**3.21 Radiator mounting rubbers and location in the engine compartment front crossmember**

### 4  Thermostat - removal, testing and refitting

**Note:** *A new thermostat cover gasket and a new thermostat sealing ring will be required on refitting.*

## Removal

**1** Disconnect the battery negative (earth) lead (see Chapter 5A).

**2** Drain the cooling system as described in Chapter 1.

**3** Release or loosen the clips and disconnect the top hose and by-pass hose from the thermostat housing cover.

**4** Unscrew the securing bolts, and lift off the thermostat housing. Recover the gasket. If necessary, disconnect the coolant hoses from the thermostat housing to enable the housing to be withdrawn.

**5** Using pliers, compress the thermostat retaining clip, and remove it from the housing.

**6** Lift the thermostat from its housing **(see illustration)**.

## Testing

**7** A rough test of the thermostat's operation may be made by suspending it with a piece of string in a container full of water. Heat the water to bring it to the boil - the thermostat must open by the time the water boils. If not, renew it.

**8** The opening temperature is usually marked on the thermostat. If a thermometer is available, the precise opening temperature of

**4.6 Thermostat components**

1  *Cover*        3  *Thermostat*
2  *Gasket*

**4.8  Testing the thermostat**

the thermostat may be determined, and compared with the value marked on the thermostat **(see illustration)**.

9  A thermostat which fails to close as the water cools must also be renewed.

### Refitting

10  Refitting is a reversal of removal, bearing in mind the following points.
  a) *Thoroughly clean the mating faces of the thermostat cover and the cylinder head.*
  b) *Refit the thermostat housing, using a new gasket.*
  c) *Refill the cooling system as described in Chapter 1.*

| 5 | Electric cooling fan - testing, removal and refitting |
|---|---|

### Testing

1  On all models, the cooling fan is controlled by the Powertrain Control Module (PCM - see Chapter 4A), using signals provided by the engine coolant temperature sensor.

2  The fan operation can be checked by connecting the fan motor directly to a 12-volt power supply. Disconnect the motor wiring plug, and apply 12-volts across the motor terminals (the black wire is the earth) - take great care not to short out the power supply wires.

3  If the fan fails to operate, the fan motor is almost certainly at fault.

4  Testing of the fan motor control circuit must be entrusted to a Ford dealer, who will have the necessary specialist diagnostic equipment to test the powertrain control system - do not attempt to test the system using conventional test equipment, as the Powertrain Control Module may be damaged.

### Removal

5  Disconnect the battery leads and remove the battery from the engine compartment with reference to Chapter 5A. Also remove the battery cover from the battery box.

6  Apply the handbrake, then jack up the front of the vehicle and support it on axle stands (see *"Jacking and Vehicle Support"*).

7  Loosen only the nuts securing the top of the

electric cooling fan shroud to the radiator.

8  At the bottom of the radiator, disconnect the wiring from the fan resistor.

9  Disconnect the wiring from the electric cooling fan motor **(see illustration)**.

10  On models with power steering, unbolt and remove the PAS hydraulic line supports from under the radiator.

11  With the securing nuts loose, push the electric cooling fan assembly upwards to release it from the studs on the radiator, then push it towards the engine to release the lower clips. Withdraw the assembly downwards from the engine compartment taking care not to damage it on the surrounding components. Note that it is not possible to obtain the fan motor separate to the shroud.

### Refitting

12  Refitting is a reversal of removal, but tighten all nuts and bolts securely.

| 6 | Cooling system electrical switches and sensors - testing, removal and refitting |
|---|---|

### Coolant temperature sensor

### Testing

1  Testing of the coolant temperature sensor circuit must be entrusted to a Ford dealer, who will have the necessary specialist diagnostic equipment to test the powertrain control system - do not attempt to test the system using conventional test equipment, as the Powertrain Control Module may be damaged.

### Removal

2  The sensor is located at the right-hand bottom corner of the inlet manifold, next to the quick release coolant stub **(see illustration)**.

3  Disconnect the battery negative (earth) lead (see Chapter 5A).

4  Drain the cooling system as described in Chapter 1.

5  Disconnect the wiring plug from the coolant temperature sensor.

**6.2  The coolant temperature sensor is located on the right-hand end of the inlet manifold**

**5.9  Wiring for the electric cooling fan motor**

6  Unscrew the sensor from the manifold.

### Refitting

7  Refitting is a reversal of removal but tighten the sensor securely, and refill the cooling system as described in Chapter 1.

### Electric cooling fan control

8  The electric cooling fan is controlled by the Powertrain Control Module (PCM), using signals provided by the engine coolant temperature sensor. Refer to Chapter 4A for information on the PCM.

| 7 | Water pump - removal and refitting |
|---|---|

### Removal

1  Disconnect the battery negative (earth) lead (see Chapter 5A).

2  Drain the cooling system as described in Chapter 1.

3  Remove both front wheel arch liners as follows. Apply the handbrake, then jack up the front of the vehicle and support it on axle stands (see *"Jacking and Vehicle Support"*). Remove both front wheels. Undo the securing screws and remove both wheel arch liners from under the wings.

4  Remove the front bumper with reference to Chapter 11.

5  Remove the front right-hand headlight with reference to Chapter 12, Section 7.

6  Pull off the cable ties from the right-hand engine mounting studs, and move the harness to one side.

7  Using a trolley jack and block of wood beneath the sump, support the weight of the engine so that all pressure is released from the right-hand engine mounting.

8  Unscrew the single bolt and two nuts, then lower the engine until the studs are free of the mounting. Unbolt the support bracket from the body, then remove the mounting by unscrewing the two bolts located beneath the right-hand front wheel arch.

9  Slacken the water pump pulley securing bolts, then remove the auxiliary drivebelt as described in Chapter 1 **(see illustration)**.

**7.9  Loosening the water pump pulley bolts before removing the auxiliary drivebelt**

**7.10  Removing the water pump pulley**

**7.12  Water pump mounting bolts**

**10** Unscrew the securing bolts, and remove the water pump pulley **(see illustration)**.
**11** Slacken the clip, and disconnect the coolant bottom hose from the water pump.
**12** Unscrew the three securing bolts, and withdraw the water pump. Recover the gasket **(see illustration)**.

### Refitting

**13** Commence refitting by thoroughly cleaning the mating faces of the water pump and the cylinder block.
**14** Refit the water pump, using a new gasket, and tighten the securing bolts to the specified torque.
**15** The remaining procedure is a reversal of removal, bearing in mind the following points.
  a) *Tighten all fixings to the specified torque.*
  b) *Refit the auxiliary drivebelt as described in Chapter 1.*
  c) *On completion, refill the cooling system as described in Chapter 1.*

## 8  Heating and ventilation system - general information

The heater/ventilation system consists of a four-speed blower motor (housed behind the facia), face-level vents in the centre and at each end of the facia, and air ducts to the front footwells.
The control unit is located in the facia, and the controls operate flap valves and a coolant valve, to deflect and mix the air flowing through the various parts of the heater/ventilation system. The flap valves are contained in the air distribution housing, which acts as a central distribution unit, passing air to the various ducts and vents. The control unit operates the flap valves by means of a distribution shaft - there are no cables in the system.
Cold air enters the system through a grille at the rear of the engine compartment.
The air (boosted by the blower fan if required) then flows through the various ducts, according to the settings of the controls. Stale air is expelled through ducts at the rear of the vehicle. If warm air is required, the cold air is passed through the heater matrix, which is heated by the engine coolant.
A recirculation switch enables the outside air supply to be closed off, while the air inside the vehicle is recirculated. This can be useful to prevent unpleasant odours entering from outside the vehicle, but should only be used briefly, as the recirculated air inside the vehicle will soon deteriorate.

## 9  Heater/ventilation system components - removal and refitting

### Heater/ventilation control unit

#### Removal

**1** Disconnect the battery negative (earth) lead (see Chapter 5A).
**2** Remove the radio/cassette player as described in Chapter 12.

**3** Working at the top of the heater/ventilation control unit, undo the two securing screws **(see illustration)**.
**4** Release the two securing clips at the sides of the panel, then pull the control panel forwards from the facia.
**5** Disconnect the air distribution shaft **(see illustration)**.
**6** Disconnect the wiring plugs from the rear of the unit **(see illustration)**.
**7** Remove the heating/air conditioning module and the blower motor switch from the facia.

#### Refitting

**8** Refitting is a reversal of removal, but check the operation of the heater/ventilation controls on completion.

### Heater blower motor switch

#### Removal

**9** Remove the heater/ventilation control unit as described previously in this Section.
**10** Working at the rear of the control unit, disconnect the multiplug then undo the screws and remove the heater blower motor switch.

#### Refitting

**11** Refitting is a reversal of removal, but check the operation of the heater/ventilation controls on completion.

### Heater blower motor

⚠ *Warning:  On  left-hand-drive models with air conditioning, read the precautions given in Section 10, and have the system discharged by a Ford*

**9.3  Undo the two securing screws . . .**

**9.5  . . . withdraw the unit and disconnect the air distribution shaft . . .**

**9.6  . . . then disconnect the wiring**

9.19 Pollen filter housing mounting bolt

9.36 Undo the screw and lift the coolant expansion tank from its position

## Air recirculation control valve motor

### Removal

**29** Remove the complete facia assembly as described in Chapter 11.
**30** Disconnect the control motor wiring plug.
**31** Unscrew the three securing screws, and withdraw the motor from the heater assembly.

### Refitting

**32** Refitting is a reversal of removal.

### Heater matrix

 **Warning: On models with air conditioning, read the precautions given in Section 10, and have the system refrigerant evacuated by a Ford dealer or an air conditioning specialist. Do not carry out the following work unless the system has been discharged.**

**Note:** *On models with air conditioning, Ford special tool No 34-003 (or a suitable alternative tool) will be required to release the refrigerant line connectors from the evaporator.*

### Removal

**33** On models with air conditioning, have the refrigerant evacuated from the system by an air conditioning specialist before commencing the following work.
**34** Disconnect the battery negative (earth) lead (see Chapter 5A).
**35** Drain the cooling system as described in Chapter 1.
**36** Undo the screw and lift the coolant expansion tank from its position in the left-hand (up to 1999) and right-hand (from 1999) rear corner of the engine compartment **(see illustration)**. Place the tank to one side without disconnecting the coolant hoses.
**37** Remove the windscreen wiper arms as described in Chapter 12.
**38** Remove the grille panel from in front of the windscreen and disconnect the windscreen washer hose from the washer jet (on models up to 1999).
**39** Undo the screws and pull the bulkhead extension forwards.
**40** On models with air conditioning, disconnect the refrigerant lines from the evaporator on the bulkhead using the special tool described in Section 10. The refrigerant lines must be properly capped while they are disconnected, and the evaporator stubs must also be plugged **(see illustration)**.
**41** Release or loosen the clips and disconnect the hoses from the heater matrix **(see illustration)**. Keep the hoses identified for position to ensure correct refitting. Tape over or plug the hoses and matrix stubs.
**42** Unscrew the bolts and remove the heater housing cover from the bulkhead **(see illustration)**.
**43** Carefully pull the heater matrix from the heater housing. On models with air conditioning, also pull out the evaporator from the housing. Take care not to damage the matrix fins on the plastic lugs in front of the matrix **(see illustrations)**.

---

dealer or an air conditioning specialist. **Do not carry out the following work unless the system had been discharged.**
**Note:** *On left-hand drive models with air conditioning, Ford special tool No 34-003 (or an alternative tool) will be required to release the refrigerant line connectors from the evaporator.*

### Removal

**12** On left-hand drive models with air conditioning, have the refrigerant evacuated from the system by an air conditioning specialist before commencing the following work.
**13** Disconnect the battery negative (earth) lead (see Chapter 5A).
**14** Undo the screws and lift the coolant expansion tank from its position in the left-hand (up to 1999) and right-hand (from 1999) rear corner of the engine compartment. Place the tank to one side without disconnecting the coolant hoses.
**15** Remove the windscreen wiper arms as described in Chapter 12.
**16** Remove the grille panel from in front of the windscreen and disconnect the windscreen washer hose from the washer jet (on models up to 1999).
**17** Unscrew the bolts and pull the bulkhead extension forwards for access to the heater blower.
**18** On left-hand drive models with air conditioning, disconnect the refrigerant lines from the evaporator on the bulkhead using the special tool described in Section 10. The refrigerant lines must be properly capped while they are disconnected, and the evaporator stubs must also be plugged.

**19** Undo the screws and remove the pollen filter housing **(see illustration)**.
**20** Unbolt the blower motor cover.
**21** Working in the passenger footwell, disconnect the wiring for the blower motor.
**22** Undo the screws and lift out the blower motor, then pull out the wiring and rubber grommet.

### Refitting

**23** Refitting is a reversal of removal, bearing in mind the following points.
 a) *Before refitting the pollen filter housing, clean the contact faces and apply a 10 mm thick bead of suitable sealer to the opening.*
 b) *On left-hand drive models, renew all O-rings and lubricate them with refrigerant oil before reconnecting the refrigerant lines. Have the air conditioning system recharged by a Ford dealer or air conditioning specialist, then check the operation of the air conditioning system.*

## Heater blower motor resistor

### Removal

**24** The resistor is located on the side of the heater assembly in the passenger's side footwell.
**25** Disconnect the battery negative (earth) lead (see Chapter 5A).
**26** Disconnect the resistor wiring plug.
**27** Unscrew the securing screw, and withdraw the resistor.

### Refitting

**28** Refitting is a reversal of removal.

9.40 Using the home-made tool to disconnect the refrigerant lines from the evaporator

9.41 Disconnecting the hoses from the heater matrix

## Refitting

**44** Refitting is a reversal of removal, but refill the cooling system as described in Chapter 1. On models with air conditioning, renew the O-rings on the evaporator stubs and coat them with refrigerant oil before reconnecting the refrigerant lines. Note that when the lines are originally fitted by the factory, plastic fitting rings drop to the bottom of the evaporator stubs - these rings can be used again when reconnecting the lines by placing them inside the coupling locking springs **(see illustration)**. Have the system recharged with refrigerant by an air conditioning specialist.

### *Coolant valve*

#### Removal

**45** Disconnect the battery negative (earth) lead (see Chapter 5A).
**46** Undo the screws and lift the coolant expansion tank from its position in the left-hand (up to 1999) and right-hand (from 1999) rear corner of the engine compartment. Place the tank to one side without disconnecting the coolant hoses.
**47** Remove the windscreen wiper arms as described in Chapter 12.
**48** Remove the grille panel from in front of the windscreen and disconnect the windscreen washer hose from the washer jet (on models up to 1999).
**49** Unscrew the bolts and pull the bulkhead extension forwards for access to the coolant valve.
**50** Disconnect the wiring plug from the coolant valve.
**51** Release or loosen the clips and disconnect the four coolant hoses from the coolant valve, then slide the valve from the heater matrix housing. Be prepared for some spillage by placing a container or cloth rags beneath the hoses. Note the locations of the hoses, to ensure correct refitting. Clamp or plug the open ends of the hoses to prevent further coolant spillage.

#### Refitting

**52** Refitting is a reversal of removal, but top up and purge the cooling system with reference to 'Weekly Checks' and Chapter 1. Finally, check the operation of the heater.

### *Heater assembly*

⚠️ **Warning: On models with air conditioning, read the precautions given in Section 10, and have the system discharged by a Ford dealer or an air conditioning specialist. Do not carry out the following work unless the system has been discharged.**
**Note:** *On models with air conditioning, Ford special tool No 34-003 will be required to release the refrigerant line connectors from the evaporator.*

#### Removal

**53** On models with air conditioning, have the refrigerant evacuated from the system by an

**9.42 Removing the heater housing cover**

air conditioning specialist before commencing the following work.
**54** Disconnect the battery negative (earth) lead (see Chapter 5A).
**55** Drain the cooling system as described in Chapter 1.
**56** Remove the complete facia assembly as described in Chapter 11.
**57** Undo the screws and lift the coolant expansion tank from its position in the left-hand (up to 1999) and right-hand (from 1999) rear corner of the engine compartment. Place the tank to one side without disconnecting the coolant hoses.
**58** Remove the windscreen wiper arms as described in Chapter 12.
**59** Remove the grille panel from in front of the windscreen and disconnect the windscreen washer hose from the washer jet (on models up to 1999).
**60** Unscrew the bolts and pull the bulkhead extension forwards.
**61** Release or loosen the clips and disconnect the heater matrix hoses from the coolant valve on the bulkhead. Keep the hoses identified for position to ensure correct refitting.
**62** On models with air conditioning, disconnect the refrigerant lines from the evaporator using the special tool described in Section 10. The refrigerant lines must be properly capped while they are disconnected, and the evaporator stubs must also be plugged.
**63** Inside the vehicle, disconnect the wiring from the blower motor, air recirculation valve control motor, and blower motor resistor.

**9.43b Removing the air conditioning evaporator**

**9.43a Removing the heater matrix**

**64** Disconnect the wiring from the control panel.
**65** Unscrew and remove the heater assembly mounting nuts, then withdraw the assembly from the bracket. Disconnect the side air ducts and release the wiring from the clips. On models with air conditioning, pull the evaporator condensation drain hose from the floor. Remove the heater assembly from inside the vehicle.

#### Refitting

**66** Refitting is a reversal of removal, but note the following additional points.
a) *The heater assembly must be sealed against the bulkhead to prevent entry of water. If the original sealing is no longer serviceable, remove it and obtain new butyl rubber adhesive strips. The side strips must be 190 mm long and the front and rear strips must be 270 mm long. On models with air conditioning, the refrigerant lines must be sealed against the heater cover with butyl rubber strips, but note that the plastic rings on the evaporator stubs must not touch the heater cover.*
b) *Refill the cooling system as described in Chapter 1.*
c) *On models with air conditioning, renew all O-rings and lubricate them with refrigerant oil before reconnecting the refrigerant lines. Have the system recharged by an air conditioning specialist.*
d) *Check the operation of the heater (and air conditioning where applicable).*

**9.44 Plastic fitting rings used when reconnecting the air conditioning couplings**

**10.2 Air conditioning components**

1 Service connection (low pressure)
2 Service connection (high pressure)
3 Fixed orifice tube
4 Accumulator/dehydrator

5 Low pressure pipe
6 Condenser
7 Compressor
8 High pressure pipe

## 10 Air conditioning system - general information and precautions

### General information

1 Air conditioning is available as an option on Ka and Ka-2 models. On Ka-3 models it is standard. The system enables the temperature of incoming air to be lowered, and also dehumidifies the air, which makes for rapid demisting and increased comfort.

2 The cooling side of the system works in the same way as a domestic refrigerator. Refrigerant gas is drawn into a belt-driven compressor, and passes into a condenser mounted in front of the radiator, where it loses heat and becomes liquid. The liquid passes through an expansion valve to an evaporator, where it changes from liquid under high pressure to gas under low pressure. This change is accompanied by a drop in temperature, which cools the evaporator. The refrigerant returns to the compressor, and the cycle begins again **(see illustration)**.

3 Air blown through the evaporator passes into the passenger compartment, to achieve the desired temperature.

4 The heating side of the system works in the same way as on models without air conditioning, the heater matrix being positioned in the heater housing together with the air conditioning evaporator.

5 The operation of the system is controlled

electronically. Any problems with the system should be referred to a Ford dealer or an air conditioning specialist.

6 During the winter months, Ford recommend that the air conditioning system be switched on for approximately 10 minutes each month, in order to keep the internal seals lubricated and effective.

### Precautions

7 It is necessary to observe special precautions whenever dealing with any part of the system, its associated components, and any items which necessitate disconnection of the system.

⚠ **Warning: The refrigeration circuit contains a liquid refrigerant which is potentially dangerous, and should only be handled by qualified persons. If it is splashed onto the skin, it can cause frostbite. It is not itself poisonous, but in the presence of a naked flame it forms a poisonous gas; inhalation of the vapour through a lighted cigarette could prove fatal. Uncontrolled discharging of the refrigerant is dangerous, and potentially damaging to the environment. It is therefore dangerous to disconnect any part of the system without specialised knowledge and equipment. If for any reason the system must be disconnected, entrust this task to an authorised dealer or an air conditioning specialist. Note also that some of the procedures described in this Manual concern disconnecting air**

**conditioning components AFTER the system has been discharged. Always wear protective gloves and goggles when working on the air conditioning components, as the system may still contain refrigerant which has evaporated from the oil left in the system and may be under pressure.**

8 Note that when the system is discharged, the air conditioning specialist will normally evacuate the refrigerant from the discharge point, and then leave the system sealed. There will still be some refrigerant and oil in the system, and it is possible for the system to slightly pressurise itself as the result of refrigerant evaporating from the oil. Ford recommend that the dehydrator is renewed if the system is opened for more than 2 hours, however, if the dehydrator is sealed immediately after discharge it may be possible to re-use the dehydrator. Seek the advice of an air conditioning specialist if in doubt.

9 When disconnecting the air conditioning refrigerant lines (only after the system has been discharged), it will be necessary to obtain a special tool to release the internal lock spring fingers. The Ford tool is shown in the accompanying illustration **(see illustration)** and consists of two semi-circular halves which clamp onto the refrigerant line connection. The tool is pushed onto the joint so that an internal collar opens the lock spring fingers away from the flared end, and the two sections of the line can then be separated from each other. It is recommended that the special Ford tool 34-003 is obtained to disconnect the lines, however it is possible to fabricate a home-made tool out of a Jubilee clip using two halves brazed to the inside of the clip. Alternatively, have the air conditioning specialist disconnect them for you with the special tool.

10 Do not operate the air conditioning system if it is known to be short of refrigerant, as this may damage the compressor.

**10.9 Ford tool 34-003 for disconnecting the A/C refrigerant lines**

*Arrow shows collar for releasing lock spring*

## 11 Air conditioning system components - removal and refitting

### Compressor

⚠️ *Warning: Read the precautions given in Section 10, and have the system discharged by a Ford dealer or an air conditioning specialist. Do not carry out the following work unless the system had been discharged.*

#### Removal

1 Have the refrigerant evacuated from the system by an air conditioning specialist before commencing the following work.

2 Disconnect the battery negative (earth) lead (see Chapter 5A).

3 Apply the handbrake, then jack up the front of the vehicle and support it on axle stands (see *"Jacking and Vehicle Support"*).

4 Remove the auxiliary drivebelt as described in Chapter 1.

5 Position a clean measuring container beneath the compressor in order to collect the escaping refrigerant oil (see illustration). Note that the same amount of oil must be added to the compressor on refitting.

6 Unscrew and remove the union bolt and disconnect the refrigerant line connector block from the compressor. The refrigerant lines must be properly capped while they are disconnected, and the compressor openings must also be plugged. Remove the drained refrigerant oil to a safe place.

7 Disconnect the compressor wiring plug.

8 Support the compressor, then unscrew the four compressor mounting bolts. Lower the compressor and withdraw it from under the vehicle.

#### Refitting

9 Refitting is a reversal of removal, but refit the auxiliary drivebelt as described in Chapter 1 and tighten all mounting bolts and unions to the specified torque. On completion, renew all union O-rings and lubricate them with refrigerant oil before refitting the unions. Have the air conditioning system recharged by the air conditioning specialist, making sure that the quantity of drained refrigerant oil is added to the system. Finally, check the operation of the air conditioning system.

### Evaporator

#### Removal and refitting

10 Removal and refitting of the evaporator is described as part of the heater matrix removal and refitting procedure in Section 9. Note that the special tool described in Section 10 will be required to disconnect the refrigerant lines from the evaporator.

### Condenser

⚠️ *Warning: Read the precautions given in Section 10, and have the system discharged by a Ford*

**11.5 The air conditioning compressor is located on the front of the engine**

*dealer or an air conditioning specialist. Do not carry out the following work unless the system had been discharged.*

#### Removal

11 Have the refrigerant evacuated from the system by an air conditioning specialist before commencing the following work.

12 The condenser is located in front of the radiator. First disconnect the battery negative (earth) lead (see Chapter 5A).

13 Apply the handbrake, then jack up the front of the vehicle and support it on axle stands (see *"Jacking and Vehicle Support"*).

14 Unscrew the nuts and disconnect the refrigerant lines from the condenser. The nuts are accessible through the cut-out in the top of the radiator grille (see illustration). The refrigerant lines must be properly capped while they are disconnected, and the condenser stubs must also be plugged.

15 Unscrew and remove the bolts securing the condenser to the bottom of the radiator.

16 At the right-hand side of the radiator, disconnect the wiring plug for the oxygen sensor.

17 Undo the fasteners and remove the cover from under the front of the vehicle, then disconnect the wiring plugs and move the wiring to one side to allow room for the condenser to be lowered.

18 Unbolt the power steering hydraulic pipe brackets from under the front valance and tie the pipes to the rear, clear of the condenser.

19 Remove the electric cooling fan downwards from the radiator with reference to Section 5.

20 Tie the radiator to the engine compartment front crossmember, so that it will remain in position while the lower radiator support is removed.

21 Unscrew the bolts securing the radiator lower support bracket to the body. There is no need to remove the bracket as the lower rubber mountings will retain it in position . Tie the bottom of the radiator back as far as possible from the condenser.

22 With the clamp bolts removed, release the condenser from the bracket by sliding it to the right then left. Carefully lower the condenser from the radiator and withdraw it from under the vehicle (see illustration).

**11.14 Refrigerant line connection on the condenser**

#### Refitting

23 Refitting is a reversal of removal, but tighten all mounting bolts and nuts to the specified torque. Renew all O-rings and lubricate them with refrigerant oil before reconnecting the refrigerant lines. On completion, have the air conditioning system recharged by the air conditioning specialist, making sure that the quantity of drained refrigerant oil is added to the system. Finally, check the operation of the air conditioning system.

### Dehydrator

⚠️ *Warning: Read the precautions given in Section 10, and have the system discharged by a Ford dealer or an air conditioning specialist. Do not carry out the following work unless the system had been discharged.*

#### Removal

24 Have the refrigerant evacuated from the system by an air conditioning specialist before commencing the following work.

25 The dehydrator is located at the right-hand rear corner of the engine compartment. First, disconnect the battery negative (earth) lead (see Chapter 5A).

26 Apply the handbrake, then jack up the front of the vehicle and support it on axle stands (see *"Jacking and Vehicle Support"*).

27 Disconnect the wiring from the low pressure switch located on top of the dehydrator (see illustration).

**11.22 The top of the A/C condenser locates in the radiator cowl**

11.27 Disconnecting the wiring from the low pressure switch located on top of the dehydrator

11.28a Using a thin rod and cloth to release the pressure from the air conditioning system (already evacuated)

11.28b Disconnecting the refrigerant line from the top of the dehydrator

28 Unscrew the nut and disconnect the refrigerant line from the top of the dehydrator (see illustrations).

⚠️ **Warning: Note that even though the system has been evacuated, some pressure will build up from refrigerant left in the system oil. Before disconnecting the system, cover the system Shrader valves with cloth and depress the valves to release any pressure.**

29 Working under the vehicle, unscrew the nut and disconnect the refrigerant line from the bottom of the dehydrator (see illustration).

30 Unscrew the mounting nuts and lower the dehydrator from the engine compartment.

Note that if the system is to be left opened, the dehydrator ports and line openings must be sealed (see illustrations).

### Refitting

31 Refitting is a reversal of removal, but tighten the mounting bolts and unions to the specified torque. Renew all O-rings and lubricate them with refrigerant oil before reconnecting the refrigerant lines. On completion, have the air conditioning system recharged by the air conditioning specialist, making sure that the previously noted quantity of drained refrigerant oil is added to the system. Finally, check the operation of the air conditioning system.

11.29 Refrigerant line connection on the bottom of the dehydrator

11.30a Unscrew the mounting nuts . . .

11.30b . . . and lower the dehydrator from the engine compartment

11.30c Seal the dehydrator ports as soon as the unit is removed

# Chapter 4 Part A:
# Fuel and exhaust systems

## Contents

## Degrees of difficulty

| Easy, suitable for novice with little experience | | Fairly easy, suitable for beginner with some experience | | Fairly difficult, suitable for competent DIY mechanic | | Difficult, suitable for experienced DIY mechanic | | Very difficult, suitable for expert DIY or professional | |
|---|---|---|---|---|---|---|---|---|---|

## Specifications

### General

| | |
|---|---|
| System type . . . . . . . . . . . . . . . . . . . . . . . . . . . . . . . . . . . . . . . . . . | Sequential Electronic Fuel injection (SEFi) |
| Application . . . . . . . . . . . . . . . . . . . . . . . . . . . . . . . . . . . . . . . . . . . | 1.3 litre JJB, J4D, JJF, J4M, JJD, and J4K Endura-E engines |

### Fuel grade

| | |
|---|---|
| Fuel octane requirement . . . . . . . . . . . . . . . . . . . . . . . . . . . . . . . | 95 RON unleaded |

### Fuel system data

| | |
|---|---|
| Regulated fuel pressure: | |
|    Pressure regulator vacuum hose disconnected . . . . . . . . . . . . . . | 2.7 ± 0.2 bar |
|    With engine running and pressure regulator vacuum hose connected . | 2.1 ± 0.2 bar |
| Hold pressure - engine stopped after five minutes . . . . . . . . . . . . . | 1.8 bars minimum |

### Torque wrench settings

| | Nm | lbf ft |
|---|---|---|
| Camshaft position sensor . . . . . . . . . . . . . . . . . . . . . . . . . . . . . . | 10 | 7 |
| Crankshaft position sensor . . . . . . . . . . . . . . . . . . . . . . . . . . . . . | 7 | 5 |
| Engine coolant temperature sensor . . . . . . . . . . . . . . . . . . . . . . . | 12 | 9 |
| Exhaust flange bolts . . . . . . . . . . . . . . . . . . . . . . . . . . . . . . . . . | 47 | 35 |
| Exhaust manifold . . . . . . . . . . . . . . . . . . . . . . . . . . . . . . . . . . . . | 23 | 17 |
| Fuel pressure regulator screws . . . . . . . . . . . . . . . . . . . . . . . . . . | 10 | 7 |
| Fuel rail-to-inlet manifold bolts . . . . . . . . . . . . . . . . . . . . . . . . . . | 18 | 13 |
| Idle air control valve . . . . . . . . . . . . . . . . . . . . . . . . . . . . . . . . . | 10 | 7 |
| Inlet manifold heat shield . . . . . . . . . . . . . . . . . . . . . . . . . . . . . . | 17 | 13 |
| Inlet manifold . . . . . . . . . . . . . . . . . . . . . . . . . . . . . . . . . . . . . . | 18 | 13 |
| Shrader valve retaining bolts . . . . . . . . . . . . . . . . . . . . . . . . . . . | 10 | 7 |
| Throttle body housing . . . . . . . . . . . . . . . . . . . . . . . . . . . . . . . . | 10 | 7 |
| TMAP sensor . . . . . . . . . . . . . . . . . . . . . . . . . . . . . . . . . . . . . . | 4 | 3 |

## 1 General information and precautions

### General information

The fuel system consists of a steel fuel tank (mounted under the body, beneath the rear seats), fuel hoses, an electric fuel pump mounted in the fuel tank, and a sequential electronic fuel injection system controlled by an EEC V engine management control module (Powertrain Control Module).

The electric fuel pump supplies fuel under pressure to the plastic moulded fuel rail, which distributes fuel to the injectors. A pressure regulator controls the system pressure in relation to inlet tract depression. From the fuel rail, fuel is injected into the inlet ports, just above the inlet valves, by four fuel injectors.

The amount of fuel supplied by the injectors is precisely controlled by the Powertrain Control Module (PCM). The module uses the signals from the crankshaft position sensor and the camshaft position sensor, to trigger each injector separately in cylinder firing order (sequential injection), with benefits in terms of better fuel economy and leaner exhaust emissions.

The Powertrain Control Module is the heart of the entire engine management system, controlling the fuel injection, ignition and emissions control systems. The module receives information from various sensors which is then computed and compared with pre-set values stored in it's memory, to determine the required period of injection.

Information on crankshaft position and engine speed is generated by a crankshaft position sensor. The inductive head of the sensor runs just above the engine flywheel and scans a series of 36 protrusions on the flywheel periphery. As the crankshaft rotates, the sensor transmits a pulse to the system's ignition module every time a protrusion passes it. There is one missing protrusion in the flywheel periphery at a point corresponding to 90° BTDC. The ignition module recognises the absence of a pulse from the crankshaft position sensor at this point to establish a reference mark for crankshaft position. Similarly, the time interval between absent pulses is used to determine engine speed. This information is then fed to the Powertrain Control Module for further processing.

The camshaft position sensor is located on the timing cover and registers with a plate located beneath the camshaft sprocket retaining bolts. The camshaft position sensor functions in the same way as the crankshaft position sensor, producing a series of pulses; this gives the Powertrain Control Module a reference point, to enable it to determine the firing order, and operate the injectors in the appropriate sequence.

On models manufactured up to mid-1999 model year, the mass air flow sensor is based on a "hot-wire" system, sending the Powertrain Control Module a constantly-varying (analogue) voltage signal corresponding to the mass of air passing into the engine. Since air mass varies with temperature (cold air being denser than warm), measuring air mass provides the module with a very accurate means of determining the correct amount of fuel required to achieve the ideal air/fuel mixture ratio. Together with the mass air flow sensor, pre-1999 models are fitted with an inlet air temperature sensor which provides the Powertrain Control Module with a signal corresponding to the temperature of air passing into the engine. This is used to refine the calculations made by the module, when determining the correct amount of fuel required to achieve the ideal air/fuel mixture ratio.

Models manufactured from mid-1999 model year onwards are fitted with a temperature manifold absolute pressure (TMAP) sensor which replaces the mass air flow and inlet air temperature sensors fitted to earlier models. The TMAP sensor consists of a pressure transducer and a temperature sensor fitted directly into the inlet manifold, and the system provides the Power Control Module with information on the inlet manifold vacuum and inlet air temperature. When the ignition is switched on with the engine stationary, the system provides the PCM with barometric pressure information.

Engine temperature information is supplied by the coolant temperature sensor located in the inlet manifold. This component is an NTC (Negative Temperature Coefficient) thermistor - that is, a semi-conductor whose electrical resistance decreases as its temperature increases. It provides the Powertrain Control Module with a constantly-varying (analogue) voltage signal, corresponding to the temperature of the engine coolant. This is used to refine the calculations made by the module, when determining the correct amount of fuel required to achieve the ideal air/fuel mixture ratio.

A throttle position sensor is mounted on the end of the throttle valve spindle, to provide the Powertrain Control Module with a constantly-varying (analogue) voltage signal corresponding to the throttle opening. This allows the module to register the driver's input when determining the amount of fuel required by the engine.

Road speed is monitored by the vehicle speed sensor. This component is a Hall-effect generator, mounted on the transmission's speedometer drive. It supplies the module with a series of pulses corresponding to the vehicle's road speed, enabling the module to control features such as the fuel shut-off on overrun.

The clutch pedal position is monitored by a switch fitted to the pedal bracket. This sends a signal to the Powertrain Control Module.

Where power steering is fitted, a pressure-operated switch is screwed into the power steering system's high-pressure pipe. The switch sends a signal to the Powertrain Control Module to increase engine speed to maintain idle speed during power steering assistance.

The oxygen sensor (located on the exhaust manifold) provides the module with constant feedback - "closed-loop" control - which enables it to adjust the mixture to provide the best possible operating conditions for the catalytic converter.

The air inlet side of the system consists of an air cleaner housing, the mass air flow sensor (pre 1999 models only), an inlet hose and duct, and a throttle housing.

The throttle valve inside the throttle housing is controlled by the driver, through the accelerator pedal. As the valve opens, the amount of air that can pass through the system increases. As the throttle valve opens further, the mass air flow sensor signal alters, and the Powertrain Control Module opens each injector for a longer duration, to increase the amount of fuel delivered to the inlet ports.

Both the idle speed and mixture are under the control of the Powertrain Control Module, and cannot be adjusted.

### Precautions

⚠️ **Warning: Many of the procedures in this Chapter require the removal of fuel lines and connections, which may result in some fuel spillage. Before carrying out any operation on the fuel system, refer to the precautions given in "Safety first!" at the beginning of this manual, and follow them implicitly. Petrol is a highly-dangerous and volatile liquid, and the precautions necessary when handling it cannot be overstressed.**
**Note:** *Residual pressure will remain in the fuel lines long after the vehicle was last used. When disconnecting any fuel line, first depressurise the fuel system as described in Section 2.*

## 2 Fuel system - depressurisation

⚠️ **Warning: Refer to the warning note in Section 1 before proceeding.**

1 The fuel system described in this Chapter includes the fuel tank and tank-mounted fuel pump/fuel gauge sender unit, the fuel filter, the fuel injectors and the pressure regulator in the injector rail, and the metal pipes and flexible hoses of the fuel lines between these components. All these contain fuel, which will be under pressure while the engine is running and/or while the ignition is switched on.
2 The pressure will remain for some time after the ignition has been switched off, and must be relieved before any of these components is disturbed for servicing work.
3 On pre-1999 models, the Ford method of depressurisation is to use service tool 23-033 fitted to the fuel rail pressure test/release fitting. The fitting consists of a Schrader-type

**2.4a Unscrew the cap . . .**

**2.4b . . . then use a piece of rod to depress the valve core**

valve with a plastic cap located on the fuel rail, and the tool acts as a tap by depressing the valve core. Access to the valve is gained by removing the air inlet duct from between the air cleaner and throttle housing.

**4** To release the pressure without using the service tool, use a suitable container and rag wrapped around the fitting to catch the fuel then use a piece of rod to depress the valve. **Do not** simply depress the valve core without wrapping rag around it, as fuel will spray out, with the consequent risk of fire, and personal injury **(see illustrations)**.

**5** The alternative method, and the only method to use on 1999-on models, is simply to disconnect the fuel pump's electrical supply while the engine is running, by removing the fuel pump fuse (number 19), and to allow the engine to idle until it dies through lack of fuel. Turn the engine over once or twice on the starter to ensure that all pressure is released, then switch off the ignition. Do not

forget to refit the fuse when work is complete.
**6** Note that, once the fuel system has been depressurised, it may take a little longer to restart the engine - perhaps several seconds of cranking - before the system is refilled and pressure restored.

## 3 Unleaded petrol - general information and usage

The fuel recommended by Ford is given in the Specifications section of this Chapter.

All models are designed to run on fuel with a minimum octane rating of 95 (RON). All models have a catalytic converter, and so must be run on unleaded fuel only. Under no circumstances should leaded fuel (UK "4-star") be used, as this will permanently damage the converter.

Super unleaded petrol (98 octane) can also be used in all models if wished, though there is no advantage in doing so.

## 4 Fuel lines and fittings - general information

⚠️ **Warning: Refer to the warning note in Section 1 before proceeding.**

**1** Quick-release couplings are employed at the fuel feed and return lines at the fuel rail. The couplings are coloured red or are identified by a red band.

**2** Before disconnecting any fuel system component, relieve the pressure in the system as described in Section 2, and equalise tank pressure by removing the fuel filler cap.
**3** Release the protruding locking lugs on each union by squeezing them together, then carefully pull the coupling apart **(see illustration)**. Use rag to soak up any spilt fuel. Note carefully which pipe is connected to which, and ensure that they are correctly reconnected on refitting.
**4** To reconnect one of these couplings, press them together until the locking lugs snap into their groove. Switch the ignition on to pressurise the system, and check for any sign of fuel leakage around the disturbed coupling before attempting to start the engine.
**5** Checking procedures for the fuel lines are included in Chapter 1.
**6** Always use genuine fuel lines and hoses when renewing sections of the fuel system. **Do not** fit substitutes constructed from inferior or inappropriate material, or you could cause a fuel leak or a fire.
**7** Before disconnecting any part of the fuel system, note the routing of all hoses and pipes, and the orientation of all clamps and clips to ensure correct refitting.

## 5 Air cleaner assembly and air inlet components - removal and refitting

### Removal

**1** Loosen the clips and disconnect the air inlet duct from between the air cleaner (or airflow meter) and throttle housing **(see illustration)**.
**2** On pre-1999 models, disconnect the wiring from the inlet air temperature sensor on the air cleaner cover and from the airflow meter **(see illustration)**.
**3** Release the clips or undo the screws and lift the cover from the air cleaner body. Remove the air cleaner element.
**4** On pre-1999 models, undo the screws and remove the airflow meter from the cover.
**5** Undo the retaining screws on the front crossmember, then depress the tang and remove the intake duct **(see illustrations)**.

**4.3 Disconnecting the fuel line couplings**

**5.1 Disconnecting the air inlet duct from between the airflow meter and throttle housing**

**5.2 Disconnecting the wiring from the air temperature sensor**

**5.5a Undo the screws . . .**

**5.5b . . . and remove the intake duct from the crossmember**

**5.6a Removing the air cleaner assembly**

**5.6b Air cleaner rear mounting grommets**

**6** Release the front of the air cleaner body from the front rubber grommet, and withdraw the body from the rear rubber grommets. Recover the intermediate air inlet tube **(see illustrations)**.

### Refitting

**7** Refitting is a reversal of removal.

---

### 6 Accelerator cable - removal, refitting and adjustment

### Removal

**1** Fold back the carpet and insulation in the driver's footwell to gain access to the accelerator pedal.
**2** Disconnect the inner cable from the top of the pedal **(see illustration)**.
**3** From within the engine compartment,

**6.2 Disconnect the accelerator cable from the top of the pedal**

**6.4 Disconnecting the inner cable from the quadrant on the throttle housing**

detach the outer cable from the adjuster/support bracket by removing the metal retaining clip **(see illustration)**.
**4** Disconnect the inner cable from the quadrant on the throttle housing by pivoting the quadrant then extracting the retaining clip **(see illustration)**.
**5** Release the cable from the supports in the engine compartment, and withdraw it from the bulkhead **(see illustration)**.

### Refitting

**6** Refitting is a reversal of removal. When the cable is reconnected at each end, adjust the cable as follows.

### Adjustment

**7** Remove the outer cable metal retaining clip at the adjuster/support bracket.
**8** Remove any slack by pulling the cable as far as possible out of the adjuster. Have an assistant depress the accelerator pedal fully -

**6.3 Detach the outer cable from the adjuster/support bracket by removing the metal retaining clip**

**6.5 Releasing the accelerator cable from the support on the inlet manifold**

the cable outer will move back into the adjuster - and hold it there while the clip is refitted.
**9** Check that the throttle quadrant moves smoothly and easily from the fully-closed to the fully-open position and back again as the assistant depresses and releases the accelerator pedal. Re-adjust the cable if required.

---

### 7 Accelerator pedal - removal and refitting

### Removal

**1** Peel back the carpet and insulation from the driver's footwell to allow access to the accelerator pedal.
**2** Detach the accelerator cable from the pedal, then release the circlip from the pivot shaft and remove the accelerator pedal.

### Refitting

**3** Refitting is a reversal of removal. On completion, check the action of the pedal and the cable to ensure that the throttle has full unrestricted movement, and fully returns when released.
**4** Check and if necessary adjust the accelerator cable as described in Section 6.

---

### 8 Fuel pump/fuel pressure - checking

⚠ *Warning: Refer to the warning note in Section 1 before proceeding.*

### Fuel pump operation check

**1** Switch on the ignition, and listen for the fuel pump (the sound of an electric motor running, audible from beneath the rear seats). Assuming there is sufficient fuel in the tank, the pump should start and run for approximately one or two seconds, then stop, each time the ignition is switched on. **Note:** *If the pump runs continuously all the time the ignition is switched on, the electronic control system is running in the backup (or "limp-home") mode referred to by Ford as "Limited Operation Strategy" (LOS). This almost* *certainly indicates a fault in the EEC V module itself, and the vehicle should therefore be taken to a Ford dealer for a full test of the complete system, using the correct diagnostic equipment; do not waste time or risk damaging the components by trying to test the system without such facilities.*

**2** Listen for fuel return noises from the fuel pressure regulator. It should be possible to feel the fuel pulsing in the regulator and in the feed hose from the fuel filter.

**3** If the pump does not run at all, check the fuse, relay and wiring (see Chapter 12). Check also that the fuel cut-off switch has not been activated and if so, reset it. The switch is located behind the carpet just in front of the right-hand door. If the switch button is in its raised position, this may have been caused by a sudden vibration or parking collision. Depress the button and check if the pump runs again.

### Fuel pressure check

**4** A fuel pressure gauge will be required for this check and should be connected in the fuel line between the fuel filter and the fuel rail, in accordance with the gauge maker's instructions. A pressure gauge equipped with an adapter to suit the Schrader-type valve on the fuel rail pressure test/release fitting (identifiable by its blue plastic cap) will be required. If the Ford special tool 23-033 is available, the tool can be attached to the valve, and a conventional-type pressure gauge attached to the tool.

**5** If using the service tool, ensure that its tap is turned fully anti-clockwise, then attach it to the valve. Connect the pressure gauge to the service tool. If using a fuel pressure gauge with its own adapter, connect it in accordance with its maker's instructions.

**6** Start the engine and allow it to idle. Note the gauge reading as soon as the pressure stabilises, and compare it with the regulated fuel pressure figures listed in the Specifications.

a) *If the pressure is high, check for a restricted fuel return line. If the line is clear, renew the fuel pressure regulator.*

b) *If the pressure is low, pinch the fuel return line. If the pressure now goes up, renew the fuel pressure regulator. If the pressure does not increase, check the fuel feed line, the fuel pump and the fuel filter.*

**9.8 Filler pipe lower vent hose on the rear of the fuel tank**

**7** Detach the vacuum hose from the fuel pressure regulator; the pressure shown on the gauge should increase. Note the increase in pressure, and compare it with that listed in the Specifications. If the pressure increase is not as specified, check the vacuum hose and pressure regulator.

**8** Reconnect the regulator vacuum hose, and switch off the engine. Verify that the hold pressure stays at the specified level for five minutes after the engine is turned off.

**9** Carefully disconnect the fuel pressure gauge, depressurising the system first as described in Section 2. Be sure to cover the fitting with a rag before slackening it. Mop up any spilt petrol.

**10** Run the engine, and check that there are no fuel leaks.

---

### 9  Fuel tank – removal, inspection and refitting

**⚠ Warning: Refer to the warning note in Section 1 before proceeding.**

### Removal

**1** Run the fuel level as low as possible prior to removing the tank.

**2** Relieve the residual pressure in the fuel system (see Section 2), and equalise tank pressure by removing the fuel filler cap.

**3** Disconnect the battery negative (earth) lead (see Chapter 5A).

**4** Where possible, syphon or pump out the

**9.9 Disconnecting the fuel supply hose quick-release fitting from the fuel filter**

remaining fuel from the fuel tank (there is no drain plug). The fuel must be emptied into a suitable container for storage.

**5** Chock the front wheels then jack up the rear of the car and support it on axle stands (see *"Jacking and Vehicle Support"*). Remove the rear roadwheels.

**6** Unhook the exhaust system mounting rubbers at the front and rear and allow the exhaust system to rest on the rear suspension crossmember. There is no need to disconnect the exhaust from the exhaust manifold/catalytic converter.

**7** Unscrew the nuts and remove the exhaust heat shields from the underbody.

**8** Loosen the clip and disconnect the filler pipe lower vent hose from the rear of the fuel tank **(see illustration)**.

**9** Position a container beneath the fuel filter at the front of the tank, then disconnect the fuel supply hose from the filter inlet by squeezing the locking lugs on the quick-release fitting **(see illustration)**. Be prepared for some loss of fuel. The supply hose remains attached to the fuel pump until the tank is lowered.

**10** At the rear of the tank, disconnect the hose leading to the evaporative emission canister from the fuel tank vent valve, then release the valve from the bracket.

**11** Support the fuel tank using a jack and block of wood.

**12** Unscrew and remove the tank mounting bolts **(see illustration)**.

**13** Unscrew the filler pipe mounting bolt, then partially lower the fuel tank and at the same time ease the filler pipe from the fuel tank rubber seal **(see illustrations)**.

**9.12 Fuel tank mounting bolt**

**9.13a Filler pipe mounting bolt**

**9.13b Filler pipe connection to the fuel tank**

9.16 Filter location on the fuel tank

10.3a Using a long metal bar to loosen the special retaining ring from the fuel pump/fuel gauge sender unit

10.3b Removing the retaining ring

**14** Squeeze the locking lugs on the quick-release fitting and disconnect the fuel return pipe. Note the return pipe is identified by a red colour band.

**15** Disconnect the wiring from the fuel pump/fuel gauge sender on top of the tank.

**16** Lower the fuel tank and withdraw it from under the vehicle. If necessary, disconnect the supply hose from the fuel pump. The filter may also be removed at this time **(see illustration)**.

**17** Check the condition of the filler pipe seal and renew it if necessary.

## Inspection

**18** Whilst removed, the fuel tank can be inspected for damage or deterioration. Removal of the fuel pump/fuel gauge sender unit (see Section 10) will allow a partial inspection of the interior. If the tank is contaminated with sediment or water, swill it out with clean fuel. Do not under any circumstances undertake any repairs on a leaking or damaged fuel tank; this work must be carried out by a professional who has experience in this critical and potentially-dangerous work.

**19** Whilst the fuel tank is removed from the vehicle, it should be placed in a safe area where sparks or open flames cannot ignite the fumes coming out of the tank. Be especially careful inside garages where a natural-gas type appliance is located, because the pilot light could cause an explosion.

**20** Check the condition of the filler pipe and renew it if necessary.

10.4 Withdrawing the fuel pump/sender unit from the tank

## Refitting

**21** Refitting is a reversal of the removal procedure, but lubricate the filler pipe seal with clean engine oil to facilitate refitting the pipe. Ensure that all connections are securely fitted. When refitting the quick-release couplings, press them together until the locking lugs snap into their groove. If evidence of contamination was found, do not return any previously-drained fuel to the tank unless it is carefully filtered first.

### 10 Fuel pump/fuel gauge sender unit - removal and refitting

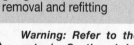
*Warning: Refer to the warning note in Section 1 before proceeding.*
**Note:** *Ford specify the use of their service tool 23-026 (a large ring spanner with projecting teeth to engage the fuel pump/sender unit retaining ring's slots) for this task. In practice it was found that a long metal bar could be used with success (see text).*

## Removal

**1** A combined fuel pump and fuel gauge sender unit is located in the top face of the fuel tank. The combined unit can only be detached and withdrawn from the tank after the tank is released and lowered from under the vehicle. Refer to Section 9 and remove the fuel tank, then proceed as follows.

**2** With the fuel tank removed, disconnect the fuel supply pipe (if still attached to the tank) from the inlet stub by squeezing the quick release lugs. Note that the fuel supply pipe connector is identified by being white or having a white band.

**3** Unscrew and remove the special retaining ring then remove the insert. Ford technicians use a special wrench to unscrew the ring, however a long metal bar may be used with success **(see illustrations)**.

**4** Carefully withdraw the fuel pump/sender unit from the fuel tank taking care not to damage the strainer and pump components **(see illustration)**.

**5** Remove the rubber seal from the periphery of the pump. The seal must be renewed

whenever the pump/sender unit is removed from the tank.

## Refitting

**6** Refitting is a reversal of removal, but fit a new rubber seal and tighten the retaining ring securely. Refit the fuel tank as described in Section 9.

### 11 Fuel tank roll-over valve - removal and refitting

*Warning: Refer to the warning note in Section 1 before proceeding.*

## Removal

**1** The roll-over valve is located in a rubber grommet in the top of the fuel tank, in the hose leading rearwards to the carbon canister. Its purpose is to prevent fuel loss if the vehicle becomes inverted in a crash.

**2** Remove the fuel tank as described in Section 9.

**3** Release the vent hose from the clip on the top of the tank **(see illustration)**.

**4** Carefully prise the roll-over valve from the rubber grommet and remove it together with the hose.

**5** Check the condition of the rubber grommet and renew it if necessary.

## Refitting

**6** Refitting is a reversal of removal, but apply a light smear of clean engine oil to the rubber grommet, to ease fitting.

11.3 Vent hose clip on the top of the fuel tank

**12.2 Filler pipe lower mounting bolt**

**12.3 View of the filler pipe with the flap open**

**13.3 Fuel cut-off switch (with trim panel removed)**

## 12 Fuel tank filler pipe - removal and refitting

 *Warning: Refer to the warning note in Section 1 before proceeding.*

### Removal

1 Remove the fuel tank as described in Section 9.
2 With the vehicle still raised, unscrew and remove the filler pipe lower mounting bolt **(see illustration)**.
3 Open the filler flap, then lift the plastic cover and unscrew the filler pipe upper mounting bolt **(see illustration)**.
4 Withdraw the filler pipe from under the vehicle.
5 If necessary, loosen the clips and disconnect the lower filler pipe and vent hose from the bottom of the filler pipe.
6 Check the condition of the filler pipe and hose and renew if necessary.

### Refitting

7 Refitting is a reversal of removal.

## 13 Fuel cut-off switch - removal and refitting

**Note:** *To reset the switch after an accident, insert a finger through the hole in the right-hand footwell side carpet, and depress the button on*

top of the switch. **Do not** *reset the switch if fuel has escaped from the fuel system.*

### Removal

1 The fuel cut-off switch is located behind the carpet on the right-hand side of the right-hand footwell.
2 Remove the trim panel from the right-hand footwell with reference to Chapter 11, Section 27.
3 Unscrew and remove the switch securing screws, then disconnect the wiring plug and remove the switch followed by the spacer pads **(see illustration)**.

### Refitting

4 Refitting is a reversal of removal, but make sure that the switch is reset. Start the engine to prove this.

## 14 Fuel injection system - checking

If a fault appears in the fuel injection system, first ensure that all the system wiring connectors are securely connected and free of corrosion. Ensure that the fault is not due to poor maintenance; ie, check that the air cleaner filter element is clean, the spark plugs are in good condition and correctly gapped, the valve clearances are correctly adjusted, the cylinder compression pressures are correct, and that the engine breather hoses are clear and undamaged, referring to Chapters 1 and 2 for further information.

If these checks fail to reveal the cause of the problem, the vehicle should be taken to a Ford dealer for testing. A test socket is incorporated in the engine management circuit, into which a special electronic diagnostic tester can be plugged. The connector is located behind the trim on the left-hand side of the left-hand passenger footwell **(see illustration)**. The tester will locate the fault quickly and simply, alleviating the need to test all the system components individually, which is a time-consuming operation that also carries a risk of damaging the EEC V engine management module.

## 15 Fuel injection system components - removal and refitting

 *Warning: Refer to the warning note in Section 1 before proceeding.*

### Throttle body housing

**Removal**

1 The housing is located on the left-hand side of the inlet manifold.
2 Loosen the clips and disconnect the air inlet duct from between the air cleaner (or airflow meter) and throttle housing **(see illustrations)**.
3 Disconnect the accelerator inner cable from the quadrant on the throttle housing by pivoting the quadrant then extracting the retaining clip.

**14.2 Diagnostic test socket (with trim panel removed)**

**15.2a Loosen the clip . . .**

**15.2b . . . and disconnect the air inlet duct from the throttle housing**

**15.4 Throttle position sensor multi-plug**

**15.5 Throttle housing mounting bolts**

**15.12 Removing the accelerator cable support bracket from the inlet manifold**

**4** Disconnect the throttle position sensor multi-plug **(see illustration)**.
**5** Unscrew and remove the mounting bolts and withdraw the throttle housing from the inlet manifold **(see illustration)**. Discard the gasket and obtain a new one.

### Refitting

**6** Refitting is a reversal of removal, but clean the mating faces and fit a new gasket, and tighten the mounting bolts to the specified torque. Check and if necessary adjust the accelerator cable as described in Section 6.

### Fuel rail and injectors

#### Removal

**7** Relieve the residual pressure in the fuel system (see Section 2), and equalise the tank pressure by removing the fuel filler cap.
**8** Disconnect the wiring from the idle air control valve. Unscrew the two bolts and remove the idle air control valve from the inlet manifold.
**9** Pull out the accelerator cable adjustment clip, then release the outer cable from the support bracket and disconnect the inner cable from the quadrant on the throttle housing. Position the accelerator cable to one side.
**10** Withdraw the air inlet resonator (where fitted) from the inlet manifold, then loosen the clips and disconnect the air inlet duct from the air cleaner and throttle housing. Remove the duct from the engine compartment.
**11** Disconnect the crankcase ventilation hoses from the inlet manifold.

**12** Unscrew the bolt and remove the accelerator cable support bracket from the inlet manifold **(see illustration)**.
**13** Disconnect the HT leads from the spark plugs, then unclip the lead supports and position the leads to one side. When disconnecting the leads, Twist the plug caps slightly to break the seal, then pull on the end fittings and not the leads.
**14** Disconnect the wiring from the throttle position sensor. To do this, depress the locking wire and pull off the plug.
**15** Disconnect the wiring from the fuel injectors **(see illustration)**, then undo the injector wiring loom retaining screws, disconnect the loom multiplug on the bulkhead, and position the loom to one side.
**16** Pull the vacuum hose from the fuel pressure regulator on the left-hand end of the fuel rail **(see illustration)**.
**17** Unscrew and remove the fuel rail mounting bolts.
**18** On pre-mid 1998 models, undo the single screw and remove the fuel supply and return pipe retaining bracket.
**19** Disconnect the fuel supply and return pipes from the fuel rail by squeezing the lugs on the special quick release fittings. Note that the supply pipe is coloured white and the return pipe is coloured red.
**20** Carefully pull the injectors from the inlet manifold and withdraw them together with the fuel rail.
**21** Remove the clips and carefully pull the injectors from the fuel rail.
**22** Using a screwdriver prise the O-rings from the grooves at each end of the injectors **(see**

illustration). Discard the O-rings and obtain new ones.

### Refitting

**23** Refitting is a reversal of removal, but note the following points:
a) Lubricate the new injector O-rings with clean engine oil to aid refitting.
b) Tighten the mounting bolts to the specified torque.
c) Ensure that the hoses and wiring are routed correctly, and secured on reconnection by any clips or ties provided.
d) Adjust the accelerator cable as described in Section 6.
e) On completion, switch the ignition on to activate the fuel pump and pressurise the system, without cranking the engine. Check for signs of fuel leaks around all disturbed unions and joints before attempting to start the engine.

### Fuel pressure regulator

#### Removal

**24** Relieve the residual pressure in the fuel system (see Section 2), and equalise tank pressure by removing the fuel filler cap.
**25** Loosen the clips and disconnect the air inlet duct from the air cleaner and throttle housing.
**26** Disconnect the vacuum hose from the fuel pressure regulator **(see illustration)**.
**27** On pre-mid 1998 models, undo the single screw and remove the fuel supply and return pipe retaining bracket.
**28** Disconnect the fuel return pipe from the fuel rail by squeezing the lugs on the special quick release fittings, then undo the two

**15.15 Disconnecting the fuel injector wiring plugs**

**15.16 Disconnecting the vacuum hose from the fuel pressure regulator**

**15.22 The injector O-rings must be renewed**

**15.26 Disconnecting the vacuum hose from the pressure regulator**

**15.32 The idle air control valve is located on the inlet manifold**

**15.33 Wiring plug to the idle air control valve**

screws and remove the fuel pressure regulator from the fuel rail.

29 On mid 1998-on models, prise out the retaining clip from the fuel pressure regulator, then pull the regulator from the fuel rail.

30 Using a screwdriver, prise out the O-ring(s) from the groove(s) in the fuel pressure regulator. Discard the O-ring(s).

### Refitting

31 Refitting is a reversal of removal, but lubricate the new O-ring(s) with clean engine oil to aid installation. On pre-mid 1998 models, tighten the mounting screws to the specified torque.

## Idle air control (IAC) valve

### Removal

32 The idle air control valve is located on the inlet manifold **(see illustration)**.

33 Depress the wire clip and disconnect the wiring from the valve **(see illustration)**.

34 Unscrew the mounting bolts and remove the valve from the inlet manifold **(see illustrations)**. If necessary, also remove the air inlet resonator.

35 Recover the O-ring seals and discard them. Obtain new seals.

### Refitting

36 Refitting is a reversal of removal, but note the following points.

a) Clean the mating surfaces, and fit new O-ring seals.

b) On completion, start the engine and allow it to idle. When it has reached normal operating temperature, check that the idle speed is stable, and that no induction (air) leaks are evident. Switch on all electrical loads (headlights, heated rear window, etc), and check that the idle speed is still satisfactory.

## Mass air flow sensor (pre 1999 models)

### Removal

37 Loosen the clip and disconnect the air inlet duct from the mass air flow sensor on the air cleaner cover. If necessary, remove the air cleaner cover for improved access.

38 Disconnect the wiring from the sensor **(see illustration)**.

**15.34a Unscrew the mounting bolts . . .**

**15.34b . . . and remove the idle air control valve from the inlet manifold**

39 Unscrew the crosshead mounting screws and remove the sensor from the air cleaner cover.

### Refitting

40 Refitting is a reversal of removal.

## Powertrain Control Module

**Note:** *The module is fragile. Take care not to drop it, or subject it to any other kind of impact. Do not subject it to extremes of temperature, or allow it to get wet.*

### Removal

41 The Module (engine management module) is located behind the front left-hand footwell side trim. First disconnect the battery negative (earth) lead (see Chapter 5A).

42 Carefully pull back the footwell floor covering for access to the powertrain control module **(see illustration)**.

**15.38 Disconnecting the wiring from the mass air flow sensor (pre 1999 models)**

43 Drill out the three rivets from the security shield, then unhook the shield and withdraw it downwards from over the module.

44 Undo the bolt and disconnect the wiring multiplug from the module. **Do not** pull on the wiring, only on the multiplug itself.

*Caution: Do not touch the module terminals, as there is the possibility of static electricity damaging the internal components.*

45 Carefully ease the module forwards then downwards from the mounting bracket. Withdraw the module from inside the vehicle.

### Refitting

46 Refitting is a reversal of removal. Take care when refitting the multiplug, and tighten the retaining bolt by hand first. Use new pop rivets when refitting the security shield.

**15.42 The Powertrain Control Module**

**15.47 The crankshaft position sensor is located on the front left-hand side of the engine cylinder block**

**15.54 Tape over the hole in the timing chain cover while the camshaft position sensor is removed**

**15.56 The engine coolant temperature sensor is located on the lower right-hand end of the inlet manifold**

## Crankshaft position sensor

### Removal

**47** The crankshaft position sensor is located on the front left-hand side of the engine cylinder block **(see illustration)**. For improved access, apply the handbrake then jack up the front of the vehicle and support it on axle stands (see *"Jacking and Vehicle Support"*).
**48** Trace the wiring back from the sensor, and disconnect the connector plug.
**49** Unscrew the mounting bolts and withdraw the sensor.

### Refitting

**50** Refitting is a reversal of removal.

## Camshaft position sensor

### Removal

**51** The sensor is located on the rear face of the timing chain cover.
**52** Depress the wire clip and disconnect the wiring from the camshaft position sensor.
**53** Unscrew the mounting bolt and withdraw the sensor from the timing chain cover.
**54** Remove the O-ring seal. Tape over the hole in the timing chain cover while the sensor is removed **(see illustration)**.

### Refitting

**55** Refitting is a reversal of removal but fit a new O-ring. Smear a little engine oil on the seal before fitting the sensor.

## Engine coolant temperature (ECT) sensor

### Removal

**56** The engine coolant temperature sensor is located on the lower right-hand end of the inlet manifold **(see illustration)**.
**57** With the engine cold, unscrew the filler cap from the coolant expansion reservoir to release any residual pressure, then refit and tighten the cap.
**58** Disconnect the wiring from the sensor.
**59** Have ready a suitable plug (or a new sensor). Unscrew the sensor from the bottom of the inlet manifold, and quickly fit the plug.

### Refitting

**60** Refitting is a reversal of removal. If necessary, clean the threads of the sensor and mounting hole, then refit the sensor and tighten it to the specified torque.

## Inlet air temperature sensor (pre 1999 models)

### Removal

**61** The sensor is located on the left-hand side of the air cleaner cover.
**62** Disconnect the wiring from the sensor, then twist the sensor through 90° and remove it **(see illustration)**.

### Refitting

**63** Refitting is a reversal of removal.

## Throttle position sensor

### Removal

**64** The throttle position sensor is located on the rear of the throttle body housing on the left-hand side of the inlet manifold. First disconnect the wiring by depressing the retaining clip **(see illustration)**.
**65** Remove the retaining screws, and withdraw the unit from the throttle housing. *Do not* force the sensor's centre to rotate past its normal operating sweep; the unit will be seriously damaged.

### Refitting

**66** Refitting is a reversal of removal, but ensure that the sensor is correctly orientated, by locating its centre on the D-shaped throttle shaft (throttle closed), and aligning the sensor body so that the bolts pass easily into the throttle housing.

## Vehicle speed sensor

### Removal

**67** The sensor is mounted on the rear of the transmission at the base of the speedometer drive cable **(see illustration)**.
**68** Undo the retaining collar and withdraw the speedometer cable from the vehicle speed sensor **(see illustration)**. Use two spanners to loosen the nut - one to counterhold the sensor, and the other to unscrew the cable nut.

**15.62 Disconnecting the wiring from the inlet air temperature sensor**

**15.64 Disconnecting the wiring from the throttle position sensor**

**15.67 The sensor is mounted on the rear of the transmission (cable disconnected)**

**15.68 Undo the retaining collar and withdraw the speedometer cable from the vehicle speed sensor**

69 Disconnect the wiring from the vehicle speed sensor, then unscrew the sensor from the top of the drive pinion.

### Refitting

70 Refitting is a reversal of removal.

## Manual transmission multi-function switch

### Removal and refitting

71 Refer to Chapter 7.

## Clutch pedal position switch

### Removal

72 Inside the vehicle, reach up under the clutch pedal and disconnect the return spring from the bracket.

73 Disconnect the wiring from the clutch switch, then twist the switch and remove it from the pedal bracket (see illustration).

### Refitting

74 Refitting is a reversal of removal.

## Power steering pressure switch

### Removal

75 The switch is located in the high pressure fluid pipe on the steering gear (see illustration). Apply the handbrake, then jack up the front of the vehicle and support it on axle stands (see "Jacking and Vehicle Support").

76 Place a container beneath the switch location to catch any escaping fluid, then disconnect the wiring. Unscrew and remove the switch from the fluid pipe. Be prepared for fluid spillage, and plug or cover the orifice in the pipe to prevent dirt entry and further fluid loss.

### Refitting

77 Refitting is a reversal of removal, but tighten the switch securely, and on completion bleed the power steering hydraulic circuit as described in Chapter 10, Section 19.

## Oxygen sensor

### Removal and refitting

78 Refer to Chapter 4B.

**15.73  Clutch position switch on the pedal bracket**

### T-MAP sensor (models from 1999)

### Removal

79 The sensor is located on the back of the inlet manifold (see illustration).

80 Disconnect the wiring from the sensor, then undo the retaining screw and remove it from the manifold.

### Refitting

81 Refitting is a reversal of removal.

## 16 Manifolds - removal and refitting

## Inlet manifold

⚠️ **Warning: Refer to the warning note in Section 1 before proceeding.**

### Removal

1 Apply the handbrake, then jack up the front of the vehicle and support it on axle stands (see "Jacking and Vehicle Support").

2 Depressurise the fuel system as described in Section 2.

3 Disconnect the battery negative (earth) lead (see Chapter 5A).

4 Drain the cooling system as described in Chapter 1.

5 Remove the air cleaner assembly complete as described in Section 5.

6 Refer to Section 6 and disconnect the

**16.13  Unscrew the bolt and detach the engine oil dipstick tube from the inlet manifold**

**15.75  The power steering pressure switch is located in the high pressure fluid pipe on the steering gear**

**15.79 Retaining screw (arrowed) securing T-MAP sensor on the inlet manifold**

accelerator cable from the throttle housing, then release the cable from the supports on the inlet manifold.

7 Release the engine wiring harness from the clips on the bulkhead.

8 Disconnect the brake servo vacuum hose from the inlet manifold, and also disconnect the evaporative emission control canister purge valve vacuum line from the inlet manifold.

9 On models with a mass air flow meter (pre 1999 models), prise the wiring connectors from the bulkhead, then disconnect the spark plug HT leads and release them from the holders (if necessary, disconnect the HT leads from the ignition coil to avoid bending them excessively).

10 On models with a temperature manifold absolute sensor (1999-on models), disconnect the wiring from the TMAP sensor.

11 Disconnect the wiring from the camshaft position (CMP) sensor, and engine coolant temperature (ECT) sensor.

12 Disconnect the quick-release coupling connecting the coolant hose to the heating matrix.

13 Unscrew the bolt and detach the engine oil dipstick tube from the inlet manifold (see illustration).

14 Disconnect the fuel supply and return lines at the quick-release connectors on the left-hand side of the bulkhead.

15 Where fitted, unbolt and remove the heatshield from the inlet manifold.

16 Progressively unscrew the mounting bolts/studs, and withdraw the inlet manifold

**17.3 Rubber mounting suspending the front exhaust pipe from the underbody**

**17.5 Wooden splint to prevent damage to the flexible joint section of the exhaust**

**17.6 Remove the flange bolts and detach the front of the exhaust pipe from the catalytic converter/downpipe**

from the cylinder head. Recover the gasket.

**17** Tape over the inlet ports on the cylinder head to prevent entry of dust and dirt. Alternatively place cloth rags in the ports.

**18** Remove the throttle body housing, the fuel rail and injectors, the idle air control valve, and the engine coolant temperature sensor as described in Section 15.

### Refitting

**19** Refitting is a reversal of removal, but note the following additional points.

a) Clean the mating faces of the inlet manifold and cylinder head and use a new gasket.

b) Tighten the bolts/studs to the specified torque.

## Exhaust manifold

### Removal

**20** The exhaust manifold is located on the front of the cylinder head. Note that the catalytic converter is integral with the exhaust manifold.

**21** Disconnect the battery negative (earth) lead (see Chapter 5A).

**22** Drain the cooling system as described in Chapter 1.

**23** On models with air conditioning, have the refrigerant evacuated from the system by an air conditioning specialist. While the system is disconnected, make sure that it is sealed adequately to prevent entry of dust, dirt and foreign matter.

 **Warning: Do not attempt to remove the refrigerant yourself - this could result in personal injury.**

**24** Remove the air cleaner assembly complete as described in Section 5.

**25** Unscrew the bolts and remove the heat shield from the exhaust manifold, then remove the oxygen sensor with reference to Chapter 4B.

**26** Disconnect the HT leads from the spark plugs. Twist the plug caps slightly to break the seal, then pull on the connector of each lead (not the lead itself), and note the order of fitting. Place the leads to one side.

**27** Apply the handbrake, then jack up the front of the vehicle and support it on axle stands (see "Jacking and Vehicle Support").

**28** Remove the radiator as described in Chapter 3.

**29** Working under the vehicle, undo the nuts and disconnect the exhaust pipe from the catalytic converter/downpipe at the flange, and recover the sealing ring. Also unscrew and remove the support bracket bolt from the transmission.

**30** Progressively unscrew the nuts, then withdraw the exhaust manifold/catalytic converter from the cylinder head. Recover the four gaskets from the studs on the cylinder head.

### Refitting

**31** Refitting is a reversal of removal, but clean the mating faces and fit new gaskets to the manifold and exhaust system flange. Tighten the bolts and nuts to the specified torque.

---

**17 Exhaust system -** general information, removal and refitting

## General information

**1** On new vehicles the exhaust system (from the manifold/downpipe rearwards) is of one-piece construction. Note that the catalytic converter, downpipe and exhaust manifold, are manufactured as a single unit, and the removal and refitting procedure is described in Section 16. The exhaust system is attached to the catalytic converter/downpipe by a flanged joint with gasket. A small tailpipe trim is also fitted to the extreme rear of the exhaust system.

**17.7a Rubber mounting located in front of the rear silencer . . .**

**2** For service replacements the exhaust system is available in two sections, however the original pipe must be cut with a hacksaw to accommodate either new section.

**3** The system is suspended throughout its entire length by rubber mountings (see illustration).

**4** To remove the complete system or a part of the system, first jack up the front and rear of the car, and support on axle stands (see "Jacking and Vehicle Support"). Alternatively, position the car over an inspection pit, or on car ramps, however if the original complete system is being removed, it will be necessary to jack up the right-hand rear of the vehicle to allow room between the underbody and rear axle.

## Complete exhaust system

### Removal

**5** Before disconnecting the exhaust pipe front flange, it is recommended that the flexible joint section is supported with a splint made from card, plastic or wood secured with jubilee clips. This will prevent damage caused by bending the joint through an excessive angle (see illustration).

**6** Unscrew and remove the flange bolts and detach the front of the exhaust pipe from the catalytic converter/downpipe (see illustration). Recover the gasket.

**7** At the rear of the exhaust system, disconnect the rubber mountings in front of and behind the rear silencer (see illustrations).

**17.7b . . . and behind the rear silencer**

**17.8 Disconnecting the rubber mountings located behind the flexible section**

**8** Disconnect the front rubber mountings located just behind the flexible section **(see illustration)**.

**9** Lower the front of the exhaust system, then lift the rear silencer over the rear axle beam and lower the system to the ground. Withdraw the system from under the vehicle.

**10** Examine the rubber mountings for damage and cracking, and renew them if necessary.

### Refitting

**11** Refitting is a reversal of removal, but fit a new flange gasket and tighten the flange bolts to the specified torque. Dip the rubber mountings in soapy water before refitting them to ease location on the metal mounting arms.

## Front exhaust pipe and silencer

### Removal

**12** If the original exhaust system is fitted, remove it as described in paragraphs 5 to 10, and use a hacksaw to cut the centre pipe at the point indicated in the accompanying illustration **(see illustration)**. Obtain a joining kit consisting of a sleeve and two clamps.

**13** If a service front exhaust pipe and silencer is fitted, before disconnecting the exhaust pipe front flange it is recommended that the flexible joint section is supported with a splint made from card, plastic or thin metal wrapped around it and secured with jubilee clips. This will prevent damage caused by bending the joint through an excessive angle.

**14** Unscrew and remove the flange bolts and detach the front of the exhaust pipe from the catalytic converter/downpipe. Recover the gasket.

**15** Unscrew the nuts and remove the clamp joining the front to the rear sections of the exhaust system.

**16** Disconnect the two front rubber mounting rings, and lower the front pipe to the ground.

**17** Use a hammer to tap around the centre joint until it is free, then twist the front pipe from the rear pipe. If the joint is very tight, it may prove easier to completely remove the system, then apply heat to the joint with a hair dryer or blow lamp.

### Refitting

**18** Refitting is a reversal of removal, but fit a new flange gasket and tighten the flange bolts to the specified torque. Make sure the intermediate and tailpipe sections are correctly aligned before tightening the clamp nuts securely. Dip the rubber mountings in soapy water before refitting them to ease location on the metal mounting arms.

## Rear exhaust pipe and silencer

### Removal

**19** If the original exhaust system is fitted, remove it as described in paragraphs 5 to 10, and use a hacksaw to cut the centre pipe at the point indicated in the accompanying illustration (see illustration 17.12). Obtain a

joining kit consisting of a sleeve and two clamps.

**20** If a service rear exhaust pipe and silencer is fitted, unscrew the nuts and remove the clamp joining the front to the rear sections of the exhaust system.

**21** At the rear of the exhaust system, disconnect the rubber mountings in front of and behind the rear silencer.

**22** Use a hammer to tap around the centre joint until it is free, then twist the rear pipe from the front pipe. If the joint is very tight, it may prove easier to completely remove the system, then apply heat to the joint with a hair dryer or blow lamp.

**23** If necessary, disconnect the centre rubber mounting(s), then withdraw the rear exhaust pipe and silencer from the rear of the car.

### Refitting

**24** Refitting is a reversal of removal, but make sure the intermediate and tailpipe sections are correctly aligned before tightening the clamp nuts securely. Dip the rubber mountings in soapy water before refitting them to ease location on the metal mounting arms.

## Heat shield(s)

### Removal and refitting

**25** The heat shields are secured to the underside of the body by special nuts. Each shield can be removed separately but note that they overlap making it necessary to loosen another section first. If a shield is being removed to gain access to a component located behind it, it may prove sufficient in some cases to remove the retaining nuts and/or bolts, and simply lower the shield, without disturbing the exhaust system. Otherwise remove the exhaust system or section as described earlier.

**17.12 The original factory-fitted exhaust must be cut at the point shown when fitting replacement sections**

# Chapter 4 Part B:
# Emission control systems

## Contents

## Degrees of difficulty

| | | | | |
|---|---|---|---|---|
| **Easy,** suitable for novice with little experience  | **Fairly easy,** suitable for beginner with some experience  | **Fairly difficult,** suitable for competent DIY mechanic  | **Difficult,** suitable for experienced DIY mechanic | **Very difficult,** suitable for expert DIY or professional  |

## Specifications

| Torque wrench setting | Nm | lbf ft |
|---|---|---|
| Oxygen (Lambda) sensor ................................... | 42 | 31 |

## 1 General information and precautions

**1** The Endura-E engine uses unleaded petrol and also has various features built into the fuel system to help minimise harmful emissions. All models are equipped with a crankcase emission-control system, a closed-loop catalytic converter and an evaporative emission control system.
**2** The emission control systems function as follows.

### Crankcase emission control

**3** To reduce the emission of unburned hydrocarbons from the crankcase into the atmosphere, the engine is sealed and the blow-by gases and oil vapour are drawn from inside the crankcase, through an oil separator and regulating (PCV - positive crankcase ventilation) valve, into the inlet manifold to be burned by the engine during normal combustion. The engine oil filler cap incorporates the oil separator and PCV valve and the gases are drawn through two hoses connected to adapters on the inlet manifold near the cylinder head.
**4** Under conditions of high manifold depression (idling, deceleration) the gases will

be sucked positively out of the crankcase. Under conditions of low manifold depression (acceleration, full-throttle running) the gases are forced out of the crankcase by the (relatively) higher crankcase pressure; if the engine is worn, the raised crankcase pressure (due to increased blow-by) will cause some of the flow to return under all manifold conditions.

### Exhaust emission control

**5** To minimise the amount of pollutants which escape into the atmosphere, all models are fitted with a catalytic converter which is integral with the exhaust manifold and downpipe **(see illustration)**. The system is of the closed-loop type, in which an oxygen (Lambda) sensor in the exhaust manifold provides the fuel-injection/ignition system Powertrain Control Module (PCM) with constant feedback, enabling the PCM to adjust the mixture to provide the best possible conditions for the converter to operate.
**6** The oxygen sensor has a built-in heating element that is controlled by the PCM through a relay to quickly bring the sensor's tip to an efficient operating temperature. The sensor's tip is sensitive to oxygen and sends the PCM a varying voltage dependant on the amount of oxygen in the exhaust gases; if the intake air/fuel mixture is too rich, the exhaust gases

are low in oxygen so the sensor sends a high-voltage signal, the voltage dropping as the mixture weakens and the amount of oxygen rises in the exhaust gases. Peak conversion efficiency of all major pollutants occurs if the intake air/fuel mixture is maintained at the chemically-correct ratio for the complete combustion of petrol of 14.7 parts (by weight) of air to 1 part of fuel (the 'stoichiometric' ratio). The sensor output voltage alters in a large step at this point, the PCM using the signal change as a reference point and correcting the intake air/fuel mixture accordingly by altering the fuel injector pulse width.

**1.5 The catalytic converter is integral with the exhaust manifold and downpipe**

**2.1 Periodically disconnect the crankcase emission control hoses on the engine oil filler cap, and check that they are clear**

**2.3 The charcoal canister is located under the rear of the vehicle, behind the fuel tank**

## Evaporative emission control

**7** To minimise the escape into the atmosphere of unburned hydrocarbons, an evaporative emissions control system is also fitted to all models. The fuel tank filler cap is sealed and a charcoal canister is mounted behind the fuel tank on the underbody. The canister collects the petrol vapours generated in the tank when the car is parked and stores them until they can be cleared from the canister (under the control of the fuel-injection/ignition system PCM) via the purge valve into the inlet tract, to be burned by the engine during normal combustion. The purge valve is located on the bulkhead in the engine compartment.

**8** To ensure that the engine runs correctly when it is cold and/or idling and to protect the catalytic converter from the effects of an over-rich mixture, the purge control valve is not opened by the PCM until the engine has warmed up, and the engine is under load; the valve solenoid is then modulated on and off to allow the stored vapour to pass into the inlet tract.

## 2  Emission control systems - testing and component renewal

### Crankcase emission control

**1** The components of this system require no attention other than to check that the hoses and PCV valve are clear and undamaged at regular intervals. If the hoses are blocked, disconnect them and clear them using an airline or pipe cleaner **(see illustration)**. If the engine oil filler cap is blocked, renew it.

### Evaporative emission control system

#### Testing

**2** If the system is thought to be faulty,

disconnect the hoses from the charcoal canister and purge control valve and check that they are clear by blowing through them. If the purge control valve or charcoal canister are thought to be faulty, they must be renewed.

### Charcoal canister - renewal

**3** The charcoal canister is located under the rear of the vehicle, behind the fuel tank **(see illustration)**. First chock the front wheels then jack up the rear of the vehicle and support it on axle stands (see "*Jacking and Vehicle Support*").

**4** Unscrew the mounting bolts and lower the canister cover from the underbody **(see illustration)**.

**5** Disconnect the hoses and remove the canister from under the vehicle.

**6** Fit the new canister using a reversal of the removal procedure.

### Purge valve - renewal

**7** The purge valve is mounted on the left-hand end of the engine compartment bulkhead, behind the brake vacuum servo unit **(see illustration)**.

**8** To renew the purge valve, first disconnect the wiring plug.

**9** Disconnect the hoses from the valve noting

their locations, then detach the valve from its mounting bracket.

**10** Fit the new purge valve using a reversal of the removal procedure.

## Exhaust emission control

### Testing

**11** The performance of the catalytic converter can be checked only by measuring the exhaust gases using a good-quality, carefully-calibrated exhaust gas analyser.

**12** If the CO level at the tailpipe is too high, the vehicle should be taken to a Ford dealer so that the complete fuel-injection and ignition systems, including the oxygen sensor, can be thoroughly checked using the special diagnostic equipment. Once these have been checked and are known to be free from faults, the fault must be in the catalytic converter, which must be renewed.

### Catalytic converter - renewal

**13** Refer to Chapter 4A, Section 16.

### Oxygen (Lambda) sensor - renewal

**Note:** *The oxygen sensor is delicate and will not work if it is dropped or knocked, if its power supply is disrupted, or if any cleaning materials are used on it.*

**2.4 Charcoal canister and mounting bolts**

**2.7 Evaporative emission control system purge valve, located on the left-hand end of the engine compartment bulkhead**

**14** Trace the wiring back from the oxygen sensor to the connector on the radiator cowling and disconnect the wiring **(see illustration)**.

**15** Unscrew the sensor and remove it from the exhaust manifold **(see illustration)**. If necessary for improved access, unbolt the heatshield first.

**16** Clean the threads of the sensor and the threads in the exhaust manifold.

**17** Insert the sensor in the manifold and tighten to the specified torque.

**18** Refit the heat shield where removed.

**19** Reconnect the wiring making sure that it is in no danger of contacting the exhaust manifold. **Note:** *On later models (from 1999), there is a second oxygen sensor fitted after the catalytic converter at the bottom of the exhaust downpipe. The renewal procedure is the same for both sensors.*

**2.14 The oxygen sensor wiring connector located on the radiator cowling**

**2.15 The oxygen sensor is located on the top of the exhaust manifold**

---

## 3 Catalytic converter -
### general information and precautions

### *General information*

**1** The catalytic converter is a reliable and simple device which needs no maintenance in itself, but there are some facts of which an owner should be aware if the converter is to function properly for its full service life.

a) *DO NOT use leaded petrol in a car equipped with a catalytic converter - the lead will coat the precious metals, reducing their converting efficiency and will eventually destroy the converter.*

b) *Always keep the ignition and fuel systems well-maintained in accordance with the manufacturer's schedule.*

c) *If the engine develops a misfire, do not drive the car at all (or at least as little as*

possible) *until the fault is cured.*

d) *DO NOT push- or tow-start the car - this will soak the catalytic converter in unburned fuel, causing it to overheat when the engine does start.*

e) *DO NOT switch off the ignition at high engine speeds.*

f) *DO NOT use fuel or engine oil additives - these may contain substances harmful to the catalytic converter.*

g) *DO NOT continue to use the car if the engine burns oil to the extent of leaving a visible trail of blue smoke.*

h) *Remember that the catalytic converter operates at very high temperatures. DO NOT, therefore, park the car in dry undergrowth, over long grass or piles of dead leaves after a long run.*

i) *Remember that the catalytic converter is FRAGILE - do not strike it with tools during servicing work.*

j) *In some cases a sulphurous smell (like that of rotten eggs) may be noticed from the exhaust. This is common to many catalytic converter-equipped cars and once the car has covered a few thousand miles the problem should disappear.*

k) *The catalytic converter, used on a well-maintained and well-driven car, should last for between 50 000 and 100 000 miles - if the converter is no longer effective it must be renewed.*

### *Precautions*

**2** For long life and satisfactory operation of the catalytic converter, certain precautions must be observed. These are as follows.

**3** Only use unleaded fuel. Leaded fuel will damage the catalytic converter and the oxygen sensor.

**4** Do not run the engine for long periods if it is misfiring. Unburnt fuel entering the catalytic converter can cause it to overheat, resulting in permanent damage. For the same reason, do not try to start the engine by pushing or towing the car, nor crank it on the starter motor for long periods.

**5** Do not strike or drop the catalytic converter. The ceramic honeycomb which forms part of its internal structure may be damaged.

**6** Always renew seals and gaskets upstream of the catalytic converter whenever they are disturbed.

# Chapter 5 Part A:
## Starting and charging systems

## Contents

## Degrees of difficulty

| Easy, suitable for novice with little experience |  | Fairly easy, suitable for beginner with some experience |  | Fairly difficult, suitable for competent DIY mechanic | | Difficult, suitable for experienced DIY mechanic |  | Very difficult, suitable for expert DIY or professional | |

## Specifications

**System type** ........................................... 12-volt, negative earth

**Battery**
Type ................................................... Low-maintenance or "maintenance free" (lead/calcium type fitted from 1999, marked Ca)

Charge condition:
Poor ................................................... 12.5 volts
Normal .................................................. 12.6 volts
Good ................................................... 12.7 volts

**Alternator**
Type ................................................... Bosch
Output .................................................. 70 or 90 amps
Regulated voltage ....................................... 13.5 to 14.8 volts

**Starter motor**
Type ................................................... Bosch
Rating .................................................. 1.1 kW

| Torque wrench settings | Nm | lbf ft |
| --- | --- | --- |
| Alternator mounting bolts | 25 | 18 |
| Auxiliary drivebelt tensioner bolt | 35 | 26 |
| Starter motor mounting bolts | 35 | 26 |
| Starter cable nut: | | |
| M8 (terminal 30) | 12 | 9 |
| M6 (terminal 50) | 6 | 4 |

## 1 General information, precautions and battery disconnection

### General information

**1** The engine electrical system consists mainly of the charging and starting systems. Because of their engine-related functions, these components are covered separately from the body electrical devices such as the lights, instruments, etc (which are covered in Chapter 12). Information on the ignition system is covered in Part B of this Chapter.

**2** The electrical system is of 12-volt negative earth type.

**3** The battery is of the low maintenance or "maintenance-free" (sealed for life) type. On models from 1999 a lead/calcium battery is used, this is marked with "Ca" on the top of the battery. When renewing this type, it has to be with a lead/calcium battery (no other type of battery is to be used). All types of battery are charged by the alternator, which is belt-driven from the crankshaft pulley.

**4** The starter motor is of the pre-engaged type incorporating an integral solenoid. On starting, the solenoid moves the drive pinion into engagement with the flywheel ring gear before the starter motor is energised. Once the engine has started, a one-way clutch prevents the motor armature being driven by the engine until the pinion disengages from the flywheel.

### Precautions

**5** Further details of the starting and charging systems are given in the relevant Sections of this Chapter. While a repair may be possible, the usual course of action is to renew the component concerned. The owner whose interest extends beyond mere component renewal should obtain a copy of the "Automobile Electrical & Electronic Systems Manual", available from the publishers of this manual.

**6** It is necessary to take extra care when working on the electrical system to avoid damage to semi-conductor devices (diodes and transistors), and to avoid the risk of personal injury. In addition to the precautions given in "Safety First!" at the beginning of this manual, observe the following when working on the system:

a) Always remove rings, watches, etc before working on the electrical system. Even with the battery disconnected, capacitive discharge could occur if a component's live terminal is earthed through a metal object. This could cause a shock or nasty burn.

b) Do not reverse the battery connections. Components such as the alternator, electronic control units, or any other components having semi-conductor circuitry could be irreparably damaged.

c) If the engine is being started using jump leads and a slave battery, connect the batteries positive-to-positive and negative-to-negative (see "Jump-starting"). This also applies when connecting a battery charger.

d) Never disconnect the battery terminals, the alternator, any electrical wiring or any test instruments when the engine is running.

e) Do not allow the engine to turn the alternator when the alternator is not connected.

f) Never "test" for alternator output by "flashing" the output lead to earth.

g) Never use an ohmmeter of the type incorporating a hand-cranked generator for circuit or continuity testing.

h) Always ensure that the battery negative lead is disconnected when working on the electrical system.

i) Before using electric-arc welding equipment on the car, disconnect the battery, alternator and components such as the fuel injection/ignition electronic control unit to protect them from the risk of damage.

### Battery disconnection

**7** Several systems fitted to the vehicle require battery power to be available at all times, either to ensure that their continued operation (such as the clock) or to maintain control unit memories (such as that in the engine management system's ECU) which would be wiped if the battery were to be disconnected. Whenever the battery is to be disconnected therefore, first note the following, to ensure that there are no unforeseen consequences of this action:

a) First, on any vehicle with central locking, it is a wise precaution to remove the key from the ignition, and to keep it with you, so that it does not get locked in, if the central locking should engage accidentally when the battery is reconnected.

b) The engine management system's ECU (Powertrain Control Module - PCM) will lose the information stored in its fault memory - referred to by Ford as the "KAM" (Keep-Alive Memory) - when the battery is disconnected. This includes idling and operating values, and any fault codes detected - in the case of the fault codes, if it is thought likely that the system has developed a fault for which the corresponding code has been logged, the vehicle must be taken to a Ford dealer for the codes to be read, using the special diagnostic equipment necessary for this. Whenever the battery is disconnected, the information relating to idle speed control and other operating values will have to be re-programmed into the unit's memory. The ECU does this by itself, but until it is fully re-programmed, there may be surging, hesitation, erratic idle and a generally inferior level of performance. To allow the ECU to relearn these values, start the engine and run it to normal operating temperature, then run it at idle speed for approximately two minutes, first with the gear lever in neutral with the air conditioning (where fitted) switched off, then with the air conditioning switched on. Next, drive the vehicle for approximately 5 miles of varied driving to complete the relearning process.

c) If the battery is disconnected while the engine immobiliser is activated, the immobiliser will remain in the same state when the battery is reconnected.

d) If a Ford "Keycode" audio unit is fitted, and the unit and/or the battery is disconnected, the unit will not function again on reconnection until the correct security code is entered. Details of this procedure, which varies according to the unit and model year, are given in the "Ford Audio Systems Operating Guide" supplied with the vehicle when new, with the code itself being given in a "Radio Passport" and/or a "Keycode Label" at the same time. Ensure you have the correct code before you disconnect the battery. For obvious security reasons, the procedure is not given in this manual. If you do not have the code or details of the correct procedure, but can supply proof of ownership and a legitimate reason for wanting this information, the vehicle's selling dealer may be able to help.

**8** Devices known as "memory-savers" (or "code-savers") can be used to avoid some of the above problems. Precise details vary according to the device used. Typically, it is plugged into the cigarette lighter (where fitted), and is connected by its own wires to a spare battery; the vehicle's own battery is then disconnected from the electrical system, leaving the "memory-saver" to pass sufficient current to maintain audio unit security codes and ECU memory values, and also to run permanently-live circuits such as the clock, all the while isolating the battery in the event of a short-circuit occurring while work is carried out.

⚠ **Warning: Some of these devices allow a considerable amount of current to pass, which can mean that many of the vehicle's systems are still operational when the main battery is disconnected. If a 'memory-saver' is used, ensure that the circuit concerned is actually "dead" before carrying out any work on it! DO NOT use a 'memory-saver' when working on air bag components.**

## 2 Electrical fault finding - general information

Refer to Chapter 12.

### 3 Battery -
testing and charging

**Note:** *Refer to the warnings given in "Safety First!" and in Section 1 of this Chapter before starting work.*

#### Standard and low maintenance battery - testing

**1** If the vehicle covers a small annual mileage it is worthwhile checking the specific gravity of the electrolyte every three months to determine the state of charge of the battery. Use a hydrometer to make the check and compare the results with the following table. Note that the specific gravity readings assume an electrolyte temperature of 15°C (60°F); for every 10°C (18°F) below 15°C (60°F) subtract 0.007. For every 10°C (18°F) above 15°C (60°F) add 0.007.

|  | Ambient temperature | |
|---|---|---|
|  | above 25°C | below 25°C |
| Fully-charged | 1.210 to 1.230 | 1.270 to 1.290 |
| 70% charged | 1.170 to 1.190 | 1.230 to 1.250 |
| Discharged | 1.050 to 1.070 | 1.110 to 1.130 |

**2** If the battery condition is suspect, first check the specific gravity of electrolyte in each cell. A variation of 0.040 or more between any cells indicates loss of electrolyte or deterioration of the internal plates.

**3** If the specific gravity variation is 0.040 or more, the battery should be renewed. If the cell variation is satisfactory but the battery is discharged, it should be charged as described later in this Section.

#### Maintenance-free battery - testing

**4** Where a "sealed for life" maintenance-free battery is fitted, topping-up and testing of the electrolyte in each cell is not possible. The condition of the battery can therefore only be tested using a battery condition indicator or a voltmeter.

**5** The battery may be fitted with a built-in charge condition indicator. The indicator is located in the top of the battery casing, and indicates the condition of the battery from its colour. If the indicator shows green, then the battery is in a good state of charge. If the indicator turns darker, eventually to black, then the battery requires charging, as described later in this Section. If the indicator shows clear/yellow, then the electrolyte level in the battery is too low to allow further use, and the battery should be renewed. **Do not** attempt to charge, load or jump start a battery when the indicator shows clear/yellow.

**6** If testing the battery using a voltmeter, connect the voltmeter across the battery and compare the result with those given in the Specifications under "charge condition". The test is only accurate if the battery has not been subjected to any kind of charge for the previous six hours. If this is not the case, switch on the headlights for 30 seconds, then

wait four to five minutes before testing the battery after switching off the headlights. All other electrical circuits must be switched off, so check that the doors and tailgate/bootlid are fully shut when making the test.

**7** If the voltage reading is less than 12.2 volts, then the battery is discharged, whilst a reading of 12.2 to 12.4 volts indicates a partially discharged condition.

**8** If the battery is to be charged, remove it from the vehicle (Section 4) and charge it as described later in this Section.

#### Standard and low maintenance battery - charging

**Note:** *The following is intended as a guide only. Always refer to the manufacturer's recommendations (often printed on a label attached to the battery), and always disconnect both terminal leads before charging a battery.*

**9** Charge the battery at a rate of 3.5 to 4 amps and continue to charge the battery at this rate until no further rise in specific gravity is noted over a four hour period.

**10** Alternatively, a trickle charger charging at the rate of 1.5 amps can safely be used overnight.

**11** Specially rapid 'boost' charges which are claimed to restore the power of the battery in 1 to 2 hours are not recommended, as they can cause serious damage to the battery plates through overheating.

**12** While charging the battery, note that the temperature of the electrolyte should never exceed 37.8°C (100°F).

#### Maintenance-free battery - charging

**Note:** *The following is intended as a guide only. Always refer to the manufacturer's recommendations (often printed on a label attached to the battery), and always disconnect both terminal leads before charging a battery.*

**13** This battery type takes considerably longer to fully recharge than the standard type, the time taken being dependent on the extent of discharge, but it can take anything up to three days.

**14** A constant voltage type charger is required, to be set, when connected, to 13.9

to 14.9 volts with a charger current below 25 amps. Using this method, the battery should be usable within three hours, giving a voltage reading of 12.5 volts, but this is for a partially discharged battery and, as mentioned, full charging can take considerably longer.

**15** If the battery is to be charged from a fully discharged state (condition reading less than 12.2 volts), have it recharged by your Ford dealer or local automotive electrician, as the charge rate is higher and constant supervision during charging is necessary.

### 4 Battery -
removal and refitting

**Note:** *Refer to the warnings given in "Safety First!" and in Section 1 of this Chapter before starting work.*

#### Removal

**1** The battery is located on the left-hand side of the engine compartment, on a platform on the vehicle structure above the transmission. It is enclosed in an insulated box **(see illustration)**.

**2** Lift the lid of the battery box and remove it, then loosen the clamp bolt and detach the earth lead from the battery negative (earth) terminal **(see illustration)**. This is the terminal to disconnect before working on, or disconnecting, any electrical component on the vehicle. Position the lead away from the battery.

**3** Loosen the positive lead clamp bolt. Detach the positive lead from the terminal and position it away from the battery.

**4** Unscrew the single nut and raise the retaining strap from the top of the battery. Lift the battery from its location, keeping it in an upright position to avoid the possibility of corrosive electrolyte spilling onto the paintwork.

**5** Remove the battery box and insulators from the platform.

**6** Clean the battery terminal posts, clamps and the battery casing. If the platform is corroded as a result of battery acid spilling onto it, clean it thoroughly and re-paint.

**7** If you are renewing the battery, make sure

**4.1 The battery is located on the left-hand side of the engine compartment**

**4.2 Disconnecting the battery negative (earth) lead**

**7.3 Removing the auxiliary drivebelt**

that you get the correct one, and dispose of the old battery in a responsible fashion. Most local authorities have facilities for the collection and disposal of such items.

### Refitting

**8** Refitting is a reversal of removal. Smear the battery terminals with a petroleum-based jelly prior to reconnecting. Always connect the positive terminal clamp first and the negative terminal clamp last.

### 5 Charging system - testing

**Note:** *Refer to the warnings given in "Safety First!" and in Section 1 of this Chapter before starting work.*

**1** If the ignition warning light fails to illuminate when the ignition is switched on, first check the alternator wiring connections for security. If satisfactory, check that the warning light bulb has not blown, and that the bulbholder is secure in its location in the instrument panel. If the light still fails to illuminate, check the continuity of the warning light feed wire from the alternator to the bulbholder. If all is satisfactory, the alternator is at fault and should be renewed or taken to an auto-electrician for testing and repair.

**2** If the ignition warning light illuminates when the engine is running, stop the engine and check that the auxiliary drivebelt is intact (see Chapter 1) and that the alternator connections are secure. If all is so far satisfactory, have the alternator checked by an auto-electrician.

**7.13 The alternator upper mounting bolt**

**3** If the alternator output is suspect even though the warning light functions correctly, the regulated voltage may be checked as follows.

**4** Connect a voltmeter across the battery terminals and start the engine.

**5** Increase the engine speed until the voltmeter reading remains steady; the reading should be approximately 12 to 13 volts, and no more than 14 volts.

**6** Switch on as many electrical accessories (eg, the headlights, heated rear window and heater blower) as possible, and check that the alternator maintains the regulated voltage at around 13 to 14 volts.

**7** If the regulated voltage is not as stated, the fault may be due to worn brushes, weak brush springs, a faulty voltage regulator, a faulty diode, a severed phase winding or worn or damaged slip rings. The alternator should be renewed or taken to an auto-electrician for testing and repair. **Note:** *Lead/calcium batteries, fitted from 1999, require a different charge rate to other batteries; ensure any new components are suitable.*

### 6 Alternator drivebelt - removal, refitting and tensioning

Refer to the procedure given for the auxiliary drivebelt in Chapter 1.

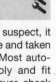

### 7 Alternator - removal and refitting

**Note:** *Refer to the warnings given in "Safety First!" and in Section 1 of this Chapter before starting work.*

### Removal

**1** The alternator is located on the right-hand front of the cylinder block. First disconnect the battery negative (earth) lead (see Chapter 5A).

**2** Apply the handbrake, then jack up the front of the vehicle and support it on axle stands (see *"Jacking and Vehicle Support"*).

**3** Using a spanner on the auxiliary drivebelt tensioner centre bolt, turn the tensioner

**7.14 One of the alternator lower mounting bolts**

clockwise to release the drivebelt tension. Note how the drivebelt is routed, then remove the belt from the pulleys **(see illustration)**.

**4** Remove the air cleaner assembly complete with air intake ducts as described in Chapter 4A.

**5** Where applicable, unscrew the bolts securing the air conditioning pipe beneath the right-hand side of the engine compartment.

**6** Unscrew the bolts securing the wiring harness beneath the right-hand side of the engine compartment.

**7** Using a suitable puller, pull the pulley from the power steering pump driveshaft (refer to Chapter 10 if necessary).

**8** Unbolt the cover from beneath the radiator.

**9** Beneath the right-hand wheel arch, undo the screw securing the radiator bottom hose support to the inner wing panel.

**10** On models with air conditioning, disconnect the wiring plug from the compressor, then unscrew the bolt and remove the clamp securing the refrigerant pipe to the compressor. Unscrew the compressor mounting bolts, and suspend the compressor to one side using wire or string.

**11** Unbolt and remove the alternator heatshield (where fitted).

**12** Note the location of the wiring on the rear of the alternator, then undo the nuts and disconnect the cables from the terminals.

**13** Unscrew and remove the alternator upper mounting bolt **(see illustration)**.

**14** Unscrew and remove the alternator lower mounting bolts, then ease the alternator away from the engine and withdraw from under the right-hand wheel arch **(see illustration)**.

### Refitting

**15** Refitting is a reversal of removal, but tighten all mounting nuts and bolts to the specified torque.

### 8 Alternator - testing and overhaul

If the alternator is thought to be suspect, it should be removed from the vehicle and taken to an auto-electrician for testing. Most auto-electricians will be able to supply and fit brushes at a reasonable cost. However, check on the cost of repairs before proceeding as it may prove more economical to obtain a new or exchange alternator. **Note:** *Lead/calcium batteries, fitted from 1999, require a different charge rate to other batteries; ensure any new components are suitable.*

### 9 Starting system - testing

**Note:** *Refer to the precautions given in "Safety First!" and in Section 1 of this Chapter before starting work.*

**1** If the starter motor fails to operate when the ignition key is turned to the appropriate position, the following possible causes may be to blame.

 a) *The battery is faulty.*
 b) *The electrical connections between the switch, solenoid, battery and starter motor are somewhere failing to pass the necessary current from the battery through the starter to earth.*
 c) *The solenoid is faulty.*
 d) *The starter motor is mechanically or electrically defective.*

**2** To check the battery, switch on the headlights. If they dim after a few seconds, this indicates that the battery is discharged - recharge (see Section 3) or renew the battery. If the headlights glow brightly, operate the starter and observe the lights. If they dim, then this indicates that current is reaching the starter motor, therefore the fault must lie in the starter motor. If the lights continue to glow brightly (and no clicking sound can be heard from the starter motor solenoid), this indicates that there is a fault in the circuit or solenoid (see following paragraphs). If the starter motor turns slowly when operated, but the battery is in good condition, then this indicates that either the starter motor is faulty, or there is considerable resistance somewhere in the circuit.

**3** If a fault in the circuit is suspected, disconnect the battery leads (including the earth connection to the body), the starter/solenoid wiring and the engine/transmission earth strap. Thoroughly clean the connections, and reconnect the leads and wiring, then use a voltmeter or test lamp to check that full battery voltage is available at the battery positive lead connection to the solenoid, and that the earth is sound. Smear petroleum jelly around the battery terminals to prevent corrosion - corroded connections are amongst the most frequent causes of electrical system faults.

**4** If the battery and all connections are in good condition, check the circuit by disconnecting the wire from the solenoid terminal. Connect a voltmeter or test lamp between the wire end and a good earth (such as the battery negative terminal), and check

**10.6  Wiring terminals on the starter solenoid**

that the wire is live when the ignition switch is turned to the `start' position. If it is, then the circuit is sound - if not, the circuit wiring can be checked as described in Chapter 12.

**5** The solenoid contacts can be checked by connecting a voltmeter or test lamp between the battery positive feed connection on the starter side of the solenoid, and earth. When the ignition switch is turned to the 'start' position, there should be a reading or lighted bulb, as applicable. If there is no reading or lighted bulb, the solenoid is faulty and should be renewed.

**6** If the circuit and solenoid are proved sound, the fault must lie in the starter motor. In this event, it may be possible to have the starter motor overhauled by a specialist, but check on the cost of spares before proceeding, as it may prove more economical to obtain a new or exchange motor.

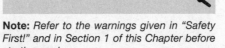

**10  Starter motor -**
**removal and refitting**

**Note:** *Refer to the warnings given in "Safety First!" and in Section 1 of this Chapter before starting work.*

### Removal

**1** The starter motor is located on the left-hand rear of the engine. First disconnect the battery negative (earth) lead (see Chapter 5A).

**2** Apply the handbrake, then jack up the front

**10.7  Starter motor lower mounting bolt**

of the vehicle and support it on axle stands (see *"Jacking and Vehicle Support"*).

**3** Remove the air cleaner assembly complete with air intake ducts as described in Chapter 4A.

**4** Unscrew and remove the starter motor upper mounting bolt. The bolt is also a transmission flange mounting bolt and secures the starter motor earth lead.

**5** Release the starter motor wiring from the clip on the air cleaner mounting bracket.

**6** Working from under the vehicle, unscrew the nuts and disconnect the wiring from the starter solenoid terminals **(see illustration)**.

**7** Unscrew the lower mounting bolt and withdraw the starter motor from the engine/transmission **(see illustration)**.

### Refitting

**8** Refitting is a reversal of removal, but tighten the mounting bolts to the specified torque.

**11  Starter motor -**
**testing and overhaul**

If the starter motor is thought to be suspect, it should be removed from the vehicle and taken to an auto-electrician for testing. Most auto-electricians will be able to supply and fit brushes at a reasonable cost. However, check on the cost of repairs before proceeding as it may prove more economical to obtain a new or exchange motor.

# Notes

# Chapter 5 Part B:
## Ignition system

## Contents

## Degrees of difficulty

| Easy, suitable for novice with little experience  | Fairly easy, suitable for beginner with some experience  | Fairly difficult, suitable for competent DIY mechanic  | Difficult, suitable for experienced DIY mechanic | Very difficult, suitable for expert DIY or professional  |

## Specifications

### General

| | |
|---|---|
| System type . . . . . . . . . . . . . . . . . . . . . . . . . . . . . . . . . . . . . . . . . . . . . . . . | Electronic distributorless ignition system (DIS) with ignition module controlled by EEC V engine management module (Powertrain control module) |
| Firing order . . . . . . . . . . . . . . . . . . . . . . . . . . . . . . . . . . . . . . . . . . | 1-2-4-3 |
| Location of No 1 cylinder . . . . . . . . . . . . . . . . . . . . . . . . . . . . . . . | Crankshaft pulley end |

### Ignition system data

| | |
|---|---|
| Ignition timing . . . . . . . . . . . . . . . . . . . . . . . . . . . . . . . . . . . . . . . . . | Controlled by the Powertrain Control Module (PCM) |
| Electronic Ignition (EI) coil resistances: | |
| Primary windings . . . . . . . . . . . . . . . . . . . . . . . . . . . . . . . . . . | 0.4 to 0.6 ohms |
| Secondary windings . . . . . . . . . . . . . . . . . . . . . . . . . . . . . . . | 10 500 to 16 500 ohms |
| Ignition voltage at spark plug: | |
| Idle . . . . . . . . . . . . . . . . . . . . . . . . . . . . . . . . . . . . . . . . . . . . . . | 8 to 14 kV |
| Peak . . . . . . . . . . . . . . . . . . . . . . . . . . . . . . . . . . . . . . . . . . . . . | 16 kV |

| Torque wrench setting | Nm | lbf ft |
|---|---|---|
| Ignition coil . . . . . . . . . . . . . . . . . . . . . . . . . . . . . . . . . . . . . . . . | 6 | 4 |

## 1 Ignition system - general information and precautions

### General information

The ignition system is integrated with the fuel injection system to form a combined engine management system under the control of the Powertrain control module (PCM) (see Chapter 4A for further information). The main ignition system components include the ignition switch, the battery, the crankshaft speed/position sensor, the camshaft position sensor, the ignition coil, and the spark plugs.

A Distributorless Ignition System (DIS) is fitted where the main functions of the conventional distributor are replaced by a computerised module within the Powertrain Control Module. The remote ignition coil unit combines a double-ended pair of coils - each time a coil receives an ignition signal, two sparks are produced, at each end of the secondary windings. One spark goes to a cylinder on compression stroke and the other goes to the corresponding cylinder on its exhaust stroke. The first will give the correct power stroke, but the second spark will have no effect (a 'wasted spark'), occurring as it does during exhaust conditions.

The information contained in this Chapter concentrates on the ignition-related components of the engine management system. Information covering the fuel, exhaust and emission control components can be found in Chapters 4A and 4B.

### Precautions

The following precautions must be observed, to prevent damage to the ignition system components and to reduce risk of personal injury.

a) Do not keep the ignition switched on for more than 10 seconds if the engine will not start.
b) Ensure that the ignition is switched off before disconnecting any of the ignition wiring.
c) Ensure that the ignition is switched off before connecting or disconnecting any ignition test equipment.
d) Do not earth the coil primary or secondary circuits.

⚠ **Warning: Voltages produced by an electronic ignition system are considerably higher than those produced by conventional ignition systems. Extreme care must be taken when working on the system with the ignition switched on. Persons with surgically-implanted cardiac pacemaker devices should keep well clear of the ignition circuits, components and test equipment.**

## 2 Ignition system - testing

1 If the engine either will not turn over at all, or only turns very slowly, check the battery and starter motor as described in Chapter 5A.
2 If the engine turns over at normal speed but will not start, check the HT circuit by connecting a timing light (following the manufacturer's instructions) and turning the engine over on the starter motor; if the light flashes, voltage is reaching the spark plugs, so these should be checked first. If the light does not flash, check the HT leads themselves using the information given in Chapter 1.
3 If there is still no spark, check the coil's primary and secondary winding resistance as described in Section 3. Renew the coil if faulty, but be careful to check carefully the wiring connections themselves before doing so, to ensure that the fault is not due to dirty or poorly-fastened connectors.
4 If these checks fail to reveal the cause of the problem the vehicle should be taken to a Ford dealer for testing. A wiring block connector is incorporated in the engine management circuit into which a special electronic diagnostic tester can be plugged. The tester will locate the fault quickly and simply, alleviating the need to test all the system components individually which is a time consuming operation that carries a high risk of damaging the PCM. If necessary, the system wiring and wiring connectors can be checked as described in Chapter 12.
5 If the engine runs but has an irregular misfire, check the low tension wiring on the ignition coil ensuring that all connections are clean and securely fastened.
6 Check that the coil HT leads are clean and dry. Check the leads themselves and the spark plugs (by substitution, if necessary).
7 Regular misfiring is probably due to a fault in the HT leads or spark plugs. Use a timing light (as described above) to check whether HT voltage is present at all leads.
8 If HT voltage is not present on any particular lead, the fault will be in that lead or in the ignition coil. If HT is present on all leads,

the fault will be in the spark plugs. Check and renew them if there is any doubt about their condition.
9 If no HT is present, check the coil, as the secondary windings may be breaking down under load.

## 3 Electronic ignition HT coil - removal, testing and refitting

### Removal

1 The ignition coil is bolted to the right-hand rear of the cylinder block, below the inlet manifold. Access to the coil is difficult, however if preferred, the vehicle may be raised and supported on axle stands (see "Jacking and Vehicle Support") for access from beneath.
2 Make sure the ignition is switched off, then disconnect the low tension wiring from the coil.
3 Identify the HT leads for position then carefully pull them from the terminals on the coil (see illustration).
4 Unscrew the mounting bolts and remove the ignition coil from the engine compartment.

### Testing

5 Using an ohmmeter, measure the resistances of the ignition coil's primary and secondary windings and compare with the information given in the Specifications. Renew the coil if necessary.

### Refitting

6 Refitting is a reversal of removal. Tighten the coil mounting bolts to the specified torque setting.

## 4 Crankshaft position sensor - removal and refitting

### Removal

1 The crankshaft position sensor is located on the front left-hand side of the engine cylinder block. For improved access, apply

the handbrake then jack up the front of the vehicle and support it on axle stands (see "Jacking and Vehicle Support").
2 Unscrew the mounting bolts and withdraw the sensor (see illustration).

### Refitting

3 Refitting is a reversal of removal.

## 5 Camshaft position sensor - removal and refitting

### Removal

1 The sensor is located on the rear of the timing chain cover. Access is limited, and if necessary the car may be raised and supported on axle stands (see "Jacking and Vehicle Support") for access from below.
2 Disconnect the wiring from the camshaft position sensor.
3 Unscrew the mounting bolt and withdraw the sensor from the timing chain cover.
4 Remove the O-ring seal.

### Refitting

5 Refitting is a reversal of removal but fit a new O-ring. Smear a little engine oil on the seal before fitting the sensor.

## 6 Ignition timing - checking and adjustment

Due to the nature of the ignition system, the ignition timing is constantly being monitored and adjusted by the engine management PCM, and nominal values cannot be given. Therefore, it is not possible for the home mechanic to check the ignition timing.

The only way the ignition timing can be checked is by using special electronic test equipment, connected to the engine management system diagnostic connector (refer to Chapter 4A). No adjustment of the ignition timing is possible. Should the ignition timing be incorrect, then a fault must be present in the engine management system.

**3.3 Ignition coil HT leads (A) and mounting bolts (B)**

**4.2 Crankshaft position sensor and mounting bolts**

# Chapter 6
# Clutch

## Contents

## Degrees of difficulty

| Easy, suitable for novice with little experience |  | Fairly easy, suitable for beginner with some experience |  | Fairly difficult, suitable for competent DIY mechanic |  | Difficult, suitable for experienced DIY mechanic | | Very difficult, suitable for expert DIY or professional | |

## Specifications

### General
Clutch type ............................................... Single dry plate, diaphragm spring, hydraulically-operated release

### Clutch disc
Diameter ................................................. 180 mm
Friction material thickness (new) ........................... 8.3 mm (approximate)

### Clutch pedal
Pedal travel:
37 kW engine (Germany and Austria) ...................... 123.0 ± 3.0 mm
44 kW engine ........................................ 125.0 ± 3.0 mm

### Torque wrench settings

| | Nm | lbf ft |
| --- | --- | --- |
| Clutch master cylinder .................................... | 14 | 10 |
| Clutch pedal bracket mounting nuts/bolts ..................... | 27 | 20 |
| Clutch slave cylinder pre-loading valve ...................... | 10 | 7 |
| Clutch slave cylinder ..................................... | 10 | 7 |
| Pressure plate to flywheel bolts ............................ | 30 | 22 |
| Slave cylinder bleed valve ................................ | 14 | 10 |

## 1  General information

The clutch consists of a friction plate, a pressure plate assembly, a release bearing and hydraulic slave cylinder, hydraulic master cylinder and a pedal assembly. With the exception of the pedal and master cylinder, the remaining components are contained in the large cast-aluminium alloy bellhousing, sandwiched between the engine and transmission.

The hydraulic master cylinder is located in the pedal bracket on the bulkhead, and the fluid reservoir is shared with the brake reservoir on the top of the brake master cylinder. Inside the reservoir each circuit has its own compartment, so that in the event of fluid loss in the clutch circuit the brake circuit remains fully operational.

The friction plate is fitted between the engine flywheel and the clutch pressure plate, and is allowed to slide on the transmission input shaft splines.

The pressure plate assembly is bolted to the engine flywheel. When the engine is running, drive is transmitted from the crankshaft, via the flywheel, to the friction plate (these components being clamped securely together by the pressure plate assembly) and from the friction plate to the transmission input shaft.

To interrupt the drive for gear changing, the spring pressure must be relaxed by the hydraulically-operated release mechanism. Depressing the clutch pedal operates the master cylinder, which in turn operates the slave cylinder and presses the release bearing against the pressure plate spring fingers. This causes the springs to deform and releases the clamping force on the pressure plate.

When the pedal is released, the diaphragm spring forces the pressure plate into contact with the friction linings on the clutch disc. The disc is now firmly sandwiched between the

**3.1a Hose clamp fitted to the clutch hydraulic pressure hose**

**3.1b Extract the clip . . .**

pressure plate and the flywheel, thus transmitting engine power to the transmission.

A pre-loading valve is fitted on the fluid inlet to the slave cylinder. This valve maintains a pressure of approximately 1.0 bar between the valve and the slave cylinder in order to keep the release bearing constantly pressed against the pressure plate. Upstream of the valve there is no pressure, in order to prevent vibrations being transmitted to the clutch pedal.

Wear of the friction material on the clutch disc is automatically compensated for by the operation of the hydraulic system. As the friction material on the disc wears, the pressure plate moves towards the flywheel causing the clutch diaphragm spring inner fingers to move outwards. When the clutch pedal is released, excess fluid is expelled through the master cylinder into the fluid reservoir.

## 2 Clutch master cylinder - removal and refitting

### Removal

1 Remove the filler cap from the brake master cylinder reservoir on top of the brake master cylinder, and syphon the hydraulic fluid from the reservoir until it is below the outlet to the clutch master cylinder. Alternatively, open the slave cylinder bleed screw, and gently pump the clutch pedal to expel the fluid through a plastic tube connected to the screw. Tighten the screw when all the fluid has been removed.

⚠ **Warning: Do not syphon the fluid by mouth, as it is poisonous; use a syringe or an old poultry baster**

2 Wipe clean the area around the master cylinder fluid stubs on the engine compartment bulkhead. Remove the clip and disconnect the hydraulic fluid supply hose from the master cylinder inlet stub. Plug the hose to prevent further loss of fluid.
3 Extract the clip from the quick release connection on the master cylinder, then remove the pressure hose and tie it to one side. Plug the end of the hose or tape over the end.
4 Unscrew and remove the pedal mounting nuts located behind the brake servo unit on the bulkhead.
5 Working inside the vehicle in the driver's footwell, reach up and extract the circlip from the inner end of the pin securing the clutch pedal to the master cylinder pushrod. Keep the pedal under slight pressure using a cable tie, then press out the pin to disconnect the pedal.
6 Unscrew the pedal mounting bracket nuts/bolts to allow the bracket to be moved away from the bulkhead when the master cylinder is removed.
7 Unscrew the clutch master cylinder mounting bolts on the left-hand side of the pedal bracket.
8 Pull the pedal mounting bracket away from the bulkhead sufficient to withdraw the clutch master cylinder downwards. Recover the sponge rubber padding from the outlets. Be prepared for some loss of hydraulic fluid by placing cloth rags on the floor.
9 Remove the master cylinder from inside the vehicle. If the master cylinder is faulty it must be renewed, as the manufacturers do not supply a repair kit.

### Refitting

10 Refitting is a reversal of removal. Apply a little grease to the clutch pushrod pin before inserting it, also check and adjust the clutch pedal travel as described in Section 6. Finally bleed the clutch hydraulic system as described in Section 5.

## 3 Clutch slave cylinder - removal and refitting

### Removal

1 Remove the transmission as described in Chapter 7. When disconnecting the clutch hydraulic pressure hose, fit a hose clamp to it to prevent loss of fluid, then extract the clip and disconnect the hose from the pre-loading valve **(see illustrations)**. Refit the clip while the hose is disconnected. Be prepared for some loss of fluid.
2 Remove the protective cap from the slave cylinder bleed screw, then unscrew and remove the bleed screw **(see illustrations)**.
3 Unscrew and remove the pre-loading valve from the slave cylinder inlet on the outside of the bellhousing **(see illustrations)**.

**3.1c . . . and disconnect the line from the pre-loading valve**

**3.1d View of the pre-loading valve with the engine removed from the car**

**3.2a Remove the protective cap . . .**

**3.2b . . . then unscrew and remove the bleed screw**

3.3a Unscrew the pre-loading valve . . .

3.3b . . . and remove it from the slave cylinder inlet

**4** Inside the bellhousing, unscrew and remove the mounting bolts, then withdraw the slave cylinder over the transmission input shaft **(see illustrations)**.

**5** With the slave cylinder removed, it is recommended that the transmission input shaft oil seal is renewed. Use a suitable tool to hook it out of the transmission casing and over the input shaft. Refer to Chapter 7 if necessary.

**6** Remove the release bearing from the slave cylinder by tapping the cylinder on the workbench or against a block of wood.

**7** If the slave cylinder is faulty it must be renewed, as the manufacturers do not supply repair kits.

### Refitting

**8** Locate the release bearing on the slave cylinder making sure it is correctly seated.

**9** Locate a new oil seal over the input shaft and into the transmission housing (refer to Chapter 7), then slide the slave cylinder onto the shaft.

**10** Insert the mounting bolts and tighten them progressively to the specified torque. As the bolts are tightened make sure that the oil seal enters the transmission housing correctly.

**11** Refit the pre-loading valve to the slave cylinder and tighten to the specified torque. *Caution: Do not exceed the torque wrench setting, otherwise the pre-loading valve may not function correctly.*

**12** Refit and tighten the bleed screw and fit the protective cap.

**13** Refit the transmission as described in Chapter 7.

**14** Refill the master cylinder reservoir with fresh fluid, then bleed the hydraulic system as described in Section 5.

## 4  Clutch hydraulic hoses - removal and refitting

*Caution: Hydraulic fluid can damage vehicle paintwork. Take the necessary precautions to prevent spillage of fluid.*

### Removal

**1** Remove the filler cap from the brake master cylinder reservoir on top of the master cylinder, and syphon the hydraulic fluid from the reservoir until it is below the outlet to the clutch master cylinder. Alternatively, open the slave cylinder bleed screw, and gently pump the clutch pedal to expel the fluid through a plastic tube connected to the screw. Tighten the screw when all the fluid has been removed.

**2** To remove the supply hose, remove the clips then disconnect the hose from the reservoir and master cylinder.

**3** To remove the pressure hose, first wipe all traces of dirt from the master cylinder and slave cylinder. Extract the clip from the quick release connections on the master cylinder and slave cylinder, then remove the hose.

### Refitting

**4** Refitting is a reversal of removal, but on completion bleed the hydraulic system as described in Section 5.

## 5  Clutch hydraulic system - bleeding

*Warning: Hydraulic fluid is poisonous - wash off immediately and thoroughly in the case of skin contact, and seek immediate medical advice if any fluid is swallowed or gets into the eyes. Certain types of hydraulic fluid are flammable, and may ignite when allowed into contact with hot components. When servicing any hydraulic system, it is safest to assume that the fluid is flammable, and to take precautions against the risk of fire. Hydraulic fluid is also an effective paint stripper, and will attack plastics - if any is spilt, it should be washed off immediately, using copious quantities of fresh water. Finally, it is hygroscopic (it absorbs moisture from the air) - old fluid may be contaminated and unfit for further use. When topping-up or renewing the fluid, always use the recommended type, and ensure that it comes from a freshly opened sealed container.*

**1** The correct operation of any hydraulic system is only possible after removing all air from the components and circuit. This is achieved by bleeding the system. Observe the following points:

a) *During the bleeding procedure, add only clean, unused hydraulic fluid of the recommended type. Never re-use fluid that has already been bled from the system. Ensure that sufficient fluid is available before starting work.*

b) *If there is any possibility of incorrect fluid being already in the system, the hydraulic circuit must be flushed completely with uncontaminated, correct fluid.*

c) *If hydraulic fluid has been lost from the system, or air has entered because of a leak, ensure that the fault is cured before continuing further.*

**2** The bleed screw is screwed into the slave cylinder extension which is positioned on the top of the transmission bellhousing. Access to the bleed screw is gained by removing the air cleaner assembly complete as described in Chapter 4A.

3.4a Unscrew the mounting bolts . . .

3.4b . . . and withdraw the slave cylinder over the transmission input shaft

3.4c The clutch slave cylinder on the bench, with the release bearing removed

**5.10 Bleeding the clutch hydraulic circuit**

3 First check that all the hydraulic hoses are in good condition and securely fitted to the master and slave cylinders. Clean any dirt from around the bleed screw.

4 Unscrew the brake master cylinder fluid reservoir cap, and top up the fluid level to the upper (MAX) level line, then refit the cap loosely. Remember to maintain the fluid level at least above the lower (MIN) level line throughout the procedure, or there is a risk of further air entering the system.

5 There are a number of one-man, do-it-yourself bleeding kits currently available from motor accessory shops. It is recommended that one of these kits is used whenever possible, as they greatly simplify the bleeding operation, and reduce the risk of expelled air and fluid being drawn back into the system. If such a kit is not available, the basic (two-man) method must be used, which is described in detail below.

6 If a kit is to be used, prepare the vehicle as described previously, and follow the kit manufacturer's instructions, as the procedure may vary slightly according to the type being used, however, generally they are as outlined below in the relevant sub-section.

### Bleeding - basic (two-man) method

7 Collect a clean glass jar, a suitable length of plastic or rubber tubing which is a tight fit over the bleed screw, and a ring spanner to fit the screw. The help of an assistant will also be required.

8 Remove the protective cap from the slave cylinder bleed screw. Fit the spanner and tube to the screw, place the other end of the tube in the jar, and pour in sufficient fluid to cover the end of the tube.

9 Ensure that the fluid level is maintained at least above the lower level line in the reservoir throughout the procedure.

10 Loosen the bleed screw half a turn, then have the assistant slowly depress and release the clutch pedal several times until fluid free of air bubbles emerges **(see illustration)**. On the final stroke have the assistant hold the pedal fully depressed. Note that the pedal must be fully depressed and fully released each time.

11 With the pedal held down, tighten the bleed screw and have the assistant fully

release the pedal slowly. Check the reservoir fluid level and top up if necessary, then check the operation of the pedal. After the initial free movement, increased pressure should be felt as the clutch pressure plate diaphragm spring is operated.

12 If the pedal feels spongy, air still remains in the hydraulic system and the bleeding operation must be repeated as described in the previous paragraphs.

13 With the hydraulic system bled, tighten the bleed screw securely then remove the tube and spanner and refit the dust cap. Do not overtighten the bleed screw.

### Bleeding - using a one-way valve kit

14 As the name implies, these kits consist of a length of tubing with a one-way valve fitted, to prevent expelled air and fluid being drawn back into the system. Some kits include a translucent container, which can be positioned so that the air bubbles can be more easily seen flowing from the end of the tube.

15 The kit is connected to the bleed screw, which is then opened. The user returns to the driver's seat, depresses the clutch pedal with a smooth, steady stroke, and slowly releases it. This is repeated until the expelled fluid is clear of air bubbles.

16 Note that these kits simplify work so much that it is easy to forget the clutch fluid reservoir level, so ensure that this is maintained at least above the lower level line at all times.

### Bleeding - using a pressure-bleeding kit

17 These kits are usually operated by the reservoir of pressurised air contained in the spare tyre. However, note that it will probably be necessary to reduce the pressure to a lower level than normal. Refer to the instructions supplied with the kit.

18 By connecting a pressurised, fluid-filled container to the brake/clutch fluid reservoir, bleeding can be carried out simply by opening the bleed screw and allowing the fluid to flow out until no more air bubbles can be seen in the expelled fluid.

19 This method has the advantage that the large reservoir of fluid provides an additional safeguard against air being drawn into the system during bleeding.

### All methods

20 When bleeding is complete, and correct pedal feel is restored, check that the bleed screw is securely tightened and wash off any spilt fluid. Refit the dust cap to the bleed screw.

21 Check the hydraulic fluid level in the master cylinder reservoir, and top-up if necessary.

22 Discard any hydraulic fluid that has been bled from the system, since it will not be fit for re-use.

### 6 Clutch pedal - removal, inspection, refitting and adjustment

### Removal

1 Disconnect the battery negative (earth) lead (see Chapter 5A).

2 Remove the steering column as described in Chapter 10.

3 Extract the clip and disconnect the accelerator cable from the top of the accelerator pedal. Remove the clip and remove the pedal.

4 Unscrew the bolts securing the clutch master cylinder to the pedal bracket.

5 Extract the clip from the left-hand end of the clutch pedal pushrod pin, then push the pushrod from the pedal to disconnect the pushrod.

6 Disconnect the wiring, then twist the stop lamp switch anticlockwise and remove it from the pedal bracket.

7 Disconnect the wiring, then twist the clutch pedal position switch anticlockwise and remove it from the pedal bracket.

8 Disconnect the brake vacuum servo/linkage pushrod from the brake pedal.

9 Move the bonnet pull cable from behind the heater duct.

10 Unscrew the pedal bracket mounting nuts from the left-hand side of the bracket. Note that the position of these nuts varies according to whether the model is right- or left-hand drive.

11 Unscrew the pedal bracket mounting nuts from the right-hand side of the bracket.

12 Unscrew the pedal bracket upper mounting bolts.

13 On left-hand drive models only, disconnect the heater duct from the heater.

14 Unhook the clutch pedal return spring from the pedal bracket.

15 Extract the clip from the right-hand end of the pedal pivot shaft.

16 Slide the pivot shaft to the left, then withdraw the brake pedal from the bracket.

17 Slide the pivot shaft out from the bracket and remove the spacer and clutch pedal.

18 If necessary, prise out the bushes from each side of the clutch pedal. Note that the bushes are different for the clutch and brake pedals.

### Inspection

19 Clean the bushes and pedal and inspect them for wear and damage. The bushes may be renewed separately, however if they are worn excessively, the pivot shaft must be checked and if necessary renewed as well.

20 Check the return spring and renew it if necessary.

### Refitting

21 Refitting is a reversal of removal, but apply multi-purpose grease to the pedal pivot shaft and bushes and make sure that the retaining

clips are fully engaged with their grooves. Tighten the mounting nuts and bolts to the specified torque. When refitting the brake stop lamp switch, first pull out the switch to its full extent, then depress the pedal and refit the switch. Slowly release the pedal, then reconnect the wiring.

## Adjustment

**22** Check that the clutch pedal operates freely and that there is no obstruction or excess matting on the floor. If the pedal is spongy, the hydraulic system must be bled to remove any air as described in Section 5.

**23** With the pedal fully released, measure the distance from the adjuster bolt on the bracket to the rubber stop located in the pedal. This distance is the pedal travel, and should be as given in the Specifications.

**24** If the pedal travel is not as given in the Specifications, adjust the position of the pedal stop screw after loosening the locknut. Tighten the locknut on completion. Note that if the pedal travel is excessive, the master cylinder will be damaged.

### 7  Clutch assembly - removal, inspection and refitting

⚠ **Warning: Dust created by clutch wear and deposited on the clutch components may contain asbestos, which is a health hazard. DO NOT blow it out with compressed air, or inhale any of it. DO NOT use petrol or petroleum-based solvents to clean off the dust. Brake system cleaner or methylated spirit should be used to flush the dust into a suitable receptacle. After the clutch components are wiped clean with rags, dispose of the contaminated rags and cleaner in a sealed, marked container.**
**Note:** *Although some friction materials may no longer contain asbestos, it is safest to* assume that they do, and to take precautions accordingly.

## Removal

**1** Unless the complete engine/transmission unit is to be removed from the car and separated for major overhaul (see Chapter 2B), the clutch can be reached by removing the transmission as described in Chapter 7.

**2** Before disturbing the clutch, use chalk or a marker pen to mark the relationship of the pressure plate assembly to the flywheel.

**3** Working in a diagonal sequence, slacken the pressure plate bolts by half a turn at a time, until spring pressure is released and the bolts can be unscrewed by hand. Hold the flywheel stationary using a suitable tool engaged with the starter ring gear teeth - a piece of metal as shown can be tightened to one of the bolt holes, or alternatively an assistant can use a wide-bladed screwdriver engaged with the teeth **(see illustrations)**.

**4** Prise the pressure plate assembly off its locating dowels, and collect the friction disc, noting which way round the disc is fitted.

## Inspection

**Note:** *Due to the amount of work necessary to remove and refit clutch components, it is usually considered good practice to renew the clutch friction disc, pressure plate assembly and release bearing as a matched set, even if only one of these is actually worn enough to require renewal. It is also worth considering the renewal of the clutch components on a preventive basis if the engine and/or transmission have been removed for some other reason.*

**5** When cleaning clutch components, read first the warning at the beginning of this Section. Remove dust using a clean, dry cloth, and working in a well-ventilated atmosphere.

**6** Check the friction disc linings for signs of wear, damage or oil contamination. If the friction material is cracked, burnt, scored or damaged, or if it is contaminated with oil or grease (shown by shiny black patches), the friction disc must be renewed. Check the depth of the rivets below the friction material surface. If any are at or near the surface of the friction material, then the friction disc must be renewed.

**7** If the friction material is still serviceable, check that the centre boss splines are unworn, that the torsion springs are in good condition and securely fastened, and that all the rivets are tight. If any wear or damage is found, the friction disc must be renewed.

**8** If the friction material is contaminated with oil, this must be due to an oil leak from the crankshaft oil seal, from the sump-to-cylinder block joint, or from the transmission input shaft. Renew the seal or repair the joint, as appropriate, as described in Chapter 2A or 7, before installing the new friction disc.

**9** Check the pressure plate assembly for obvious signs of wear or damage; shake it to check for loose rivets or worn or damaged fulcrum rings, and check that the drive straps securing the pressure plate to the cover do not show signs of overheating (such as a deep yellow or blue discoloration). If the diaphragm spring is worn or damaged, or if its pressure is in any way suspect, the pressure plate assembly should be renewed.

**10** Examine the machined bearing surfaces of the pressure plate and of the flywheel. They should be clean, completely flat, and free from scratches or scoring. If either is discoloured from excessive heat, or shows signs of cracks, it should be renewed - although minor damage of this nature can sometimes be polished away using emery paper.

**11** Check that the release bearing contact surface rotates smoothly and easily, with no sign of noise or roughness. Also check that the surface itself is smooth and unworn, with no signs of cracks, pitting or scoring. If there is any doubt about its condition, the bearing must be renewed.

**7.3a  Home-made tool for holding the flywheel stationary while loosening the clutch pressure plate bolts**

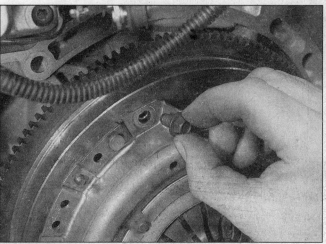

**7.3b  Unscrewing the bolts retaining the clutch pressure plate**

**7.13a 'Flywheel Side' marking on the friction disc hub**

**7.13b Using the centralising tool to hold the friction disc on the flywheel**

## Refitting

**12** On reassembly, ensure that the disc contact surfaces of the flywheel and pressure plate are completely clean, smooth, and free from oil or grease. Use solvent to remove any protective grease from new components.

**13** Fit the friction disc so that its spring hub assembly faces away from the flywheel. There may also be a marking showing which way round the plate is to be refitted. Depending on the type of centralising tool being used, the friction disc may be held in position at this stage **(see illustrations)**.

**14** Refit the pressure plate assembly, aligning the marks made on dismantling (if the original pressure plate is re-used), and locating the pressure plate on its locating dowels **(see illustration)**. Fit the pressure plate bolts, but tighten them only finger-tight, so that the friction disc can still be moved.

**15** The friction disc must now be centralised, so that when the transmission is refitted, its input shaft will pass through the splines at the centre of the friction disc.

**16** Centralisation can be achieved by passing a screwdriver or other long bar through the friction disc and into the hole in the crankshaft. The friction disc can then be moved around until it is centred on the crankshaft hole. Alternatively, a clutch-aligning tool (obtainable from most accessory shops) can be used to eliminate the guesswork. The normal type consists of a spigot bar with several different adapters, but a more recent type consists of a tool which clamps the friction disc to the pressure plate before locating the two items on the flywheel. A home-made aligning tool can be fabricated from a length of metal rod or wooden dowel which fits closely inside the crankshaft hole, and has insulating tape wound around it to match the diameter of the friction disc splined hole.

**17** When the friction disc is centralised, tighten the pressure plate bolts evenly and in a diagonal sequence to the specified torque setting **(see illustration)**.

**18** Apply a thin smear of molybdenum disulphide grease to the splines of the friction

disc and the transmission input shaft.
*Caution: Do not apply too much grease as there is a risk that it will contaminate the friction disc material.*

**19** Refit the transmission as described in Chapter 7.

## 8 Clutch release bearing - removal, inspection and refitting

### Removal

**1** For access to the clutch release bearing, the transmission must be removed as described in Chapter 7.

**2** Withdraw the release bearing from the slave cylinder inside the transmission bellhousing. If necessary, use a screwdriver to carefully prise out the bearing **(see illustration)**.

### Inspection

**3** Note that it is often considered worthwhile to renew the release bearing as a matter of course regardless of its condition, considering the amount of work necessary to access it. Check that the contact surface rotates smoothly and easily, with no sign of noise or roughness, and that the surface itself is smooth and unworn, with no signs of cracks, pitting or scoring. If there is any doubt about its condition, the bearing must be renewed.

### Refitting

**4** Align the tag with the cut-out in the slave cylinder, then slide the release bearing fully into position.

**5** Refit the transmission with reference to Chapter 7.

**7.14 Refitting the pressure plate assembly onto the friction disc**

**7.17 Tightening the clutch pressure plate bolts**

**8.2 Removing the release bearing from the clutch slave cylinder**

# Chapter 7
# Manual transmission

## Contents

## Degrees of difficulty

| Easy, suitable for novice with little experience |  | Fairly easy, suitable for beginner with some experience |  | Fairly difficult, suitable for competent DIY mechanic |  | Difficult, suitable for experienced DIY mechanic |  | Very difficult, suitable for expert DIY or professional | |
|---|---|---|---|---|---|---|---|---|---|

## Specifications

### General

| | |
|---|---|
| Type | Manual, five forward speeds and reverse. Synchromesh on all forward speeds |
| Designation | IB5 |

**Note:** *The transmission code is stamped on a plate attached to the transmission unit.*

### Gear set ratio

| | |
|---|---|
| 1st | 3.15 to 1 |
| 2nd | 1.93 to 1 |
| 3rd | 1.28 to 1 |
| 4th | 0.95 to 1 |
| 5th | 0.76 to 1 |
| Reverse | 3.62 to 1 |

### Final drive ratio

| | |
|---|---|
| 1.3 Endura-E engine (37 kW) | 4.06 to 1 |
| 1.3 Endura-E engine (44 kW) | 3.59 to 1 |

*Note that the 37 kW engine is only marketed in Germany and Austria.*

### Lubrication

| | |
|---|---|
| Capacity | 2.8 litres |
| Recommended oil | See "Lubricants and fluids" |

### Torque wrench settings

| | Nm | lbf ft |
|---|---|---|
| Front suspension upper mounting nut | 50 | 37 |
| Gearchange clamp bolt | 23 | 17 |
| Gearchange mounting to underbody | 24 | 18 |
| Gearchange stabiliser bar to transmission | 55 | 41 |
| Gearchange stabiliser bar to lever housing | 12 | 9 |
| Left-hand mounting to transmission | 32 | 24 |
| Left-hand mounting to battery support bracket | 68 | 50 |
| Lower suspension arm to hub carrier clamp bolt | 51 | 38 |
| Multi-function switch | 6 | 4 |
| Rear roll restrictor centre bolt | 120 | 89 |
| Right-hand engine mounting: | | |
|   Nuts | 63 | 47 |
|   Bolt | 50 | 37 |
| Starter motor | 35 | 26 |
| Transmission filler/level plug | 35 | 26 |
| Transmission to engine bolts | 44 | 32 |

2.3 Unscrewing the oil filler/level plug from the front of the transmission

2.4 Using an Allen key to check that the oil level is between 10 mm and 15 mm below the bottom edge of the filler/level plug hole

# 1 General information

The transmission is contained in a cast-aluminium alloy casing bolted to the engine's left-hand end, and consists of the gearbox and final drive differential. The transmission unit type is stamped on a plate attached to the transmission.

Drive is transmitted from the crankshaft via the clutch to the input shaft, which has a splined extension to accept the clutch friction plate, and rotates in sealed ball-bearings. From the input shaft, drive is transmitted to the output shaft, which rotates in a roller bearing at its left-hand end, and a taper roller bearing at its right-hand end. From the output shaft, the drive is transmitted to the differential crownwheel, which rotates with the differential and planetary gears, thus driving the sun gears and driveshafts. The rotation of the planetary gears on their shaft allows the inner roadwheel to rotate at a slower speed than the outer roadwheel when the car is cornering.

The input and output shafts are arranged side by side, parallel to the crankshaft and driveshafts, so that their gear pinion teeth are in constant mesh. In the neutral position, the output shaft gear pinions rotate freely, so that drive cannot be transmitted to the crownwheel.

Gear selection is via a floor-mounted lever and selector rod mechanism.

The transmission selector rod causes the appropriate selector fork to move its respective synchro-sleeve along the output shaft, to lock the gear pinion to the synchro-hub. Since the synchro-hubs are splined to the output shaft, this locks the pinion to the shaft, so that drive can be transmitted. To ensure that gear-changing can be made quickly and quietly, a synchro-mesh system is fitted to all forward gears, consisting of baulk rings and spring-loaded fingers, as well as the gear pinions and synchro-hubs. The synchro-mesh cones are formed on the mating faces of the baulk rings and gear pinions.

# 2 Oil level - checking

1 Note that there is no oil drain plug fitted to the transmission as it is 'filled for life'.
2 Park the car on level ground, switch off the ignition and apply the handbrake firmly. For improved access, jack up the front of the car

and support it securely on axle stands (see "Jacking and Vehicle Support").
3 Remove all traces of dirt then use an Allen key to unscrew the filler/level plug from the front face of the transmission. Note it is the plug furthest from the engine - do not confuse it with the blanking plug near the bellhousing (see illustration).
4 The level must be between 5 mm and 10 mm below the bottom edge of the filler/level plug hole (use a cranked tool such as an Allen key to check the level). When the level is correct, refit the filler/level plug and tighten it to the specified torque (see illustration).
5 Lower the car to the ground.

# 3 Gearchange linkage - adjustment

1 Firmly apply the handbrake, then jack up the front of the vehicle and support it securely on axle stands (see "Jacking and Vehicle Support"). Engage 4th gear.
2 Unbolt the heatshield(s) from the underbody for access to the bottom of the gear lever. It is not necessary to completely remove the heatshields, only pull down one side of them (see illustration).
3 Loosen the clamp bolt and disconnect the gearchange rod from the transmission selector shaft.
4 Confirm that the selector shaft is in 4th as follows. Slide the selector shaft back and forth to find its central position, then turn the selector shaft to the right and left to find the central position in the transverse plane. Hold the selector shaft in the centralised position, then insert a suitable rod (or punch) into the hole in the selector shaft in the transmission, and move it as far forwards as possible. This is the 4th gear position.
5 Locate the gearchange rod on the selector shaft, then have an assistant position the gear lever approximately in the 4th position.
6 Using a 9 mm drill bit inserted through the special hole in the bottom cover of the gear lever housing, lock the gear lever in 4th position. It will be necessary for the assistant to move the gear lever slightly until the drill locates correctly (see illustrations).

3.2 Unscrew the special nuts in order to bend down the underbody heatshields

3.6a Cross-section showing 9 mm drill location in gear lever

3.6b Inserting the 9 mm drill bit through the special hole in the bottom cover

**7** With the gearchange rod and gear lever in 4th, tighten the clamp bolt to the specified torque.

**8** Check the adjustment, by moving the gear lever in all positions.

**9** Refit the heatshields, then lower the car to the ground.

## 4 Gearchange linkage and lever - removal, overhaul and refitting

### Removal

**1** Working inside the vehicle carefully unscrew the knob from the top of the gear lever, then lift the gaiter from the floor (see illustration).

**2** Remove the inner gaiter over the gear lever.

**3** Apply the handbrake, then jack up the front of the vehicle and support it on axle stands (see "Jacking and Vehicle Support").

**4** The front exhaust system rubber mountings must now be unhooked, however it is important not to bend the exhaust flexible section through an excessive angle. Support the section with a splint made from card, plastic or thin metal wrapped around it and secured with jubilee clips. With the splint in place, unhook the rubber mountings, then support the exhaust on an axle stand.

**5** Unbolt the front heatshield from the underbody for access to the bottom of the gear lever.

**6** Unscrew the bolt securing the gearchange stabiliser rod to the transmission and tie the rod to one side (see illustration). Note that the washer is located next to the transmission.

**7** Mark the position of the gearchange rod clamp on the transmission selector shaft, then unscrew and remove the clamp bolt and disconnect the gearchange rod (see illustrations).

**8** Unscrew the gear lever support bracket mounting bolts on the underbody, and withdraw the gearchange linkage from under the car.

### Overhaul

**9** Unbolt the stabiliser rod from the gear lever housing.

**4.1 Gearchange linkage and lever**

| | | | |
|---|---|---|---|
| 1 Assembly | 7 Bolt | 11 Boot | 18 Boot retainer |
| 2 Gear lever | 8 Gearchange rod | 12 Gearchange rod | 19 Boot |
| 3 Bearing | clamp bolt | 13 Stabiliser bar | 20 Gaiter |
| 4 Support | 9 Stabiliser bar | 14 Bush | 21 Screw |
| bracket | pivot bolt and | 15 Washer | 22 Knob |
| 5 Housing | washer | 16 Nut | 23 Clamp |
| 6 Bolt | 10 Bush | 17 Insert | 24 Screw |

**4.6 Unscrewing the bolt securing the gearchange stabiliser rod to the transmission**

**4.7a Mark the position of the gearchange rod clamp on the transmission selector shaft**

**4.7b Unscrew and remove the clamp bolt and disconnect the gearchange rod**

**5.7  Prising the oil seal from the transmission**

**5.9  Locating a new oil seal on the transmission aperture**

10  Withdraw the noise damping pad over the gear lever, and remove the support bracket from the rear of the housing.

11  Using a screwdriver carefully press out the locking lugs, then withdraw the gear lever from the top of the housing.

12  Mount the inverted gear lever in a vice, then lever off the mounting sleeve using two screwdrivers.

13  Remove the rubber boot from the gearchange rod, then lever off the housing cover and remove the rod.

14  Clean all components and examine them for wear and damage. Obtain new items as necessary.

15  If necessary the bush in the stabiliser rod can be removed by pressing it out using suitable diameter metal tubes and a vice. Press in the new bush using the same method.

16  Reassemble the linkage using a reversal of dismantling, but apply a little grease to the bearing surfaces.

### Refitting

17  Refitting is a reversal of removal, but tighten all nuts and bolts to the specified torque, and adjust the linkage as described in Section 3.

---

## 5  Oil seals -
### renewal

1  Oil leaks frequently occur due to wear or deterioration of the differential side gear seals and/or the transmission selector shaft oil seal and speedometer drive pinion O-ring. Renewal of these seals is relatively easy, since the repairs can be performed without removing the transmission from the vehicle, however if the input shaft oil seal requires renewal the transmission must be removed.

### Differential side gear oil seals

*Caution: If both driveshafts are removed at the same time during the following procedure, the differential gears must be retained in position with a suitable doweled rod (refer to Chapter 8).*

2  The differential side gear oil seals are located at the sides of the transmission,

where the driveshafts enter the transmission. If leakage at the seal is suspected, raise the vehicle and support it securely on axle stands (see *"Jacking and Vehicle Support"*). If the seal is leaking, oil will be found on the side of the transmission below the driveshaft.

3  Unscrew the relevant front suspension upper mounting locknut five turns, while using an Allen key to hold the shock absorber piston rod stationary. This is necessary to prevent damage to the upper mounting when disconnecting the driveshaft.

4  The front suspension lower arm must now be disconnected from the hub carrier. To do this, unscrew the nut from the clamp bolt, drive out the bolt with a soft-metal drift, and carefully lever the lower arm down from the hub carrier. Note that the head of the clamp bolt faces the rear of the car.

5  Insert a lever between the inner driveshaft joint and the transmission housing, positioning a thin piece of wood between the lever and housing to protect it. Carefully lever the driveshaft inner joint out of the differential, taking care not to damage the transmission housing. Position a container beneath the transmission to collect the spilt oil, and tie the driveshaft to one side or support it on an axle stand.

*Caution: The inner driveshaft joint must not be bent more than 18° and the outer joint by more than 45°.*

6  Wipe clean the old oil seal and note its fitted depth below the casing edge. This is necessary to determine the correct fitted position of the new oil seal. The fitted depth will be approximately 5 mm.

**5.10  Driving the new oil seal into the transmission casing. Note the adhesive tape to indicate the fitting depth**

7  Using a large screwdriver or lever, carefully prise the oil seal out of the transmission casing, taking care not to damage the casing **(see illustration)**. If the oil seal is reluctant to move, it is sometimes helpful to carefully drive it *into* the transmission a little way, applying the force at one point only. This will have the effect of swivelling the seal out of the casing, and it can then be pulled out. If the oil seal is particularly difficult to remove, an oil seal removal tool may be obtained from a garage or accessory shop.

8  Wipe clean the oil seal seating in the transmission casing.

9  Dip the new oil seal in clean oil, then press it a little way into the casing by hand, making sure that it is square to its seating with its closed end facing outwards **(see illustration)**.

10  Using suitable tubing or a large socket, carefully drive the oil seal fully into the casing up to its previously-noted fitted depth **(see illustration)**. Wipe clean the oil seal.

**HAYNES HINT**  *Wrap adhesive tape around the socket to indicate the depth to fit the oil seal*

11  If necessary, renew the driveshaft retaining circlip, then carefully insert the driveshaft into the differential gear splines and push in until the retaining circlip is felt to engage. Ford supply a fitting sleeve with new oil seals, which should be located in the oil seal before fitting the driveshaft. With the driveshaft fully inserted, the fitting sleeve can be removed.

12  Refit the front suspension lower arm to the hub carrier, insert the clamp bolt, and tighten to the specified torque. Make sure the clamp bolt is inserted with its head facing the rear of the car.

13  Tighten the front suspension upper mounting locknut to the specified torque.

14  Lower the vehicle to the ground. Check and top-up the transmission oil level if necessary, with reference to Section 2 and Chapter 1.

### Transmission selector shaft oil seal

15  Apply the handbrake, then jack up the front of the vehicle and support it on axle stands (see *"Jacking and Vehicle Support"*).

16  Mark the position of the gearchange rod clamp on the transmission selector shaft.

17  Unscrew and remove the clamp bolt and disconnect the gearchange rod.

18  Remove the rubber boot for access to the oil seal.

19  Using a suitable tool or grips, pull the oil seal out of the transmission casing. Ford technicians use a slide hammer, with an end fitting which locates over the oil seal extension. In the absence of this tool, if the oil seal is particularly tight, drill one or two small holes in the oil seal, and screw in self-tapping screws. The oil seal can then be removed from the casing by pulling on the screws.

**20** Wipe clean the oil seal seating in the transmission.
**21** Dip the new oil seal in clean oil, then press it a little way into the casing by hand, making sure that it is square to its seating and with its closed end facing outwards.
**22** Using suitable tubing or a large socket, carefully drive the oil seal fully into the casing.
**23** Locate the rubber boot over the selector shaft.
**24** The gearchange linkage rod can now be reconnected and adjusted using the procedure described in Section 3.

### Speedometer drive pinion oil seal
**25** The procedure is covered in Section 7.

### Input shaft oil seal (transmission removed)
**26** Remove the clutch slave cylinder from the transmission as described in Chapter 6.
**27** Hook out the oil seal using a suitable tool, taking care not to damage the input shaft. If it is tight, drill one or two small holes in the oil seal, and screw in self-tapping screws. The oil seal can then be removed from the casing by pulling on the screws.
**28** Wipe clean the oil seal seating in the transmission.
**29** Dip the new oil seal in clean oil, then locate it over the input shaft and press it a little way into the casing by hand, making sure that it is square to its seating and with its closed end facing outwards.
**30** Locate the clutch slave cylinder over the input shaft and refit it with reference to Chapter 6. The action of tightening the mounting bolts evenly, presses the oil seal into the transmission casing.

## 6 Reversing light switch and multi-function switch - testing, removal and refitting

### Reversing light switch (1999-on models)

#### Testing
**1** The reversing light circuit is controlled by a plunger-type switch that is screwed into the front of the transmission casing, near the bellhousing. If a fault develops in the circuit, first ensure that the circuit fuse has not blown.
**2** To test the switch, disconnect the wiring connector, and use a multimeter (set to the resistance function) or a battery-and-bulb test circuit to check that there is continuity between the switch terminals only when reverse gear is selected. If this is not the case, and there are no obvious breaks or other damage to the wires, the switch is faulty, and must be renewed.

#### Removal
**3** Apply the handbrake, then jack up the front of the vehicle and support it on axle stands (see *"Jacking and Vehicle Support"*).

**6.16 When refitting the multi-function switch, insert a 4.0 mm diameter drift (1) through the hole, and tap lightly into position with a hammer (2), then insert the bolts (3)**

**4** Disconnect the wiring from the reversing light switch.
**5** Unscrew the switch from the front of the transmission.

#### Refitting
**6** Clean the location in the transmission, and the threads of the switch.
**7** Insert the switch and tighten securely.
**8** Reconnect the wiring.
**9** Check and top-up the transmission oil level if necessary, with reference to Section 2 and Chapter 1.
**10** Lower the vehicle to the ground.

### Multi-function switch (pre-1999 models)

#### Testing
**11** The multi-function switch is located on the left-hand front of the transmission, and is incorporated in the engine management system. Refer to Chapter 4A for information on fault codes. The switch locates on the end of the auxiliary selector shaft.

#### Removal
**12** Apply the handbrake, then jack up the front of the vehicle and support it on axle stands (see *"Jacking and Vehicle Support"*).
**13** Disconnect the wiring from the multi-function switch.
**14** Select 4th gear, then unscrew the switch mounting bolts and slightly lift it.

**7.3 Vehicle speed sensor on the rear of the transmission**

**15** Insert a 4.0 diameter drift or metal dowel through the hole in the shaft, then select 3rd gear and remove the multi-function switch from the transmission.

#### Refitting
**16** Select 4th gear, and insert the 4.0 mm diameter drift/dowel in the hole in the shaft. Carefully tap the drift with a light hammer until the switch snaps into place in the auxiliary selector shaft. Insert the bolts and tighten to the specified torque **(see illustration)**.
**18** Reconnect the wiring to the switch.
**19** Lower the vehicle to the ground.

## 7 Speedometer drive - removal and refitting

### Removal
**1** Access to the speedometer drive may be gained from the top by first removing the air cleaner assembly and duct (see Chapter 4A), or from beneath by raising the front of the vehicle and supporting on axle stands (see *"Jacking and Vehicle Support"*).
**2** Undo the retaining collar, and withdraw the speedometer cable from the vehicle speed sensor on the top, rear face of the transmission. Use two spanners to loosen the nut - one to counterhold the sensor, and the other to unscrew the cable nut.
**3** Disconnect the wiring from the vehicle speed sensor, then unscrew the sensor from the top of the drive pinion **(see illustration)**.
**4** Grip the drive pinion retaining roll pin with self-locking grips or pliers, and withdraw it from the drive pinion housing.
**5** Pull the drive pinion and bearing out of the housing, but take care not to tilt it, because the pinion and bearing are not secured and can easily be separated if the pinion is snagged **(see illustration)**.
**6** Using a small screwdriver, prise the O-ring from the groove in the bearing. Obtain a new O-ring for reassembly.
**7** Wipe clean the drive pinion and bearing, also the seating bore in the transmission casing.

**7.5 Speedometer drive pinion (A), pinion bearing (B) and drive cable (C)**

**7.8 Insert the speedometer drive pinion/bearing (A) and secure with a new retaining pin (B)**

### Refitting

**8** Refitting is a reversal of the removal procedure, but lightly oil the new O-ring before inserting the assembly in the transmission casing. Drive in the retaining roll pin using a hammer **(see illustration)**.

## 8  Manual transmission - removal and refitting

### Removal

**1** The manual transmission is removed downwards from the engine compartment, after disconnecting it from the engine. Due to the weight of the unit, it will be necessary to have a suitable method of supporting the transmission as it is lowered during removal and subsequently raised during its refitting. A trolley jack fitted with a suitable saddle to support the transmission as it is removed will be ideal, but failing this, an engine lift hoist and sling will suffice. The weight of the engine will also need to be supported whilst the transmission is detached from it - an engine support bar fitted in the front wing drain channel each side is ideal for this purpose, but care must be taken not to damage the wings or paintwork. If this type of tool is not available, the engine can be supported by blocks or a second jack from underneath.

**2** Apply the handbrake, then jack up the front of the vehicle and support it on axle stands (see *"Jacking and Vehicle Support"*).

**3** Remove the air cleaner assembly and air inlet duct as described in Chapter 4A.

**4** Disconnect and remove the battery as described in Chapter 5A.

**5** Disconnect the wiring for the vehicle speed sensor at the connector on the right-hand rear of the engine.

**6** Unscrew the bolt and detach the earth lead from the top of the transmission.

**7** Fit a hose clamp to the clutch hydraulic hose on the transmission, then extract the clip and disconnect the hose from the pre-loading valve. Be prepared for some loss of fluid. Refit the clip while the hose is disconnected, and detach the hose from the support on the transmission.

**8** Unscrew the left-hand front suspension upper mounting locknut five turns, while using an Allen key to hold the shock absorber piston rod stationary **(see illustration)**. This is necessary to prevent damage to the upper mounting when disconnecting the driveshaft.

**9** The left-hand front suspension lower arm must now be disconnected from the hub carrier. To do this, unscrew the nut from the clamp bolt, drive out the bolt with a soft-metal drift, and carefully lever the lower arm down from the hub carrier. Note that the head of the clamp bolt faces the rear of the car.

**10** Where necessary unbolt the heat shield from over the exhaust manifold.

**11** Disconnect the wiring from the multi-function switch (pre-1999 models) or the reversing light switch (1999-on models) **(see illustration)**. Also pull the earth lead from the spade connector on the transmission.

**12** Carefully cut and remove the inner (large) clips from the driveshaft inner gaiters on both driveshafts **(see illustration)**.

**13** Carefully pull out the left- and right-hand driveshaft tripodes from the inner joints and tie the driveshafts (together with the strut/hub carriers) to one side away from the area beneath the engine compartment. If necessary, scoop out the grease from the joints and fill with new grease on refitting. Protect the joints and housings by tying plastic bags over them **(see illustrations)**.

*Caution: The inner driveshaft joint must not be bent more than 18° and the outer joint by more than 45°.*

**14** Where necessary, undo the nuts and remove the exhaust heatshield from the underbody.

**15** Unscrew the bolt and detach the gear-change stabiliser bar from the rear of the trans-

**8.8 Loosen the left-hand front suspension upper mounting locknut five turns**

**8.11 Disconnecting the wiring from the multi-function switch**

**8.12 Cut free the driveshaft inner gaiter clips**

**8.13a Pull out the driveshaft tripodes from the inner joints on both sides**

**8.13b Protect the driveshaft tripodes . . .**

**8.13c . . . and housings by tying plastic bags over them**

**8.16 Unscrew the collar nut and disconnect the speedometer cable from the speed transmitter**

**8.18 Removing the rear roll restrictor bracket from the transmission**

**8.25 Withdrawing the transmission from the engine**

mission. At the same time, mark the position of the gearchange linkage/universal joint on the transmission selector rod, then unscrew and remove the clamp bolt and slide the linkage from the selector rod. Support the stabiliser bar and gearchange linkage to one side away from the area beneath the engine compartment.

**16** Unscrew the collar nut and disconnect the speedometer cable from the rear of the transmission **(see illustration)**.

**17** Support the weight of the engine using one of the methods described in paragraph 1.

**18** Unscrew and remove the centre bolt from the engine rear roll restrictor (mounting), then unbolt the mounting brackets from the transmission and underbody **(see illustration)**.

**19** Unbolt the starter motor from the engine/transmission. Tie the starter motor to one side, or alternatively disconnect the wiring and completely remove it.

**20** Unscrew the nuts securing the left-hand engine/transmission mounting bracket to the battery support bracket. Unscrew the bolts and remove the mounting bracket from the transmission.

**21** Pull the wiring cable supports from the top of the right-hand engine mounting, then unscrew the single bolt and two nuts, and remove the engine mounting upper bracket.

**22** Carefully lower the engine/transmission until there is sufficient room to allow the transmission to be removed from the engine.

**23** Unscrew and remove the two upper bolts securing the transmission to the engine.

**24** Make sure that the transmission is supported adequately, then unscrew the remaining bolts securing the transmission to the engine.

**25** With the help of an assistant withdraw the transmission directly from the engine until the input shaft is clear of the clutch pressure plate assembly, then lower it to the ground and remove from under the car **(see illustration)**.

## Refitting

**26** Refitting is a reversal of removal, but note the following additional points:

a) *Make sure that all mating faces are clean.*
b) *Apply a smear of high-melting-point grease to the splines of the transmission input shaft. Do not apply too much, otherwise there is the possibility of the grease contaminating the clutch friction disc.*
c) *Ensure that the engine adapter plate is correctly seated on the locating dowels on the engine.*
d) *When raising the transmission, guide the location pin into the battery support bracket before refitting the mounting nuts.*
e) *When reconnecting the driveshafts to the inner joints, pack each joint with 100 grams of CV joint grease before refitting the gaiters. New clips must be fitted. The driveshaft tripodes must be fully inserted into their joints, then pulled out 20 mm before tightening the clips. Any trapped air must be released first by lifting the gaiter lips with a screwdriver. Ford technicians use a special tool to squeeze the clips tight, however if this tool is not available, the clips can be carefully tightened using a pair of pincers.*
f) *Refit the engine mountings with reference to Chapter 2A.*
g) *Check and if necessary adjust the gearchange as described in Section 3.*
h) *Check and if necessary top up the transmission oil level with reference to Section 2 and Chapter 1.*
i) *Top up and bleed the clutch hydraulic system as described in "Weekly checks" and Chapter 6.*
j) *Tighten all nuts and bolts to the specified torque setting.*

**9  Manual transmission overhaul -** general information

**1** Overhauling a manual transmission unit is a difficult and involved job for the DIY home mechanic. In addition to dismantling and reassembling many small parts, clearances must be precisely measured and, if necessary, changed by selecting shims and spacers. Internal transmission components are also often difficult to obtain, and in many instances, extremely expensive. Because of this, if the transmission develops a fault or becomes noisy, the best course of action is to have the unit overhauled by a specialist repairer, or to obtain an exchange reconditioned unit.

**2** Nevertheless, it is not impossible for the more experienced mechanic to overhaul the transmission, provided the special tools are available, and the job is done in a deliberate step-by-step manner, so that nothing is overlooked.

**3** The tools necessary for an overhaul include internal and external circlip pliers, bearing pullers, a slide hammer, a set of pin punches, a dial test indicator, and possibly a hydraulic press. In addition, a large, sturdy workbench and a vice will be required.

**4** During dismantling of the transmission, make careful notes of how each component is fitted, to make reassembly easier and more accurate.

**5** Before dismantling the transmission, it will help if you have some idea what area is malfunctioning. Certain problems can be closely related to specific areas in the transmission, which can make component examination and replacement easier. Refer to the *"Fault finding"* Section at the rear of this manual for more information.

# Chapter 8
# Driveshafts

## Contents

## Degrees of difficulty

| Easy, suitable for novice with little experience  | Fairly easy, suitable for beginner with some experience  | Fairly difficult, suitable for competent DIY mechanic  | Difficult, suitable for experienced DIY mechanic  | Very difficult, suitable for expert DIY or professional 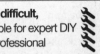 |

## Specifications

### General
Driveshaft type .......................................... Solid steel shafts with inner and outer constant velocity (CV) joints, both outer joints are of the ball-and-cage type and the inner joints of the tripode type.

### Lubricant
Type/specification ....................................... Ford grease specification WSD-M1C230-A (supplied in sachets with gaiter kits)

Quantity (per joint):
Inner joint .............................................. 100 g
Outer joint .............................................. 40 g

### Torque wrench settings

| | Nm | lbf ft |
|---|---|---|
| Front hub nut | 270 | 200 |
| Front suspension strut upper mounting nut | 50 | 37 |
| Lower suspension arm to hub carrier clamp bolt | 51 | 38 |
| Roadwheel nuts | 85 | 63 |
| Steering track-rod end to hub carrier | 37 | 27 |

## 1  General information

Drive is transmitted from the differential to the front wheels by means of two, unequal-length driveshafts.

Each driveshaft is fitted with an inner and outer constant velocity (CV) joint. The inner constant velocity joint is of the tripode type and the outer joint is of the ball-and-cage type. Each outer joint is splined to engage with the wheel hub, and is threaded so that it can be fastened to the hub by a large nut. The inner joint is also splined to engage with the differential sunwheel.

## 2  Driveshaft - removal and refitting

### Removal

**Note:** *A new front hub nut and inner retaining circlip will be required on refitting. Also, the*

*driveshaft outer joint splines may be a tight fit in the hub and it is possible that a puller/extractor will be required to draw the hub assembly off the driveshaft during removal.*
**Caution: If both driveshafts are removed at the same time during the following procedure, the differential gears must be retained in position with a suitable doweled rod inserted from one side. If this precaution is not taken, it is possible for the differential gears to move out of position and drop into the bottom of the transmission.**

1 Remove the relevant wheel trim, or the wheel centre plate (alloy wheels) for access to the front hub nut.
2 Ensure that the handbrake is applied, then relieve the staking on the front hub nut, using a suitable punch. Slacken the hub nut using a socket and extension bar. **Do not** remove the hub nut at this stage.
**Caution: Take care, as the hub nut is tightened to a very high torque.**
3 Working in the engine compartment, unscrew the relevant front suspension upper mounting locknut five turns, while using an Allen key to hold the shock absorber piston rod stationary **(see illustration)**. This is

necessary to prevent damage to the upper mounting when disconnecting the driveshaft.
4 Loosen the relevant front wheel nuts, then jack up the front of the vehicle, and support securely on axle stands (see *"Jacking and Vehicle Support"*). Remove the roadwheel.
5 Have to hand a suitable plug that can be quickly inserted into the transmission oil seal when the driveshaft is removed. Position a container beneath the transmission to catch any spilt oil.

**2.3 Loosen the left-hand front suspension upper mounting locknut five turns**

**2.6 Unscrew the clamp nut and bolt securing the hub carrier to the lower arm balljoint**

**2.9 Levering the driveshaft inner joint out of the differential**

**2.11 Removing the circlip from the left-hand driveshaft inner joint**

**6** The front suspension lower arm must now be disconnected from the hub carrier. To do this, unscrew the nut from the clamp bolt **(see illustration)**, drive out the bolt with a soft-metal drift, and carefully lever the lower arm down from the hub carrier. Note that the head of the clamp bolt faces the rear of the car.

**7** Unscrew the hub nut and remove the washer.

**8** The hub must now be freed from the end of the driveshaft. It should be possible to pull the hub off the driveshaft, but if the end of the driveshaft is tight in the hub, temporarily refit the hub nut to protect the driveshaft threads, then tap the end of the driveshaft with a soft-faced hammer, or use a suitable puller to free it. After removing the driveshaft from the hub, support it on an axle stand or tie it to the coil spring with wire or string.

**Caution: The inner driveshaft joint must not be bent more than 18° and the outer joint by more than 45°.**

**9** Insert a lever between the inner driveshaft joint and the transmission housing, positioning a thin piece of wood between the lever and housing to protect it. Carefully lever the driveshaft inner joint out of the differential, taking great care not to damage the transmission housing or to damage the oil seal **(see illustration)**. Manoeuvre the driveshaft out of position, ensuring that the constant velocity joints are not placed under excessive strain, and remove the driveshaft from underneath the vehicle. Whilst the driveshaft is removed, plug the differential aperture to prevent entry of dust and dirt.

### Refitting

**10** Before refitting the driveshaft, examine the driveshaft oil seal in the transmission for signs of damage or deterioration and, if necessary, renew it, referring to Chapter 7 for further information.

**11** Remove the circlip from the end of the driveshaft inner joint splines and discard it. Fit a new circlip, making sure it is correctly located in the groove **(see illustration)**.

**12** Thoroughly clean the driveshaft splines, and the apertures in the transmission and hub assembly. Apply a thin film of grease to the oil seal lips, and to the driveshaft splines and shoulders. Check that all gaiter clips are securely fastened.

**13** Offer up the driveshaft, and locate the joint splines with those of the differential sun gear, taking great care not to damage the oil seal. Push the joint fully into position, then check that the circlip is correctly located and securely holds the joint in position. If available, use an oil seal fitting sleeve to protect the oil seal as the driveshaft is inserted (see Chapter 7, Section 5).

**14** Align the outer constant velocity joint splines with those of the hub, and slide the joint back into position in the hub.

**15** Fit the washer and a new hub nut, and tighten the nut to draw the outer joint fully into position in the hub.

**16** Locate the lower arm balljoint in the hub carrier and refit the clamp bolt and nut, tightening it to the specified torque.

**17** Reconnect the track-rod end balljoint to the hub carrier, and tighten a new retaining nut to the specified torque.

**18** The remainder of the refitting procedure is a reversal of removal, but note the following additional points.

 a) *Do not fully tighten the hub nut until the vehicle is resting on its wheels.*
 b) *Tighten all nuts/bolts to the specified torque.*
 c) *On completion, top-up the transmission with the specified type and amount of oil, and check the level using the information given in Chapter 1.*

## 3 Driveshaft inner joint gaiter - renewal

**1** The inner joint gaiter can be renewed either with the driveshaft fitted in the vehicle or with it on the bench. If it is wished to fully remove the driveshaft, refer to Section 2 for details.

### Renewal without removing the driveshaft

**2** Remove the relevant wheel trim or the wheel centre plate (alloy wheels), then slacken the relevant front wheel nuts. Apply the handbrake, then jack up the front of the vehicle, and support securely on axle stands (see *"Jacking and Vehicle Support"*). Remove the roadwheel.

**3** Working in the engine compartment, unscrew the relevant front suspension upper mounting locknut five turns, while using an Allen key to hold the shock absorber piston rod stationary. This is necessary to prevent damage to the upper mounting when disconnecting the driveshaft.

**4** The front suspension lower arm must now be disconnected from the hub carrier. To do this, unscrew the nut from the clamp bolt, drive out the bolt with a soft-metal drift, and carefully lever the lower arm down from the hub carrier. Note that the head of the clamp bolt faces the rear of the car.

**5** Cut the gaiter clips free and remove them. Slide the gaiter from the inner joint housing **(see illustration)**.

**6** Carefully pull the driveshaft outwards, and remove the tripode and bearings from the joint housing **(see illustration)**. Support the driveshaft on an axle stand. As the tripode is

**3.5 Cut free the driveshaft inner gaiter clips**

**3.6 Pull out the driveshaft tripode from the inner joint**

**3.7a Make alignment marks between the tripode joint and the driveshaft . . .**

**3.7b . . . then prise the circlip from the end of the driveshaft**

being withdrawn, take precautions to prevent the bearing rollers falling off, and if necessary wrap tape around them.

*Caution: The inner driveshaft joint must not be bent more than 18° and the outer joint by more than 45°.*

**7** Extract the circlip from the groove on the inner end of the driveshaft, using circlip pliers or two screwdrivers **(see illustrations)**. It is recommended that the circlip is renewed.

**8** Mark the tripode and driveshaft for position to ensure correct refitting, then slide the tripode from the splines on the driveshaft.

**9** Slide the inner joint gaiter from the driveshaft.

**10** Wipe clean the driveshaft and scoop out the grease from the inner joint housing and tripode. If necessary, thoroughly clean the constant velocity joint components using paraffin, or a suitable solvent, and dry the components thoroughly. Carry out a visual inspection of all the components.

**11** Check the tripode, rollers and outer member for signs of wear, pitting or scuffing on their bearing surfaces. Also check that the rollers rotate smoothly and easily, with no traces of roughness.

**12** If on inspection, the components reveal signs of wear or damage, it will be necessary to renew the complete driveshaft as an assembly, since no components are available separately. If the joint components are in satisfactory condition, obtain a repair kit from your Ford dealer, consisting of a new gaiter, retaining clips, tripod circlip and the correct type and quantity of grease.

**13** Slide the new gaiter on the driveshaft together with new clips.

**14** Slide the tripode and bearings onto the driveshaft splines, chamfered side first, making sure that the previously made marks are aligned. Fit the new circlip in the groove to secure the tripode. Where applicable, remove the tape from the bearings.

**15** Pack the tripode bearings and joint housing with 100 grams of the specified CV joint grease.

**16** Carefully locate the tripode fully into the joint housing. Locate the gaiter on the housing, then pull out the tripode 20 mm and tighten the gaiter clips. Any trapped air must be released first by lifting the gaiter lips with a screwdriver.

Ford technicians use a special tool to squeeze the clips tight, however if this tool is not available, the clips can be carefully tightened using a pair of pincers.

**17** Locate the lower arm balljoint in the hub carrier and refit the clamp bolt and nut, tightening it to the specified torque.

**18** Tighten the front suspension upper mounting nut to the specified torque.

**19** Refit the roadwheel and lower the vehicle to the ground. Tighten the wheel nuts to the specified torque and refit the wheel trim.

### Renewal with the driveshaft on the bench

**20** Mount the driveshaft in a vice and remove all traces of dirt from the outside of the inner joint.

**21** Cut the inner gaiter clips free and remove them. Slide the gaiter from the inner joint housing.

**22** Carefully pull the joint housing from the tripode star and bearings. As the joint housing is being withdrawn, take precautions to prevent the bearing rollers falling off, and if necessary wrap tape around them.

**23** Extract the circlip from the groove on the inner end of the driveshaft, using circlip pliers or two screwdrivers. It is recommended that the circlip is renewed.

**24** Mark the tripode and driveshaft for position to ensure correct refitting, then slide the tripode from the splines on the driveshaft.

**25** Slide off the inner joint gaiter.

**26** Wipe clean the driveshaft and scoop out the grease from the inner joint housing and tripode. If necessary, thoroughly clean the constant velocity joint components using paraffin, or a suitable solvent, and dry the components thoroughly. Carry out a visual inspection of all the components.

**27** Check the tripode, rollers and outer member for signs of wear, pitting or scuffing on their bearing surfaces. Also check that the rollers rotate smoothly and easily, with no traces of roughness.

**28** If on inspection, the components reveal signs of wear or damage, it will be necessary to renew the complete driveshaft as an assembly, since no components are available separately. If the joint components are in satisfactory condition, obtain a repair kit from

your Ford dealer, consisting of a new gaiter, retaining clips, tripod circlip and the correct type and quantity of grease.

**29** Slide the new gaiter on the driveshaft together with new clips.

**30** Slide the tripode and bearings onto the driveshaft splines, chamfered side first, making sure that the previously made marks are aligned. Fit the new circlip in the groove to secure the tripode. Where applicable, remove the tape from the bearings.

**31** Pack the tripode bearings and joint housing with 100 grams of the specified CV joint grease.

**32** Carefully locate the joint housing fully onto the tripode bearings. Locate the gaiter on the housing, then pull out the housing 20 mm and tighten the gaiter clips. Any trapped air must be released first by lifting the gaiter lips with a screwdriver. Ford technicians use a special tool to squeeze the clips tight, however if this tool is not available, the clips can be carefully tightened using a pair of pincers.

**33** The driveshaft is now ready to be refitted to the vehicle.

### 4  Driveshaft outer joint gaiter - renewal

**1** The inner joint gaiter can be renewed either with the driveshaft fitted in the vehicle or with it on the bench. If it is wished to fully remove the driveshaft, refer to Section 2 for details.

### Renewal without removing the driveshaft

**2** Remove the relevant wheel trim or the wheel centre plate (alloy wheels), then slacken the relevant front wheel nuts. Apply the handbrake, then jack up the front of the vehicle, and support securely on axle stands (see *"Jacking and Vehicle Support"*). Remove the roadwheel.

**3** Working in the engine compartment, unscrew the relevant front suspension upper mounting locknut five turns, while using an Allen key to hold the shock absorber piston rod stationary. This is necessary to prevent damage to the upper mounting when disconnecting the driveshaft.

**4** The front suspension lower arm must now be disconnected from the hub carrier. To do this, unscrew the nut from the clamp bolt, drive out the bolt with a soft-metal drift, and carefully lever the lower arm down from the hub carrier. Note that the head of the clamp bolt faces the rear of the car.

**5** Cut the gaiter clips free and remove them. Slide the gaiter along the driveshaft, away from the outer joint housing.

**6** Wipe the grease from the outer joint, then use circlip pliers to prise open the retaining circlip **(see illustration)**. With the circlip held open, pull the hub carrier outwards and slide the driveshaft out from the joint hub. Close the

**4.6 Expand the driveshaft outer joint circlip whilst pulling the hub assembly outwards**

**4.11 Fit a new circlip (arrowed) to the joint hub groove**

circlip and remove it from the groove in the joint hub - a new one must be fitted on reassembly.

**7** Slide the outer joint gaiter from the driveshaft.

**8** Wipe clean the driveshaft and scoop out as much grease as possible from the constant velocity joint. Thoroughly clean the joint components using paraffin, or a suitable solvent, and dry them thoroughly. Carry out a visual inspection of the joint components. Move the joint hub from side to side to expose each ball in turn at the top of its track. Examine the balls for cracks, flat spots, or signs of surface pitting. Inspect the ball tracks on the inner and outer members. If the tracks have widened, the balls will no longer be a tight fit. At the same time, check the ball cage windows for wear or cracking between the windows.

**9** If on inspection, any of the constant velocity joint components are found to be worn or damaged, it will be necessary to renew the complete joint assembly, or even

the complete driveshaft if the splines are worn. Refer to your Ford dealer for further information on parts availability. If the joint is in satisfactory condition, obtain a repair kit consisting of a new gaiter, circlip, retaining clips, and the correct type and quantity of grease.

**10** Slide the new gaiter onto the driveshaft together with new clips.

**11** Locate the new circlip in the joint hub groove **(see illustration)**.

**12** Pack the outer joint with 40 grams of the specified CV joint grease **(see illustration)**.

**13** Align the driveshaft splines with those of the outer joint hub. Slide the joint onto the driveshaft until the circlip clicks into the driveshaft groove **(see illustration)**.

**14** Slide the gaiter along the driveshaft, and locate it in the recesses on the driveshaft and joint outer member.

**15** Locate and tighten the gaiter clips. Any trapped air must be released first by lifting the gaiter lips with a screwdriver. Ford technicians use a special tool to squeeze the clips tight,

however if this tool is not available, the clips can be carefully tightened using a pair of pincers.

**16** Locate the lower arm balljoint in the hub carrier and refit the clamp bolt and nut, tightening it to the specified torque.

**17** Tighten the front suspension upper mounting nut to the specified torque.

**18** Refit the roadwheel and lower the vehicle to the ground. Tighten the wheel nuts to the specified torque and refit the wheel trim.

### Renewal with the driveshaft on the bench

**19** Mount the driveshaft in a vice and remove all traces of dirt from the outside of the inner joint.

**20** Cut the outer gaiter clips free and remove them. Slide the gaiter along the driveshaft, away from the outer joint housing.

**21** Wipe the grease from the outer joint, then use circlip pliers to prise open the retaining circlip. With the circlip held open, pull the outer joint housing outwards off the

**4.12 Pack the outer joint with CV joint grease**

**4.13 Slide the joint onto the driveshaft until the circlip (A) engages with the driveshaft groove (B)**

driveshaft. Close the circlip and remove it from the groove in the joint hub - a new one must be fitted on reassembly.

**22** Slide the outer joint gaiter from the driveshaft.

**23** Wipe clean the driveshaft and scoop out as much grease as possible from the constant velocity joint. Thoroughly clean the joint components using paraffin, or a suitable solvent, and dry them thoroughly. Carry out a visual inspection of the joint components. Move the joint hub from side to side to expose each ball in turn at the top of its track. Examine the balls for cracks, flat spots, or signs of surface pitting. Inspect the ball tracks on the inner and outer members. If the tracks have widened, the balls will no longer be a tight fit. At the same time, check the ball cage windows for wear or cracking between the windows.

**24** If on inspection, any of the constant velocity joint components are found to be worn or damaged, it will be necessary to renew the complete joint assembly, or even the complete driveshaft if the splines are worn. Refer to your Ford dealer for further information on parts availability. If the joint is in satisfactory condition, obtain a repair kit consisting of a new gaiter, circlip, retaining clips, and the correct type and quantity of grease.

**25** Slide the new gaiter onto the driveshaft together with new clips.

**26** Locate the new circlip in the joint hub groove.

**27** Pack the outer joint with 40 grams of the specified CV joint grease.

**28** Align the driveshaft splines with those of the outer joint hub. Slide the joint onto the driveshaft until the circlip clicks into the driveshaft groove.

**29** Slide the gaiter along the driveshaft, and locate it in the recesses on the driveshaft and joint outer member.

**30** Locate and tighten the gaiter clips. Any trapped air must be released first by lifting the gaiter lips with a screwdriver. Ford technicians use a special tool to squeeze the clips tight, however if this tool is not available, the clips can be carefully tightened using a pair of pincers.

**31** The driveshaft is now ready to be refitted to the vehicle.

| 5 | Driveshaft - checking and overhaul |  |

## Checking

**1** First remove the wheel trim or centre cap (alloy wheels).

**2** If the hub nut staking is still effective, the driveshaft nut should be correctly tightened - if in doubt, relieve the staking using a suitable punch, then tighten the nut to the specified torque and re-stake the nut (ideally, a new nut should be fitted). Refit the wheel trim or centre cap (as applicable), and repeat the check on the remaining front hub nut.

**3** Road test the vehicle, and listen for a metallic clicking from the front as the vehicle is driven slowly in a circle on full-lock. If a clicking noise is heard, this indicates wear in the outer constant velocity joint. This means that the joint must be renewed since reconditioning is not possible.

**4** If vibration, consistent with road speed, is felt through the car when accelerating, there is a possibility of wear in the inner constant velocity joints.

## Overhaul

**5** To check the joints thoroughly for wear, remove them and dismantle them as described in Section 3 and 4. If any wear or free play is found, the affected joint must be renewed. In the case of the inner joints, this means that the complete driveshaft assembly must be renewed, as the joints are not available separately. The outer joints can be renewed separately. Refer to your Ford dealer for information on the availability of driveshaft components.

# Chapter 9
# Braking system

## Contents

## Degrees of difficulty

| Easy, suitable for novice with little experience  | Fairly easy, suitable for beginner with some experience  | Fairly difficult, suitable for competent DIY mechanic  | Difficult, suitable for experienced DIY mechanic  | Very difficult, suitable for expert DIY or professional |

## Specifications

### Front brakes

Brake pad friction material minimum thickness . . . . . . . . . . . . . . 1.5 mm

| Disc thickness: | New | Minimum |
| --- | --- | --- |
| Models with solid discs | 12.0 mm | 8.0 mm |
| Models with ventilated discs | 20.0 mm | 18.0 mm |

Maximum disc run-out . . . . . . . . . . . . . . . . . . . . . . . . . . . . 0.1 mm

### Rear brakes

Brake shoe friction material minimum thickness . . . . . . . . . . . . . 1.0 mm

| Drum internal diameter: | New | Maximum after machining |
| --- | --- | --- |
| Models not fitted with ABS | 180 mm | 181 mm |
| Models with ABS | 203 mm | 204 mm |

### Torque wrench settings

| | Nm | lbf ft |
| --- | --- | --- |
| ABS hydraulic unit | 23 | 17 |
| ABS hydraulic unit bracket nuts | 10 | 7 |
| ABS wheel sensor retaining bolt | 10 | 7 |
| Front brake caliper: | | |
| Guide pin bolts | 25 | 18 |
| Mounting bolts | 58 | 43 |
| Handbrake lever retaining nuts | 24 | 18 |
| Hydraulic pipe/hose union | 13 | 11 |
| Master cylinder retaining nuts | 25 | 18 |
| Rear brake pressure regulating valve | 13 | 11 |
| Rear hub nut | 235 | 173 |
| Rear hub to axle | 66 | 49 |
| Roadwheel nuts | 85 | 63 |
| Vacuum servo support stay | 25 | 18 |
| Vacuum servo unit mounting nuts | 25 | 18 |

## 1 General information

The braking system is of the servo-assisted, dual-circuit hydraulic type. The arrangement of the hydraulic system is such that each circuit operates one front and one rear brake from a tandem master cylinder. Under normal circumstances, both circuits operate in unison. However, in the event of hydraulic failure in one circuit, full braking force will still be available at two wheels.

All models are fitted with front disc brakes and rear drum brakes. The front disc brakes are actuated by single-piston sliding type calipers, which ensure that equal pressure is applied to each disc pad. The rear drum brakes incorporate leading and trailing shoes, which are actuated by twin-piston wheel cylinders. A self-adjust mechanism is incorporated, to automatically compensate for brake shoe wear. As the brake shoe linings wear, the footbrake operation automatically operates the adjuster mechanism, which effectively lengthens the shoe strut and repositions the brake shoes, to remove the lining-to-drum clearance.

On models **not** fitted with an anti-lock braking system (ABS) a pressure conscious reducing valve (PCRV) is situated in the hydraulic circuit to each rear brake. The valves, which are located on the rear underbody, regulate the hydraulic pressure applied to the rear brakes and so help to prevent rear wheel lock-up during emergency braking. Refer to Section 20 for further information on the ABS system.

The cable-operated handbrake provides an independent mechanical means of rear brake application.

⚠ *Warning: When servicing any part of the system, work carefully and methodically; also observe scrupulous cleanliness when overhauling any part of the hydraulic system. Always renew components (in axle sets, where applicable) if in doubt about their condition, and use only genuine Ford replacement parts, or at least those of known good quality. Note the warnings given in "Safety first" and at relevant points in this Chapter concerning the dangers of asbestos dust and hydraulic fluid.*

## 2 Hydraulic system - bleeding

⚠ *Warning: Hydraulic fluid is poisonous; wash off immediately and thoroughly in the case of skin contact, and seek immediate medical advice if any fluid is swallowed or gets into the eyes. Certain types of hydraulic fluid*

*are inflammable, and may ignite when allowed into contact with hot components. When servicing any hydraulic system, it is safest to assume that the fluid is inflammable, and to take precautions against the risk of fire as though it is petrol that is being handled. Hydraulic fluid is also an effective paint stripper, and will attack plastics. If any fluid is spilt, it should be washed off immediately, using copious quantities of fresh water. Finally, it is hygroscopic (it absorbs moisture from the air) - old fluid may be contaminated and unfit for further use. When topping-up or renewing the fluid, always use the recommended type, and ensure that it comes from a freshly-opened sealed container.*
*Caution: On models equipped with ABS, disconnect the battery before disconnecting any braking system hydraulic union and do not reconnect the battery until after the hydraulic system has been bled. Failure to do this could lead to air entering the ABS hydraulic unit requiring the unit to be bled using special Ford test equipment FDS 2000.*

### General

1 The correct operation of any hydraulic system is only possible after removing all air from the components and circuit; this is achieved by bleeding the system.
2 During the bleeding procedure, add only clean, unused hydraulic fluid of the recommended type; never re-use fluid that has already been bled from the system. Ensure that sufficient fluid is available before starting work.
3 If there is any possibility of incorrect fluid being already in the system, the brake components and circuit must be flushed completely with uncontaminated, correct fluid, and new seals should be fitted to the various components.
4 If hydraulic fluid has been lost from the system, or air has entered because of a leak, ensure that the fault is cured before proceeding further.
5 Park the vehicle over an inspection pit or on car ramps. Alternatively, apply the handbrake then jack up the front and rear of the vehicle and support it on axle stands (see "*Jacking and Vehicle Support*"). For improved access with the vehicle jacked up, remove the roadwheels.
6 Check that all pipes and hoses are secure, unions tight and bleed screws closed. Clean any dirt from around the bleed screws.
7 Disconnect the low fluid warning light wiring, then unscrew the master cylinder reservoir cap and top-up the master cylinder reservoir to the "MAX" level line. Refit the cap loosely, and remember to maintain the fluid level at least above the "MIN" level line throughout the procedure, otherwise there is a risk of further air entering the system.

8 There are a number of one-man, do-it-yourself brake bleeding kits currently available from motor accessory shops. It is recommended that one of these kits is used whenever possible, as they greatly simplify the bleeding operation, and also reduce the risk of expelled air and fluid being drawn back into the system. If such a kit is not available, the basic (two-man) method must be used, which is described in detail below.
9 If a kit is to be used, prepare the vehicle as described previously, and follow the kit manufacturer's instructions, as the procedure may vary slightly according to the type being used. Generally, the procedures are as outlined below in the relevant sub-section.
10 Whichever method is used, the same sequence must be followed (paragraphs 11 and 12) to ensure the removal of all air from the system.

### Bleeding sequence

11 If the system has been only partially disconnected, and suitable precautions were taken to minimise fluid loss, it should only be necessary to bleed that part of the system. On non-ABS models, each diagonal circuit (ie primary or secondary) can be bled individually. On ABS models, each wheel circuit can be bled individually.
12 If the complete system is to be bled, then it should be done working in the following sequence:

#### Models without ABS

a) Left-hand front brake.
b) Right-hand rear brake.
c) Right-hand front brake.
d) Left-hand rear brake.

#### Models with ABS

a) Left-hand front brake.
b) Right-hand front brake.
c) Right-hand rear brake.
d) Left-hand rear brake.

*Caution: On models with ABS, if a normal firm brake pedal is not restored after carrying out the conventional bleeding operation described in the following paragraphs, it will be necessary to have the ABS hydraulic unit bled by a Ford dealer using the Ford FDS 2000 diagnostic test equipment. The electronic test equipment allows the hydraulic unit to be switched into a special mode which purges the unit of all trapped air - it is not possible to remove trapped air from the unit by bleeding the system conventionally. After bleeding the hydraulic unit, the complete circuit must again be bled before using the vehicle on the road.*

### Bleeding - basic (two-man) method

13 Collect together a clean glass jar, a suitable length of plastic or rubber tubing which is a tight fit over the bleed screw, and a ring spanner to fit the screw. The help of an assistant will also be required.

**14** Remove the dust cap from the first bleed screw in the sequence **(see illustration)**. Fit the spanner and tube to the screw, place the other end of the tube in the jar, and pour in sufficient fluid to cover the end of the tube.

**15** Ensure that the master cylinder reservoir fluid level is maintained at least above the "MIN" level mark throughout the procedure.

**16** Have the assistant fully depress and release the brake pedal several times to build up initial pressure in the system and to release vacuum from the vacuum servo.

**17** Unscrew the bleed screw approximately half a turn then have the assistant slowly depress the brake pedal down to the floor and hold it there. Tighten the bleed screw and have the assistant slowly release the pedal to its rest position.

**18** Repeat the procedure given in paragraph 17 until the fluid emerging from the bleed screw is free from air bubbles. After every two or three depressions of the pedal, check the level of fluid in the reservoir and top up if necessary.

**19** When no more air bubbles appear, securely tighten the bleed screw, remove the tube and spanner, and refit the dust cap. Do not overtighten the bleed screw.

**20** Repeat the procedure on the remaining screws in the sequence, until all air is removed from the system and the brake pedal feels firm again.

### Bleeding - using a one-way valve kit

**21** As the name implies, these kits consist of a length of tubing with a one-way valve fitted, to prevent expelled air and fluid being drawn back into the system; some kits include a translucent container, which can be positioned so that the air bubbles can be more easily seen flowing from the end of the tube.

**22** The kit is connected to the bleed screw, which is then opened **(see illustration)**. The user returns to the driver's seat, depresses the brake pedal with a smooth, steady stroke, and slowly releases it. This is repeated until the expelled fluid is clear of air bubbles.

**23** Note that these kits simplify work so much that it is easy to forget the master cylinder reservoir fluid level. Ensure that this is maintained at least above the "MIN" level line at all times.

### Bleeding - using a pressure-bleeding kit

**24** These kits are usually operated by a reservoir of pressurised air contained in the spare tyre. However, note that it will probably be necessary to reduce the pressure to a lower level than normal. Refer to the instructions supplied with the kit.

**25** By connecting a pressurised, fluid-filled container to the master cylinder reservoir, bleeding can be carried out simply by opening each screw in turn (in the specified sequence), and allowing the fluid to flow out until no more air bubbles can be seen in the expelled fluid.

**2.14  Removing a brake caliper bleed screw dust cap**

**26** This method has the advantage that the large reservoir of fluid provides an additional safeguard against air being drawn into the system during bleeding.

**27** Pressure-bleeding is particularly effective when bleeding "difficult" systems, or when bleeding the complete system at the time of routine fluid renewal.

### All methods

**28** When bleeding is complete, and firm pedal feel is restored, wipe off any spilt fluid, securely tighten the bleed screws, and refit the dust caps.

**29** Check the hydraulic fluid level in the master cylinder reservoir, and top-up if necessary (see "Weekly checks").

**30** Discard any hydraulic fluid that has been bled from the system; it will not be fit for re-use.

**31** Check the feel of the brake pedal. If it feels at all spongy, air must still be present in the system, and further bleeding is required. Failure to bleed satisfactorily after a reasonable repetition of the bleeding procedure may be due to worn master cylinder seals.

---

**3  Hydraulic pipes and hoses - renewal**

**Caution: On models equipped with ABS, disconnect the battery before disconnecting any braking system hydraulic union and do not reconnect the battery**

**3.2a  Front brake pipe connection**

**2.22  Bleeding the hydraulic system using a one-way valve kit**

*until after the hydraulic system has been bled. Failure to do this could lead to air entering the ABS hydraulic unit requiring the unit to be bled using special Ford test equipment (see Section 2).*

⚠ *Warning: Refer to the warning at the start of Section 2 regarding the safe handling of brake hydraulic fluid.*

**1** If any pipe or hose is to be renewed, minimise fluid loss by first removing the master cylinder reservoir cap, then tightening it down onto a piece of polythene to obtain an airtight seal. Alternatively, flexible hoses can be sealed using a proprietary brake hose clamp, or metal brake pipe unions can be plugged or capped immediately after they are disconnected. Place a wad of rag under any union that is to be disconnected, to catch any spilt fluid.

**2** If a front flexible hose is to be disconnected, unscrew the rigid brake pipe union nut before removing the spring clip which secures the hose to its mounting bracket, then unscrew the hose union from the front brake caliper and detach the support rubber grommet from the front suspension strut **(see illustration)**. To remove a rear flexible hose on models with ABS, loosen the rigid pipe union nut and remove the spring clip securing the hose to its mounting bracket, then unscrew the hose from the rear wheel cylinder. On non-ABS models, additionally the pressure reducing valve must be unscrewed from the hose and rigid pipe **(see illustration)**.

**3** To unscrew the union nuts, it is preferable to obtain a brake pipe spanner of the correct size

**3.2b  Rear brake pipe connection**

**4.2 Prising the pad spring from the caliper**

**4.3 Prise out the plastic covers . . .**

**4.4a . . . then slacken . . .**

**4.4b . . . and remove the guide pin bolts . . .**

**4.4c . . . and lift the caliper from the disc**

**4.5a Remove the outer pad from the caliper mounting bracket . . .**

**4.5b . . . then unclip the inner pad from the caliper piston**

**4.6 Measure the thickness of the brake pad friction material**

(available from most large motor accessory shops). Failing this, a close-fitting open-ended spanner will be required, though if the nuts are tight or corroded, their flats may be rounded-off if the spanner slips. In such a case, a self-locking wrench is often the only way to unscrew a stubborn union, but it follows that the pipe and the damaged nuts must be renewed on reassembly. Always clean a union and surrounding area before disconnecting it. If disconnecting a component with more than one union, make a careful note of the connections before disturbing any of them.

4 If a brake pipe is to be renewed, it can be obtained, cut to length and with the union nuts and end flares in place, from Ford dealers. All that is then necessary is to bend it to shape, following the line of the original, before fitting it to the car. Alternatively, most motor accessory shops can make up brake pipes from kits, but this requires very careful measurement of the original, to ensure that the replacement is of the correct length. The safest answer is usually to take the original to the shop as a pattern.

5 On refitting, do not overtighten the union nuts. It is not necessary to exercise brute force to obtain a sound joint.

6 Ensure that the pipes and hoses are correctly routed, with no kinks, and that they are secured in the clips or brackets provided. After fitting, remove the polythene from the reservoir, and bleed the hydraulic system as described in Section 2. Wash off any spilt fluid, and check carefully for fluid leaks. On models with ABS, if any pipe is disconnected from the hydraulic unit, the unit must be bled as described in Section 2.

## 4 Front brake pads - renewal

⚠ *Warning: Renew BOTH sets of front brake pads at the same time - NEVER renew the pads on only one wheel, as uneven braking may result. Note that although Ford brake pads do not contain asbestos, the dust created by wear of non-genuine pads may be a health hazard. Do not use compressed air to blow out brake dust and debris - use a brush. Avoid inhaling any of the dust, and wear an approved filtration mask. Use only proprietary brake cleaner fluid or methylated spirits to clean the brake components, DO NOT use petrol or any other petroleum-based product as this will damage the rubber seals.*

1 Chock the rear wheels, apply the handbrake, then jack up the front of the vehicle and support it on axle stands (see *"Jacking and Vehicle Support"*). Remove the front roadwheels.

2 Using a flat-bladed screwdriver, carefully prise the pad spring out from the caliper noting its correct fitted position **(see illustration)**.

3 Remove the plastic covers from the ends of the guide bushes to gain access to the caliper guide pin bolts **(see illustration)**.

4 Slacken and remove the guide pin bolts, then lift the caliper assembly away from the disc **(see illustrations)**. Suspend the caliper from suspension strut coil spring using a suitable piece of wire or string; do not allow the caliper to hang down by the hose.

5 Remove the outer pad from the caliper mounting bracket, then unclip the inner pad from the caliper piston **(see illustrations)**.

6 Measure the thickness of the friction material on each brake pad **(see illustration)**.

If either pad is worn at any point to the specified minimum thickness or less, all four pads must be renewed. Also, the pads should be renewed if any are fouled with oil or grease; there is no satisfactory way of degreasing friction material, once contaminated. If any of the brake pads are worn unevenly, or are fouled with oil or grease, trace and rectify the cause before reassembly.

**7** If the brake pads are still serviceable, carefully clean them using a clean, fine wire brush or similar, paying particular attention to the sides and back of the metal backing plate. Clean out the grooves in the friction material, and pick out any large embedded particles of dirt or debris. Carefully clean the pad locations in the caliper and piston.

**8** Brush the dust and dirt from the caliper and piston, but **do not** inhale it, as it is injurious to health. Inspect the dust seal around the piston for damage, and the piston for evidence of fluid leaks, corrosion or damage. If attention is necessary, refer to Section 8.

**9** Prior to fitting the pads, check that the guide pin bolts are a reasonably tight-fit in the caliper bushes. If there is any sign of excessive freeplay between either bush and bolt, both the bushes and bolts should be renewed - the bushes are a push-fit in the caliper body.

**10** If new brake pads are to be fitted, the caliper piston must be pushed back into the cylinder to make room for them. Either use a G-clamp or similar tool, or use suitable pieces of wood as levers. Provided that the master cylinder reservoir has not been overfilled with hydraulic fluid, there should be no spillage, but keep a careful watch on the fluid level while retracting the piston. If the fluid level rises above the "MAX" level line at any time, the surplus should be siphoned off, or ejected via a plastic tube connected to one of the bleed screws (see Section 2).

 *Warning: Do not syphon the fluid by mouth, as it is poisonous; use a syringe or an old poultry baster.*

**11** Fit the outer pad to the caliper mounting bracket, ensuring that the pad friction material is against the brake disc, then clip the inner pad into position in the caliper piston.

**12** Slide the caliper into position over the brake disc, and install the guide pin bolts. Tighten both guide pin bolts to the specified torque setting, then refit the plastic caps to the ends of the guide bushes.

**13** Engage the pad spring with the outer pad, then engage the spring ends correctly in the caliper body holes, as noted before removal.

**14** Depress the brake pedal repeatedly until the pads are pressed into firm contact with the brake disc, and normal (non-assisted) pedal pressure is restored.

**15** Repeat the procedure on the remaining front brake caliper.

**16** Refit the roadwheels, then lower the vehicle to the ground and tighten the road-wheel nuts to the specified torque setting.

**5.3a Bolts securing the rear stub axle to the rear axle**

**17** Check the hydraulic fluid level as described in "Weekly checks".

 *New pads will not give full braking efficiency until they have bedded in. Be prepared for this, and avoid hard braking as far as possible for the first hundred miles or so after pad renewal.*

### 5 Rear brake shoes - renewal

 *Warning: Brake shoes must be renewed on both rear wheels at the same time - NEVER renew the shoes on only one wheel, as uneven braking may result. Note that although Ford brake shoes do not contain asbestos, the dust created by wear of non-genuine shoes may be a health hazard. Do not use compressed air to blow out brake dust and debris - use a brush. Avoid inhaling any of the dust, and wear an approved filtration mask. Use only proprietary brake cleaner fluid or methylated spirits to clean the brake components, DO NOT use petrol or any other petroleum-based product as this will damage the rubber seals.*

**Note:** *The following paragraphs describe two methods for renewal of the rear brake shoes. Method 1 is quickest and will prevent renewal of the hub dust cap which is damaged during removal. If Method 2 is used, a torque wrench capable of tightening the hub nut to 235 Nm will be required.*

#### Method 1

**1** Working inside the car, pull up the gaiter from the handbrake lever to expose the handbrake cable adjustment nut. Fully loosen the nut (but do not remove it) so that the rear brake shoes are fully retracted.

**2** Chock the front wheels, then jack up the rear of the vehicle and support it on axle stands (see "Jacking and Vehicle Support"). Remove both rear roadwheels.

**3** Unscrew the bolts securing the rear stub axle to the rear axle, then withdraw the stub axle together with the hub/brake drum over the

**5.3b Removing the stub axle together with the hub/brake drum over the brake shoes**

brake shoes **(see illustrations)**. Note that the backplate and spacer plate are riveted to the rear axle. On models with ABS, take care not to damage the ABS sensor bolted to the backplate.

**4** Working carefully, and taking the necessary precautions to avoid inhalation of dust, remove all traces of brake dust from the brake drum, backplate and shoes **(see illustration)**.

**5** Measure the thickness of the friction material of each brake shoe at several points; if either shoe is worn at any point to the specified minimum thickness or less, all four shoes must be renewed as a set. The shoes should also be renewed if any are fouled with oil or grease; there is no satisfactory way of degreasing friction material, once contaminated.

**6** If either of the brake shoes are worn unevenly, or fouled with oil or grease, trace and rectify the cause before reassembly.

**7** Note the position of each shoe, and the location of each of the springs. Also make a note of the self-adjuster component locations, to aid refitting later.

**8** Using a pair of pliers, remove the shoe retainer springs by depressing and sliding them downwards, then withdraw the retainer pins from the brake backplate **(see illustration)**.

**9** Ease the shoes out one at a time from the lower anchor point, to release the tension of the return spring, then disconnect the lower return spring from both shoes, using pliers if necessary **(see illustration)**.

**10** Ease the upper end of both shoes out from the wheel cylinder pistons, taking care

**5.4 Rear brake shoes with the drum/hub removed**

**5.8 Rear brake shoes retainer spring**

**5.9 Lower return spring**

**5.10 Handbrake cable connected to the lever on the trailing shoe**

not to damage the wheel cylinder seals, and disconnect the handbrake cable from the lever on the trailing shoe **(see illustration)**. The brake shoe and adjuster strut assembly can then be manoeuvred out of position and away from the backplate. Do not depress the brake pedal until the brakes are reassembled; fit a strong elastic band around the wheel cylinder pistons to retain them.

11 With the shoe and adjuster strut assembly on the bench, make a note of the correct fitted positions of the springs and adjuster strut, to use as a guide on reassembly. Unhook and remove the upper return spring then detach the leading shoe from the trailing shoe and strut assembly. Unhook the adjuster strut from the trailing shoe, and remove its spring noting which way round it is fitted **(see illustrations)**.

12 Carefully examine the adjuster strut assembly for signs of wear or damage, paying particular attention to the self-adjusting ratchet mechanism, and renew if necessary.

13 Depending on the brake shoes being installed, it may be necessary to remove the handbrake lever from the original trailing shoe, and install it on the new shoe. Secure the lever in position with a new retaining clip. All return springs should be renewed, regardless of their apparent condition. Note that spring kits are available from Ford dealers.

14 Fit the adjuster strut retaining spring to the trailing shoe, ensuring that the shorter hook of the spring is engaged with the shoe.

15 Fully extend the adjuster strut ratchet, then engage the adjuster strut with the leading shoe, and fully release the ratchet.

16 Attach the adjuster strut to the retaining spring on the trailing shoe, then ease the strut into position in its slot in the trailing shoe.

17 Hook the leading shoe onto the return spring, then manipulate the shoes until the return spring can be connected to the trailing shoe.

18 Remove the elastic band fitted to the wheel cylinder. Peel back the rubber protective caps, and check the wheel cylinder for fluid leaks or other damage. Also check that both cylinder pistons are free to move easily. Refer to Section 9, if necessary, for information on wheel cylinder renewal.

19 Prior to installation, clean the backplate and apply a thin smear of high-temperature brake grease to all those surfaces of the backplate which bear on the shoes, particularly the wheel cylinder pistons and lower anchor point. Do not use too much lubricant, and don't allow the lubricant to foul the friction material.

20 Ensure that the adjuster strut self-adjust mechanism is fully released then manoeuvre the shoe and strut assembly into position and attach the handbrake cable to the lever on the trailing shoe. Engage the upper ends of both shoes with the wheel cylinder pistons, then fit the lower return spring to both shoes and ease the shoes into position on the lower anchor point.

21 Centralise the shoes relative to the backplate by tapping them. Refit the shoe retainer pins and secure them in position with the springs.

22 Locate the hub/brake drum and stub axle assembly over the brake shoes, then insert

the retaining bolts and tighten to the specified torque.

23 Repeat the procedure on the remaining rear brake.

24 Refit the roadwheels and lower the car to the ground. Adjust the lining-to-drum clearance by repeatedly depressing the brake pedal. Whilst doing this, have an assistant listen to the rear drums, to check that the adjuster strut is functioning correctly - a clicking sound should be emitted by the strut as the pedal is operated.

25 Adjust the handbrake as described in Section 14, then refit the handbrake lever gaiter.

> **HAYNES HiNT** *New shoes will not give full braking efficiency until they have bedded-in. Be prepared for this, and avoid hard braking as far as possible for the first hundred miles or so after shoe renewal.*

### Method 2

26 Remove the brake drum as described in Section 7.

27 Working carefully, and taking the necessary precautions to avoid inhalation of dust, remove all traces of brake dust from the brake drum, backplate and shoes.

28 Measure the thickness of the friction material of each brake shoe at several points; if either shoe is worn at any point to the specified minimum thickness or less, all four shoes must be renewed as a set. The shoes should also be renewed if any are fouled with oil or grease. There is no satisfactory way of degreasing friction material, once contaminated.

29 If either of the brake shoes are worn unevenly, or fouled with oil or grease, trace and rectify the cause before reassembly.

30 To renew the brake shoes, note the position of each shoe and the location of each of the springs. Also make a note of the self-adjuster component locations, to aid refitting later.

31 Using a pair of pliers, remove the shoe retainer springs by depressing and sliding them downwards, then withdraw the retainer pins from the brake backplate **(see illustration)**.

**5.11a Upper return spring location on the trailing shoe**

**5.11b Upper return spring location on the leading shoe**

**5.31 Remove the shoe retaining springs and the pins**

**5.32 Disconnect the lower return spring from both shoes**

**5.33a Disconnecting the handbrake cable from the lever on the trailing shoe**

**5.33b Wrap a strong elastic band around the wheel cylinder pistons to retain them**

**5.37a Adjuster strut components correctly assembled for refitting**

**5.37b Fit the adjuster strut retaining spring**

**32** Ease the shoes out one at a time from the lower anchor point, to release the tension of the return spring, then disconnect the lower return spring from both shoes, using pliers if necessary **(see illustration)**.

**33** Ease the upper end of both shoes out from the wheel cylinder pistons, taking care not to damage the wheel cylinder seals, and disconnect the handbrake cable from the lever on the trailing shoe. The brake shoe and adjuster strut assembly can then be manoeuvred out of position and away from the backplate. Do not depress the brake pedal until the brakes are reassembled; fit a strong elastic band around the wheel cylinder pistons to retain them **(see illustrations)**.

**34** With the shoe and adjuster strut assembly on the bench, make a note of the correct fitted positions of the springs and adjuster strut, to use as a guide on reassembly. Unhook and remove the upper return spring then detach

the leading shoe from the trailing shoe and strut assembly. Unhook the adjuster strut from the trailing shoe, and remove its spring noting which way around it is fitted.

**35** Carefully examine the adjuster strut assembly for signs of wear or damage, paying particular attention to the self-adjusting ratchet mechanism, and renew if necessary.

**36** Depending on the type of brake shoes being installed, it may be necessary to remove the handbrake lever from the original trailing shoe, and install it on the new shoe. Secure the lever in position with a new retaining clip. All return springs should be renewed, regardless of their apparent condition. Note that spring kits are available from Ford dealers.

**37** Fit the adjuster strut retaining spring to the trailing shoe, ensuring that the shorter hook of the spring is engaged with the shoe **(see illustrations)**.

**38** Fully extend the adjuster strut ratchet, then engage the adjuster strut with the leading shoe, and fully release the ratchet **(see illustration)**.

**39** Attach the adjuster strut to the retaining spring on the trailing shoe, then ease the strut into position in its slot in the trailing shoe **(see illustration)**.

**40** Hook the leading shoe onto the return spring, then manipulate the shoes until the return spring can be connected to the trailing shoe **(see illustration)**.

**41** Remove the elastic band fitted to the wheel cylinder. Peel back the rubber protective caps, and check the wheel cylinder for fluid leaks or other damage. Also check that both cylinder pistons are free to move easily. Refer to Section 9, if necessary, for information on wheel cylinder renewal.

**42** Prior to installation, clean the backplate and apply a thin smear of high-temperature

**5.38 Engage the adjuster strut with the leading shoe**

**5.39 Ease the strut into position in its slot in the trailing shoe**

**5.40 Fitting the upper shoe return spring**

**5.43 Fit the lower return spring and ease the shoes into position over the lower anchor point**

brake grease to all those surfaces of the backplate which bear on the shoes, particularly the wheel cylinder pistons and lower anchor point. Do not use too much lubricant, and don't allow the lubricant to foul the friction material.

43 Ensure that the adjuster strut self-adjust mechanism is fully released then manoeuvre the shoe and strut assembly into position and attach the handbrake cable to the lever on the trailing shoe. Engage the upper ends of both shoes with the wheel cylinder pistons, then fit the lower return spring to both shoes and ease the shoes into position on the lower anchor point **(see illustration)**.

44 Centralise the shoes relative to the backplate by tapping them. Refit the shoe retainer pins and secure them in position with the springs.

45 Refit the brake drum as described in Section 7.

46 Repeat the procedure on the remaining rear brake.

47 Once the brake drums have been refitted, adjust the lining-to-drum clearance by repeatedly depressing the brake pedal. Whilst doing this, have an assistant listen to the rear drums, to check that the adjuster strut is functioning correctly - a clicking sound should be emitted by the strut as the pedal is operated.

48 Adjust the handbrake as described in Section 14.

## 6 Front brake disc - inspection, removal and refitting

⚠️ **Warning: Refer to the warning at the beginning of Section 4 concerning the dangers of asbestos dust.**

### Inspection

**Note:** *If either disc requires renewal, BOTH should be renewed at the same time, to ensure even and consistent braking. New brake pads should also be fitted.*

1 Apply the handbrake, then jack up the front of the car and support it on axle stands (see *"Jacking and Vehicle Support"*). Remove the appropriate front roadwheel.

2 Slowly rotate the disc so that the full area of both sides can be checked. Remove the brake pads if better access is required to the inboard surface. Light scoring is normal in the area swept by the brake pads, but if heavy scoring or cracks are found, the disc must be renewed.

3 It is normal to find a lip of rust and brake dust around the disc's perimeter - this can be scraped off if required. If, however, a lip has formed due to excessive wear of the brake pad swept area, then the disc's thickness must be measured using a micrometer. Take measurements at several places around the disc, at the inside and outside of the pad swept area. If the disc has worn at any point to the specified minimum thickness or less, the disc must be renewed.

4 If the disc is thought to be warped, it can be checked for run-out. Using spacers, refit at least two wheel nuts and tighten them securely to seat the disc in position. Either use a dial gauge mounted on any convenient fixed point, while the disc is slowly rotated, or use feeler blades to measure (several points around the disc) the clearance between the disc and a fixed point, such as the caliper mounting bracket **(see illustration)**. If the measurements obtained are more than the specified maximum, the disc is excessively warped, and must be renewed, however, it is worth checking first that the hub bearing is in good condition (see Chapters 1 and 10). Remove the nuts and spacers.

5 Check the disc for cracks, especially around the wheel stud holes, and any other wear or damage, and renew if necessary.

### Removal

6 With the front of the vehicle raised and the wheel removed, slacken and remove the two bolts securing the brake caliper mounting bracket to the hub carrier. Slide the caliper assembly (complete with the brake pads) off of the disc, and suspend the assembly from the suspension strut coil spring, using a piece of wire or string, to avoid placing any strain on the hydraulic brake hose.

7 Use chalk or paint to mark the relationship of the disc to the hub then, where applicable, remove the retaining clip(s) from the wheel studs, and remove the disc. If the disc is tight,

**6.4 Checking brake disc run-out using a dial gauge**

lightly tap its rear face with a hide or plastic mallet.

### Refitting

8 Ensure that the mating surfaces of the disc and hub are clean and flat, then locate the disc on the studs.

9 If a new disc has been fitted, use a suitable solvent to wipe any preservative coating from the disc, before refitting the caliper and pads.

10 Slide the caliper into position, making sure the pads pass either side of the disc, and tighten the caliper bracket bolts to the specified torque setting.

11 Refit the roadwheel then lower the vehicle to the ground and tighten the wheel nuts to the specified torque. Apply the footbrake several times to force the pads back into contact with the disc before driving the vehicle.

## 7 Rear brake drum - removal, inspection and refitting

⚠️ **Warning: Refer to the warning at the beginning of Section 5 concerning the dangers of asbestos dust.**

### Removal

1 The rear brake drum incorporates the rear hub and wheel bearings in one unit. To remove it, first pull up the gaiter from the handbrake lever to expose the handbrake cable adjustment nut. Loosen the nut so that the rear brake shoes are fully retracted.

2 Chock the front wheels, then jack up the rear of the vehicle and support it on axle stands (see *"Jacking and Vehicle Support"*). Remove the relevant rear roadwheel.

3 Using a screwdriver or small cold chisel, remove the dust cap from the centre of the hub/brake drum **(see illustration)**. This is a difficult task that will usually result in the cap being damaged. If necessary, obtain a new cap for the refitting procedure.

4 Unscrew and remove the hub nut **(see illustrations)**. *Caution: Take care, as the hub nut is tightened to a very high torque.*

5 Withdraw the hub/brake drum from the stub

**7.3 Prise out the dust cap . . .**

axle **(see illustration)**. If the drum is tight (this should not be the case if the handbrake cable has been backed off sufficiently), this may be due to the tightness of the hub bearing on the stub axle, or due to the brake shoes binding on the inner circumference of the drum. If the bearing is tight, tap the periphery of the hub/brake drum using a hide or plastic mallet, or use a universal puller, secured to the hub/brake drum with the wheel nuts, to pull it off. If the brake shoes are binding, proceed as follows.

**6** Remove the small rubber grommet from the bottom of the rear backplate (not the grommet for checking the lining thickness). Insert a screwdriver through the hole and release the handbrake operating lever by twisting the screwdriver so that the lever stop lug can pass over the surface of the shoe, allowing the brake shoes to retract fully. The hub/brake drum should then be free to be removed.

### Inspection

**7** Remove all traces of brake dust from the drum, but avoid inhaling the dust, as it is injurious to health.

**8** Clean the outside of the drum, and check it for obvious signs of wear or damage such as cracks around the roadwheel stud holes. Renew the drum if necessary.

**9** Examine carefully the inside of the drum. Light scoring of the friction surface is normal, but if heavy scoring is found, the drum must be renewed. It is usual to find a lip on the drum's inboard edge which consists of a mixture of rust and brake dust; this should be scraped away to leave a smooth surface. If the lip is due to excessive wear of the friction surface, then the drum must be refinished (within the specified limits) or renewed.

**10** If the drum is thought to be excessively worn or oval, its internal diameter must be measured at several points using an internal micrometer. Take measurements in pairs, the second at right-angles to the first, and compare the two for signs of ovality. Minor ovality can be corrected by machining, otherwise renew the hub/brake drum.

### Refitting

**11** If a new hub/brake drum is to be installed, use a suitable solvent to remove any preservative coating that may have been

**8.5 Unscrewing a caliper guide pin bolt**

**7.4 . . . then unscrew the rear hub nut . . .**

applied to its interior friction surface.

**12** Apply a smear of gear oil to the stub axle, and slide on the hub/brake drum, being careful not to get oil onto the brake shoes or the friction surface of the drum.

**13** Fit the rear hub nut, tightening it to the specified torque setting, and tap the new dust cap securely into position in the centre of the hub/brake drum.

**14** Depress the footbrake pedal several times to operate the self-adjusting mechanism until normal pedal action returns. Refit the roadwheel then lower the vehicle to the ground and tighten the wheel nuts to the specified torque.

**15** On completion, adjust the handbrake as described in Section 14.

### 8  Front brake caliper - removal, overhaul and refitting

⚠ **Warning: Refer to the warning at the start of Section 2 regarding the safe handling of brake hydraulic fluid, and to the warning at the beginning of Section 4 concerning the dangers of asbestos dust.**
**Caution: On models equipped with ABS, disconnect the battery before disconnecting any braking system hydraulic union and do not reconnect the battery until after the hydraulic system has been bled. Failure to do this could lead to air entering the ABS hydraulic unit requiring the unit to be bled using special Ford test equipment (see Section 2).**

**8.6 Lift the caliper away from the disc**

**7.5 . . . and withdraw the hub/brake drum**

### Removal

**1** Apply the handbrake, then jack up the front of the vehicle and support it on axle stands (see *"Jacking and Vehicle Support"*). Remove the appropriate roadwheel.

**2** Minimise fluid loss by first removing the master cylinder reservoir cap, and then tightening it down onto a piece of polythene, to obtain an airtight seal. Alternatively, use a brake hose clamp to clamp the flexible hose running to the caliper.

**3** Clean the area around the caliper hose union, then loosen the union nut.

**4** Using a flat-bladed screwdriver, carefully prise the pad spring out from the caliper noting its correct fitted position.

**5** Remove the plastic covers from the ends of the guide bushes to gain access to the caliper guide pin bolts, then unscrew and remove the guide pin bolts **(see illustration)**.

**6** Lift the caliper assembly away from the disc **(see illustration)** and unclip the inner pad from the caliper piston. Unscrew the caliper from the end of the brake hose and remove it from the vehicle. Plug or cover the end of the hose to minimise fluid loss and to prevent dirt entry.

### Overhaul

**7** With the caliper on the bench, wipe away all traces of dust and dirt, but *avoid inhaling the dust, as it is injurious to health.*

**8** Withdraw the partially ejected piston from the caliper body **(see illustration)**.

**8.8 Brake caliper components**

A  *Dust cover*    C  *Piston*
B  *Piston seal*    D  *Caliper body*

**If the piston cannot be withdrawn by hand, it can be pushed out by applying compressed air to the brake hose union hole. Only low pressure should be required, such as is generated by a foot pump. As the piston is expelled take great care not to trap your fingers between the piston and caliper.**

9 Using a small screwdriver, prise the dust seal from the piston, then extract the piston hydraulic seal from the caliper bore, taking great care not to damage the bore.
10 Thoroughly clean all components, using only methylated spirit, isopropyl alcohol or clean hydraulic fluid as a cleaning medium. Never use mineral-based solvents such as petrol or paraffin, as they will attack the hydraulic system rubber components. Dry the components immediately, using compressed air or a clean, lint-free cloth. Use compressed air to blow clear the fluid passages.
11 Check all components, and renew any that are worn or damaged. Check particularly the cylinder bore and piston - these should be renewed if they are scratched, worn or corroded in any way (note that this means the renewal of the complete caliper body assembly). Similarly, check the condition of the guide pin bolts and their bushes - both bolts should be undamaged and (when cleaned) a reasonably tight sliding fit in their bushes. If there is any doubt about the condition of any component, renew it.
12 If the assembly is fit for further use, obtain the appropriate repair kit. The components are available from Ford dealers. All rubber seals should be renewed as a matter of course.
13 Before commencing reassembly, ensure that all components are clean and dry.
14 Dip the piston and the new seal in clean hydraulic fluid. Smear clean fluid on the cylinder bore surface.
15 Fit the new seal using only your fingers to manipulate it into the cylinder bore groove.
16 Fit the new dust seal to the piston groove, then carefully ease the piston squarely into the cylinder bore, using a twisting motion to help it enter the seal. Press the piston fully into position then seat the outer lip of the dust seal on the caliper body.

### Refitting

17 Screw the caliper body fully onto the flexible hose union.
18 Ensure that the outer brake pad is still correctly fitted in the caliper mounting bracket, and clip the inner pad into position in the caliper piston.
19 Slide the caliper over the disc, making sure that the pads remain correctly positioned, and fit the guide pin bolts. Tighten both guide pin bolts to the specified torque, then refit the plastic covers to the ends of the guide bushes.

20 Engage the pad spring with the outer pad and engage the spring ends correctly in the caliper body holes, as noted before removal.
21 Tighten the brake hose union, then remove the brake hose clamp or polythene (where fitted). Make sure that the hose is not twisted after tightening the union.
22 Bleed the hydraulic system as described in Section 2. Note that, provided precautions were taken to minimise brake fluid loss, it should only be necessary to bleed the relevant front brake.
23 Refit the roadwheel, then lower the vehicle to the ground and tighten the roadwheel nuts to the specified torque.

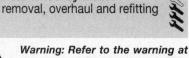

## 9 Rear wheel cylinder -
### removal, overhaul and refitting

⚠️ **Warning: Refer to the warning at the start of Section 2 regarding the safe handling of brake hydraulic fluid, and to the warning at the beginning of Section 5 concerning the dangers of asbestos dust.**
**Caution: On models equipped with ABS, disconnect the battery before disconnecting any braking system hydraulic union and do not reconnect the battery until after the hydraulic system has been bled. Failure to do this could lead to air entering the ABS hydraulic unit requiring the unit to be bled using special Ford test equipment (see Section 2).**

### Removal

1 Remove the brake drum as described in Section 7.
2 Minimise fluid loss by first removing the master cylinder reservoir cap, and then tightening it down onto a piece of polythene, to obtain an airtight seal. Alternatively, use a brake hose clamp to clamp the flexible hose at the nearest convenient point to the wheel cylinder.
3 Carefully unhook the brake shoe upper return spring, and remove it from both brake shoes **(see illustration)**. Pull the upper ends of the shoes away from the wheel cylinder to disengage them from the pistons.
4 Wipe away all traces of dirt around the brake pipe union at the rear of the wheel cylinder, and unscrew the union nut. Carefully ease the pipe out of the wheel cylinder, and plug or tape over its end to prevent dirt entry. Wipe off any spilt fluid immediately.
5 Unscrew the two wheel cylinder retaining bolts from the rear of the backplate, and remove the cylinder, taking great care not to allow surplus hydraulic fluid to contaminate the brake shoe linings **(see illustration)**.

### Overhaul

6 It is not possible to overhaul the cylinder, since no components are available separately. If faulty, the complete wheel cylinder assembly must be renewed.

**9.3 Unhook the brake shoe upper return spring (arrowed)**

### Refitting

7 Ensure that the backplate and wheel cylinder mating surfaces are clean and dry then spread the brake shoes and manoeuvre the wheel cylinder into position. Engage the brake pipe, and screw in the union nut two or three turns to ensure that the thread has started.
8 Insert the two wheel cylinder retaining bolts, tightening them securely, then tighten the brake pipe union nut to the specified torque.
9 Remove the clamp from the flexible brake hose, or the polythene from the master cylinder reservoir (as applicable).
10 Ensure that the brake shoes are correctly located in the cylinder pistons, then carefully refit the brake shoe return spring, ensuring it is correctly located in both shoes. Also check that the adjuster strut components are correctly located on the shoes.
11 Refit the brake drum as described in Section 7.
12 Bleed the brake hydraulic system as described in Section 2. Providing suitable precautions were taken to minimise loss of fluid, it should only be necessary to bleed the relevant rear brake.

## 10 Master cylinder -
### removal, overhaul and refitting

⚠️ **Warning: Refer to the warning at the start of Section 2 regarding the safe handling of brake fluid.**

**9.5 Rear wheel cylinder retaining bolts on the backplate**

**Caution:** *On models equipped with ABS, disconnect the battery before disconnecting any braking system hydraulic union and do not reconnect the battery until after the hydraulic system has been bled. Failure to do this could lead to air entering the ABS hydraulic unit requiring the unit to be bled using special Ford test equipment (see Section 2).*

## Removal

**1** Exhaust the vacuum present in the brake servo unit by repeatedly depressing the brake pedal.

**2** Disconnect the wiring connector from the brake fluid level sender unit in the reservoir cap, then unscrew and remove the cap and syphon all the hydraulic fluid from the reservoir. Alternatively, open any convenient bleed screw in the system, and gently pump the brake pedal to expel the fluid through a plastic tube connected to the bleed screw (see Section 2).

 **Warning:** *Do not syphon the fluid by mouth, as it is poisonous; use a syringe or an old poultry baster.*

**3** Release the retaining clip and disconnect the clutch master cylinder fluid supply hose from the side of the reservoir **(see illustration)**. Be prepared for a little fluid spillage, and plug the hose to prevent entry of dust and dirt.

**4** Wipe clean the area around the brake pipe unions on the side of the master cylinder, and place absorbent rags beneath the pipe unions to catch any surplus fluid. Make a note of the correct fitted positions of the unions, then unscrew the union nuts and carefully withdraw the pipes **(see illustration)**. Note that on models with ABS, the pipes between the master cylinder and ABS hydraulic unit are manufactured of nylon, whereas on non-ABS models, they are manufactured of steel. The ABS pipes should be tied to the bulkhead so that the fluid will not drain from them. Plug or tape over the pipe ends and master cylinder ports, to minimise the loss of brake fluid, and to prevent the entry of dust and dirt into the system. Wash off any spilt fluid immediately with cold water.

**5** Unscrew and remove the nuts securing the master cylinder to the vacuum servo unit. Remove the master cylinder from the engine compartment together with the reservoir. Recover the sealing ring and discard it - a new one must be used on refitting.

## Overhaul

**6** Ford do not supply a repair kit for the master cylinder, although it may be possible to obtain one from a motor factor. If a kit is obtained, note the locations of all components when dismantling to ensure correct refitting, and lubricate the new seals using clean brake fluid. Follow the assembly instructions supplied with the repair kit.

**10.3 The clutch master cylinder hose on the side of the brake fluid reservoir**

## Refitting

**7** Ensure the mating surfaces are clean and dry then fit the new sealing ring to the rear of the master cylinder.

**8** Carefully fit the master cylinder to the servo unit, ensuring that the servo unit pushrod enters the master cylinder bore centrally. Fit the retaining nuts and tighten them to the specified torque setting.

**9** Reconnect the brake pipes to the master cylinder and tighten the union nuts to the specified torque. Make sure that the pipes are correctly reconnected as noted before removal.

**10** Reconnect the clutch fluid hose to the side of the reservoir, and secure with the clip.

**11** Refill the master cylinder reservoir with new fluid, then bleed the complete hydraulic system as described in Section 2. Thoroughly check the operation of the braking system before using the vehicle on the road.

## 11 Brake pedal - removal and refitting

**Note:** *Removal of the clutch pedal and pedal bracket is described in Chapter 6.*

### Removal

**1** Disconnect the battery negative (earth) lead (see Chapter 5A).

**2** Inside the car, reach up and disconnect the wiring from the stop lamp switch, then twist the switch and remove it from the pedal bracket.

**3** Extract the clip securing the brake vacuum servo/linkage pushrod to the brake pedal, and disconnect the pushrod **(see illustration)**. If necessary, recover the bush and spacer.

**4** Extract the shaft securing clip from the right-hand end of the pedal pivot shaft, then push the shaft to the left until the brake pedal can be withdrawn from the bracket.

**5** Remove the pivot bushes from either side of the pedal.

**6** Inspect the pedal for signs of wear or damage, paying particular attention to the pivot bushes, and renew worn components as necessary.

**10.4 Brake pipe unions on the side of the master cylinder**

### Refitting

**7** Apply some multi-purpose grease to the bearing surfaces of the pedal, pivot shaft and bushes. Fit the bushes to the pedal.

**8** Manoeuvre the pedal into the bracket, then align it with the pivot shaft and slide the shaft fully to the right. Refit the retaining clip.

**9** Engage the brake vacuum servo/linkage pushrod with the pedal, and secure with the clip. Make sure the bush and spacer are correctly located.

**10** Refit the stop lamp switch to the bracket then adjust it as follows. First pull out the switch to its full extent, then depress the pedal and refit the switch. Slowly release the pedal, then reconnect the wiring.

**11** Reconnect the battery negative (earth) lead (see Chapter 5A).

**12** Check the operation of the brake pedal before using the vehicle on the road.

## 12 Vacuum servo unit - testing, removal and refitting

### Testing

**1** To test the operation of the servo unit, depress the footbrake several times to exhaust the vacuum, then start the engine whilst keeping the pedal firmly depressed. As the engine starts, there should be a noticeable "give" in the brake pedal as the vacuum builds up. Allow the engine to run for at least two minutes, then switch it off. If the brake pedal

**11.3 The pushrod-to-brake pedal retaining clip**

is now depressed it should feel normal, but further applications should result in the pedal feeling firmer, with the pedal stroke decreasing with each application.

**2** If the servo does not operate as described, first inspect the servo unit check valve as described in Section 13.

**3** If the servo unit still fails to operate satisfactorily, the fault lies within the unit itself. Repairs to the unit are not possible - if faulty, the servo unit must be renewed.

### Removal

**4** Remove the master cylinder as described in Section 10.

**5** Carefully ease the vacuum hose end fitting out from the servo unit, taking care not to displace the rubber grommet.

**6** Unscrew and remove the nuts securing the vacuum servo unit to the bracket on the bulkhead, and move the unit slightly forwards from the bracket **(see illustration)**.

**7** On left-hand-drive models, working inside the car extract the clip securing the brake vacuum servo pushrod to the brake pedal, and disconnect the pushrod. Withdraw the servo unit from the rubber grommet on the bulkhead and remove from the engine compartment.

**8** On right-hand drive models, use a length of wood to hold the brake pedal fully depressed. Working in the engine compartment, extract the clip and remove the pin securing the servo unit pushrod clevis to the brake pedal cross-shaft. Withdraw the servo unit from the engine compartment.

**9** If the servo unit is faulty it must be renewed - overhaul of the unit is not possible.

### Refitting

**10** On right-hand-drive models, apply a little multi-purpose grease to the servo unit clevis and clevis pin. Manoeuvre the unit into position, then refit the clevis pin and secure it in position with the retaining clip. Seat the unit on the bracket and tighten its mounting nuts to the specified torque.

**11** On left-hand-drive models, carefully manoeuvre the servo unit into position, making sure that the pushrod is located through the rubber grommet. Ensure that the pushrod is correctly located, then refit the servo unit

**12.6 Nuts securing the vacuum servo unit to the bracket on the bulkhead**

securing nuts and tighten them to the specified torque. Secure the pushrod to the pedal with the retaining clip.

**12** Carefully ease the vacuum hose end fitting into the servo unit.

**13** Refit the master cylinder as described in Section 10 and bleed the complete hydraulic system as described in Section 2.

### 13 Vacuum servo unit check valve - removal, testing and refitting

### Removal

**1** The valve is integral with the servo vacuum hose.

**2** Carefully ease the vacuum hose end fitting out from its rubber grommet on the front of the servo unit.

**3** Work back along the vacuum hose, freeing it from any relevant retaining clips, then unscrew the union nut securing the hose to the inlet manifold and remove the hose from the engine compartment. The check valve and hose cannot be separated.

### Testing

**4** Examine the check valve and hose for signs of damage, and renew if necessary. The valve may be tested by blowing through the hose in both directions. Air should flow through the valve in one direction only - when blown through from the servo unit end of the hose. Renew the valve and hose assembly if this is not the case.

**5** Examine the servo unit rubber sealing grommet for signs of damage or deterioration, and renew as necessary.

### Refitting

**6** Manoeuvre the hose assembly into position and connect the engine end of the hose to the inlet manifold. Tighten the union nut securely.

**7** Ensure the hose is correctly routed and fit the sealing grommet into position in the servo unit. Ease the hose end fitting into position in the servo, taking care not to displace the grommet.

**8** On completion, start the engine and check that there are no air leaks.

### 14 Handbrake - adjustment

*Caution: If the handbrake is incorrectly adjusted, the rear brake automatic adjustment mechanism will not be able to function correctly. This will lead to the brake shoe-to-drum clearance becoming excessive as the shoe linings wear, resulting in excessive brake pedal travel.*

**1** Fully release the handbrake then apply the footbrake firmly several times to ensure that the self-adjust mechanism is fully adjusted.

**2** Lift the handbrake lever gaiter from the floor to gain access to the adjuster nut on the side of the lever **(see illustration)**.

**3** From the fully-released position, pull the handbrake lever up noting the number of clicks emitted from the handbrake ratchet mechanism. Position the handbrake lever on the sixth notch of the mechanism then slacken the adjusting nut until it rotates freely. Adjust the handbrake by tightening the adjuster nut to 4.0 Nm then refit the gaiter **(see illustration)**.

### 15 Handbrake lever - removal and refitting

### Removal

**1** Chock the wheels to prevent the vehicle rolling whilst the handbrake is released.

**2** Inside the vehicle, unclip the hand-brake lever gaiter and remove it from the lever.

**3** Unscrew and remove the cable adjusting nut from the side of the lever, then unscrew the two lever retaining nuts **(see illustration)**. Manoeuvre the lever assembly out of position, disconnecting the warning light switch wiring connector as it becomes accessible.

**4** With the handbrake lever removed, make sure that the front cable end fitting remains engaged with the equalizer bar. If it becomes disengaged, it will be necessary to jack up the front of the car and remove the exhaust front and centre heatshields in order to relocate it.

**14.2 Lift the handbrake lever gaiter from the floor**

**14.3 Handbrake adjusting nut**

**15.3 Handbrake lever securing nuts**

**16.2 Handbrake front cable (carpet removed)**

**16.5 Handbrake equalizer bar mechanism (arrowed)**

## Refitting

**5** Refitting is a reversal of removal, tightening the lever retaining nuts to the specified torque. Prior to refitting the gaiter, adjust the handbrake cable as described in Section 14.

## 16 Handbrake cables - removal and refitting

**1** The handbrake cable consists of three sections, a short front section which connects the lever to the equalizer plate and the left- and right-hand rear sections which link the equalizer plate to each rear brake. Each section can be removed individually as follows.

### Front cable

#### Removal

**2** Remove the handbrake lever as described in Section 15 (see illustration).
**3** Chock the front wheels, then jack up the rear of the vehicle and support it on axle stands (see "Jacking and Vehicle Support").
**4** To gain access to the equalizer bar which links the front ends of the handbrake cables, unscrew the nuts and remove the exhaust system front and centre heatshields.
**5** Detach the front cable from the equalizer bar (see illustration), then free the cable grommet from the underbody and remove the cable from the vehicle.

#### Refitting

**6** Refitting is a reversal of the removal procedure, but refit the handbrake lever and adjust the handbrake (see Section 14) before refitting the heatshields. Make sure that the cable end fitting is correctly located in the equalizer bar.

### Rear cables

#### Removal

**7** Chock the front wheels, then jack up the rear of the vehicle and support it on axle stands (see "Jacking and Vehicle Support"). Remove both rear roadwheels.
**8** Unscrew the nuts and remove the exhaust system front and centre heatshields.

**9** Inside the vehicle, unclip the handbrake lever gaiter and remove it from the lever.
**10** Fully loosen the handbrake lever adjustment nut but do not remove it.
**11** Working on one side at a time, unscrew the bolts securing the rear stub axle to the rear axle, then withdraw the stub axle together with the hub/brake drum over the brake shoes. Note that the backplate and spacer plate are riveted to the rear axle. On models with ABS, take care not to damage the ABS sensor bolted to the backplate.
**12** Remove the rear brake shoes with reference to Section 5 (Method 1).
**13** Unscrew and remove the handbrake cable rear support bolts.
**14** Release the cable rear retaining rings from the brake backplates, and pull out the cables from the backplates.
**15** Work back along the cables and release them from the support clips (see illustration).
**16** At the front of the cables, disconnect the front cable end fitting from the equalizer bar.
**17** Release the rear outer cables from the underbody bracket and guide the inner cables through the slots. If necessary, remove the equalizer bar from the inner cable end fittings. Note that the two rear cables and equalizer bar are supplied as one assembly by Ford.

#### Refitting

**18** Refitting is a reversal of the removal procedure, bearing in mind the following points.
a) Ensure that the cable is correctly routed and retained by all the relevant clips.
b) Refit the rear brake shoes with reference to Section 5.

**16.15 Handbrake rear cable support clip**

c) Prior to refitting the handbrake lever gaiter and exhaust heatshields, adjust the handbrake as described in Section 14.

## 17 Rear brake pressure-regulating valve - testing, removal and refitting

⚠️ *Warning: Refer to the warning at the start of Section 2 regarding the safe handling of brake hydraulic fluid.*

### Testing

**1** On models not equipped with ABS, a pressure regulating valve is fitted into the hydraulic circuit to each rear brake. The valves are located between the rear rigid lines and flexible hoses (see illustration). The valves regulate the hydraulic pressure applied to the rear brakes to help prevent rear wheels locking up under hard braking.
**2** Specialist equipment is required to check the performance of the valves, therefore if the valves are thought to be faulty the car should be taken to a Ford dealer for testing. Repairs are not possible and, if faulty, the valves must be renewed.

### Removal

**3** Exhaust the vacuum present in the servo unit by repeatedly depressing the brake pedal.
**4** Minimise fluid loss by first removing the master cylinder reservoir cap, and then tightening it down onto a piece of polythene, to obtain an airtight seal.

**17.1 The rear brake pressure regulating valves are located between the rigid lines and flexible hoses**

**5** Chock the front wheels, then jack up the rear of the vehicle and support it on axle stands (see "Jacking and Vehicle Support"). Remove the relevant rear roadwheel.
**6** Clean the surrounding area, then unscrew the union nut and disconnect the rigid line from the top of the pressure regulating valve. Be prepared for some loss of hydraulic fluid.
**7** Hold the flexible hose end fitting stationary with a spanner, then unscrew the pressure regulating valve from the hose and remove it from the support bracket.
**8** Plug or tape over the ends of the pipe and hose to prevent entry of dust and dirt.

### Refitting

**9** Ensure that the threads of the valve, rigid pipe and hose end fitting are clean and dry. Locate the hose end fitting in the support bracket, then screw on the pressure regulating valve and tighten securely while holding the end fitting stationary with a second spanner.
**10** Refit the rigid pipe to the top of the valve and tighten the union nut to the specified torque while holding the valve stationary.
**11** Remove the polythene from the master cylinder, then bleed the hydraulic system as described in Section 2.
**12** Refit the roadwheel and lower the car to the ground.

### 18 Stop-light switch - removal, refitting and adjustment

### Removal

**1** The stop-light switch is located on the pedal bracket beneath the facia (see illustration).
**2** Disconnect the battery negative (earth) lead (see Chapter 5A).
**3** Reach up and disconnect the wiring connector from the switch on the bracket.
**4** Rotate the switch slightly anti-clockwise and remove it from the bracket.

### Refitting and adjustment

**5** On left-hand-drive models, insert the switch in the bracket aperture, then pull the brake pedal fully upwards (to its rest position) and push down the switch until the plunger is fully depressed. Turn the switch 40° clockwise to back it off 1.0 mm and lock it.
**6** On right-hand-drive models, insert the switch in the bracket aperture, then support the brake pedal in its rest position. Push the switch fully downwards while still supporting the pedal, so that the switch plunger is fully depressed. Turn the switch 40° clockwise to back it off 1.0 mm and lock it.
**7** Reconnect the wiring to the switch.
**8** Reconnect the battery negative (earth) lead (see Chapter 5A), and check the stop-light operation by switching on the ignition.

**18.1 Brake stop-light switch**

### 19 Handbrake "on" warning light switch - removal and refitting

### Removal

**1** Lift the handbrake lever gaiter from the floor.
**2** Remove the securing screw, and withdraw the switch (see illustration).

### Refitting

**3** Refitting is a reversal of removal, but adjust the handbrake cable as described in Section 14.

### 20 Anti-lock braking system (ABS) - general information

ABS is available as an option on all models. The system comprises the hydraulic unit, four wheel sensors and four sensor rings. The hydraulic unit incorporates hydraulic solenoid valves (one set for each brake), a brake pressure pump and the ABS control module. The purpose of the system is to prevent wheel lock-up during heavy braking at speeds in excess of 3 mph. This is achieved by automatic release of the brake on the relevant wheel followed by re-application of the brake, this cycle occurring many times a second.

The solenoid valves are controlled by the ECU, which itself receives signals from the four wheel sensors (fitted to the wheel hubs), which monitor the speed of rotation of each

**19.2 Handbrake lever switch location**

wheel. By comparing these signals, the ECU can determine the speed at which the vehicle is travelling. It can then use this speed to determine when a wheel is decelerating at an abnormal rate, compared to the speed of the vehicle, and therefore predicts when a wheel is about to lock. During normal operation, the system functions in the same way as a non-ABS braking system.

If the ECU senses that a wheel is about to lock, it operates the relevant solenoid valves in the hydraulic unit to reduce the hydraulic pressure on the wheel which is about to lock. If the wheel speed now increases to an acceptable rate, the pressure pump increases the hydraulic pressure to the wheel to equal the pressure applied by the brake pedal.

The action of the solenoid valves and pump creates pulses in the hydraulic circuit. When the ABS system is functioning, these pulses can be felt through the brake pedal.

The operation of the ABS system is entirely dependent on electrical signals. If an inaccurate signal or low battery voltage is detected, the system is automatically shut down, and the warning light on the instrument panel is illuminated to inform the driver that the system is not operational. However, normal braking is still available.

If a fault does develop in the ABS control system, the vehicle must be taken to a Ford dealer for fault diagnosis and repair.

### 21 Anti-lock braking system components - removal and refitting

### Hydraulic unit

⚠ **Warning: After refitting the hydraulic unit and carrying out the initial conventional bleeding procedure, the hydraulic unit must be bled by a Ford dealer using the special Ford test equipment FDS 2000, followed by a further conventional bleeding procedure (see Section 2).**

### Removal

**1** Apply the handbrake, then jack up the front of the vehicle and support it on axle stands (see "Jacking and Vehicle Support"). Remove both front roadwheels.
**2** Disconnect the wiring connector from the brake fluid level sender unit in the reservoir cap, then unscrew and remove the cap and syphon all the hydraulic fluid from the reservoir.

⚠ **Warning: Do not syphon the fluid by mouth, as it is poisonous; use a syringe or an old poultry baster.**

**3** Drain the hydraulic fluid from the front brake lines as follows. Collect together a clean glass jar, a suitable length of plastic or rubber tubing which is a tight fit over the bleed screw, and a ring spanner to fit the screw. The help of an assistant will also be required.

Working on each side at a time, connect the tube to the front caliper bleed screws, then have an assistant depress the brake pedal slowly several times until all fluid has been removed.

**4** Unhook the exhaust rubber mountings and allow the exhaust to rest on the rear axle beam.

**5** Working beneath the car, unscrew the nuts and remove the rear exhaust heatshield from the underbody.

**6** Disconnect the hydraulic unit wiring at the multiplug, then unscrew the cable support bracket from the unit mounting bracket.

**7** Release the brake lines leading to the hydraulic unit from the underbody clips.

**8** Unscrew the bolts securing the unit mounting bracket to the underbody, and lower it sufficient to disconnect the wiring at the multiplug.

**9** Identify the brake lines for location, then unscrew the union nuts and disconnect the lines **(see illustration)**. Plug or tape over the line ends and unit apertures to prevent entry of dust and dirt.

**10** With the unit on the bench, unscrew the nuts and remove the unit from the rubber mountings on the bracket.

### Refitting

**11** Refitting is a reversal of removal, but carry out the initial bleeding procedure as described in Section 2, then have the hydraulic unit bled by a Ford dealer using the FDS 2000 test equipment (see Section 2). Finally, bleed the complete system again conventionally.

## Wheel sensor (front)

### Removal

**12** Apply the handbrake, then jack up the front of the vehicle and support it on axle stands (see *"Jacking and Vehicle Support"*). Remove the relevant front roadwheel.

**13** Trace the wheel sensor wiring back into the engine compartment, and disconnect it. Release the wiring from the clip and support bracket.

**14** Unscrew the mounting bolt and remove the wheel sensor from its housing.

### Refitting

**15** Ensure that the mating faces of the sensor and the housing are clean, and apply a little multi-purpose grease to the housing bore before refitting.

**16** Make sure the sensor tip is clean, then ease the sensor into position in the housing. Refit the retaining bolt and tighten it to the specified torque.

**17** Locate the wiring in the support bracket and clip and reconnect it to the main wiring harness.

**18** Refit the roadwheel, then lower the vehicle to the ground.

## Wheel sensor (rear)

### Removal

**19** Chock the front wheels, then jack up the rear of the vehicle and support it on axle stands (see *"Jacking and Vehicle Support"*). Remove the relevant rear roadwheel.

**20** Trace the wheel sensor wiring back to the

**21.9 Hydraulic brake line connections on the ABS hydraulic unit (arrowed)**

multiplug and disconnect it. Release the wiring from the support clips.

**21** Unscrew the mounting bolt and remove the wheel sensor from the rear brake backplate.

### Refitting

**22** Ensure that the mating faces of the sensor and the backplate are clean, and apply a little multi-purpose grease to the location bore before refitting.

**23** Make sure the sensor tip is clean, then locate the sensor into position. Refit the retaining bolt and tighten it to the specified torque.

**24** Locate the wiring in the support clips and reconnect it to the main wiring harness.

**25** Refit the roadwheel, then lower the vehicle to the ground.

**Notes**

# Chapter 10
# Suspension and steering

## Contents

## Degrees of difficulty

| Easy, suitable for novice with little experience | | Fairly easy, suitable for beginner with some experience | | Fairly difficult, suitable for competent DIY mechanic | | Difficult, suitable for experienced DIY mechanic | | Very difficult, suitable for expert DIY or professional | |
|---|---|---|---|---|---|---|---|---|---|
| |  | |  | |  | |  | | |

## Specifications

### General

| | |
|---|---|
| Front suspension type ................................... | Independent, with MacPherson struts, integral shock absorbers, coil springs and anti-roll bar |
| Rear suspension type ................................... | Semi-independent, trailing arms integral with 'twist beam', struts with shock absorbers and coil springs |
| Steering type ......................................... | Rack and pinion steering, power-assisted on most models |

### Wheel alignment and steering angles

|  | Tolerance | Nominal |
|---|---|---|
| Front wheel castor: | | |
| Manual steering .......................................... | 1°47' to -0°43' | 0°32' |
| Power steering ........................................... | 4°02' to 1°32' | 2°47' |
| Maximum variation side-to-side ............................ | 1°00' | |
| Front wheel camber: | | |
| Manual steering .......................................... | 1°24' to -1°24' | 0°00' |
| Power steering ........................................... | 1°27' to -1°21' | 0°03' |
| Maximum variation side-to-side ............................ | 1°15' | |
| Front wheel toe-setting: | | |
| Allowable tolerance ...................................... | 0°35' (3.5 mm) toe-in to -0°15' (-1.5 mm) toe-out | |
| Setting value ............................................ | 0°10' (1.0 mm) toe-in ± 0°10' (1.0 mm) | |
|  | Tolerance | Nominal |
| Rear wheel camber ......................................... | -0°30' to -2°00' | -1°00' |
| Maximum variation side-to-side ............................ | 1°15' | |
| Rear wheel toe-setting: | | |
| Allowable tolerance ...................................... | 0°43' (4.3 mm) to 0°03' (0.3 mm) toe-in | |
| Setting value ............................................ | 0°24' (2.3 mm) toe-in | |

## Torque wrench settings

| | Nm | lbf ft |
|---|---|---|
| **Front suspension** | | |
| Anti-roll bar clamp bolts | 25 | 18 |
| Anti-roll bar drop link nuts | 52 | 38 |
| Front hub nut | 270 | 200 |
| Front suspension lower arm mounting bracket | 85 | 63 |
| Hub carrier-to-suspension strut clamp bolt | 51 | 38 |
| Lower arm inner bolts: | | |
|    Stage 1 | 50 | 37 |
|    Stage 2 | Angle-tighten 90° | |
| Lower arm-to-hub carrier clamp bolt and nut | 51 | 38 |
| Suspension strut piston rod locknut | 59 | 44 |
| Suspension strut top mounting nut | 50 | 37 |
| **Rear suspension** | | |
| Rear axle assembly mounting bracket-to-trailing arm bolts | 68 | 50 |
| Rear axle assembly mounting bracket-to-floor bolts | 50 | 37 |
| Rear hub nut | 235 | 173 |
| Stub axle-to-trailing arm bolts | 66 | 49 |
| Suspension strut lower securing bolt | 120 | 89 |
| Suspension strut top mounting nut | 34 | 25 |
| **Steering** | | |
| Brake vacuum servo support stay | 25 | 18 |
| Column lower universal joint clamp bolt | 28 | 21 |
| Power steering cooler left-hand union nut | 17 | 13 |
| Power steering cooler right-hand union nut | 65 | 48 |
| Power steering fluid pressure switch | 11 | 8 |
| Power steering gear fluid pipe unions | 31 | 23 |
| Power steering pump securing bolts | 25 | 18 |
| Steering column securing nuts | 12 | 9 |
| Steering gear securing nuts and bolts | 84 | 62 |
| Steering wheel securing bolt | 45 | 33 |
| Track-rod end to track-rod locknut | 63 | 46 |
| Track-rod end-to-steering arm nut | 26 | 19 |
| **Roadwheels** | | |
| Wheel nuts | 85 | 63 |

## 1 General information

The front suspension is of independent type, with MacPherson struts, lower arms, and an anti-roll bar. The lower arms and anti-roll bar are mounted on side brackets bolted to the underbody The struts, which incorporate coil springs and integral shock absorbers, are attached at their upper ends to the reinforced strut mountings on the body shell. The lower end of each strut is attached to the top of a cast hub carrier by a clamp bolt. The hub carriers incorporate the hubs, brake discs and calipers. The hubs run within non-adjustable bearings in the hub carriers. The lower end of each hub carrier is attached, via a balljoint, to a pressed-steel lower arm

assembly. The balljoints are integral with the lower arms. The lower arms are attached at their inboard ends to side brackets, via flexible rubber bushes. The lower arms control both lateral and fore and aft movement of the front wheels. The anti-roll bar is mounted on the side brackets, and is connected to the suspension struts via vertical drop links.

The rear suspension is semi-independent, and consists of a beam welded between trailing arms. This beam allows a limited torsional flexibility, giving each rear wheel a certain degree of independent movement, whilst maintaining optimum track and wheel camber control. This type of arrangement is called a "twist beam" rear axle. The axle is attached to the body via rubber bushes. The rear suspension struts, which are similar to the MacPherson struts used at the front, are attached at their upper ends to the reinforced

strut mountings in the luggage compartment. At their lower ends, the struts are attached to the rear of the trailing arms. The rear hubs are integral with the brake drums, and the hub/drums run on stub axles which are bolted to the rear of the trailing arms.

The steering is of conventional rack-and-pinion type, incorporating a collapsible safety column **(see illustration)**. The column is joined to the steering gear via a flexible coupling. The steering gear is mounted on the underbody, below the bulkhead. The steering gear track-rods are attached via the track-rod ends to the steering arms on the hub carriers.

Up to June 1997, power steering was available as an option on base models, however, from this date all models are fitted with power steering **(see illustration)**. The power steering pump is belt-driven from the crankshaft pulley.

### 1.3  Steering system components

1  Track rod
2  Steering gear
3  Track rod end
4  Gaiter
5  Coupling
6  Steering column
7  Steering wheel

### 1.4  Power steering components

1  Hydraulic fluid reservoir
2  Power steering pump
3  Fluid cooler pipes
4  Track rod end
5  Track rod
6  Steering gear gaiter
7  Steering gear
8  Universal joint
9  Steering column assembly
10  Steering wheel
11  Pressure switch

**2.2 Relieve the staking on the front hub nut**

**2.3 Loosen the suspension strut top mounting nut five turns**

**2.5 The brake hose is attached to the bracket on the suspension strut with a rubber grommet**

## 2 Front hub carrier -
removal and refitting

### Removal

**Note:** *A balljoint separator tool will be required to disconnect the track-rod end from the steering arm. A new hub nut will be required on refitting.*

**1** Remove the relevant wheel trim, or the wheel centre plate (alloy wheels) for access to the front hub nut.

**2** Ensure that the handbrake is applied, then relieve the staking on the front hub nut, using a suitable punch **(see illustration)**. Slacken the hub nut using a suitable socket and extension bar. Do not remove the hub nut at this stage.

*Caution: Take care, as the hub nut is tightened to a very high torque.*

**3** Working in the engine compartment, slacken the relevant suspension strut top mounting nut five turns, using a ring spanner. Counterhold the strut piston rod using a suitable Allen key or hexagon bit. **Do not** remove the nut **(see illustration)**.

**4** Slacken the relevant front wheel nuts, then jack up the front of the vehicle, and support securely on axle stands (see *"Jacking and Vehicle Support"*). Remove the roadwheel.

**5** Working under the wheel arch, disconnect the brake hose from the bracket on the suspension strut. Take care not to damage the rubber grommet **(see illustration)**.

**6** Unscrew the bolts securing the brake caliper mounting bracket to the hub carrier, then slide the caliper/bracket assembly from the hub carrier and brake disc (there is no need to remove the brake pads) **(see illustration)**. Suspend the caliper/bracket assembly from the strut coil spring using wire or string - do not

allow the caliper to hang on the brake hose.

**7** Extract the split pin, then unscrew the track-rod end balljoint nut as far as the ends of the threads **(see illustration)**.

**8** Disconnect the track-rod end balljoint from the hub carrier using a balljoint separator tool (leave the nut fitted to protect the threads), taking care not to damage the balljoint rubber seal **(see illustration)**. Once the balljoint has been released, remove the balljoint nut.

**9** Where applicable, unbolt the ABS wheel sensor from the hub carrier, and tie it clear of the working area.

**10** Unscrew the hub nut from the end of the driveshaft, and remove the washer **(see illustration)**.

**11** Where applicable, prise the locating clip from the wheel stud, then lift off the brake disc.

**12** Unscrew and remove the clamp bolt securing the hub carrier to the lower arm balljoint - note that the bolt head is facing the

**2.6 Unscrew the bolts securing the brake caliper mounting bracket to the hub carrier**

**2.7 Track-rod end balljoint and nut**

**2.8 Using a balljoint separator tool to release the track-rod end**

**2.10 Unscrew the hub nut and remove the washer**

**2.12a Unscrew the clamp bolt and nut securing the hub carrier to the lower arm balljoint . . .**

**2.12b . . . then push the end of the lower arm down to free the balljoint from the hub carrier**

front of the car. Push the end of the lower arm down to free the balljoint from the hub carrier **(see illustrations)**. If the balljoint is very tight, it may be necessary to use a long lever or similar tool, but take care not to damage the balljoint rubber seal.

**13** The hub must now be freed from the end of the driveshaft. It should be possible to pull the hub carrier off the driveshaft, but if the end of the driveshaft is tight in the hub, temporarily refit the hub nut to protect the driveshaft threads, then tap the end of the driveshaft with a soft-faced hammer, or use a suitable puller to free it. Support the driveshaft using wire or string - **do not** allow the driveshaft to hang down under its own weight, as this may result in damage to the constant velocity joints.

*Caution: When freeing the driveshaft from the hub, make sure that the driveshaft does not disengage from the inner constant velocity joint.*

**14** Unscrew the clamp bolt securing the hub carrier to the lower end of the suspension strut **(see illustration)**. Using a suitable lever, or a large screwdriver, spread the slot in the top of the hub carrier, until the hub carrier can be pulled from the end of the strut. If necessary, tap the hub carrier down to free it from the strut, using a soft-faced mallet.

### Refitting

**15** Refitting is a reversal of removal, but note the following points.
   a) Use a new hub nut.
   b) Make sure that the slot for the clamp bolt in the strut aligns with the corresponding holes in the hub carrier.

**3.2  Driving the hub from the hub bearing**

**3.4  Remove the bearing circlip from the inner face of the hub carrier**

**2.14  Clamp bolt securing the hub carrier to the lower end of the suspension strut**

   c) Do not fully tighten the hub nut until the vehicle is resting on its wheels.
   d) Fit a new split pin to the track rod end nut.
   e) Tighten all nuts and bolts to the specified torque, referring to the relevant Chapter of this Manual where necessary.

### 3  Front hub bearings - renewal

**Note:** *A press and puller, or similar improvised tools will be required for this operation. Obtain a new bearing and bearing retaining clip before proceeding.*

**1** Remove the hub carrier as described in Section 2.
**2** The hub must now be removed from the bearing/hub carrier assembly. It is preferable to use a press to do this, but it is possible to drive out the hub using a metal tube of suitable diameter. First, support the hub carrier with the inner face uppermost, then use a metal bar or tube of suitable diameter to press or drive the hub from the hub bearing **(see illustration)**. Alternatively, use a puller to separate the hub from the bearing. On models with ABS, take care not to damage the ABS sensor ring. Note that the inner bearing race will remain on the hub.
**3** Using a suitable puller, pull the inner bearing race from the hub. Alternatively, support the bearing race on suitably thin

**4.4  Unscrew the nut securing the anti-roll bar drop link to the suspension strut**

metal bars, and press or drive the hub from the bearing race.
**4** Remove the bearing retaining circlip from the inner face of the hub carrier - discard the circlip, a new one must be used on refitting **(see illustration)**.
**5** Using a puller, pull the bearing from the hub carrier. Alternatively, support the hub carrier, and press or drive out the bearing.
**6** Before fitting the new bearing, thoroughly clean the bearing location in the hub carrier.
**7** Using a press or a suitable puller, fit the new bearing to the hub carrier. The outer face of the bearing should contact the shoulder in the hub carrier. It may be possible to improvise a suitable puller using a socket, nut, washers, and length of threaded bar.
**8** Fit a new bearing retaining clip to the inner face of the hub carrier.
**9** Press or draw the hub into the bearing while supporting the bearing inner track.
**10** Refit the hub carrier as described in Section 2.

### 4  Front suspension strut - removal, overhaul and refitting

### Removal

**1** Apply the handbrake, then jack up the front of the vehicle and support it on axle stands (see *"Jacking and Vehicle Support"*). Remove the relevant roadwheel.
**2** On models with ABS, disconnect the sensor wiring and release it from the clips and support bracket, then position it to one side.
**3** Carefully release the hydraulic brake hose from the support bracket on the strut. Take care not to damage the rubber grommet.
**4** Unscrew the nut and disconnect the anti-roll bar link from the strut **(see illustration)**.
**5** Unscrew the bolts securing the brake caliper mounting bracket to the hub carrier, then slide the caliper/bracket assembly from the hub carrier and brake disc (there is no need to remove the brake pads) **(see illustration)**. Support the caliper/bracket assembly on an axle stand.

**4.5  Unscrew the bolts securing the brake caliper mounting bracket to the hub carrier**

4.6a Unscrew the clamp nut and bolt securing the hub carrier to the lower arm balljoint

4.6b . . . then push the end of the lower arm down to free the balljoint from the hub carrier

4.9 The top mounting insulator may be stuck in position under the wheel arch

**6** Unscrew and remove the clamp nut and bolt securing the hub carrier to the lower arm balljoint - note that the bolt head is facing the front of the car. Push the end of the lower arm down to free the balljoint from the hub carrier **(see illustrations)**. If the balljoint is very tight, it may be necessary to use a long lever or similar tool, but take care not to damage the balljoint rubber seal.

**7** Unscrew the clamp bolt securing the hub carrier to the lower end of the suspension strut. Using a suitable lever, or a large screwdriver, spread the slot in the top of the hub carrier, until the hub carrier can be pulled from the end of the strut. If necessary, tap the hub carrier down to free it from the strut, using a soft-faced mallet. With the hub carrier released, support it on an axle stand making sure that the driveshaft joints are not bent excessively.

**Caution: The inner driveshaft joint must not be bent more than 18°, and the outer joint by more than 45°.**

**8** Support the strut then, working in the engine compartment, unscrew and remove the top mounting nut, using a ring spanner. Counterhold the strut piston rod using an Allen key. Lower the strut from the top

mounting and withdraw it from under the wheel arch.

**9** Remove the top mounting insulator from the body **(see illustration)**. Also remove the mounting cup from the top of the strut.

## Overhaul

**Note:** *A spring compressor tool will be required for this operation.*

**10** With the suspension strut resting on a bench, or clamped in a vice, fit a spring compressor tool, and compress the coil spring to relieve the pressure on the spring seats **(see illustration)**. Ensure that the compressor tool is securely located on the spring, in accordance with the tool manufacturer's instructions.

⚠ **Warning: Do not attempt to dismantle the strut without using an approved spring compressor tool.**

**11** Counterhold the strut piston rod with the Allen key used during removal, then unscrew and remove the piston rod nut **(see illustration)**.

**12** Remove the thrust bearing, the upper spring seat, the spring (with compressor tool still fitted), the gaiter, the rubber bump stop,

and the dust cover - note that the gaiter clips into the dust cover.

**13** With the strut assembly now completely dismantled, examine all the components for wear, damage or deformation, and check the thrust bearing for smoothness of operation. Renew any of the components as necessary.

**14** Examine the strut for signs of fluid leakage. Check the strut piston for signs of pitting along its entire length, and check the strut body for signs of damage. While holding it in an upright position, test the operation of the strut shock absorber by moving the piston through a full stroke, and then through short strokes of 50 to 100 mm. In both cases, the resistance felt should be smooth and continuous. If the resistance is jerky or uneven or if there is any visible sign of wear or damage to the strut, renewal is necessary.

**15** If any doubt exists as to the condition of the coil spring, carefully remove the spring compressors and check the spring for distortion and signs of cracking. Renew the spring if it is damaged or distorted, or if there is any doubt as to its condition.

**16** Inspect all other components for damage or deterioration, and renew any that are suspect.

4.10 Spring compressor tools fitted to suspension strut coil spring

4.11 Counterhold the strut piston rod with the Allen key and unscrew the piston rod nut

4.17a  Slide on the dust cover . . .

4.17b  . . . followed by the bump stop . . .

4.17c  . . . and the gaiter

4.19a  Slide the spring over the strut . . .

4.19b  . . . and position it so that the lower end of the spring is resting against the stop (arrowed)

4.20  Refit the upper spring seat . . .

**17** Slide the dust cover onto the strut piston, followed by the rubber bump stop and gaiter **(see illustrations)**. Clip the gaiter into position on the dust cover.

**18** If the spring compressor tool has been removed from the spring, refit it and compress the spring sufficiently to enable it to be refitted to the strut.

**19** Fit the spring over the strut, and position it so that the lower end of the spring is resting against the stop on the lower seat **(see illustrations)**.

**20** Refit the upper spring seat, and rotate it as necessary to position the stop against the upper end of the spring **(see illustration)**.

**21** Refit the thrust bearing, then refit the piston rod nut, and tighten to the specified torque **(see illustrations)**. Counterhold the

piston rod using an Allen key as during removal.

**22** Slowly slacken the spring compressor tool to relieve the tension in the spring. Check that the ends of the spring locate correctly against the stops on the spring seats. If necessary, turn the spring and the upper seat so that the components locate correctly before the compressor tool is removed. Remove the compressor tool when the spring is fully seated.

### Refitting

**23** Refitting is a reversal of removal, bearing in mind the following points.

a) *Make sure that the slot for the clamp bolt in the strut aligns with the corresponding holes in the hub carrier* **(see illustration)**.

b) *Make sure that the top mounting insulator is correctly seated on the strut mounting in the engine compartment.*

c) *Tighten the nuts and bolts to the specified torque.*

### 5  Front suspension anti-roll bar - removal and refitting

### Removal

**1** Apply the handbrake, then jack up the front of the vehicle and support it on axle stands (see *"Jacking and Vehicle Support"*). Remove both front roadwheels.

**2** The front suspension lower arms must be

4.21a  . . . followed by the thrust bearing . . .

4.21b  . . . and the piston rod nut

4.23  Make sure that the slot (A) for the clamp bolt in the strut aligns with the holes (B) in the hub carrier

**5.4 Anti-roll bar mounting on the lower arm**

**6.2 Push the lower arm down to free the balljoint from the hub carrier**

disconnected from the hub carriers on both sides. To do this, unscrew and remove the clamp bolts, then push the end of the lower arm down to free the balljoint from the hub carrier. If a balljoint is very tight, it may be necessary to use a long lever or similar tool, but take care not to damage the balljoint rubber seal. Note that the heads of the bolts face the front of the car.

**3** Unscrew the nuts securing the drop links to the anti-roll bar ends and disconnect the drop links.

**4** Unscrew the bolts securing the anti-roll bar to the lower arm mounting brackets **(see illustration)**.

**5** Unbolt the left- and right-hand side lower arm mounting brackets from the underbody, and remove them together with the lower arms attached.

**6** Withdraw the anti-roll bar from under the vehicle.

**7** If desired, the drop links can be removed from the struts by unscrewing the retaining nuts. If necessary, counterhold the drop link pins using a spanner on the flats provided.

*Refitting*

**8** Refitting is a reversal of removal, bearing in mind the following points.
   a) *Tighten the nuts and bolts to the specified torque.*
   b) *Refit the front suspension lower arm mounting brackets as described in Section 7.*

**7.5 Front suspension lower arm mounting bracket**

### 6  Front suspension lower arm - removal and refitting

*Removal*

**1** Remove the wheel trims or the wheel centre plates (alloy wheels), then slacken the front wheel nuts. Apply the handbrake, then jack up the front of the vehicle, and support securely on axle stands (see *"Jacking and Vehicle Support"*). Remove the relevant roadwheel.

**2** Unscrew and remove the clamp bolt securing the hub carrier to the lower arm balljoint - note that the bolt head is facing the front of the car. Push the end of the lower arm down to free the balljoint from the hub carrier **(see illustration)**. If the balljoint is very tight, it may be necessary to use a long lever or similar tool, but take care not to damage the balljoint rubber seal.

**3** Unscrew the two nuts and bolts and remove the lower arm from the mounting bracket.

*Refitting*

**4** Refitting is a reversal of removal, but renew self-locking nuts and tighten the nuts and bolts to the specified torque.

### 7  Front suspension lower arm mounting bracket - removal and refitting

*Removal*

**1** Apply the handbrake, then jack up the front of the vehicle and support it on axle stands (see *"Jacking and Vehicle Support"*). Remove the relevant front roadwheel.

**2** Unscrew and remove the clamp bolt securing the hub carrier to the lower arm balljoint - note that the bolt head is facing the front of the car. Push the end of the lower arm down to free the balljoint from the hub carrier. If the balljoint is very tight, it may be necessary to use a long lever or similar tool, but take care not to damage the balljoint rubber seal.

**3** Unscrew the nut securing the drop link to the anti-roll bar end and disconnect the drop link.

**4** Unscrew the bolts securing the anti-roll bar to the lower arm mounting bracket.

**5** Unbolt the lower arm mounting bracket from the underbody **(see illustration)**, and withdraw together with the lower arm attached. Note that the single bolt which is shorter than the others is the alignment bolt.

**6** Unscrew the bolts and remove the lower arm from the mounting bracket. Note that the bolt heads are facing downwards.

*Refitting*

**7** Locate the lower arm in the mounting bracket, and insert the bolts making sure their heads face the bottom of the bracket. Screw on the nuts and tighten to the specified torque in the two stages given.

**8** Locate the mounting bracket (and lower arm) on the underbody so that the peg enters the location hole centrally. Insert the alignment bolt and tighten moderately.

**9** Insert the remaining bolts, then tighten all of the bolts to the specified torque.

**10** Refit the anti-roll bar mounting and tighten the bolts to the specified torque.

**11** Reconnect the drop link to the anti-roll bar and tighten the nut to the specified torque.

**12** Lift the lower arm and locate the balljoint in the hub carrier. Make sure the balljoint is fully entered, then insert the clamp bolt from the front of the car and tighten the nut to the specified torque.

**13** Refit the roadwheel and lower the vehicle to the ground.

### 8  Rear hub/brake drum assembly - removal and refitting

**1** An integral hub and brake drum assembly is used, which incorporates the rear wheel bearings.

**2** Removal and refitting of the rear brake drum/hub assembly is described in Chapter 9.

### 9  Rear hub bearings - renewal

**Note:** *A press and puller, or similar improvised tools will be required for this operation. Obtain a new bearing and bearing grease seal before proceeding.*

**1** Remove the rear brake drum/hub as described in Chapter 9.

**2** On models with ABS, prise the sensor ring from the inboard end of the hub/brake drum using a screwdriver or similar tool. Discard the sensor ring - a new one must be used on refitting.

**3** Carefully prise out the grease seal from the inboard hub bore, using a screwdriver **(see illustration)**. Take great care not to damage the bore surface.

**9.3 Prising the grease seal from the inboard hub bore**

**9.4 Lifting out the outer bearing cone**

**9.5 Driving out a bearing cup**

**4** Lift the inner and outer bearing cones out from the hub bore **(see illustration)**.

**5** The bearing cups must now be removed from the hub bore by driving them out with a suitable punch. Drive each cup out from its respective end, by tapping alternately at diagonally opposite points **(see illustration)**. Do not allow the cups to tilt in the bore, or the surfaces may become burred and prevent the new bearings from seating correctly as they are fitted.

**6** Clean the hub bore and the stub axle thoroughly before commencing reassembly.

**7** Carefully tap the new bearing cups into position in the hub bore, using a piece of tubing of a slightly smaller diameter than the bearing cups. Make sure that the cups are fitted squarely, and that they abut their respective shoulders in the hub.

**8** Pack the inner bearing cone with suitable grease, then fit the bearing cone to the cup in the hub.

**9** Lubricate the inner lip of the new grease seal, then lightly tap the seal into position using a block of wood. Note that the seal lips should face in towards the bearings in the hub.

**10** On models with ABS, fit the new sensor ring to the inboard end of the brake drum/hub. Press the sensor ring into position using a tube of suitable diameter. Make sure that the ring seats correctly on the hub shoulder.
*Caution: The sensor ring teeth are easily damaged - take great care to avoid damage when fitting. It is not advisable to*

*tap the ring into position, as this may cause damage.*

**11** Pack the outer bearing cone with grease, then fit it to the bearing cone in the hub.

**12** Refit the brake drum/hub as described in Chapter 9.

## 10 Rear strut - removal, overhaul and refitting

### Removal

**1** Remove the relevant rear wheel trim or the wheel centre plate (alloy wheels), then slacken the relevant rear wheel nuts. Chock the front wheels, then jack up the rear of the vehicle, and support on axle stands (see "*Jacking and Vehicle Support*"). Remove the rear roadwheel.

**2** Open the tailgate and remove the rear parcel shelf, then remove the shelf support trim from the relevant side of the luggage compartment with reference to Chapter 11, Section 27.

**3** Support the trailing arm using a trolley jack, then unscrew the strut top mounting nut inside the luggage compartment **(see illustration)**.

**4** Unscrew the bolt securing the lower end of the strut assembly to the trailing arm, and withdraw the rear strut from the vehicle **(see illustration)**.

**5** Remove the top mounting insulator from the body.

### Overhaul

**Note:** *A spring compressor tool will be required for this operation.*

**6** With the suspension strut resting on a bench, or clamped in a vice, fit a spring compressor tool, and compress the coil spring to relieve the pressure on the spring seats. Ensure that the compressor tool is securely located on the spring, in accordance with the tool manufacturer's instructions.

 *Warning: Do not attempt to dismantle the strut without using an approved spring compressor tool.*

**7** Remove the strut top mounting retaining circlip using circlip pliers.

**8** Remove the top mounting, followed by the circlip, upper spring seat, the spring (with compressor tool still fitted), the gaiter, the rubber bump stop, and the dust cover.

**9** With the strut assembly now completely dismantled, examine all the components for wear, damage or deformation. Renew any of the components as necessary.

**10** Examine the strut for signs of fluid leakage. Check the strut piston for signs of pitting along its entire length, and check the strut body for signs of damage. While holding it in an upright position, test the operation of the strut shock absorber by moving the piston through a full stroke, and then through short strokes of 50 to 100 mm. In both cases, the resistance felt should be smooth and continuous. If the resistance is jerky or uneven or if there is any visible sign of wear or damage to the strut, renewal is necessary.

**11** If any doubt exists as to the condition of the coil spring, carefully remove the spring compressors and check the spring for distortion and signs of cracking. Renew the spring if it is damaged or distorted, or if there is any doubt as to its condition.

**12** Inspect all other components for damage or deterioration, and renew any that are suspect.

**13** Slide the dust cover, followed by rubber bump stop and the gaiter, onto the strut piston **(see illustration)**.

**10.3 The rear strut top mounting**

**10.4 The rear strut lower securing bolt**

**10.13 Rear suspension strut components**

| | |
|---|---|
| 1 Circlip | 5 Strut body |
| 2 Top mounting | 6 Bump stop |
| 3 Circlip | 7 Gaiter |
| 4 Upper spring seat | 8 Dust cover |

**14** If the spring compressor tool has been removed from the spring, refit it and compress the spring sufficiently to enable it to be refitted to the strut.

**15** Slide the spring over the piston rod, and position it so that the lower end of the spring is resting against the stop on the lower seat.

**16** Refit the upper spring seat, and rotate it as necessary to position the stop against the upper end of the spring.

**17** Fit a new circlip, followed by the top mounting and a further new circlip.

**18** Slowly slacken the spring compressor tool to relieve the tension in the spring. Check that the ends of the spring locate correctly against the stops on the spring seats. If necessary, turn the spring and the upper seat so that the components locate correctly before the compressor tool is removed. Remove the compressor tool when the spring is fully seated.

**11.5 Bolts securing the rear stub axle to the rear axle**

## Refitting

**19** Refitting is a reversal of removal, bearing in mind the following points.
a) *Make sure that the top mounting insulator is correctly seated.*
b) *Delay fully tightening the upper mounting nut and lower mounting bolt until the weight of the car is on the rear suspension.*

## 11 Rear axle assembly - removal and refitting

### Removal

**1** Working inside the car, lift the handbrake lever gaiter and back off the handbrake cable adjustment nut to the end of the thread.

**2** Remove the wheel trims or the wheel centre plates (alloy wheels), then slacken the rear wheel nuts. Chock the front wheels, then jack up the rear of the vehicle, and support it securely on axle stands (see *"Jacking and Vehicle Support"*). Remove the rear road-wheels.

**3** Minimise brake fluid loss by removing the master cylinder reservoir cap, and tightening it down onto a piece of polythene to obtain an airtight seal.

**4** On models with ABS, loosen the rigid pipe union nuts and remove the spring clips securing the rear brake flexible hoses to their mounting brackets on each side, then unscrew the hoses from the rear wheel cylinders. On non-ABS models, additionally the pressure reducing valve must be unscrewed from the hose and rigid pipe. Tape over or plug the pipe ends and wheel cylinder ports to prevent entry of dust and dirt.

**5** Working on each side at a time, unscrew the bolts securing the rear stub axles to the rear axle, then withdraw the stub axles together with the hub/brake drum over the brake shoes **(see illustration)**. Note that the backplate and spacer plate are riveted to the rear axle. On models with ABS, disconnect the wiring from the ABS sensors. Identify each stub axle assembly to ensure they are refitted to the correct sides.

**6** Remove the rear brake shoes, handbrake cables and wheel cylinders with reference to Chapter 9.

**7** Support the rear axle with a trolley jack and block of wood, then unscrew the bolts from the rear strut bottom mountings.

**8** With the help of an assistant, support the trailing arms. Unscrew the bolts securing the front mountings to the underbody. Lower the rear axle to the ground and withdraw from under the vehicle.

**9** Unscrew and remove the bolts, nuts and washers and remove the front mounting brackets from the trailing arms. Note that the bolts are fitted with their heads facing inwards.

**10** If required, the brake backplates can be

removed from the rear axle by drilling out the rivets. Keep the backplates identified for location to ensure correct refitting, and obtain new rivets. Renewal of the pivot bushes is described in Section 12.

## Refitting

**11** Refitting of the rear axle is a reversal of the removal procedure, but note the following additional points.
a) *Use new rivets to secure the brake backplates to the trailing arms.*
b) *When refitting the front mounting brackets, make sure the heads of the bolts are facing inwards.*
c) *Adjust the handbrake cable as described in Chapter 9.*
d) *Bleed the brake hydraulic system as described in Chapter 9.*
e) *Do not fully tighten the front pivot and strut bottom bolts until the weight of the car is on the rear suspension.*

## 12 Rear axle assembly pivot bushes - renewal

**1** Remove the rear wheel trims or the wheel centre plates (alloy wheels), then slacken the rear wheel nuts. Chock the front wheels, then jack up the rear of the vehicle and support it securely on axle stands (see *"Jacking and Vehicle Support"*). Remove both rear road-wheels.

**2** Support the rear axle assembly using a jack positioned beneath the axle beam. Use a block of wood between the jack and the axle beam to spread the load.

**3** Working on each side of the vehicle in turn, release the handbrake cable from the clips on the trailing arms.

**4** Unscrew the through-bolts and nuts (on both sides of the vehicle) securing the trailing arms to the mounting brackets on the underbody. Note that the heads of the bolts face inwards **(see illustration)**.

**5** Using the jack, carefully lower the axle assembly until the pivot bushes (in the trailing arms) are clear of the axle mounting brackets and the body side members. Take care not to place the brake fluid lines under strain.

**12.4 Rear suspension trailing arm front mounting bracket**

**12.6 Prise the pivot bush dust cover (arrowed) from the trailing arm**

**6** Carefully prise the pivot bush outer dust cover from the relevant trailing arm **(see illustration)**.

**7** Make an alignment mark on the bush housing on the trailing arm corresponding to the position of the alignment arrow on the end of the bush **(see illustration)**.

**8** Using a metal tube of suitable diameter, flat washers and a long bolt and nut, draw the bush out of its location in the trailing arm.

**9** Thoroughly clean the bush housing in the trailing arm.

**10** Carefully prise the outer dust cover from the new bush, then mark a line along the side of the bush, corresponding with the alignment arrow on the end of the bush.

**11** Lubricate the bush housing, and the new bush, with a soapy solution (eg, washing-up liquid) to aid fitting.

**12** Locate the new bush in position against the housing, together with the metal tube,

washers, bolt and nut used for removal. Align the line made on the side of the bush with the alignment mark made before removal on the trailing arm, then draw the bush into the housing until it is fully engaged.

**13** Fit the outer dust cover to the bush.

**14** If desired, repeat the procedure given in paragraphs 6 to 13 for the remaining bush.

**15** Further refitting is a reversal of removal, but do not fully tighten the trailing arm-to-mounting bracket through-bolts and nuts to the specified torque until the weight of the vehicle is resting on its wheels.

## 13 Steering wheel - removal and refitting

> ⚠️ **Warning: Refer to Chapter 12 and note the precautions to be observed when working with an air bag. If the steering wheel is left fitted to the steering column, handle the assembly with care, and note the precautions given for storing an air bag.**

### Removal

**1** Disconnect the battery negative (earth) lead (see Chapter 5A), then wait at least two minutes before proceeding. If this waiting period is not observed, there is a danger of accidentally activating the air bag(s) and/or seat belt tensioners.

**2** Undo the screws and remove the upper and lower steering column shrouds.

**12.7 Make an alignment mark on the bush housing corresponding to the alignment arrow on the bush**

**3** Remove the air bag unit from the steering wheel as described in Chapter 12.

**4** Ensure that the front wheels are pointing in the straight-ahead position, then remove the ignition key and engage the steering lock.

**5** Disconnect the wiring plug and remove the securing screw, then withdraw the anti-theft immobiliser transceiver unit from the ignition switch/steering lock assembly **(see illustrations)**.

**6** Disconnect the air bag module wiring at the connector beneath the instrument panel **(see illustration)**.

**7** Unscrew and remove the steering wheel securing bolt **(see illustration)**.

**8** Turn the ignition key to position "I" and withdraw the steering wheel from the column. Grip the steering wheel on each side, then pull and withdraw it from the splines on the end of the column **(see illustration)**.

**9** Once the steering wheel has been removed, turn the ignition key back to position "0".

**10** If a new steering wheel is to be fitted, remove the air bag clockspring assembly from the old wheel, as described in Chapter 12, and fit it to the new steering wheel. If the clockspring is left in position, be careful not to depress the red locking button otherwise the central position of the clockspring may be disturbed and damage may occur to the clockspring. If the button is accidentally depressed, re-centralise it with reference to Chapter 12.

### Refitting

**11** Where applicable, fit the air bag clockspring assembly, and make sure that the

**13.5a Undo the securing screw . . .**

**13.5b . . . and remove the anti-theft immobiliser transceiver unit**

**13.6 Disconnecting the air bag module wiring beneath the instrument panel**

**13.7 Removing the steering wheel securing bolt**

**13.8 Removing the steering wheel**

**14.4  Steering column lower universal joint viewed from the engine compartment**

**14.7  Bonnet release lever and cable located on the steering column**

**14.8  Steering column upper mounting**

assembly is centralised, as described in Chapter 12.

12  Make sure that the front wheels are pointing in the straight-ahead position, and turn the ignition key to position "I", then fit the steering wheel to the column, making sure that the air bag clockspring tabs engage correctly over the steering lock plunger assembly.

13  Refit the steering wheel securing bolt, and tighten to the specified torque, then turn the ignition key back to position "0".

14  The remainder of the refitting procedure is a reversal of removal, but refit the air bag unit as described in Chapter 12.

### 14  Steering column - removal and refitting

#### Removal

⚠️ *Warning: Refer to Chapter 12 and note the precautions to be observed when working with an air bag. If the steering wheel is left fitted to the steering column, handle the assembly with care, and note the precautions given for storing an air bag.*

1  Disconnect the battery negative (earth) lead (see Chapter 5A), then wait at least two minutes before proceeding. If this waiting period is not observed, there is a danger of accidentally activating the air bag(s) and/or seat belt tensioner(s).

2  Remove the steering wheel and clockspring

as described in Section 13. This work is not essential, however if the steering wheel is left on the column, refer to the safety precautions described in Chapter 12, and make sure that the steering wheel is not turned from its central position otherwise the air bag clockspring will be damaged.

3  Apply the handbrake, then jack up the front of the vehicle and support it on axle stands (see *"Jacking and Vehicle Support"*). Turn the front roadwheels to the straight-ahead position, then remove the ignition key to lock the column.

4  Working beneath the vehicle, reach up behind the engine and unscrew the clamp bolt securing the steering column lower universal joint to the steering gear pinion shaft **(see illustration)**. Slide the joint upwards off the pinion shaft.

5  Inside the car, undo the screws and remove the upper and lower steering column shrouds.

6  Disconnect the wiring from the air bag unit, the anti-theft immobiliser transceiver unit, the multi-function switch and the ignition switch.

7  Disconnect the bonnet release cable from the steering column by releasing the outer cable clip, then unhooking the cable from the lever **(see illustration)**.

8  Unscrew the two column mounting nuts from the bulkhead studs **(see illustration)**.

9  Remove the rubber grommet from the bulkhead, then withdraw the steering column from the mounting studs **(see illustrations)**. Note that there is very little room to manoeuvre the steering column due to the proximity of the lower support bush to the mounting bracket.

10  Unscrew the clamp bolt and remove the lower universal joint from the bottom of the inner column. Mark the joint in relation to the column to ensure correct refitting.

#### Refitting

11  Refitting is a reversal of removal, but tighten the mounting nuts and clamp bolts to the specified torque. Make sure that the clamp bolts are correctly located through the cut-aways in the inner column and pinion shaft.

### 15  Steering gear rubber gaiters - renewal

1  Remove the relevant front wheel trim or the wheel centre plate (alloy wheels), then loosen the wheel nuts. Apply the handbrake, then jack up the front of the vehicle, and support it securely on axle stands (see *"Jacking and Vehicle Support"*). Remove the roadwheel.

2  Extract the split pin, then loosen the track-rod end balljoint nut, and unscrew it as far as the ends of the threads.

3  Disconnect the track-rod end balljoint from the steering arm on the hub carrier using a balljoint separator tool (leave the nut fitted to protect the threads), taking care not to damage the balljoint rubber seal. Once the balljoint has been released, remove the balljoint nut.

4  Slacken the track-rod end locknut, then unscrew the track-rod end from the track-rod, counting the number of turns necessary to remove it. Unscrew the locknut from the track-rod.

5  Remove the inner and outer securing clips, then slide the gaiter off the end of the track-rod.

6  Thoroughly clean the track-rod, then slide the new gaiter into position.

7  Fit the gaiter securing clips, using new clips if necessary, making sure that the gaiter is not twisted.

8  Screw the locknut onto the track-rod, then screw on the track-rod end the number of turns noted during removal. Tighten the locknut while holding the balljoint in position.

9  Engage the track-rod end balljoint pin with the steering arm, then refit the securing nut.

**14.9a  Steering column rubber grommet on the bulkhead**

**14.9b  Showing the upper universal joint on the inner steering column**

Tighten the nut to the specified torque then fit a new split pin and bend over its ends to secure.

**10** Refit the roadwheel, then lower the vehicle to the ground, and tighten the wheel nuts.

**11** Check the front wheel alignment (see Section 22) at the earliest opportunity.

## 16 Steering gear -
### removal and refitting

## Models without power steering

### Removal

**1** Ensure that the front wheels are pointing in the straight-ahead position, then remove the ignition key and engage the steering lock.

**2** Remove the front wheel trims or the wheel centre plates (alloy wheels), then loosen the wheel nuts. Apply the handbrake, then jack up the front of the vehicle, and support it securely on axle stands (see *"Jacking and Vehicle Support"*). Remove both front roadwheels.

**3** Working on each side at a time, extract the split pin, then loosen the track-rod end balljoint nut, and unscrew it as far as the ends of the threads.

**4** Disconnect the track-rod end balljoints from the steering arms on the hub carriers using a balljoint separator tool.

**5** Reach up behind the engine and unscrew the clamp bolt securing the steering column lower universal joint to the steering gear pinion shaft. Slide the joint upwards off the pinion shaft.

**6** Unscrew the mounting bolts and remove the steering gear from the bulkhead, then withdraw it from one side of the car.

### Refitting

**7** Make sure that the steering gear rack is in its central position.

**8** Locate the steering gear on the bulkhead and insert the mounting bolts. Note that one of the mounting brackets has a hook on it which locates in a corresponding hole in the bulkhead **(see illustration)**. Tighten the mounting bolts to the specified torque.

**9** Engage the steering column lower universal joint with the pinion shaft splines, then insert the clamp bolt and tighten to the specified torque. Note that the joint can only be refitted in one position as there is a master spline.

**10** Working on each side at a time, engage the track-rod end balljoint pin with the steering arm, then refit the securing nut. Tighten the nut to the specified torque then fit a new split pin and bend over its ends to secure.

**11** Refit the roadwheels and lower the vehicle to the ground.

**12** Check the front wheel alignment (see Section 22) at the earliest opportunity.

**16.8 The steering gear mounting bracket hook engages a hole (1) in the bulkhead**

## Models with power steering

### Removal

**13** Ensure that the front wheels are pointing in the straight-ahead position, then remove the ignition key and engage the steering lock.

**14** Remove the front wheel trims or the wheel centre plates (alloy wheels), then loosen the wheel nuts. Apply the handbrake, then jack up the front of the vehicle, and support it securely on axle stands (see *"Jacking and Vehicle Support"*). Remove both front roadwheels.

**15** Position a suitable clean container beneath the left-hand side of the engine compartment, then unscrew the union nut and disconnect the hydraulic fluid pressure line from the oil cooler pipes **(see illustration)**. Allow the fluid to drain into the container.

**16** Working on each side of the vehicle at a time, extract the split pin, then loosen the track-rod end balljoint nut, and unscrew it as far as the ends of the threads.

**17** Disconnect the track-rod end balljoints from the steering arms on the hub carriers using a balljoint separator tool.

**18** Reach up behind the engine and unscrew the clamp bolt securing the steering column lower universal joint to the steering gear pinion shaft. Slide the joint upwards off the pinion shaft.

**19** Undo the screw and release the power steering hydraulic pipes from the support on the bulkhead.

**20** Position a container beneath the steering gear. Identify the pipes on the steering gear for position, then unscrew the unions and disconnect the pipes. Allow the fluid to drain into the container.

**21** Unscrew the nut and disconnect the link from the anti-roll bar on the driver's side, then unscrew the anti-roll bar mounting bolts from the lower arm mounting bracket.

**22** Unscrew and remove the bolts from the lower arm mounting bracket on the driver's side (ie RHS on RHD, LHS on LHD), but leave the rearmost bolt in position (but loose) to support the bracket and lower arm.

**23** Where a brake vacuum servo support stay is fitted, unscrew the nut from the steering gear mounting bolt and move the stay to one side.

**16.15 Disconnecting the power steering hydraulic fluid pressure line on the left-hand side of the transmission**

**24** Unbolt the steering gear support brackets from the bulkhead **(see illustration)**.

**25** Unscrew the mounting bolts and remove the steering gear from the bulkhead, then withdraw it from the driver's side of the car. Recover the support brackets. Note the location of the steering gear mounting bolt with the stud extension (for the vacuum servo support stay).

**26** If necessary, remove the insulator bushes from the steering gear. Check the bushes for wear and renew them if necessary.

**27** If the steering gear is being renewed, unscrew the union nuts and remove the hydraulic pipes from the old unit, then transfer them to the new unit. New O-ring seals must be fitted to the unions - wrap tape around the union threads to prevent damage to the seals when fitting them.

### Refitting

**28** Make sure that the steering gear rack is in its central position.

**29** Where removed, refit the insulator bushes to the steering gear.

**30** Locate the steering gear on the bulkhead and insert the mounting bolts together with support brackets, making sure that the bolt with the stud extension is located on the left-hand side. Note that one of the steering gear mounting brackets has a hook on it which locates in a corresponding hole in the bulkhead.

**31** With the support brackets located on the studs, refit the nuts and tighten to the specified torque.

**16.24 Support bracket securing the steering gear to the bulkhead**

**32** Tighten the steering gear mounting bolts to the specified torque.

**33** Engage the steering column lower universal joint with the pinion shaft splines, then insert the clamp bolt and tighten to the specified torque. Note that the joint can only be refitted in one position as there is a master spline.

**34** Where fitted, refit the brake vacuum servo support stay and tighten the nut.

**35** Refit the lower arm mounting bracket, making sure that the location peg engages the hole in the underbody correctly. Tighten the bolts to the specified torque.

**36** Refit the anti-roll bar to the lower arm mounting bracket and tighten the bolts to the specified torque.

**37** Refit the link to the anti-roll bar and tighten the nut to the specified torque.

**38** Fit new O-ring seals to the unions, then reconnect the feed and return pipes to the steering gear.

**39** Fit the pipe support to the bulkhead and tighten the screw.

**40** Working on each side at a time, engage the track-rod end balljoint pin with the steering arm, then refit the securing nut. Tighten the nut to the specified torque then fit a new split pin and bend over its ends to secure.

**41** Reconnect the hydraulic fluid pressure line to the oil cooler and tighten the union nut.

**42** Refit the roadwheels and lower the vehicle to the ground.

**43** Bleed the power steering hydraulic system as described in Section 19.

**44** Check the front wheel alignment (see Section 22) at the earliest opportunity.

## 17 Power steering pump - removal and refitting

### Removal

**1** Disconnect the battery negative (earth) lead (see Chapter 5A).

**2** Remove the right-hand headlight as described in Chapter 12, Section 7.

**3** Note how the auxiliary drivebelt is fitted. Using a spanner, turn the auxiliary drivebelt

**17.4a Power steering pump pulley**

tensioner centre bolt clockwise, then slip the drivebelt from the pulleys (refer to Chapter 1 if necessary).

**4** Using a suitable puller, draw the pulley from the power steering pump driveshaft. Ford technicians use tool 13-022 for this job **(see illustrations)**.

**5** Use a brake hose clamp to clamp the hydraulic fluid hose from the fluid reservoir **(see illustration)**. Alternatively, syphon the fluid from the reservoir.

**6** Position a container beneath the pump, then loosen the clip and disconnect the supply hose. Also unscrew the union and disconnect the high pressure pipe from the pump.

**7** Unscrew the four mounting bolts and withdraw the power steering pump from the engine **(see illustration)**. Remove the pump from the engine compartment.

### Refitting

**8** If a new pump is being fitted, remove the transit union plugs. Before refitting the pump, fit new O-ring seals to the unions - wrap tape around the union threads to prevent damage to the seals when fitting them.

**9** Locate the pump on the engine and insert the mounting bolts. Progressively tighten the bolts to the specified torque.

**10** Reconnect the high pressure pipe and tighten the union nut to the specified torque.

**11** Reconnect the supply hose to the pump and tighten the clip. Remove the brake hose clamp from the hose.

**12** Press the pulley onto the pump driveshaft until flush with the end. Ford use tool 21-192

**17.4b Ford tool 13-022 for removing the power steering pump pulley**

for this job, however a suitable bolt, washer and nut can be used instead.

**13** Turn the tensioner clockwise and refit the auxiliary drivebelt on the pulleys. Release the tensioner, making sure that the drivebelt is correctly located in the pulley grooves. Refer to Chapter 1 if necessary.

**14** Refit the right-hand headlight as described in Chapter 12, Section 7.

**15** Reconnect the battery negative (earth) lead (see Chapter 5A).

**16** Bleed the power steering hydraulic system as described in Section 19.

## 18 Power steering fluid cooler pipes - removal and refitting

### Removal

**1** The fluid cooler takes the form of a pipe assembly fitted beneath the radiator.

**2** Disconnect the battery negative (earth) lead (see Chapter 5A).

**3** Apply the handbrake, then jack up the front of the vehicle and support it on axle stands (see *"Jacking and Vehicle Support"*).

**4** Position a suitable container beneath the right-hand side of the radiator.

**5** Disconnect the return pipe quick release union from the fluid cooler and allow the fluid to drain into the container. Ford technicians use tool 17-049 to do this **(see illustration)**,

**17.5 Using a brake hose clamp to clamp the hydraulic fluid hose from the fluid reservoir**

**17.7 Power steering pump location on the right-hand front of the engine**

**18.5 Using Ford tool 17-049 to disconnect the quick release couplings**

*1 Tool 17-049*
*2 Disconnecting the pipe*

**18.10 Power steering hydraulic cooler pipe connections at the left-hand side of the transmission**

however it may be possible to use a home-made split collar inserted into the union to release it from the cooler.

6 Remove the right-hand headlight as described in Chapter 12, Section 7.

7 Note how the auxiliary drivebelt is fitted. Using a spanner, turn the auxiliary drivebelt tensioner centre bolt clockwise, then slip the drivebelt from the pulleys (refer to Chapter 1 if necessary).

8 Using a suitable puller, draw the pulley from the power steering pump driveshaft. Ford technicians use tool 13-022 for this job.

9 At the right-hand side of the radiator, loosen and disconnect the high-pressure union from the fluid cooler.

10 Disconnect both unions from the left-hand end of the fluid cooler pipes. Note that one of the unions is of hexagonal type, and the other is of quick-release type **(see illustration)**.

11 Unscrew the mounting bolts and withdraw the fluid cooler from the bottom of the radiator.

### Refitting

12 Refitting is a reversal of removal, but on completion bleed the power steering hydraulic system as described in Section 19. Fit new O-ring seals to the unions - wrap tape around the union threads to prevent damage to the seals when fitting them.

### 19 Power steering hydraulic system - bleeding

**Note:** *Ford recommend that the power steering system is bled using a hand-operated vacuum pump connected to the reservoir filler neck - this should only be necessary if persistent problems are experienced with air in the hydraulic system.*

### Conventional bleeding

1 Check the power steering fluid level as described in "Weekly Checks".

2 Turn the steering wheel quickly from lock-to-lock several times, then re-check the fluid level and top-up if necessary.

3 Start the engine and allow it to idle, then *slowly* turn the steering wheel from lock-to-

lock several times - do not hold the steering wheel on full lock for more than 15 seconds at a time. Check for air bubbles in the fluid reservoir - if air bubbles are visible, the system requires further bleeding.

4 Stop the engine, then lower the vehicle to the ground, and re-check the fluid level.

5 If air bubbles appear in the reservoir when the system is operated, or if the pump is noisy in operation (not to be confused with a slipping drivebelt), repeat the bleeding procedure.

### Bleeding using a vacuum pump

**Note:** *During the bleeding procedure, the pressure will drop, so adequate vacuum should be maintained using the vacuum pump. If the pressure increases by more than 0.07 bar in 5 minutes, the system should be checked for leaks.*

6 Check the power steering fluid level as described in "Weekly Checks".

7 Start the engine and allow it to idle, then slowly turn the steering wheel from lock-to-lock several times - do not hold the steering wheel on full lock for more than 15 seconds at a time.

8 Switch off the engine, then recheck the fluid level and top up if necessary.

9 Connect a vacuum pump to the fluid reservoir filler neck using a suitable adapter (Ford Tool No 13-016 is available for this purpose).

10 Start the engine, and slowly turn the steering to the right, just off full right lock.

11 Stop the engine, and apply a vacuum of 0.51 bar, using the vacuum pump, until the air is purged from the system (this will take at least 5 minutes).

12 Release the vacuum, then repeat the procedure given in paragraphs 10 and 11 with the steering turned to just off full left lock.

13 Disconnect the vacuum pump from the fluid reservoir, and top up the fluid level if necessary.

14 Start the engine, and turn the steering wheel from lock-to-lock. If the system is excessively noisy in operation, repeat the bleeding procedure.

15 If problems with air in the system persist, leave the vehicle overnight, then repeat the bleeding procedure.

**21.2 Track-rod end locknut**

**20.1 The power steering pressure switch is located in the high pressure fluid pipe on the steering gear**

### 20 Power steering fluid pressure switch - removal and refitting

### Removal

1 The power steering fluid pressure switch provides a signal to the engine management electronic control unit, which is used to reduce the engine speed if the power steering fluid pressure becomes too high. The switch is located in the high pressure fluid pipe on the steering gear **(see illustration)**.

2 Place a container beneath the switch location to catch any escaping fluid, then disconnect the wiring.

3 Unscrew and remove the switch from the fluid pipe. Be prepared for fluid spillage, and plug or cover the orifice in the pipe to prevent dirt entry and further fluid loss.

### Refitting

4 Refitting is a reversal of removal, but tighten the switch securely, and on completion bleed the power steering hydraulic circuit as described in Section 19.

### 21 Track-rod end - removal and refitting

**Note:** *A balljoint separator tool will be required for this operation.*

### Removal

1 Remove the relevant front wheel trim or the wheel centre plate (alloy wheels), then slacken the wheel nuts. Apply the handbrake, then jack up the front of the vehicle, and support it securely on axle stands (see "Jacking and Vehicle Support"). Remove the relevant roadwheel.

2 Loosen the track-rod end locknut by a quarter turn **(see illustration)**.

3 Extract the split pin, then loosen the track-rod end balljoint nut and unscrew it as far as the ends of the threads **(see illustration)**.

4 Disconnect the track-rod end balljoint from the steering arm on the hub carrier using a balljoint separator tool (leave the nut fitted to

**21.3 Track-rod end balljoint nut**

**21.4 Using a balljoint separator tool to release the balljoint from the steering arm**

**22.2 Wheel alignment and steering angles**

protect the threads), taking care not to damage the balljoint rubber seal. Once the balljoint has been released, remove the balljoint nut **(see illustration)**.

5 Unscrew the track-rod end from the track-rod, counting the number of turns necessary to remove it.

### Refitting

6 Screw the track-rod end onto the track-rod the number of turns noted during removal, then tighten the locknut while holding the balljoint in position.

7 Engage the track-rod end balljoint pin with the steering arm on the hub carrier, then fit the securing nut. Tighten the nut to the specified torque and fit a new split pin.

8 Refit the roadwheel, then lower the vehicle to the ground, and tighten the wheel nuts.

9 Check the front wheel alignment (see Section 22) at the earliest opportunity.

### 22 Wheel alignment and steering angles - general information

### Front wheel alignment

1 Accurate front wheel alignment is essential to good steering and for even tyre wear. Before considering the steering angles, check that the tyres are correctly inflated, that the front wheels are not buckled, the hub bearings are not worn and that the steering linkage is in good order. without slackness or wear at the joints.

2 Wheel alignment consists of four factors **(see illustration)**:

*Camber,* is the angle at which the roadwheels are set from the vertical when viewed from the front or rear of the vehicle. Positive camber is the angle (in degrees) that the wheels are tilted outwards at the top from the vertical. The camber angle is given for reference only and cannot be adjusted.

*Castor,* is the angle between the steering axis and a vertical line when viewed from each side of the vehicle. Positive castor is indicated when the steering axis is inclined towards the rear of the vehicle at its upper end. This angle is not adjustable.

*Steering axis inclination (kingpin inclination),*

is the angle, when viewed from the front or rear of the vehicle, between the vertical and an imaginary line drawn between the upper and lower front suspension strut mountings. This angle is not adjustable.

*Toe,* is the amount by which the distance between the front inside edges of the roadwheel rim differs from that between the rear inside edges. If the distance between the front edges is less than that at the rear, the wheels are said to toe-in. If the distance between the front inside edges is greater than that at the rear, the wheels toe-out.

3 Owing to the need for precision gauges to measure the small angles of the steering and suspension settings, it is preferable that checking of camber and castor is left to a service station having the necessary equipment. Camber and castor is set during production of the vehicle, and any deviation from the specified angle will be due to accident damage or gross wear in the suspension mountings.

4 To check the front wheel alignment, first make sure that the lengths of both track-rods are equal when the steering is in the straight-ahead position. The track-rod lengths can be adjusted if necessary by releasing the locknuts from the track-rod ends and rotating the track-rods. If necessary, self-locking grips can be used to rotate the track-rods.

5 Obtain a tracking gauge. These are available in various forms from accessory stores, or one can be fabricated from a length of steel tubing suitably cranked to clear the sump and transmission, and having a setscrew and locknut at one end.

6 With the gauge, measure the distances between the two wheel inner rims (at hub height) at the rear of the wheel. Push the vehicle forward to rotate the wheel through 180° (half a turn) and measure the distance between the wheel inner rims, again at hub height, at the front of the wheel. This last measurement should differ from the first by the appropriate toe-in which is given in the Specifications. The vehicle must be on level ground.

7 If the toe-in is found to be incorrect, release the track-rod end locknuts and turn both track-rods equally. Only turn them a quarter-of-a-turn at a time before re-checking the alignment. If necessary use self-locking grips to turn the track-rods - **do not** grip the threaded part of the track-rod during adjustment. It is important not to allow the track-rods to become unequal in length during adjustment, otherwise the alignment of the steering wheel will become incorrect and tyre scrubbing will occur on turns.

8 On completion tighten the locknuts without disturbing the setting. Check that the balljoint is at the centre of its arc of travel, and that the gaiters are not twisted.

### Rear wheel alignment

9 Figures are provided in the Specifications for rear wheel camber and toe-setting for reference only. No adjustment is possible.

# Chapter 11
# Bodywork and fittings

## Contents

## Degrees of difficulty

| | | | | |
|---|---|---|---|---|
| **Easy,** suitable for novice with little experience  | **Fairly easy,** suitable for beginner with some experience  | **Fairly difficult,** suitable for competent DIY mechanic  | **Difficult,** suitable for experienced DIY mechanic  | **Very difficult,** suitable for expert DIY or professional |

## Specifications

| Torque wrench settings | Nm | lbf ft |
|---|---|---|
| Front seat mounting bolts | 22 | 16 |
| Front seat slide to frame | 25 | 18 |
| Inertia reel Torx bolts | 38 | 28 |
| Rear seat backrest to hinge | 25 | 18 |
| Rear seat hinge | 50 | 37 |
| Seat belt anchor bolts | 38 | 28 |
| Seat belt stalk bolts | 38 | 28 |
| Tailgate hinge bolts | 12 | 9 |

## 1  General information

The bodyshell is of three-door Hatchback design, and is made of pressed steel sections. Most components are welded together, but some use is made of structural adhesives.

The bonnet, doors and some other vulnerable panels are made of zinc-coated metal, and are further protected by being coated with an anti-chip primer prior to being sprayed.

Extensive use is made of plastic materials, mainly in the interior, but also in exterior components. The front and rear bumpers and the front grille are injection-moulded from a synthetic material which is very strong, and yet light. Plastic components such as wheel arch liners are fitted to the underside of the vehicle, to improve the body's resistance to corrosion.

## 2  Maintenance - bodywork and underframe

The general condition of a vehicle's bodywork is the one thing that significantly affects its value. Maintenance is easy, but needs to be regular. Neglect, particularly after minor damage, can lead quickly to further deterioration and costly repair bills. It is important also to keep watch on those parts of the vehicle not immediately visible, for instance the underside, inside all the wheel arches, and the lower part of the engine compartment.

The basic maintenance routine for the bodywork is washing - preferably with a lot of water, from a hose. This will remove all the loose solids which may have stuck to the vehicle. It is important to flush these off in such a way as to prevent grit from scratching the finish. The wheel arches and underframe need washing in the same way, to remove any accumulated mud which will retain moisture and tend to encourage rust. Paradoxically enough, the best time to clean the underframe and wheel arches is in wet weather, when the mud is thoroughly wet and soft. In very wet weather, the underframe is usually cleaned of large accumulations automatically, and this is a good time for inspection.

Periodically, except on vehicles with a wax-based underbody protective coating, it is a good idea to have the whole of the underframe of the vehicle steam-cleaned, engine compartment included, so that a thorough inspection can be carried out to see what minor repairs and renovations are necessary. Steam-cleaning is available at many garages, and is necessary for the removal of the accumulation of oily grime, which sometimes is allowed to become thick in certain areas. If steam-cleaning facilities are

not available, there are one or two excellent grease solvents available, which can be brush-applied; the dirt can then be simply hosed off. Note that these methods should not be used on vehicles with wax-based underbody protective coating, or the coating will be removed. Such vehicles should be inspected annually, preferably just prior to Winter, when the underbody should be washed down, and any damage to the wax coating repaired. Ideally, a completely fresh coat should be applied. It would also be worth considering the use of such wax-based protection for injection into door panels, sills, box sections, etc, as an additional safeguard against rust damage, where such protection is not provided by the vehicle manufacturer.

After washing paintwork, wipe off with a chamois leather to give an unspotted clear finish. A coat of clear protective wax polish will give added protection against chemical pollutants in the air. If the paintwork sheen has dulled or oxidised, use a cleaner/polisher combination to restore the brilliance of the shine. This requires a little effort, but such dulling is usually caused because regular washing has been neglected. Care needs to be taken with metallic paintwork, as special non-abrasive cleaner/polisher is required to avoid damage to the finish. Always check that the door and ventilator opening drain holes and pipes are completely clear, so that water can be drained out. Brightwork should be treated in the same way as paintwork. Windscreens and windows can be kept clear of the smeary film which often appears, by the use of proprietary glass cleaner. Never use any form of wax or other body or chromium polish on glass.

## 3  Maintenance - upholstery and carpets

Mats and carpets should be brushed or vacuum-cleaned regularly, to keep them free of grit. If they are badly stained, remove them from the vehicle for scrubbing or sponging, and make quite sure they are dry before refitting. Seats and interior trim panels can be kept clean by wiping with a damp cloth. If they do become stained (which can be more apparent on light-coloured upholstery), use a little liquid detergent and a soft nail brush to scour the grime out of the grain of the material. Do not forget to keep the headlining clean in the same way as the upholstery. When using liquid cleaners inside the vehicle, do not over-wet the surfaces being cleaned. Excessive damp could get into the seams and padded interior, causing stains, offensive odours or even rot. If the inside of the vehicle gets wet accidentally, it is worthwhile taking some trouble to dry it out properly, particularly where carpets are involved. *Do not leave oil or electric heaters inside the vehicle for this purpose.*

## 4  Minor body damage - repair

### *Repairs of minor scratches in bodywork*

If the scratch is very superficial, and does not penetrate to the metal of the bodywork, repair is very simple. Lightly rub the area of the scratch with a paintwork renovator, or a very fine cutting paste, to remove loose paint from the scratch, and to clear the surrounding bodywork of wax polish. Rinse the area with clean water.

Apply touch-up paint to the scratch using a fine paint brush; continue to apply fine layers of paint until the surface of the paint in the scratch is level with the surrounding paintwork. Allow the new paint at least two weeks to harden, then blend it into the surrounding paintwork by rubbing the scratch area with a paintwork renovator or a very fine cutting paste. Finally, apply wax polish.

Where the scratch has penetrated right through to the metal of the bodywork, causing the metal to rust, a different repair technique is required. Remove any loose rust from the bottom of the scratch with a penknife, then apply rust-inhibiting paint, to prevent the formation of rust in the future. Using a rubber or nylon applicator, fill the scratch with bodystopper paste. If required, this paste can be mixed with cellulose thinners, to provide a very thin paste which is ideal for filling narrow scratches. Before the stopper-paste in the scratch hardens, wrap a piece of smooth cotton rag around the top of a finger. Dip the finger in cellulose thinners, and quickly sweep it across the surface of the stopper-paste in the scratch; this will ensure that the surface of the stopper-paste is slightly hollowed. The scratch can now be painted over as described earlier in this Section.

### *Repairs of dents in bodywork*

When deep denting of the vehicle's bodywork has taken place, the first task is to pull the dent out, until the affected bodywork almost attains its original shape. There is little point in trying to restore the original shape completely, as the metal in the damaged area will have stretched on impact, and cannot be reshaped fully to its original contour. It is better to bring the level of the dent up to a point which is about 3 mm below the level of the surrounding bodywork. In cases where the dent is very shallow anyway, it is not worth trying to pull it out at all. If the underside of the dent is accessible, it can be hammered out gently from behind, using a mallet with a wooden or plastic head. Whilst doing this, hold a suitable block of wood firmly against the outside of the panel, to absorb the impact from the hammer blows and thus prevent a large area of the bodywork from being "belled-out".

Should the dent be in a section of the bodywork which has a double skin, or some other factor making it inaccessible from behind, a different technique is called for. Drill several small holes through the metal inside the area - particularly in the deeper section. Then screw long self-tapping screws into the holes, just sufficiently for them to gain a good purchase in the metal. Now the dent can be pulled out by pulling on the protruding heads of the screws with a pair of pliers.

The next stage of the repair is the removal of the paint from the damaged area, and from an inch or so of the surrounding "sound" bodywork. This is accomplished most easily by using a wire brush or abrasive pad on a power drill, although it can be done just as effectively by hand, using sheets of abrasive paper. To complete the preparation for filling, score the surface of the bare metal with a screwdriver or the tang of a file, or alternatively, drill small holes in the affected area. This will provide a really good "key" for the filler paste.

To complete the repair, see the Section on filling and respraying.

### Repairs of rust holes or gashes in bodywork

Remove all paint from the affected area, and from an inch or so of the surrounding "sound" bodywork, using an abrasive pad or a wire brush on a power drill. If these are not available, a few sheets of abrasive paper will do the job most effectively. With the paint removed, you will be able to judge the severity of the corrosion, and therefore decide whether to renew the whole panel (if this is possible) or to repair the affected area. New body panels are not as expensive as most people think, and it is often quicker and more satisfactory to fit a new panel than to attempt to repair large areas of corrosion.

Remove all fittings from the affected area, except those which will act as a guide to the original shape of the damaged bodywork (eg headlamp shells etc). Then, using tin snips or a hacksaw blade, remove all loose metal and any other metal badly affected by corrosion. Hammer the edges of the hole inwards, in order to create a slight depression for the filler paste.

Wire-brush the affected area to remove the powdery rust from the surface of the remaining metal. Paint the affected area with rust-inhibiting paint; if the back of the rusted area is accessible, treat this also.

Before filling can take place, it will be necessary to block the hole in some way. This can be achieved by the use of aluminium or plastic mesh, or aluminium tape.

Aluminium or plastic mesh, or glass-fibre matting is probably the best material to use for a large hole. Cut a piece to the approximate size and shape of the hole to be filled, then position it in the hole so that its edges are below the level of the surrounding bodywork. It can be retained in position by several blobs of filler paste around its periphery.

Aluminium tape should be used for small or very narrow holes. Pull a piece off the roll, trim it to the approximate size and shape required, then pull off the backing paper (if used) and stick the tape over the hole; it can be overlapped if the thickness of one piece is insufficient. Burnish down the edges of the tape with the handle of a screwdriver or similar, to ensure that the tape is securely attached to the metal underneath.

### Bodywork repairs - filling and respraying

Before using this Section, see the Sections on dent, deep scratch, rust holes and gash repairs.

Many types of bodyfiller are available, but generally speaking, those proprietary kits which contain a tin of filler paste and a tube of resin hardener are best for this type of repair. A wide, flexible plastic or nylon applicator will be found invaluable for imparting a smooth and well-contoured finish to the surface of the filler.

Mix up a little filler on a clean piece of card or board - measure the hardener carefully (follow the maker's instructions on the pack), otherwise the filler will set too rapidly or too slowly. Using the applicator, apply the filler paste to the prepared area; draw the applicator across the surface of the filler to achieve the correct contour and to level the surface. As soon as a contour that approximates to the correct one is achieved, stop working the paste - if you carry on too long, the paste will become sticky and begin to "pick-up" on the applicator. Continue to add thin layers of filler paste at 20-minute intervals, until the level of the filler is just proud of the surrounding bodywork.

Once the filler has hardened, the excess can be removed using a metal plane or file. From then on, progressively-finer grades of abrasive paper should be used, starting with a 40-grade production paper, and finishing with a 400-grade wet-and-dry paper. Always wrap the abrasive paper around a flat rubber, cork, or wooden block - otherwise the surface of the filler will not be completely flat. During the smoothing of the filler surface, the wet-and-dry paper should be periodically rinsed in water. This will ensure that a very smooth finish is imparted to the filler at the final stage.

At this stage, the "dent" should be surrounded by a ring of bare metal, which in turn should be encircled by the finely "feathered" edge of the good paintwork. Rinse the repair area with clean water, until all of the dust produced by the rubbing-down operation has gone.

Spray the whole area with a light coat of - this will show up any imperfections in the surface of the filler. Repair these imperfections with fresh filler paste or bodystopper, and once more smooth the surface with abrasive paper. If bodystopper is used, it can be mixed with cellulose thinners, to form a really thin paste which is ideal for filling small holes. Repeat this spray-and-repair procedure until you are satisfied that the surface of the filler, and the feathered edge of the paintwork, are perfect. Clean the repair area with clean water, and allow to dry fully.

The repair area is now ready for final spraying. Paint spraying must be carried out in a warm, dry, windless and dust-free atmosphere. This condition can be created artificially if you have access to a large indoor working area, but if you are forced to work in the open, you will have to pick your day very carefully. If you are working indoors, dousing the floor in the work area with water will help to settle the dust which would otherwise be in the atmosphere. If the repair area is confined to one body panel, mask off the surrounding panels; this will help to minimise the effects of a slight mis-match in paint colours. Bodywork fittings (eg chrome strips, door handles etc) will also need to be masked off. Use genuine masking tape, and several thicknesses of newspaper, for the masking operations.

Before commencing to spray, agitate the aerosol can thoroughly, then spray a test area (an old tin, or similar) until the technique is mastered. Cover the repair area with a thick coat of primer; the thickness should be built up using several thin layers of paint, rather than one thick one. Using 400 grade wet-and-dry paper, rub down the surface of the primer until it is really smooth. While doing this, the work area should be thoroughly doused with water, and the wet-and-dry paper periodically rinsed in water. Allow to dry before spraying on more paint.

Spray on the top coat, again building up the thickness by using several thin layers of paint. Start spraying in the centre of the repair area, and then, using a circular motion, work outwards until the whole repair area and about 2 inches of the surrounding original paintwork is covered. Remove all masking material 10 to 15 minutes after spraying on the final coat of paint.

Allow the new paint at least two weeks to harden, then, using a paintwork renovator or a very fine cutting paste, blend the edges of the paint into the existing paintwork. Finally, apply wax polish.

### Plastic components

With the use of more and more plastic body components by the vehicle manufacturers (eg bumpers. spoilers, and in some cases major body panels), rectification of more serious damage to such items has become a matter of either entrusting repair work to a specialist in this field, or renewing complete components. Repair of such damage by the DIY owner is not really feasible, owing to the cost of the equipment and materials required for effecting such repairs. The basic technique involves making a groove along the line of the

**6.2a Undo the screws . . .**

crack in the plastic, using a rotary burr in a power drill. The damaged part is then welded back together, using a hot air gun to heat up and fuse a plastic filler rod into the groove. Any excess plastic is then removed, and the area rubbed down to a smooth finish. It is important that a filler rod of the correct plastic is used, as body components can be made of a variety of different types (eg polycarbonate, ABS, polypropylene).

Damage of a less serious nature (abrasions, minor cracks etc) can be repaired by the DIY owner using a two-part epoxy filler repair. Once mixed in equal, this is used in similar fashion to the bodywork filler used on metal panels. The filler is usually cured in twenty to thirty minutes, ready for sanding and painting.

If the owner is renewing a complete component himself, or if he has repaired it with epoxy filler, he will be left with the problem of finding a suitable paint for finishing which is compatible with the type of plastic used. At one time, the use of a universal paint was not possible, owing to the complex range of plastics encountered in body component applications. Standard paints, generally speaking, will not bond to plastic or rubber satisfactorily, but suitable paints to match any plastic or rubber finish, can be obtained from dealers. However, it is now possible to obtain a plastic body parts finishing kit which consists of a pre-primer treatment, a primer and coloured top coat. Full instructions are normally supplied with a kit, but basically, the method of use is to first apply the pre-primer to the component concerned, and allow it to dry for up to 30 minutes. Then the primer is

applied, and left to dry for about an hour before finally applying the special-coloured top coat. The result is a correctly-coloured component, where the paint will flex with the plastic or rubber, a property that standard paint does not normally posses.

## 5 Major body damage - repair

Where serious damage has occurred, or large areas need renewal due to neglect, it means that complete new panels will need welding-in, and this is best left to professionals. If the damage is due to impact, it will also be necessary to check completely the alignment of the bodyshell, and this can only be carried out accurately by a Ford dealer using special jigs. If the body is left misaligned, it is primarily dangerous, as the car will not handle properly, and secondly, uneven stresses will be imposed on the steering, suspension and possibly transmission, causing abnormal wear, or complete failure, particularly to such items as the tyres.

## 6 Bumpers - removal and refitting

### *Front bumper*

#### Removal

1 Apply the handbrake, then jack up the front of the vehicle and support it on axle stands (see *"Jacking and Vehicle Support"*). Remove both front roadwheels.
2 Working on each side in turn, undo the screws and remove the wheel arch liners from under the front wings **(see illustrations)**.
3 Undo and remove the bumper retaining screws located at the bottom of the wheel arches and prise out the expanders **(see illustration)**. The screws are located in front of and behind the front wheels.
4 Undo the screws and remove the front number plate. Undo the retaining screw on the number plate area, and the two screws

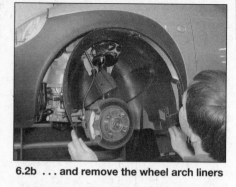

**6.2b . . . and remove the wheel arch liners**

located below the outer edges of the area.
5 Undo the screws from the upper edge of the front bumper.
6 Using a screwdriver, release the four retaining clips located beneath the outer edges of the wheel arches on each side. The clips are very tight and the inner halves of the clips may come away from the body. Also release the plastic clips located at the upper front of the bumper by pressing in the bumper and lowering the clips **(see illustrations)**. If necessary for easier access, remove the headlight unit as described in Chapter 12, Section 7.
7 With the help of an assistant, carefully withdraw the front bumper from the front of the car.

#### Refitting

8 Refitting is a reversal of removal.

### *Rear bumper*

#### Removal

9 Chock the front wheels, then jack up the rear of the vehicle and support it on axle stands (see *"Jacking and Vehicle Support"*). Remove both rear roadwheels.
10 Working on each side in turn, undo the screws located at the front lower edge of the wheel arch.
11 Drill out the retaining rivets located beneath each wheel arch **(see illustration)**. There are three upper ones and one rear lower one.
12 Drill out the two retaining rivets located beneath the centre of the rear bumper.

**6.3 Removing the expanders from the bottom of the wheel arches**

**6.6a Releasing the front bumper from the plastic clips on the wheel arch**

**6.6b The upper front retaining clips on the front bumper**

**6.11 Drilling out the rear bumper retaining rivets located beneath the rear wheel arch**

**6.13 The rear bumper is secured with rivets**

**8.1 On later models, disconnect the washer hose (arrowed)**

**13** With the tailgate open, drill out the three retaining rivets located on the top of the rear bumper **(see illustration)**.

**14** Remove the rear light clusters as described in Chapter 12, Section 7, then remove the clips from the brackets in the rear light cluster apertures.

**15** Release the clips in the wheel arches.

**16** Squeeze the plastic tabs and remove the number plate lights from the rear bumper.

**17** With the help of an assistant, carefully withdraw the rear bumper from the rear of the car. Where fitted, disconnect the wiring for the ultrasonic park distance sensor.

### Refitting

**18** Refitting is a reversal of removal.

---

### 7 Radiator grille panels - removal and refitting

#### *Removal*

**1** The radiator grille panels are located on the rear of the front bumper. The upper oval shaped panel has a Ford badge clipped to it. The lower panel is located behind the air intake grids.

**2** Remove the front bumper as described in Section 6, then unclip the panels.

#### *Refitting*

**3** Refitting is a reversal of removal.

---

### 8 Bonnet - removal, refitting and adjustment

#### *Removal*

**1** Open the bonnet, and support it on its stay. On later models, disconnect the washer hose from the washer jets **(see illustration)**.

**2** Using a marker pen or pencil, mark around the hinge positions on the bonnet **(see illustration)**.

**3** With the aid of an assistant, support the bonnet, and unscrew the four bolts securing the bonnet to the hinges.

**4** Lift off the bonnet.

**8.2 Bonnet hinge bolts**

#### *Refitting*

**5** Align the marks made on the bonnet before removal, with the hinges, then refit and tighten the bonnet securing bolts.

**6** Check the bonnet adjustment as follows.

#### *Adjustment*

**7** Close the bonnet, and check that there is an equal gap at each side, between the bonnet and the wing panels. Check also that the bonnet sits flush in relation to the surrounding body panels.

**8** The bonnet should close smoothly and positively without excessive pressure. If this is not the case, adjustment will be required.

**9** To adjust the bonnet alignment, slacken the bonnet securing bolts, and move the bonnet on the bolts as required (the bolt holes in the hinges are elongated). To adjust the bonnet closure, adjustable bump stops are fitted to the body front panel **(see illustration)**. These may be raised or lowered by screwing in or out as necessary.

---

### 9 Bonnet release cable - removal and refitting

#### *Removal*

**1** With the bonnet open, pull up the bonnet release outer cable from the bonnet lock on the centre of the engine compartment front crossmember.

**2** Unhook the inner cable end stop from the bonnet lock **(see illustration)**.

**3** Working inside the car, undo the screws and remove the upper and lower shrouds from the steering column.

**8.9 Bonnet adjustable bump stop**

**4** Release the outer cable from the clip near the ignition switch/lock, then disconnect the inner cable from the lever.

**5** In the engine compartment, prise out the rubber grommet from the right-hand side of the bulkhead. Also release the cable from the support clip.

**6** Tie a length of string to the end of the cable inside the car, then carefully pull the cable through the bulkhead into the engine compartment.

**7** Withdraw the bonnet release cable into the engine compartment and remove from the car.

**8** Untie the string from the end of the cable and leave it in position to aid refitting.

#### *Refitting*

**9** Refitting is a reversal of removal, but tie the string to the release lever end of the cable, and use the string to pull the cable into position. Ensure that the cable is routed as noted before removal, and make sure that the bulkhead grommet is correctly seated.

**9.2 Unhook the inner cable end stop from the bonnet lock**

**10.3 Bonnet lock and retaining nuts/bolt**

**11.1 Disconnecting the wiring harness from the front door**

**11.2 Door check strap**

### 10 Bonnet lock -
removal and refitting

#### Removal

1 With the bonnet open, pull up the bonnet release outer cable from the bonnet lock on the centre of the engine compartment front crossmember.
2 Unhook the inner cable end stop from the bonnet lock.
3 Unscrew the nuts and bolt and withdraw the bonnet lock from the crossmember **(see illustration)**. Recover the washers.

#### Refitting

4 Refitting is a reversal of removal.

### 11 Door -
removal and refitting

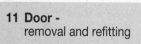

#### Removal

1 With the door open, unscrew the collar and disconnect the wiring harness connector from the front door pillar **(see illustration)**.
2 Using a Torx key, unscrew the bolt and remove the door check strap from the door pillar **(see illustration)**.
3 Ensure that the door is adequately supported, with the aid of an assistant, or using wooden blocks or similar under the bottom edge of the door (take care not to damage the paintwork).
4 Using a Torx socket, unscrew the bolts securing the pivot pins in the hinges. Note

**11.4 Door hinge**

that the hinges are welded to the door and front door pillar **(see illustration)**.
5 Drive out the door hinge pins using a suitable drift, and lift the door from the vehicle.

#### Refitting

6 Refitting is a reversal of removal, but check the condition of the hinge pins, and renew if necessary. Check that the door closes over the striker centrally, and if necessary reposition the striker by loosening the screws **(see illustration)**.

### 12 Door inner trim panel -
removal and refitting

#### Removal

1 Disconnect the battery negative (earth) lead (see Chapter 5A).
2 On models with manual windows, fully close the window and note the position of the window regulator handle. Carefully pull the handle from the regulator shaft.

**11.6 Door striker**

3 On models with electric windows, remove the cover (where fitted), undo the lower handle screw, and carefully prise out the upper half of the door pull handle. This is extremely difficult to do without breaking the plastic retaining tags, however the plastic upper half is not expensive to replace. It may be possible to prise out the plastic insert or electric window switch for access to the trim retaining screw, however on early models this is a difficult task which carries the risk of breaking the switch which will be more expensive than the upper half. Protect the trim panel with cloth or a piece of card and use a wide-blade screwdriver when levering. Note that a revised door handle upper half is fitted to later models which does not need to be removed to access the trim retaining screw, and a small hole is provided in the lower half to enable the plastic insert or electric window switch to be pushed out using a bent length of welding rod or a similar instrument. With the handle removed where necessary, disconnect the wiring from the electric window switch **(see illustrations)**.

**12.3a Prise out the cover (where fitted) . . .**

**12.3b . . . then undo the retaining screw**

**12.3c Protect the trim panel with cloth while prising off the upper half of the door pull handle**

12.3d Disconnecting the wiring from the electric window switch

12.4a Undo the upper screw . . .

12.4b . . . front screw . . .

12.4c . . . and lower screw from the trim panel

12.5a Removing the door inner trim panel

12.5b Door inner trim panel retaining clip

4 Undo the three retaining screws located on the circular area of the trim panel (see illustrations).
5 Using a forked tool or wide-blade screwdriver, carefully prise the trim panel from the inner door. To prevent damage to the inner surface of the trim panel, only lever near the clip positions (see illustrations).
6 If work is to be carried out on the components inside the door it will be necessary to peel back the protective sheeting from the door, however the inner door handle should be removed from the inner panel first (see illustration). Do not touch the self-adhesive surfaces otherwise re-bonding will be impaired.

### Refitting

7 Refitting is a reversal of removal. Make sure that the protective plastic sheeting is pressed securely back into position on the door.

### 13 Door handles and lock components - removal and refitting

#### Door inner handle

##### Removal

1 Remove the door inner trim panel, and locally peel back the protective plastic sheeting as described in Section 12.
2 Undo the screw securing the inner handle to the inner door (see illustration).
3 Slide the handle forwards and unclip it from the door (see illustration).
4 Release the cable from the clip, then disconnect it from the inner handle by turning the inner cable to align with the removal slot. Withdraw the handle.

### Refitting

5 Refitting is a reversal of removal.

### Front door exterior handle

Note: New rivets will be required to secure the window rear guide channel on refitting.

#### Removal

6 Fully close the front door window.
7 Remove the door inner trim panel, and locally peel back the protective plastic sheeting as described in Section 12.
8 Note that the door lock shield is integral with the window rear guide channel. Using a sharp knife, carefully cut through the sealant between the lock shield and door outer skin (see illustration).
9 On the rear edge of the door, drill out the two rivets securing the window guide channel to the door (see illustration).

12.6 Carefully peel back the protective sheeting

13.2 Undo the screw . . .

13.3 . . . and slide forwards the inner door handle to release it from the door

**13.8 Using a sharp knife, carefully cut through the sealant between the lock shield and door outer skin**

**13.9 Drill out the two rivets securing the window guide channel to the door**

**13.22 Position the 'V' cut-out on the retaining plate facing downwards**

10 Manoeuvre out the window guide channel and lock shield through the aperture in the inner door panel.

11 Prise off the clip and disconnect the door lock operating rod from the door lock. Unhook the rod from the exterior door handle.

12 Undo the screws, then carefully withdraw the exterior handle from the outside of the door.

**Refitting**

13 Refitting is a reversal of removal, but if necessary apply additional sealant between the lock shield and door outer skin.

### Front door lock cylinder

**Note:** *New rivets will be required to secure the window rear guide channel on refitting.*

**Removal**

14 Fully close the front door window.

15 Remove the door inner trim panel, and locally peel back the protective plastic sheeting as described in Section 12.

16 Note that the door lock shield is integral with the window rear guide channel. Using a sharp knife, carefully cut through the sealant between the lock shield and door outer skin.

17 On the rear edge of the door, drill out the two rivets securing the window guide channel to the door.

18 Manoeuvre out the window guide channel and lock shield through the aperture in the inner door panel.

19 Prise off the clip and disconnect door lock cylinder operating rod from the door lock.

20 Using a suitable pin-punch engaged with one of the holes in the lock cylinder retaining plate, tap the retaining plate collar anti-clockwise to release it from the lock cylinder.

21 Withdraw the retaining plate, then withdraw the lock cylinder from the outside of the door.

**Refitting**

22 Refitting is a reversal of removal, but make sure that the lock cylinder is fitted correctly by positioning the 'V' cut-out on the retaining plate facing downwards **(see illustration)**. Secure the window guide channel with new rivets, and if necessary apply additional sealant between the lock shield and door outer skin. Check the

operation of the lock mechanism before refitting the plastic sheeting and inner door trim panel.

### Front door lock and motor

**Note:** *New rivets will be required to secure the window rear guide channel on refitting.*

**Removal**

23 Fully close the front door window.

24 Remove the door inner trim panel, and locally peel back the protective plastic sheeting as described in Section 12.

25 Note that the door lock shield is integral with the window rear guide channel. Using a sharp knife, carefully cut through the sealant between the lock shield and door outer skin.

26 On the rear edge of the door, drill out the two rivets securing the window guide channel to the door.

27 Manoeuvre out the window guide channel and lock shield through the aperture in the inner door panel.

28 Prise off the clips and disconnect the exterior door and lock cylinder operating rods from the door lock.

29 Release the central locking wiring from the clip.

30 Undo the screw securing the inner door handle, then slide the handle forwards and unclip it from the door. Release the cable from the clip, then disconnect it from the inner handle by turning the inner cable to align with the removal slot. Withdraw the inner handle.

31 Support the door lock, then unscrew the mounting screws from the rear edge of the door.

**14.3 Prise off the small gaiter from the door mirror control lever**

32 Withdraw the door lock through the aperture in the inner door panel, then disconnect the central locking wiring.

33 With the lock on the bench, carefully prise out the inner door handle grommet from the lock shield.

34 Undo the screws and withdraw the lock shield.

35 Undo the screws and withdraw the lock motor from the lock.

36 Lift the inner door handle outer cable from the slot and disconnect the inner cable from the lever.

**Refitting**

37 Refitting is a reversal of removal, but secure the window guide channel with new rivets and if necessary apply additional sealant between the lock shield and door outer skin. Check the operation of the lock mechanism before refitting the plastic sheeting and inner door trim panel.

---

**14 Door window glass and regulator -** removal and refitting

### Front door window

**Removal**

1 Remove the door inner trim panel as described in Section 12. Peel back the protective plastic sheeting from the bottom of the access hole in the door inner panel.

2 On models with manually-operated windows, temporarily refit the window winder handle. On models with electric windows, temporarily reconnect the battery negative lead, and the door window switch. Lower the window so that the lower edge of the glass is visible at the bottom of the aperture in the inner panel.

3 Using a screwdriver, carefully prise off the small gaiter from the door mirror control lever **(see illustration)**.

4 Using the screwdriver, carefully prise off the door mirror inner trim panel, starting at the front upper edge **(see illustration)**.

5 Undo the lock screw then undo the retaining nut and withdraw the exterior mirror from the outside of the door. Carefully prise off the mirror external trim panel.

**14.4 Removing the exterior mirror trim panel**

**14.6 Removing the window weatherstrips**

**14.7a Undo the lower channel screws . . .**

**14.7b . . . then tilt the glass and remove it from the door**

**14.8 With the window shut, loosen then tighten the channel screws through the access holes**

**14.15 Drilling out the window regulator mechanism retaining rivets**

6 Carefully prise the window weatherstrips from the outside and inside of the door (see illustration).

7 Undo the two screws securing the glass lower channel to the regulator. Tilt the glass forwards to release it from the window channels, then carefully lift the glass and withdraw it from the outside of the door (see illustrations).

### Refitting

8 Refitting is a reversal of removal, but check that the edges of the window glass engage correctly with the guide channels. Before refitting the door trim panel, temporarily reconnect the switch and fully raise the window. With the window shut, loosen the glass lower channel screws through the holes in the inner panel (see illustration), then settle the glass in its guide channels and re-tighten the screws. Check that the window regulator mechanism operates correctly.

### *Front door regulator*

**Note:** *New rivets will be required to secure the regulator mechanism to the door on refitting.*

### Removal

9 Disconnect the battery negative (earth) lead (see Chapter 5A).

10 Remove the door inner trim panel and protective plastic sheeting as described in Section 12.

11 Undo the screws and withdraw the radio loudspeaker so that the wiring multiplug can be disconnected. Remove the loudspeaker.

12 Undo the screw securing the inner handle

to the inner door. Slide the handle forwards and unclip it from the door.

13 On models with manually-operated windows, temporarily refit the window winder handle. On models with electric windows, temporarily reconnect the battery negative lead, and the door window switch. Lower the window so that the lower edge of the glass is visible at the bottom of the aperture in the inner panel.

14 Manually lift the window glass until it is almost in the closed position. Retain the glass in this position using adhesive tape.

15 Drill out the rivets securing the regulator mechanism to the door (see illustration).

16 On models with power windows, unscrew the regulator retaining nuts and also disconnect the wiring at the multiplug.

17 Manipulate the regulator mechanism out through the aperture in the door inner panel.

### Refitting

18 Refitting is a reversal of removal, but check the operation of the window regulator mechanism before refitting the door trim panel, and use new rivets to secure the regulator mechanism.

### 15 Opening rear quarter windows - removal and refitting

### *Removal*

1 Open the window, then undo the screws securing the latch to the side body panel (see illustration).

2 Using a screwdriver, prise off the screw covers from the glass hinges (see illustration).

**15.1 Removing the latch securing screws**

**15.2 Removing the opening rear quarter window glass hinge covers**

**17.0 On later models, wiring is threaded through wiring harness grommets (arrowed)**

**17.2 Removing the cover from the top of the tailgate for access to the washer jet**

**17.4 Tailgate hinge**

**3** Support the window glass, then undo the screws and withdraw the quarter window from the car. Recover the spacers and washers, noting their locations.

**4** If desired, the hinges may be removed from the body by prising out the rivet covers and drilling out the rivets.

## Refitting

**5** Refitting is a reversal of removal, but where necessary use new rivets to secure the hinges.

**16 Fuel filler flap -**
removal and refitting

## Removal

**1** Open the fuel filler flap and remove the filler cap.

**2** Undo the screw retaining the filler neck to the body.

**3** Turn the filler flap housing anticlockwise approximately 30°, then withdraw the housing from the body.

 **Warning: As a safety precaution, refit the filler cap while the housing is removed.**

**4** Using a screwdriver inserted through the hole, prise out the flap spigot, then twist the flap and remove it from the housing.

## Refitting

**5** Refitting is a reversal of removal.

**17.10a Lever off the retaining clip . . .**

**17 Tailgate and support struts -**
removal, refitting and adjustment

**Note:** *On later models, the wiring for the rear wiper motor, heated rear window and lock mechanism are through wiring grommets at the top of the tailgate aperture (see illustration). On this type the wiring will have to be disconnected from the components and threaded through the tailgate as described in paragraph 3.*

### Tailgate

#### Removal

**1** Open the tailgate, then unhook the straps and remove the parcel shelf.

**2** Using a screwdriver and protective pad, carefully prise out the cover from the top of the tailgate for access to the washer jet and tube **(see illustration). Note:** *On later models, remove the high-level stop-light as described in Chapter 12, Section 5. Disconnect the tube from the jet.*

**3** Squeeze together the washer/cable grommet and disconnect it from the tailgate. Pull the washer fluid hose through, and withdraw the hose from the tailgate. If desired, to aid refitting, tie a length of string to the end of the hose before pulling it through, then pull the hose from the tailgate, and untie the string, leaving the string in position in the tailgate.

**4** Using a pencil or marker pen, mark the position of the hinges on the tailgate to aid refitting **(see illustration).**

**5** If necessary, prise the washer nozzle from the tailgate.

**17.10b . . . and disconnect the strut from the tailgate**

**6** Support the tailgate, and disconnect the support struts, as described later in this Section.

**7** Ensure that the tailgate is adequately supported, ideally with the aid of an assistant, then unscrew the bolts securing the hinges to the tailgate, and lift the tailgate from the vehicle.

#### Refitting and adjustment

**8** Refitting is a reversal of removal, but note the following points.

  a) *Make sure that the hinges are aligned with the marks made before removal.*
  b) *Where applicable, use the string to pull the wiring harness and the washer fluid hose into position in the tailgate.*
  c) *On completion, check the alignment of the tailgate with the surrounding body panels and, if necessary, adjust the position of the tailgate hinges within the elongated holes until satisfactory alignment is achieved.*

### Support struts

#### Removal

**9** Open the tailgate, and support it in the open position, using a wooden prop or similar tool. Note that the tailgate is heavy, and will fall closed if either of the support struts are disconnected.

**10** Working at the top end of the strut, lever off the retaining clip, and disconnect the end of the strut from the lug on the tailgate **(see illustrations).**

**11** Repeat the procedure at the bottom end of the strut, and withdraw the strut.

#### Refitting

**12** Refitting is a reversal of removal.

**18 Tailgate lock components -**
removal and refitting

### Lock cylinder and handle
#### Removal

**1** With the tailgate open, prise out the fixing peg located near the tailgate closing recess, then carefully pull the trim panel from the tailgate to release the remaining securing clips **(see**

18.1a Remove the fixing peg . . .

18.1b . . . then carefully pull the trim panel and release the retaining clips

18.2a Disconnect the outer cable . . .

18.2b . . . and inner cable

18.3a Unscrew the nuts . . .

18.3b . . . and remove the lock cylinder from the handle

18.3c Removing the tailgate handle

18.7a Remove the two lock motor retaining screws (arrowed) . . .

18.7b . . . then unclip the operating cable from the lock motor lever

**illustrations).** Start pulling at the top edge of the trim panel which is secured by six clips, then pull off the lower edge which is secured by two clips.
2 Working through the access hole, slide the lock operating outer cable from the bracket, then use pliers to squeeze the tabs and disconnect the inner cable from the lock cylinder lever **(see illustrations).**

3 Unscrew the nuts, and remove the lock cylinder from the handle. If necessary, the lock handle may be removed by unscrewing the nuts. Note that the upper part of the handle is secured with double-sided tape **(see illustrations).**

**Refitting**
4 Refitting is a reversal of removal.

### Lock/motor assembly
#### Removal
5 With the tailgate open, prise out the fixing peg (as shown in illustration 18.1a), then carefully pull the trim panel from the tailgate to release the remaining securing clips. Start pulling at the top edge of the trim panel which is secured by six clips, then pull off the lower edge which is secured by two clips.
6 Working through the access hole, slide the lock operating outer cable from the bracket, then depress the tabs and disconnect the inner cable from the lock cylinder lever.
7 On models with tailgate locking motor, undo the two retaining screws and disconnect the operating cable from the locking motor lever **(see illustration).**
8 Using a Torx key, unscrew the lock mounting screws, then withdraw the lock (together with the operating cable) from the tailgate **(see illustrations).**

18.8a Unscrew the lock mounting screws . . .

18.8b . . . and withdraw the lock and operating cable from the tailgate

**18.9 Disconnecting the operating cable from the tailgate lock**

**9** Disconnect the cable and remove it from the lock **(see illustration).**

### Refitting

**10** Refitting is a reversal of removal, but check the operation of the lock mechanism before refitting the tailgate trim panel.

## 19 Central locking system components - general information

**1** Central locking is fitted as standard to Ka-2 and Ka-3 models. On early models, it operates on the front doors, and the tailgate can only be opened by the ignition key (the tailgate locks automatically when it is closed). On later models, the doors and the tailgate locks are operated by central locking motors.
**2** The removal and refitting procedure for the door lock motors is described as part of the door lock removal and refitting procedure in Section 13, and the tailgate lock/motor is in Section 18.

## 20 Electric window components - removal and refitting

### Window operating switches

**1** Refer to Chapter 12, Section 4.

### Window regulator motors

**2** The motors are integral with the regulator assemblies, and if faulty, the complete regulator assembly must be renewed. Removal and refitting of the regulator assemblies is described in Section 14.

## 21 Windscreen and tailgate window glass - general information

These areas of glass are secured by the tight fit of the weatherseal in the body aperture, and are bonded in position with a

special adhesive. Renewal of such fixed glass is a difficult, messy and time-consuming task, which is considered beyond the scope of the home mechanic. It is difficult, unless one has plenty of practice, to obtain a secure, waterproof fit. Furthermore, the task carries a high risk of breakage; this applies especially to the laminated glass windscreen. In view of this, owners are strongly advised to have this sort of work carried out by one of the many specialist windscreen fitters.

## 22 Sunroof - removal and refitting

### Sliding Sunroof

**Note:** *If the sunroof stops working, it can be closed manually. Remove the round trim cover in the roof console, then insert the handle (supplied in the storage compartment) and turn it anti-clockwise to close the roof.*

### Removal

**1** With the sunroof closed, disconnect the battery negative (earth) lead (see Chapter 5A).
**2** Carefully prise the sliding roof surround panel from the headlining, using fingers only at each corner. With the surround detached from the headlining, disconnect the wiring from the sunroof operating switch.
**3** Disconnect the wiring from the sliding roof motor, then undo the screws and remove the motor.
**4** Undo the screw and remove the relay bracket, then undo the screws on each side and remove the glass from the top of the car.
**5** Using the sequence shown **(see illustration)**, undo the screws and remove the clamp frame from the roof.
**6** Lift the mainframe and weatherstrip from the roof.
**7** Remove the foam seal from the roof opening. It is recommended that the seal is renewed.

### Refitting

**8** Refitting is a reversal of removal.

**22.5 Sunroof clamp frame screw loosening sequence**

### Folding Sunroof

**9** Due to the complexity of the sunroof mechanism, considerable expertise is needed to repair, renew or adjust the sunroof components successfully. Removal of the sunroof may first require removing the headlining, which is a complex and tedious operation. Therefore any problems with the sunroof should be referred to a Ford dealer.

## 23 Exterior mirrors and associated components - removal and refitting

### Mirror glass

#### Removal

**1** On models with electric mirrors, make sure that the ignition is switched off.
**2** Push the inboard edge of the mirror glass fully into the mirror housing, to leave a gap at the outboard edge of the glass.
**3** Carefully pull the outboard edge of the glass outwards, and at the same time, pull the glass towards the outboard edge of the housing, until the glass is released from the mirror. Where applicable, disconnect the wiring from the glass.

#### Refitting

**4** Where applicable, reconnect the wiring to the glass.
**5** Locate the inboard edge of the glass on the mounting in the mirror housing.
**6** With the glass in position, press the outboard edge of the glass into the housing until an audible click is heard, and the glass locks in position.

### Mirror

#### Removal

**7** On models with stalk-operated mirrors, carefully prise the control stalk grommet from the inner trim panel.
**8** Using a screwdriver, carefully prise off the mirror inner trim panel starting at the upper front corner.
**9** Undo the lock screw then unscrew the retaining nut and withdraw the mirror assembly from the outside of the door **(see illustrations)**.

**23.9a Undo the lock screw ...**

23.9b . . . then unscrew the retaining nut . . .

23.9c . . . and withdraw the mirror assembly from the outside of the door

23.10  Removing the exterior mirror outer trim panel

**10** If necessary, carefully prise off the outer trim panel **(see illustration)**.

### Refitting

**11** Refitting is a reversal of removal.

---

## 24 Body exterior fittings - removal and refitting

### Front wheel arch liner

#### Removal

**1** Apply the handbrake, then jack up the front of the vehicle and support it on axle stands (see *"Jacking and Vehicle Support"*). Remove the roadwheel.

24.2  Removing the wheel arch liner

**2** Undo the screws and manoeuvre the liner out from under the wheel arch **(see illustration)**. The liner is secured by 7 screws.

### Refitting

**3** Refitting is a reversal of removal.

---

## Body mouldings and decals

### Removal and refitting

**4** The door mouldings are held in position with double-sided self-adhesive tape, and the various decals have adhesive on their inner surfaces. Removal requires the moulding or decal to be heated to soften the adhesive. Due to the high risk of damage to the vehicle paintwork during this operation, it is recommended that this task should be entrusted to a Ford dealer.

25.1a  Remove the side carpet/trim . . .

### Front badge

#### Removal and refitting

**5** The front badge is attached to the radiator grille. Refer to Section 7 for details of removing and refitting the radiator grille.

---

## 25 Seats - removal and refitting

### Front seat

#### Removal

**1** Adjust the front seat fully forwards for access to the rear mounting bolts. Remove the side carpet/trim, then unscrew and remove the rear mounting bolts **(see illustrations)**.

**2** Adjust the front seat fully rearwards for access to the front mounting bolts. Unscrew and remove the front mounting bolts **(see illustration)**.

**3** Lift the seat, complete with the rails, from the vehicle.

#### Refitting

**4** Refitting is a reversal of removal, but tighten the seat mounting bolts to the specified torque.

### Rear seat cushion

#### Removal

**5** Working at the front lower edge of the seat

25.1b . . . then unscrew the front seat rear outer mounting bolt . . .

25.1c . . . and rear inner mounting bolt

25.2  Removing the front seat front mounting bolts

**25.5 Removing the rear seat cushion mounting screws**

cushion, remove the two screws securing the seat cushion to the floor **(see illustration)**.
**6** Release the catch and fold the left-hand rear backrest forwards. This is necessary in order to provide room for the cushion to be released from the rear hooks. If necessary, unscrew the hinge bolts using a Torx key to allow the cushion to be raised.
**7** Lift the front of the seat cushion, and push it sharply towards the rear of the vehicle to release the retainers from the hooks. At the same time lift up the rear edge of the cushion.
**8** Withdraw the cushion and guide the seat belt buckles through the apertures **(see illustration)**.

### Refitting
**9** Refitting is a reversal of removal, but tighten the rear backrest hinge bolts to the specified torque.

**25.8 Remove the rear seat cushion and guide the seat belt buckles through the apertures**

## *Rear seat backrest*
### Removal
**10** Release the catches, and fold the rear seat backrest forwards.
**11** Using a Torx key, unscrew the hinge bolts, then withdraw the backrest from the vehicle **(see illustration)**.

### Refitting
**12** Refitting is a reversal of removal.

## *Rear seat catch*
### Removal
**13** Release the catch and fully lower the rear seat.
**14** Unscrew and remove the centre bolt/ striker and remove the catch from the rear seat.

### Refitting
**15** Locate the centre bolt/striker on the rear seat and hand-tighten the centre bolt.
**16** Raise and lower the rear seat to set the striker position, then fully tighten the centre bolt.

---

**26 Seat belt components -** removal and refitting

## *Front seat belt and inertia reel/pretensioner*

> ⚠ *Warning: Disconnect the battery negative (earth) lead (see Chapter 5A), then wait at least 2 minutes before proceeding.*

### Removal
**1** Pull off the plastic cover, then unscrew the upper seat belt anchor bolt using a Torx key **(see illustrations)**.
**2** Unbolt the lower seat belt anchor rail bolt, then raise it and remove from the side panel. Slide the seat belt from the rail **(see illustrations)**.
**3** Undo the screws, then carefully pull away the side trim panel and release it from the front clips. Note that the rear of the panel is secured by a rivet **(see illustrations)**.
**4** Unscrew the inertia reel anchor bolt using a

**25.11 Rear seat backrest hinge bolts**

**26.1a Remove the plastic cover . . .**

**26.1b . . . then unscrew the upper seat belt anchor bolt using a Torx key**

**26.2a Unscrew the lower seat belt anchor rail bolt . . .**

**26.2b . . . then raise it and remove it from the side panel**

**26.3a Removing the screws from the side trim panel**

26.3b The rear of the panel is secured by a rivet

26.3c Unclip the front of the side trim panel

26.4 The front seat belt inertia reel located on the door pillar

26.6 The front seat belt stalk is located on the side of the front seat

26.13 Rear seat lower anchor bolt

26.14 Remove the plastic cover for access to the rear seat belt upper anchor bolt

Torx key, and withdraw the reel from the door pillar **(see illustration)**.

### Refitting

**5** Refitting is a reversal of removal, but tighten the bolts to the specified torque.

## Front seat belt stalk

### Removal

**6** Using a Torx key, unscrew the bolt and withdraw the seat belt stalk from the side of the front seat **(see illustration)**.

### Refitting

**7** Refitting is a reversal of removal, but tighten the bolt to the specified torque.

## Front seat belt height

### Adjustment

**Note:** *The front seat upper anchor bolt may be*

*positioned in one of two different locations.*
**8** Pull off the plastic cover, then unscrew the upper seat belt anchor bolt using a Torx key.
**9** Prise the plug from the unused location hole.
**10** Insert the plug in the unused location hole.
**11** Refit the seat belt buckle and insert the upper anchor bolt. Tighten the bolt to the specified torque.

## Rear seat belt and inertia reel

### Removal

**12** Working in the rear passenger compartment, undo the screws and carefully pull away the side trim panel and release it from the clips.
**13** Using a Torx key, unscrew the seat belt lower anchor bolt **(see illustration)**.
**14** Pull off the plastic cover, then unscrew the upper seat belt anchor bolt using a Torx key **(see illustration)**.

**15** Open the tailgate and remove the parcel shelf.
**16** Release the fasteners and drill out the rivets, then remove the relevant rear parcel shelf support bracket for access to the inertia reel **(see illustration)**.
**17** Unscrew the inertia reel anchor bolt using a Torx key, and withdraw the reel from the rear panel **(see illustration)**.

### Refitting

**18** Refitting is a reversal of removal.

## Rear seat belt stalks

### Removal

**19** Remove the rear seat cushion as described in Section 25.
**20** Using a Torx key, unscrew the bolt and withdraw the seat belt stalks **(see illustration)**.

26.16 The rear parcel shelf support bracket is secured with rivets

26.17 Rear seat belt inertia reel anchor bolt

26.20 Rear seat belt stalks

27.3a Undo the screws . . .

27.3b . . . and remove the upper steering
column shroud

27.4a Undo the remaining screws . . .

27.4b . . . and remove the lower steering
column shroud

### Refitting

21 Refitting is a reversal of removal.

## 27 Interior trim -
### removal and refitting

### General

1 The interior trim panels are secured by a combination of clips and screws. Removal and refitting is generally self-explanatory, noting that it may be necessary to remove or loosen surrounding panels to allow a particular panel to be removed. The following paragraphs describe the removal and refitting of the major panels in more detail.

### Door inner trim panels

2 Refer to Section 12.

## *Steering column shrouds*
### Removal

3 Working under the steering column, undo the two screws located nearest to the steering wheel, and lift off the upper shroud (see illustrations).
4 Undo the two remaining screws and remove the lower shroud from the steering column (see illustrations).

### Refitting

5 Refitting is a reversal of removal, but make sure that the upper and lower shrouds engage correctly.

## *Front pillar trim panel*
### Removal

6 Open the door, and carefully prise the weatherseal from the edge of the door aperture.

7 Starting at the top, carefully prise the trim panel from the pillar to release the three securing clips, then unhook the panel from the facia.

### Refitting

8 Refitting is a reversal of removal.

## *Rear parcel shelf support bracket*
### Removal

9 Open the tailgate and remove the parcel shelf.
10 Drill out the pop-rivets and remove the rear parcel shelf support bracket.

### Refitting

11 Refitting is a reversal of removal, but use new pop-rivets to secure the support bracket.

## *Rear quarter trim panel*
### Removal

12 Open the tailgate and remove the parcel shelf.
13 Lower the rear seat backrest into the luggage compartment.
14 Carefully drill out the upper front rivet securing the trim panel to the body.
15 Undo the two trim panel retaining screws. Note that one of the screws is located in the side pocket.
16 Pull out the trim panel and release it from the clips.

### Refitting

17 Refitting is a reversal of removal, but use a new rivet.

## *Carpet*
### Removal

18 Remove both front seats as described in Section 25.
19 Working on each side in turn, use a Torx key to unscrew the bolts from the front seat belt anchor rails, then slide out the rear ends of the rails.
20 Unscrew and remove the gear lever knob (see illustration).
21 Release the gear lever gaiter from the floor, and remove it from the top of the gear lever (see illustration).
22 Pull the handbrake lever gaiter from the floor (see illustration).

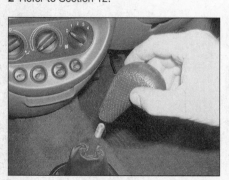

27.20 Unscrewing the gear lever knob

27.21 Release the gear lever gaiter from
the floor

27.22 Removing the handbrake lever
gaiter from the floor

**27.23  Pull up the door weatherstrips from the sills on each side**

**27.25  Unclip the lower trim from the inner sill on each side of the car**

**27.26  Releasing the carpet side clips**

**23** Pull up the door weatherstrips from the sills on each side **(see illustration)**. Do not completely remove the weatherstrips.
**24** Lower the rear seat backrests into the luggage compartment.
**25** Unclip the lower trim from the inner sill on each side of the car **(see illustration)**.
**26** Release the carpet side clips **(see illustration)**.
**27** On the driver's side footwell, remove the side trim panel.
**28** With the tailgate open, withdraw the carpet from the rear of the car **(see illustration)**.

### Refitting

**29** Refitting is a reversal of removal, but tighten the seat belt anchor rail bolts to the specified torque.

## Headlining

### Removal

**30** Working on each side at a time, undo the screws and remove the sun visors and retaining clips.
**31** Remove the front pillar trim panels as described above.
**32** On the passenger side, lift the covers then undo the screws and remove the grab handle from the headlining.
**33** Where fitted, remove the sunroof as described in Section 22.
**34** In the rear passenger compartment, lift the covers then undo the screws and remove the rear coat hooks from the headlining.
**35** Carefully prise the interior lamp from the headlining, and disconnect the wiring.

**36** At the rear of the headlining, prise out the three retaining clips.
**37** Pull down the door weatherstrips from the headlining on each side. Do not completely remove the weatherstrips.
**38** Open the tailgate and pull down the tailgate weatherstrip from the rear of the headlining.
**39** Carefully withdraw the headlining from the rear of the car, taking care not to bend it excessively.

### Refitting

**40** Refitting is a reversal of removal.

---

**28  Facia assembly -**
removal and refitting

> ⚠ **Warning: Refer to Chapter 12 and note the precautions to be observed when working with an air bag.**

### Removal

**Note:** *This is a difficult procedure, as the wiring harness and heater/ventilation ducting must be released from the rear of the facia (and attached on refitting) with the facia pulled back from the bulkhead, before the assembly can be removed. Access is very difficult, and it is suggested that this Section is read through thoroughly before starting the procedure.*
**1** Disconnect the battery negative (earth) lead

**27.28  Removing the carpet from inside the car**

(see Chapter 5A). Wait for two minutes before carrying out any further work.
**2** Remove the steering column as described in Chapter 10.
**3** Remove the instrument panel as described in Chapter 12.
**4** Working on each side at a time, pull the weatherstrip from the door apertures **(see illustration)**.
**5** Remove the upper front pillar trim panels by carefully prising them away with a wide-blade screwdriver **(see illustration)**. This is a difficult task as the retaining clips are very tight and are likely to be broken on removal. However, replacement panels are not expensive.
**6** Using a screwdriver, prise out the small side covers from each end of the facia **(see illustration)**.
**7** Open and remove the fusebox lid, then undo the fusebox retaining screws and

**28.4  Pulling the weatherstrip from the door pillar**

**28.5  Removing the upper front pillar trim panels**

**28.6  Prising out the facia side covers**

28.7a Open and remove the fusebox lid . . .

28.7b . . . then undo the fusebox retaining screws . . .

28.7c . . . and release the fusebox from the facia

release the fusebox from the facia **(see illustrations)**.

**8** Fold back the front of the carpet from the area below the facia. Refer to Section 27 if necessary.

**9** Unscrew the facia mounting bolts. Two bolts are located at each end of the facia, two bolts are located beneath the heater control

28.9 Unscrewing the facia mounting bolts

panel, and two bolts are located beneath the instrument panel position. Do not confuse the bolts with the facia retaining screws which secure the facia to the bulkhead safety bar. Note that the facia is removed together with the safety bar, and if necessary the bar removed later **(see illustration)**.

**10** With the bonnet open, undo the screws securing the vent cowling to the bulkhead in front of the windscreen.

**11** Close the bonnet and remove the windscreen wiper arms and blades as described in Chapter 12, then open the bonnet again.

**12** With the screws removed, remove the right and left vent cowlings and disconnect the washer jet supply tube.

**13** With the vent cowling removed, unscrew and remove the three facia mounting nuts located on the bulkhead.

**14** During the following paragraphs, note the location of all wiring plugs to ensure correct refitting.

**15** Disconnect the central wiring multiplug, then with the help of an assistant lift the facia away from the bulkhead sufficient for access to its rear. Cut the plastic cable ties holding the wiring to the facia.

**16** Remove the sound insulation.

**17** Disconnect the wiring from the cigar lighter and clock.

**18** On models fitted with a passenger airbag, carefully disconnect the two wires from it.

**19** Disconnect the multiplug from the airbag control module by pressing the locking tag upwards and pulling over the retaining strap.

**20** Undo the screws from under the front of the facia, and remove the heater ducting.

**21** Release the wiring harness from the facia clips and cable ties.

**22** With the help of an assistant, withdraw the facia from one side of the vehicle.

### Refitting

**23** Refitting is a reversal of removal, referring to the relevant Chapters as necessary.

# Chapter 12
## Body electrical system

## Contents

## Degrees of difficulty

| **Easy,** suitable for novice with little experience |  | **Fairly easy,** suitable for beginner with some experience |  | **Fairly difficult,** suitable for competent DIY mechanic |  | **Difficult,** suitable for experienced DIY mechanic |  | **Very difficult,** suitable for expert DIY or professional | |
|---|---|---|---|---|---|---|---|---|---|

## Specifications

### General
System type ............................................. 12-volt negative earth

### Fuses
See Section 3 and the Wiring Diagrams at the end of this Chapter.

### Relays

| Number | Colour | Circuits |
|---|---|---|
| 1 | Green | Electric cooling fan motor |
| 2 | Red | Windscreen wiper interval |
| 3 | - | Not used |
| 4 | - | Not used |
| 5 | Green | Ignition |
| 6 | Green | Heated rear screen |
| 7 | Green | Start inhibitor |
| 8 | White | 'Lights-on' warning chime |
| A | Brown | Dipped beam |
| B | Brown | Main beam |
| C | Brown | Fuel and ignition |
| D | Brown | Fuel pump |
| E | Brown | Air conditioning switch |
| F | Brown | Remote luggage compartment release |
| G | - | Not used |

| Bulbs | Type | Wattage |
|---|---|---|
| Headlight: | | |
|   Main beam | H1 | 55 |
|   Dipped beam | H7 | 55 |
| Front sidelight | Push-fit | 5 |
| Front direction indicator light | Bayonet-fit | 21 |
| Front direction indicator side repeater light | Push-fit | 5 |
| Tail light | Bayonet-fit | 5 |
| Stop-light | Bayonet-fit | 21 |
| Rear direction indicator light | Bayonet-fit | 21 |
| Reversing light | Bayonet-fit | 21 |
| Rear foglight | Bayonet-fit | 21 |
| High-mounted stop-light | Push-fit | 5 |
| Number plate light | Push-fit | 10 |
| Courtesy light | Festoon | 10 |

| Torque wrench settings | Nm | lbf ft |
|---|---|---|
| Air bag electronic control unit | 4 | 3 |
| Driver's air bag to steering wheel | 4 | 3 |
| Headlight | 6 | 4 |
| Passenger air bag to facia | 4 | 3 |
| Tailgate wiper motor | 8 | 6 |
| Wiper arm nut: | | |
|   Windscreen | 18 | 13 |
|   Tailgate | 15 | 10 |
| Windscreen wiper motor: | | |
|   To bracket | 10 | 7 |
|   To bulkhead | 8 | 6 |
|   Lever to motor | 24 | 18 |

## 1 General information and precautions

**Warning: Before carrying out any work on the electrical system, read through the precautions given in "Safety first!" at the beginning of this manual, Chapter 5A, and the air bag precautions given in Section 24 of this Chapter. Before disconnecting the battery, refer to the information given in Chapter 5A.**

### General information

The electrical system is of the 12-volt negative earth type and comprises a 12-volt battery, an alternator with integral voltage regulator, a starter motor and related electrical accessories, components and wiring. This Chapter covers repair and service procedures for the various electrical components not associated with engine. Information on the battery, alternator and starter motor can be found in Chapter 5A.

All models are fitted with a driver's air bag, which is designed to prevent serious chest and head injuries to the driver during an accident. A similar bag for the front seat passenger is also available. The combined sensor and electronics for the air bag is located next to the steering column inside the vehicle, and contains a back-up capacitor, crash sensor, decelerometer, safety sensor, integrated circuit and microprocessor. The air bag is inflated by a gas generator, which forces the bag out of the module cover in the centre of the steering wheel. A "clock spring" ensures that a good electrical connection is maintained with the air bag at all times - as the steering wheel is turned in each direction, the spring winds and unwinds.

All models are fitted with a Passive Anti-Theft System (PATS) which prevents the engine being started without the correct key. A miniature transponder embedded in the ignition key acts as a short range radio transmitter, which activates a transceiver module mounted around the ignition lock barrel. The transponder requires no independent power supply, as it is activated by an electrical field emitted by the transceiver module.

While some repair procedures are given, the usual course of action is to renew a defective component. The owner whose interest extends beyond mere component renewal should obtain a copy of the *Automobile Electrical & Electronic Systems Manual*, available from the publishers of this Manual.

### Precautions

Prior to removing any component in the electrical system, the battery negative terminal should first be disconnected, to prevent the possibility of electrical short-circuits and/or fires. Refer to Chapter 5A for information on disconnecting the battery.

In addition to the precautions given in "*Safety first!*" at the beginning of this Manual, observe the following when working on the electrical system:

a) Always remove rings, watches, etc. before working on the electrical system. Even with the battery disconnected, capacitive discharge could occur if a component's live terminal is earthed through a metal object. This could cause a shock or nasty burn.
b) Do not reverse the battery connections. Components such as the alternator, fuel injection/ignition system ECU, or any other having semi-conductor circuitry could be irreparably damaged.
c) Do not allow the engine to turn the alternator when the alternator is not connected.
d) Always ensure that the battery negative lead is disconnected when working on the electrical system.
e) Before using electric-arc welding equipment on the vehicle, disconnect the battery, alternator and components such as the fuel injection/ignition system ECU to protect them.

## 2 Electrical fault-finding - general information

**Note:** *The following tests relate to testing of the main electrical circuits, and should not be used to test delicate electronic circuits (such as anti-lock braking systems), particularly where an electronic control module is used.*

### General

1 A typical electrical circuit consists of an electrical component, any switches, relays, motors, fuses, fusible links or circuit breakers related to that component, and the wiring and

connectors which link the component to both the battery and the chassis. To help to pinpoint a problem in an electrical circuit, wiring diagrams are included at the end of this Chapter.

**2** Before attempting to diagnose an electrical fault, first study the appropriate wiring diagram, to obtain a more complete understanding of the components included in the particular circuit concerned. The possible sources of a fault can be narrowed down by noting whether other components related to the circuit are operating properly. If several components or circuits fail at one time, the problem is likely to be related to a shared fuse or earth connection.

**3** Electrical problems usually stem from simple causes, such as loose or corroded connections, a faulty earth connection, a blown fuse, a melted fusible link, or a faulty relay (refer to Section 3 for details of testing relays). Visually inspect the condition of all fuses, wires and connections in a problem circuit before testing the components. Use the wiring diagrams to determine which terminal connections will need to be checked, in order to pinpoint the trouble-spot.

**4** The basic tools required for electrical fault-finding include a circuit tester or voltmeter (a 12-volt bulb with a set of test leads can also be used for certain tests); a self-powered test light (sometimes known as a continuity tester); an ohmmeter (to measure resistance); a battery and set of test leads; and a jumper wire, preferably with a circuit breaker or fuse incorporated, which can be used to bypass suspect wires or electrical components. Before attempting to locate a problem with test instruments, use the wiring diagram to determine where to make the connections.

**5** To find the source of an intermittent wiring fault (usually due to a poor or dirty connection, or damaged wiring insulation), a "wiggle" test can be performed on the wiring. This involves wiggling the wiring by hand, to see if the fault occurs as the wiring is moved. It should be possible to narrow down the source of the fault to a particular section of wiring. This method of testing can be used in conjunction with any of the tests described in the following sub-Sections.

**6** Apart from problems due to poor connections, two basic types of fault can occur in an electrical circuit - open-circuit, or short-circuit.

**7** Open-circuit faults are caused by a break somewhere in the circuit, which prevents current from flowing. An open-circuit fault will prevent a component from working, but will not cause the relevant circuit fuse to blow.

**8** Short-circuit faults are caused by a "short" somewhere in the circuit, which allows the current flowing in the circuit to "escape" along an alternative route, usually to earth. Short-circuit faults are normally caused by a breakdown in wiring insulation, which allows a feed wire to touch either another wire, or an earthed component such as the bodyshell. A short-circuit fault will normally cause the relevant circuit fuse to blow.

### Finding an open-circuit

**9** To check for an open-circuit, connect one lead of a circuit tester or voltmeter to either the negative battery terminal or a known good earth.

**10** Connect the other lead to a connector in the circuit being tested, preferably nearest to the battery or fuse.

**11** Switch on the circuit, bearing in mind that some circuits are live only when the ignition switch is moved to a particular position.

**12** If voltage is present (indicated either by the tester bulb lighting or a voltmeter reading, as applicable), this means that the section of the circuit between the relevant connector and the battery is problem-free.

**13** Continue to check the remainder of the circuit in the same fashion.

**14** When a point is reached at which no voltage is present, the problem must lie between that point and the previous test point with voltage. Most problems can be traced to a broken, corroded or loose connection.

### Finding a short-circuit

**15** To check for a short-circuit, first disconnect the load(s) from the circuit (loads are the components which draw current from a circuit, such as bulbs, motors, heating elements, etc).

**16** Remove the relevant fuse from the circuit, and connect a circuit tester or voltmeter to the fuse connections.

**17** Switch on the circuit, bearing in mind that some circuits are live only when the ignition switch is moved to a particular position.

**18** If voltage is present (indicated either by the tester bulb lighting or a voltmeter reading, as applicable), this means that there is a short-circuit.

**19** If no voltage is present, but the fuse still blows with the load(s) connected, this indicates an internal fault in the load(s).

### Finding an earth fault

**20** The battery negative terminal is connected to "earth" - the metal of the engine/transmission unit and the car body - and most systems are wired so that they only receive a positive feed, the current returning via the metal of the car body. This means that the component mounting and the body form part of that circuit. Loose or corroded mountings can therefore cause a range of electrical faults, ranging from total failure of a circuit, to a puzzling partial fault. In particular, lights may shine dimly (especially when another circuit sharing the same earth point is in operation), motors (eg wiper motors or the radiator cooling fan motor) may run slowly, and the operation of one circuit may have an apparently-unrelated effect on another. Note that on many vehicles, earth straps are used between certain components, such as the engine/transmission and the body, usually where there is no metal-to-metal contact between components, due to flexible rubber mountings, etc.

**21** To check whether a component is properly earthed, disconnect the battery, and connect one lead of an ohmmeter to a known good earth point. Connect the other lead to the wire or earth connection being tested. The resistance reading should be zero; if not, check the connection as follows.

**22** If an earth connection is thought to be faulty, dismantle the connection, and clean back to bare metal both the bodyshell and the wire terminal or the component earth connection mating surface. Be careful to remove all traces of dirt and corrosion, then use a knife to trim away any paint, so that a clean metal-to-metal joint is made. On reassembly, tighten the joint fasteners securely; if a wire terminal is being refitted, use serrated washers between the terminal and the bodyshell, to ensure a clean and secure connection. When the connection is remade, prevent the onset of corrosion in the future by applying a coat of petroleum jelly or silicone-based grease, or by spraying on (at regular intervals) a proprietary ignition sealer.

## 3  Fuses and relays - general information

### Fuses

**1** Fuses are designed to break a circuit when a predetermined current is reached, in order to protect the components and wiring which could be damaged by excessive current flow. Any excessive current flow will be due to a fault in the circuit, usually a short-circuit (see Section 2).

**2** The fuses are located in the fusebox, below the driver's side of the facia. Additional fuses are located on the rear of the fusebox.

**3** For access to the fuses, pull out the bottom of the fusebox cover and unhook it **(see illustration)**.

**4** A blown fuse can be recognised from its melted or broken wire.

**5** To remove a fuse, first ensure that the relevant circuit is switched off.

**6** Using the plastic tool provided on the

**3.3 Pull out the bottom of the fusebox cover and unhook**

3.6a  Remove the plastic tool from the fusebox cover . . .

3.6b  . . . and pull the fuse from its location

3.10  Relays and fuses located in the top of the main fusebox

3.11a  Undo the securing screws . . .

3.11b  . . . and lower the fusebox from the facia

## 4  Switches - removal and refitting

**Note:** *Disconnect the battery negative lead, with reference to Chapter 5A before removing any switch, and reconnect the lead after refitting the switch.*

### Ignition switch/steering column lock

#### Removal

1  Undo the screws and withdraw the upper and lower shrouds from around the steering column.

2  Disconnect the wiring plug and remove the securing screw, then withdraw the anti-theft immobiliser transceiver unit from the ignition switch/steering lock assembly.

3  Insert the ignition key, and turn it to position "I".

4  Using a small screwdriver, depress the locking pin at the top of the lock housing, then pull out the lock cylinder using the key.

5  To refit the lock cylinder, push the assembly into the lock housing, until the locking pin engages, then turn the ignition key to position "0" and withdraw the key. Refit the anti-theft immobiliser transceiver unit and the steering column shrouds.

6  To remove the ignition switch, separate the wiring connectors, then release the securing clips using a small screwdriver, and withdraw the switch from the end of the lock housing.

#### Refitting

7  Refitting is a reversal of removal.

fusebox cover, pull the fuse from its location **(see illustrations)**.

7  Before renewing a blown fuse, trace and rectify the cause, and always use a fuse of the correct rating. Never substitute a fuse of a higher rating, or make temporary repairs using wire or metal foil; more serious damage, or even fire, could result.

8  Note that the fuses are colour-coded as follows. Refer to the markings on the fusebox cover for details of the circuits protected and to the Wiring Diagrams.

| Colour | Rating |
|---|---|
| Orange | 5A |
| Red | 10A |
| Blue | 15A |
| Yellow | 20A |
| Clear or white | 25A |
| Green | 30A |

### Relays

9  A relay is an electrically-operated switch, which is used for the following reasons:

a) *A relay can switch a heavy current remotely from the circuit in which the current is flowing, allowing the use of lighter-gauge wiring and switch contacts.*

b) *A relay can receive more than one control input, unlike a mechanical switch.*

c) *A relay can have a timer function - for example, the intermittent wiper relay.*

10  Most of the relays are located under the facia, on the fusebox **(see illustration)**, however, some engine-related relays are located on the bulkhead in the engine compartment. The lights-on warning buzzer is located on the top of the fusebox.

11  Access to the relays in the fusebox can be

obtained by removing the two securing screws, then releasing the securing clips, and lowering the fusebox from the facia **(see illustrations)**.

12  If a circuit or system controlled by a relay develops a fault, and the relay is suspect, operate the system. If the relay is functioning, it should be possible to hear it "click" as it is energised. If this is the case, the fault lies with the components or wiring of the system. If the relay is not being energised, then either the relay is not receiving a main supply or a switching voltage, or the relay itself is faulty. Testing is by the substitution of a known good unit, but be careful - while some relays are identical in appearance and in operation, others look similar but perform different functions.

13  To remove a relay, first ensure that the relevant circuit is switched off. The fusebox-mounted relays can simply be pulled out from their sockets, and pushed back into position. The engine compartment mounted relays can be removed by detaching the mountings and disconnecting the wiring - refitting is a reversal of removal.

4.9  Remove the securing screw from the top of the combination switch . . .

4.10  . . . then disconnect the wiring from the indicator switch . . .

4.11 . . . and from the washer switch

4.29a Undo the screw . . .

4.29b . . . and remove the door courtesy light switch from the door pillar

### Steering column combination switch assembly

**Removal**

8 Undo the screws and withdraw the upper and lower shrouds from around the steering column.
9 Remove the securing screw from the top of the switch assembly (see illustration)
10 Disconnect the wiring plugs from the rear of the indicator switch (see illustration).
11 Disconnect the wiring plug from the rear of the washer switch (see illustration).
12 Lift the switch assembly from the steering column.

**Refitting**

13 Refitting is a reversal of removal.

### Centre facia-mounted pushbutton switches

**Note:** *The following procedure applies to the air conditioning, rear fog lamp, heated rear screen and recirculation switches.*

**Removal**

14 Remove the radio/cassette player as described in Section 20.
15 Working at the top of the heater/ventilation control unit, unscrew the two securing screws.
16 Release the two securing clips at the sides of the panel, then pull the control panel forwards from the facia.
17 Disconnect the wiring plug from the rear of the unit.
18 Release the air distribution shaft from the clip.
19 Remove the heating/air conditioning module and the blower motor switch from the facia.

20 On the rear of the assembly, disconnect the multiplug then undo the four screws and remove the switch assembly.

**Refitting**

21 Refitting is a reversal of removal.

### Headlight leveller

**Removal**

22 Carefully prise the switch from the facia using a small screwdriver, and disconnect the wiring plug. Alternatively, if it is very tight, remove the instrument panel surround first then push the leveller from it.

**Refitting**

23 Refitting is a reversal of removal.

### Heater blower motor switch

**Removal and refitting**

24 Refer to Chapter 3, Section 9.

### Stop-light switch and handbrake "on" warning light switch

**Removal and refitting**

25 Refer to Chapter 9.

### Electric window switches

**Removal**

26 Remove the door inner trim panel as described in Chapter 11.
27 Disconnect the wiring plug from the switch, then push the switch out from the trim panel.

**Refitting**

28 Refitting is a reversal of removal.

### Door courtesy light switch

**Removal**

29 With the door open, unscrew the switch securing screw, then pull the switch from the door pillar, and disconnect the wiring plug (see illustrations).
30 It is advisable to tape or tie the switch wiring in position, to prevent it from dropping down into the door pillar.

**Refitting**

31 Refitting is a reversal of removal.

### Hazard warning switch (up to 1999)

**Removal**

32 Remove the radio/cassette player as described in Section 20.
33 Depress the plastic tabs and push the hazard flasher switch out of the radio surround (see illustration).

**Refitting**

34 Refitting is a reversal of removal.

### Hazard warning switch (from 1999)

35 The hazard switch is part of the steering column combination switch assembly. To remove the switch assembly, follow the procedures as described in paragraphs 8 to 13 in this Section.

### Heated front windscreen switch

**Removal**

36 Remove the radio/cassette player as described in Section 20.
37 Depress the plastic tabs and push the heated front windscreen switch out of the radio surround.

**Refitting**

38 Refitting is a reversal of removal.

### Luggage compartment release switch

**Removal**

39 Remove the fusebox cover.
40 Depress the plastic tabs, and push the switch out from inside the fusebox aperture (see illustration).

**Refitting**

41 Refitting is a reversal of removal.

4.33 Removing the hazard flasher switch from the radio surround

4.40 The switch is released at the rear of the facia

5.1a Pull up the retaining spring clip . . .

5.1b . . . and lift the plastic cover from the rear of the headlight

### 5 Bulbs (exterior lights) - renewal

⚠ **Warning: Ensure all exterior lights are switched off before disconnecting the wiring connectors. Note that if a bulb fails, and has just been in use, it will still be extremely hot, particularly in the case of a headlight bulb.**

#### Headlight

1 With the bonnet open, pull the retaining spring clip upwards and remove the plastic cover from the rear of the headlight (see illustrations).

2 The top bulb is for the dipped beam, and the bottom bulb is for the main beam. To remove a bulb, first disconnect the wiring plug from the bulb terminals (see illustration).

3 Release the spring clip and withdraw the bulb from the reflector housing (see illustrations).

4 When handling the new bulb, use a tissue or clean cloth, to avoid touching the glass with the fingers; moisture and grease from the skin can cause blackening and rapid failure of this type of bulb. If the glass is accidentally touched, wipe it clean using methylated spirit.

5 Fit the new bulb, ensuring that its locating tabs are correctly seated in the housing cut-outs. Secure the bulb in position with the spring clip, and reconnect the wiring plug.

6 Refit the plastic cover and secure with the clip.

#### Front sidelight

7 With the bonnet open, pull the retaining spring clip upwards and remove the plastic cover from the rear of the headlight.

8 Carefully pull the bulbholder from the reflector (see illustration).

9 Pull the wedge-type bulb from the bulbholder (see illustration).

10 Press the new bulb firmly into the bulbholder, then locate the bulbholder in the reflector.

11 Refit the plastic cover and secure with the clip.

#### Front direction indicator light

12 With the bonnet open, reach down through the access hole in the front cross-member and turn the bulbholder anticlockwise to release it from the side of the headlight. Note that the bulbholder has two extensions to make it easier to turn (see illustration).

13 Depress the wire clip and disconnect the wiring plug from the bulbholder.

14 Depress and twist the bulb to remove it from the bulbholder (see illustration). The bulb is a bayonet-fit in the bulbholder.

15 Fit the new bulb and turn it clockwise. Make sure it is securely fitted in the bulbholder.

16 Press the wiring plug firmly onto the bulbholder, then fit the bulbholder to the headlight and turn it clockwise to secure.

#### Front direction indicator side repeater light

17 Carefully slide the side repeater light to the rear of the car, and withdraw it from the front wing (see illustration). In practice, the light may be a very tight fit in the wing, and in this case it is recommended that the wheel arch liner be removed in order that the

5.2 Disconnecting the wiring plug from the dipped beam bulb terminals

5.3a Release the spring clip . . .

5.3b . . . and withdraw the bulb from the reflector housing

5.8 Pull the front sidelight bulbholder from the reflector . . .

5.9 . . . then pull the wedge-type bulb from the bulbholder

5.12 Remove the front direction indicator light bulbholder . . .

5.14 ... then depress and twist the bulb to remove it

5.17 Remove the front direction indicator side repeater light ...

5.18a ... then remove the bulbholder ...

5.18b ... and pull out the wedge-type bulb

5.21 Squeeze together the tags to remove the rear light bulbholder

5.22 Removing a bulb from the rear light bulbholder

retaining tabs can be depressed and the light pushed out from inside the wheel arch.
**18** Turn the bulbholder anticlockwise from the lens unit, then pull out the wedge-type bulb **(see illustrations)**.
**19** Press the new bulb firmly into the bulbholder, then insert the bulbholder in the lens unit and turn clockwise.
**20** Insert the side repeater light into the front wing, and press in firmly so that the retaining tags are correctly engaged.

### Rear lights

**21** Open the tailgate. Working in the luggage compartment, squeeze together the tags in the centre of the rear light bulbholder and withdraw the bulbholder from the rear light **(see illustration)**.
**22** The top outer bulb is the stop-light, the

top inner bulb is the tail light, the bottom outer bulb is the direction indicator, and the bottom inner bulb is the reversing light. Depress and twist the relevant bulb to remove it **(see illustration)**. The bulb is a bayonet-fit in the bulbholder.
**23** Fit the new bulb and turn it clockwise. Make sure it is securely fitted in the bulbholder.
**24** Locate the bulbholder plate on the rear light and make sure that the tags engage correctly.

### Rear number plate light

**25** Using a small screwdriver in the hole provided, carefully prise the rear number plate light down from the tailgate **(see illustration)**.
**26** Turn the bulbholder anticlockwise and remove it from the lens unit **(see illustration)**.

**27** Pull the wedge-type bulb from the bulbholder **(see illustration)**.
**28** Press the new bulb firmly into the bulbholder, then insert the bulbholder in the lens unit and turn clockwise.

### High-mounted stop-light (where fitted)

**29** Open the tailgate. Undo the screws and remove the complete stop-light.
**30** Flex the housing outwards and unclip the light module, then press out the reflector.
**31** Pull out the relevant wedge-type bulb.
**32** Press the new bulb firmly into position, and refit the reflector followed by the light module.
**33** Locate the stop-light on its bracket and secure with the screws.

5.25 Prise the rear number plate light down from the tailgate ...

5.26 ... then remove the bulbholder from the lens unit ...

5.27 ... and pull the wedge-type bulb from the bulbholder

## 6 Bulbs (interior lights) - renewal

⚠️ **Warning: Ensure all interior lights are switched off before disconnecting the wiring connectors. Note that if a bulb fails, and has just been in use, it will still be extremely hot.**

### Courtesy light

1 Using a screwdriver, carefully prise the courtesy light unit from the headlining (**see illustration**).
2 Pull the bulb from the spring contacts (**see illustration**).
3 Fit the new bulb using a reversal of the removal procedure.

### Instrument panel illumination and warning light bulbs

4 Remove the instrument panel as described in Section 10.
5 Twist the relevant bulbholder anti-clockwise to remove it from the rear of the panel (**see illustration**).
6 Remove the bulb from the bulbholder (**see illustration**).
7 Fit the new bulb using a reversal of the removal procedure. Refit the instrument panel with reference to Section 10.

### Clock illumination bulb

8 Remove the clock as described in Section 13.
9 Remove the bulb from the rear of the clock.
10 Fit the new bulb using a reversal of the removal procedure. Refit the clock with reference to Section 13.

### Pushbutton switch illumination bulbs

11 The bulbs are integral with the switches, and cannot be renewed separately.

### Cigarette lighter illumination bulb

12 Open the ashtray, then undo the screws, withdraw the ashtray and disconnect the wiring.
13 Working at the rear of the assembly, carefully prise the bulbholder from the cigarette lighter body. The bulb is a push-fit in the bulbholder.

**6.1 Remove the courtesy light unit from the headlining . . .**

**6.5 Twist the bulbholder from the rear of the instrument panel . . .**

14 Fit the new bulb using a reversal of the removal procedure.

### Heater/ventilation control unit illumination bulbs

15 Remove the heater control unit as described in Chapter 3.
16 Twist the relevant bulbholder anticlockwise and remove it from the rear of the panel. The bulb is a push-fit in the bulbholder (**see illustrations**).
17 Fit the new bulb using a reversal of the removal procedure.

### Heater blower motor switch illumination bulb

18 Pull the knob from the blower switch for access to the bulb.
19 The bulb is a push-fit in the switch.
20 Fit the new bulb using a reversal of the removal procedure.

**6.2 . . . then pull the bulb from the spring contacts**

**6.6 . . . then remove the bulb from the bulbholder**

## 7 Exterior light units - removal and refitting

### Headlight

#### Removal

1 At the rear of the wheel arch, unscrew and remove the lower bolt securing the front bumper to the body, then release the bumper from the four clips on the wheel arch. This procedure is particularly difficult as the clips can be easily broken, or can come out of the front wing completely.
2 With the bonnet open, undo the centre and side screws securing the front bumper/radiator grille to the front crossmember.
3 Unscrew and remove the headlight upper mounting bolt (**see illustration**).

**6.16a Remove the bulbholder from the rear of the heater/ventilation control unit . . .**

**6.16b . . . and pull the wedge-type bulb from the bulbholder**

**7.3 The headlight upper mounting bolt**

**7.5 Headlight lower mounting bolt**

**7.6a Headlight side mounting bolt**

**7.6b Removing the headlight**

**7.7 Disconnecting the wiring from the headlight**

**7.12 Disconnecting the wiring from the rear light cluster**

4 Reach down through the access hole in the front crossmember and turn the front indicator light bulbholder anticlockwise to release it from the side of the headlight. Note that the bulbholder has two extensions to make it easier to turn.

5 With the indicator light bulbholder removed, unscrew and remove the lower mounting bolt **(see illustration)**.

6 Unscrew the side mounting bolt, and carefully withdraw the headlight unit. Note the location of the guide pin **(see illustrations)**.

7 Disconnect the wiring at the multiplug and withdraw the headlight unit from the front of the car **(see illustration)**.

8 If necessary, the headlight levelling control motor may be removed from the light with reference to Section 8. The headlight polycarbonate lens is not available separately as it is bonded to the light housing.

### Refitting

9 Refitting is a reversal of removal, but have the headlight beam checked and if necessary adjusted as described in Section 9.

### Front direction indicator light

#### Removal and refitting

10 The front direction indicator light is integral with the headlight and the procedure is described above.

### Front direction indicator side repeater light

#### Removal and refitting

11 The procedure is described as part of the bulb renewal procedure in Section 5.

### Rear light cluster

**Note:** *A new rubber seal should be used on refitting.*

#### Removal

12 With the tailgate open, disconnect the wiring from the rear light cluster **(see illustration)**. If necessary the bulbholder can be removed at this stage by squeezing together the central tags.

13 Unscrew the three mounting nuts and withdraw the light cluster from the rear of the car **(see illustration)**. Recover the rubber seal.

#### Refitting

14 Refitting is a reversal of removal, but use a new rubber seal, and make sure that the seal is seated correctly.

### Rear number plate light

15 The procedure is described as part of the bulb renewal procedure in Section 5.

**7.13 Removing the rear light cluster**

## 8 Headlight beam leveller components - removal and refitting

### Beam leveller switch

1 Refer to Section 4, paragraphs 22 and 23.

### Beam leveller control motor

#### Removal

2 Remove the headlight as described in Section 7.

3 Remove the cover from the rear of the headlight.

4 Disconnect the wiring plug from the control motor.

5 Twist the control motor anticlockwise and remove it from the rear of the headlight. The motor has a bayonet fitting **(see illustration)**.

#### Refitting

6 Refitting is a reversal of removal but refit the headlight with reference to Section 7.

## 9 Headlight beam alignment - general information

1 Most models are equipped with a four-position electrical vertical beam adjuster unit. The unit can be used to adjust the headlight beam, to compensate for the relevant load which the vehicle is carrying. An adjuster switch is provided on the facia. The switch should be positioned according to the load

**8.5 Removing the beam leveller control motor from the rear of the headlight**

10.5a Undo the upper securing screws . . .

10.5b . . . and lower securing screws . . .

10.5c . . . then withdraw the surround . . .

10.5d . . . and disconnect the wiring from the headlight levelling switch

10.6a Undo the screws and withdraw the instrument panel . . .

10.6b . . . then disconnect the speedometer cable . . .

being carried in the vehicle. Refer to the vehicle handbook for further information. Note that the switch must be set to zero, and the vehicle must be unladen, before adjusting the headlight beam as described in the following paragraphs.

2 Accurate adjustment of the headlight beam is only possible using optical beam-setting equipment, and this work should therefore be carried out by a Ford dealer or suitably-equipped workshop.

3 For reference, the headlights can be finely adjusted by rotating the adjuster screws fitted to the rear of each light unit. The screws are accessible with the bonnet open. The vertical adjustment screw is mounted at the inner end of the headlight and faces to the rear. The horizontal adjustment screw is mounted on top of the headlight and is accessible through the crossmember. Note that if the vertical adjustment is altered, this will also affect the horizontal adjustment.

## 10 Instrument panel - removal and refitting

### Removal

1 Disconnect the battery negative (earth) lead (see Chapter 5A).
2 Undo the screws and remove the upper and lower steering column shrouds with reference to Chapter 10.

3 Remove the radio as described in Section 20.
4 Undo the screws and release the clips, then withdraw the heater control panel from the facia. Unhook the control cable and disconnect the wiring plugs. Remove the control panel.
5 Undo the screws securing the instrument panel surround to the facia. There are two above the instrument panel, and three lower ones. Withdraw the surround sufficient to disconnect the wiring plug from the headlight levelling switch, then remove the surround (see illustrations).
6 Undo the screws securing the instrument panel to the facia, then withdraw the panel sufficient to disconnect the speedometer cable and wiring multiplug. Remove the instrument panel (see illustrations).

### Refitting

7 Refitting is a reversal of removal.

10.6c . . . and wiring multiplug

## 11 Instrument panel components - removal and refitting

1 With the instrument panel removed as described in Section 10, proceed as follows (see illustration).

### Lens assembly

#### Removal

2 Twist the main bulbholder anticlockwise, and remove it from the bottom of the instrument panel. Remove the printed circuit from the lens.
3 Carefully release the clips and withdraw the lens from the instrument panel.

#### Refitting

4 Refitting is a reversal of removal.

11.1 Rear view of the instrument panel

13.2a  Use a screwdriver and wad of cloth . . .

13.2b  . . . to prise the clock from the facia panel . . .

13.3  . . . then disconnect the wiring plug

## Fuel gauge

### Removal

5  Remove the lens as described in paragraphs 2 and 3.
6  Undo the two screws and carefully remove the fuel gauge from its contacts.

### Refitting

7  Refitting is a reversal of removal.

## Speedometer head

### Removal

8  Remove the fuel gauge as described in paragraphs 5 and 6.
9  Undo the remaining screw and remove the speedometer head from the instrument panel.

### Refitting

10  Refitting is a reversal of removal.

## Printed circuit

### Removal

11  Remove the speedometer head as described in paragraphs 8 and 9.
12  Using a screwdriver, press in the tabs then remove the multiplug housing.
13  Twist the remaining bulbholders anti-clockwise and remove them from the printed circuit.
14  Carefully release the fuel gauge contacts, then prise out the retaining lugs and remove the printed circuit.
15  Remove the fuel gauge contacts from the printed circuit.
*Caution: Do not bend the printed circuit excessively, otherwise it may be permanently damaged.*

### Refitting

16  Refitting is a reversal of removal.

## Illumination/warning light bulbs

### Removal

17  Twist the bulbholders anti-clockwise to remove them from the printed circuit. The bulbs are integral with the bulbholders.

### Refitting

18  Refitting is a reversal of removal.

### 12  Cigarette lighter - removal and refitting

### Removal

1  Disconnect the battery negative (earth) lead (see Chapter 5A).
2  Open the ashtray, and pull out the ashtray liner by lifting its rear edge. Pull out the lighter element.
3  Undo the retaining screws and lift out the ashtray sufficient to disconnect the wiring multiplug.
4  With the ashtray on the bench, undo the screws and remove the cover.
5  Using a screwdriver, carefully prise the bulbholder from the cigarette lighter body.
6  Turn the cigarette lighter body 30° anti-clockwise (viewed from the rear), and push it out approximately 10 mm. Now turn the body clockwise 30° and push it completely out of the ashtray.
7  The illumination ring can now be pulled from the ashtray.

14.1  The horn and mounting bracket (front bumper removed)

14.4  Horn mounting bracket bolt

### Refitting

8  Refitting is a reversal of removal.

### 13  Clock - removal and refitting

### Removal

1  Disconnect the battery negative (earth) lead (see Chapter 5A).
2  Using a small screwdriver or similar tool, carefully prise the clock from the facia - protect the facia with a cloth pad while doing this **(see illustrations)**.
3  Disconnect the wiring plug and withdraw the unit **(see illustration)**.

### Refitting

4  Refitting is a reversal of removal.

### 14  Horn - removal and refitting

### Removal

1  The horn is located under the left-hand corner of the front bumper **(see illustration)**.
2  Remove the front bumper as described in Chapter 11.
3  Disconnect the wiring plug from the horn.
4  Unscrew the securing nut, and remove the horn from its mounting bracket. Alternatively, unbolt the bracket from the body and remove it together with the horn **(see illustration)**.

### Refitting

5  Refitting is a reversal of removal.

### 15  Speedometer cable - removal and refitting

### Removal

1  Remove the instrument panel as described in Section 10.
2  Remove the air cleaner assembly and air

**16.3a Lift the cover . . .**

**16.3b . . . then unscrew the windscreen wiper arm retaining nut**

**16.4a Remove the tailgate spindle nut cover . . .**

duct as described in Chapter 4A.

**3** Reach down behind the engine and unscrew the collar nut securing the speed-ometer cable to the speed sensor on the rear of the transmission. Pull out the inner cable.

**4** Withdraw the cable through the bulkhead panels into the engine compartment.

**5** Release the cable from any brackets or clips, noting its routing, then withdraw the cable.

### Refitting

**6** Refitting is a reversal of removal, but ensure that the cable is routed as noted before removal, and refit the instrument panel as described in Section 10.

**16.4b . . . then unscrew the retaining nut . . .**

**16.4c . . . and remove the washer**

## 16 Wiper arms -
removal and refitting

### Removal

**1** Operate the wiper motor, then switch it off so that the wiper arm returns to its rest position.

 **HAYNES HiNT** *Stick a piece of masking tape along the edge of the wiper blade, to use as an alignment aid on refitting.*

**2** To remove the windscreen wiper arms, open the bonnet then pull the rubber seal from the engine compartment rear panel. Undo the screws securing the windscreen grille cowl to the bulkhead and move the cowl forwards as

far as possible. This is necessary to provide access to the wiper arm securing nut.

**3** For windscreen wiper arm removal, lift up the wiper arm spindle nut cover, then unscrew and remove the spindle nut. Recover the washer **(see illustrations)**.

**4** For tailgate wiper arm removal, release the spindle nut cover and slide it down from the arm, then unscrew and remove the spindle nut and washer **(see illustrations)**.

**5** Lift the blade off the glass, and ease the wiper arm off its spindle by rocking it side to side **(see illustrations)**.

### Refitting

**6** Ensure that the wiper arm and spindle splines are clean and dry, then refit the arm to the spindle. Align the wiper blade with the tape fitted on removal.

**7** Refit the spindle nut, tightening it securely, then refit the nut cover.

**8** Ford technicians use a special tool to check the setting of the windscreen wiper arm to ensure the wiper blade angle on the wind-screen is correct **(see illustration)**. Without this tool it will be impossible to check the angle, however it is unlikely that the arm will bend under normal operating conditions.

**9** Where necessary, reposition the wind-screen grille cowls then insert and tighten the screws. Refit the rubber seal to the engine compartment rear panel.

## 17 Windscreen wiper motor and linkage -
removal and refitting

⚠ *Warning: Make sure the ignition is switched off before starting this procedure.*

**16.5a Removing the windscreen wiper arm**

**16.5b Removing the tailgate wiper arm**

**16.8 Ford tool for checking the windscreen wiper arm setting**

## Removal

**1** Remove the wiper arms as described in Section 16.

**2** Remove the weatherstrip, then unscrew the retaining screws and lift the windscreen grille cowls from the bulkhead **(see illustrations)**. On models up to 1999, disconnect the washer hose and jet.

**3** On models up to 1999, with power steering, unscrew the bolt and move the power steering fluid reservoir to one side **(see illustration)**. Do not open the reservoir.

**4** Unscrew the bolt and move the coolant expansion tank to one side **(see illustrations)**. Do not open the reservoir (**Note:** *The coolant expansion tank shown is on the left-hand side, on models after 1999 it was fitted to the right-hand side*).

**5** Note the location of the wiring harness on

**17.2a  Remove the weatherstrip . . .**

**17.2b  . . . then prise out the covers . . .**

the rear engine cross panel, then unclip it. Also unclip the relay from the right-hand end of the cross panel. Undo the retaining screws and move the cross panel forwards as far as

possible. Note that two of the retaining screws are located on the wing inner panels **(see illustrations)**.

**6** Disconnect the wiring plug from the

**17.2c  . . . and undo the cowl retaining screws**

**17.2d  Lift the cowl sections from the bulkhead . . .**

**17.2e  . . . and disconnect the washer hose and jet**

**17.3  Unscrew the bolt and move the power steering fluid reservoir to one side**

**17.4a  Undo the bolt . . .**

**17.4b  . . . and move the coolant expansion tank to one side**

**17.5a  Unclip the wiring from the rear engine cross panel . . .**

**17.5b  . . . and unclip the relay**

**17.5c  Unscrewing the cross panel support bracket**

**17.6 Disconnecting the wiring from the washer pump**

**17.7a Unscrew the windscreen wiper motor and linkage upper mounting bolts . . .**

the bolt and detach the reservoir from the wiper motor and linkage assembly **(see illustration)**.

**9** Use a pencil to mark the motor crank lever in relation to the plate to ensure correct refitting. Hold the lever stationary then unscrew the nut and remove the lever from the motor spindle **(see illustration)**. Note that the lever locates in a groove in the spindle.

**10** Unscrew the bolts and remove the motor from the linkage.

### Refitting

**11** Refitting is a reversal of removal, bearing in mind the following points.

a) *Ensure that the motor is in the "parked" position before refitting.*

b) *If the motor has been removed from the linkage, ensure that the marks made on the linkage drive link and motor spindle are aligned on refitting.*

c) *Refit the wiper arms with reference to Section 16.*

**17.7b . . . and lower mounting bolts**

**17.8 Unscrew the bolt to detach the reservoir from the wiper motor and linkage**

windscreen wiper motor and washer pump **(see illustration)**.

**7** Unscrew and remove the windscreen wiper motor and linkage mounting bolts, then lift the assembly from the bulkhead and disconnect

the hoses from the washer pump **(see illustrations)**. Quickly block the pump outlet then remove the assembly and drain its contents into a suitable container.

**8** With the assembly on the bench, unscrew

### 18 Tailgate wiper motor - removal and refitting

⚠️ *Warning: Make sure the ignition is switched off before starting this procedure.*

### Removal

**1** Remove the wiper arm as described in Section 16, then lift off the plastic cover and unscrew the wiper motor spindle nut.

**2** With the tailgate open, prise out the fixing peg located near the tailgate closing recess, then carefully pull the trim panel from the tailgate to release the remaining securing clips. Start pulling at the top edge of the trim panel which is secured by six clips, then pull off the lower edge which is secured by two clips **(see illustrations)**.

**3** Disconnect the wiring plug for the motor and also disconnect the earth lead **(see illustration)**.

**4** Unscrew the mounting bolts and withdraw the wiper motor from the tailgate **(see illustration)**.

**17.9 Windscreen wiper motor linkage**

**18.2a Prise out the fixing peg located near the contact prongs . . .**

**18.2b . . . then pull the trim panel from the tailgate to release the securing clips**

**18.3 Disconnecting the tailgate wiper motor wiring**

**18.4 Unscrewing the tailgate wiper motor retaining bolts**

## Refitting

**5** Refitting is a reversal of removal, but tighten the motor mounting bolts to the specified torque, and refit the wiper arm with reference to Section 16.

### 19 Windscreen/tailgate washer system components - removal and refitting

## Washer fluid reservoir

### Removal and refitting

**1** The washer fluid reservoir is attached to the windscreen wiper motor linkage. The removal and refitting procedure is described in Section 17.

## Washer fluid pump

### Removal

**2** Refer to Section 17 and remove the windscreen washer wiper motor and linkage together with the reservoir. Empty the contents of the reservoir in a suitable container.
**3** Pull the pump from the reservoir, and recover the rubber sealing grommet **(see illustration)**.

### Refitting

**4** Examine the rubber sealing grommet, and renew if necessary.
**5** Refitting is a reversal of removal, but coat the rubber grommet with soapy water before inserting the pump. Make sure that the fluid hose is securely reconnected.

## Windscreen washer nozzle (up to 1999)

### Removal

**6** Remove the windscreen wiper arms as described in Section 16. This procedure includes removing the retaining screws for the grille cowl sections.
**7** Lift the grille cowl sections over the wiper linkage spindles, and at the same time release the washer nozzle where the two sections join. Disconnect the washer tube from the nozzle.

### Refitting

**8** Refitting is a reversal of removal, but make sure that the nozzle is located correctly in the grille section. On completion, check that the jets of water are directed at the top of the wiper blade strokes, and if necessary adjust them using a pin.

## Windscreen washer nozzle (from 1999)

### Removal

**9** With the bonnet open, disconnect the supply hose from the washer nozzle.
**10** Depress the tabs at the rear of the washer nozzle, then prise the nozzle from the bonnet taking care not to damage the paintwork.

**19.3  The washer fluid pump is located on the side of the reservoir**

### Refitting

**11** Refitting is a reversal of removal, making sure that the nozzle is located correctly in the bonnet. On completion check that the jets of water are directed at the top of the wiper blade strokes, and if necessary adjust them using a pin.

## Tailgate washer nozzle

### Removal

**12** With the tailgate open, use a screwdriver to prise out the rubber grommet from the tailgate inner skin. Use a wad of cloth to lever against to prevent damage to the paintwork **(see illustration)**. **Note:** *On later models, remove the high-level stop-light as described in Chapter 12, Section 5.*
**13** Disconnect the washer tube from the tailgate nozzle. Take care not to allow the washer tube to drop down inside the tailgate - if necessary tie a piece of string to it.

**20.2  Inserting the DIN removal tools in the radio/cassette player**

**20.5b  . . . aerial . . .**

**19.12  Remove the rubber grommet for access to the tailgate washer nozzle**

**14** Carefully prise the nozzle from the tailgate, taking care not to damage the paintwork.

### Refitting

**15** Refitting is a reversal of removal, but make sure that the fluid hose is securely reconnected.

### 20 Radio/cassette player - removal and refitting

**Note:** *On models with a security-coded radio/cassette player, once the battery has been disconnected, the unit cannot be re-activated until the appropriate security code has been entered. Do not remove the unit unless the appropriate code is known. The following information applies to radio/cassette players having standard DIN fixings. Two DIN removal tools will be required for this operation.*

**20.5a  Disconnect the wiring plugs . . .**

**20.5c  . . . and hazard warning switch wiring**

21.2a Undo the screws and withdraw the loudspeaker . . .

21.2b . . . then disconnect the wiring

## Removal

1 Disconnect the battery negative (earth) lead (see Chapter 5A).
2 Insert the DIN removal tools into the holes on each side of the radio/cassette player, and push them until they click into place (see illustration).
3 Pull the tools gently to the left and right to release the locking tangs.
4 Gently pull the radio/cassette player from the facia, using the removal tools.
5 Disconnect the wiring plugs and the aerial lead, and withdraw the unit. Do not forget to disconnect the wiring plug from the hazard warning switch (see illustrations).

## Refitting

6 Reconnect the wiring plugs and the aerial lead, then push the unit into its housing until the securing clips engage.
7 On completion, reconnect the battery negative lead and, where applicable enter the security code.

## 21 Loudspeakers - removal and refitting

### Removal

1 The loudspeakers are mounted in the front doors. First remove the relevant door inner trim panel, as described in Chapter 11.
2 Unscrew the four loudspeaker securing screws, then withdraw the loudspeaker from the door and disconnect the wiring plug (see illustrations).

### Refitting

3 Refitting is a reversal of removal.

## 22 Radio aerial - removal and refitting

### Removal

1 Disconnect the battery negative (earth) lead (see Chapter 5A).
2 Carefully prise the courtesy light assembly from the front of the headlining. Disconnect

the wiring plugs, and remove the courtesy light assembly.
3 Using a Torx key, unscrew the now-exposed securing screw, and disconnect the aerial lead from the base of the aerial.
4 Withdraw the aerial from the roof panel and recover the gasket, then press out the plastic ring. Note that the aerial mast can be unscrewed from the aerial body if desired.

### Refitting

5 Refitting is a reversal of removal but make sure the plastic ring is correctly located in the roof panel before refitting the aerial and securing screw.

## 23 Anti-theft alarm system and engine immobiliser - general information

All models are fitted with a Passive Anti-Theft System (PATS) which prevents the engine being started without the correct ignition key. A miniature transponder embedded in the ignition key acts as a short range radio transmitter, which activates a transceiver module mounted around the ignition lock barrel. The transponder requires no independent power supply, as it is activated by an electrical field emitted by the transceiver module.

The operation of the PATS system is controlled by the Powertrain Control Module. It is not possible to access the coded signal of the PATS system, therefore it is not possible to copy key coding.

When the ignition is switched on, an LED in the analogue clock face illuminates for approximately three seconds indicating that the PATS system is operating correctly. The LED flashes periodically when the ignition is switched off to indicate that the system is armed.

On models manufactured up to mid-1998, one red master key and two black keys are supplied with each car. If the PATS module is renewed at any time, the red master key must be the first one inserted in the ignition switch for the system to function correctly. From mid-1998 on, only two black keys are provided with each car and both are required to programme additional keys (alternatively a Ford dealer can programme the key using FDS 2000 test equipment).

To programme a key on models manufactured up to mid-1998, insert the red master key in the switch and turn it to position II. When the LED comes on, turn the key to position 0 and remove it. The LED will now go off and then come on again for 2 seconds. The system is now in programming mode for 10 seconds. Insert the new key and turn it to position II. The LED will now flash once to indicate that the key has been successfully programmed, and after the key has been turned to position 0 it can be removed.

To programme a key on models manufactured from mid-1998 on, insert the first black key in the ignition switch and turn to position II, then turn it to position 0 and remove it. Insert the second black key in the ignition switch and turn to position II, then turn it to position 0 and remove it. Insert the new key and turn it to position II, then return it to position 0 and remove it.

## 24 Airbag system - general information, precautions and system de-activation

### General information

A driver's air bag is fitted as standard equipment on all models, the air bag is fitted to the steering wheel centre pad. Similarly, a passenger's air bag is fitted as standard equipment, or as an option, depending on model. On certain later models, side air bags, mounted in the sides of the front seat, are available as an option.

The system is armed only when the ignition is switched on, however, a reserve power source maintains a power supply to the system in the event of a break in the main electrical supply. The system is activated by a deceleration sensor and safing sensor connected in parallel in the circuit. In the event of an accident, both sensors must be activated for the air bag to be deployed. Note that the electronic control unit also controls the front seat belt tensioners. The air bags are inflated by gas generators, which force the bags out from their locations in the steering wheel, and the passenger's side facia, where applicable.

### Precautions

⚠ Warning: The following precautions must be observed when working on vehicles equipped with an air bag system, to prevent the possibility of personal injury.

### General precautions

The following precautions must be observed when carrying out work on a vehicle equipped with an air bag.
a) Do not disconnect the battery with the engine running.
b) Before carrying out any work in the vicinity of the air bag, removal of any of the air bag components, or any welding work on

the vehicle, de-activate the system as described in the following sub-Section.

c) Do not attempt to test any of the air bag system circuits using test meters or any other test equipment.

d) If the air bag warning light comes on, or any fault in the system is suspected, consult a Ford dealer without delay. **Do not** attempt to carry out fault diagnosis, or any dismantling of the components.

## Precautions to be taken when handling an air bag

a) Transport the air bag by itself, bag upward.

b) Do not put your arms around the air bag.

c) Carry the air bag close to the body, bag outward.

d) Do not drop the air bag or expose it to impacts.

e) Do not attempt to dismantle the air bag unit.

f) Do not connect any form of electrical equipment to any part of the air bag circuit.

## Precautions to be taken when storing an air bag unit

a) Store the unit in a cupboard with the air bag upward.

b) Do not expose the air bag to temperatures above 80° C.

c) Do not expose the air bag to flames.

d) Do not attempt to dispose of the air bag - consult a Ford dealer.

e) Never refit an air bag which is known to be faulty or damaged.

### De-activation of air bag system

The system must be de-activated as follows, before carrying out any work on the air bag components or surrounding area.

 **Warning: Do not fit any battery powered key code saving device while working on the air bag system.**

a) Switch off the ignition and remove the ignition key.

b) Switch off all electrical equipment.

c) Disconnect the battery negative lead, with reference to Chapter 5A.

d) Insulate the battery negative terminal and the end of the battery negative lead to prevent any possibility of contact.

e) Wait for at least 2 minutes before carrying out any further work on the air bag system components, however, wait 15 minutes if the air bag control module multiplug is to be disconnected.

## 25 Airbag system components - removal and refitting

### Driver's side air bag unit

 **Warning: Refer to the precautions given in Section 24 before attempting to carry out work on the air bag components.**

**25.4 Use a Torx key to unscrew the driver's air bag securing screws**

**25.5a Withdraw the air bag . . .**

**25.5b . . . then disconnect the yellow multiplug . . .**

**25.5c . . . and remaining two wires**

### Removal

1 The air bag unit is an integral part of the steering wheel centre pad. First make sure that the front roadwheels are in their straight-ahead position.

2 De-activate the air bag system as described in Section 24. Wait at least 2 minutes after disconnecting the battery.

3 Undo the screws and remove the upper and lower shrouds from around the steering column.

4 Turn the steering wheel so that one of the air bag retaining screws is positioned at the top rear of the steering wheel. Unscrew and remove the screw using a Torx key (see illustration). Similarly remove the other retaining screw.

5 Withdraw the air bag unit from the steering wheel, then disconnect the central (yellow) multiplug from the air bag. Also disconnect the remaining two wires from the terminals on the steering wheel. Note the routing of the wiring (see illustrations).

6 Remove the air bag unit from the vehicle, making sure that it is carried with its outer cover uppermost. Store it in a safe place, with reference to the precautions given in Section 24.

### Refitting

7 Refitting is a reversal of removal, but tighten the retaining screws to the specified torque. Make sure that the wiring connector is securely reconnected and the wiring routed correctly. When switching on the ignition for the first time after reconnecting the battery, it is recommended that you reach in through the driver's door window as a precaution against the air bag deploying.

### Passenger's side air bag unit

 **Warning: Refer to the precautions given in Section 24 before attempting to carry out work on the air bag components.**

### Removal

8 De-activate the air bag system as described in Section 24. Wait at least 2 minutes after disconnecting the battery.

9 Using a screwdriver, carefully release the two clips on the rear edge of the air bag cover. Protect the facia with a wad of cloth while doing this. Lift the rear of the cover, then release the three front retaining clips.

10 Using a Torx key, undo the air bag retaining screws - there are two at the rear of the air bag and one each side.

11 Lift the air bag together with the cover and disconnect the two wiring multiplugs. Note the routing of the wiring.

12 Remove the air bag unit from the vehicle, making sure that it is carried with its outer cover uppermost. Store it in a safe place, with reference to the precautions given in Section 24. Do not twist the cover retaining strap.

### Refitting

13 Refitting is a reversal of removal, but tighten the retaining screws to the specified torque. Make sure that the wiring connectors are securely reconnected and the wiring routed correctly. When switching on the ignition for the first time after reconnecting the

25.16 Removing the air bag electronic control unit securing screws

25.22 Releasing the tangs securing the air bag clockspring to the steering wheel

25.23 Air bag clockspring locking pin (arrowed)

battery, it is recommended that you reach in through the driver's door window as a precaution against the air bag deploying.

## Electronic control unit

 **Warning: After disconnecting the battery, wait 15 minutes before proceeding.**

### Removal

**14** De-activate the air bag system as described in Section 24. Wait at least 15 minutes after disconnecting the battery.
**15** Fold back the carpet from the front passenger footwells for access to the electronic control unit located beneath the centre of the facia.
**16** Undo the control unit securing screws and withdraw the unit to the extent of the wiring **(see illustration)**.
**17** Disconnect the wiring multiplug by first depressing the tang, then lifting and unhooking the plug.

### Refitting

**18** Refitting is a reversal of removal, but tighten the retaining screws to the specified torque. When switching on the ignition for the first time after reconnecting the battery, it is recommended that you reach in through the driver's door window as a precaution against the air bag deploying.

## Air bag clockspring

### Removal

**19** The clockspring is located on the rear of the steering wheel. First de-activate the air bag system as described in Section 24. Wait at least 2 minutes after disconnecting the battery.
**20** Remove the driver's air bag as described earlier in this Section, then remove the steering wheel as described in Chapter 10.
**21** Note the location of the wires on the clockspring and through the steering wheel, then disconnect and release them from the plastic cable ties.
**22** Using a screwdriver, carefully release the three tangs from the holes in the steering wheel, then remove the clockspring **(see illustration)**. As the clockspring is removed, note the routing of the wiring.

### Refitting

**Caution: The clockspring centralising procedure described in the following paragraphs must be carried out before refitting the assembly.**

**23** Depress the red locking pin at the lower left-hand corner of the clockspring **(see illustration)**.
**24** Rotate the inner rotor fully anti-clockwise against the outer rotor until tight.
**25** Rotate the inner rotor 3.75 turns clock-

wise, then release the locking pin. Ensure that the inner rotor is locked in position.
**26** Locate the clockspring on the steering wheel and insert the wiring as previously noted. Press in the clockspring and make sure that the tangs engage correctly.
**27** Reconnect the wiring and secure with the cable ties.
**28** Refit the steering wheel as described in Chapter 10, then refit the air bag with reference to the paragraphs at the beginning of this Section.
**29** Reconnect the battery, then switch on the ignition to check that the air bag warning lamp extinguishes. When switching on the ignition for the first time after disconnecting the battery, it is recommended that you reach in through the driver's door window as a precaution against the air bag deploying.

## Side air bag units

 **Warning: Refer to the precautions given in Section 24 before attempting to carry out work on the air bag components.**

### Removal

**30** The removal of the side airbags involves partially dismantling the seat upholstery; it is therefore recommended that this work is carried out by a Ford dealer.

## Key to symbols

| | | | |
|---|---|---|---|
| Bulb | ⊗ | Item no. | **7** |
| Switch | ⊸○ ○⊸ | Pump/motor | Ⓜ |
| Multiple contact switch (ganged) | | Earth | |
| | | Gauge/meter | |
| Fuse/ fusible link | F10 | Diode | ▸|⊢ |
| | | Resistor | |
| Variable resistor | | Wire splice | |
| Internal connection | | Solenoid actuator | |

Denotes alternative wiring variation (brackets)

Wire colour (Green with yellow tracer) — Gn/Ye —

Connections to other circuits (e.g. diagram 3/grid location B2. Direction of arrow denotes current flow.) **3/B2**

## Earth locations

| | |
|---|---|
| E1 | LH compartment |
| E2 | RH front engine compartment |
| E3 | LH side of vehicle rear end |
| E4 | LH sill |
| E5 | RH side of vehicle rear end |
| E6 | LH sill |
| E7 | RH sill |
| E8 | LH front engine compartment |
| E9 | RH 'A' pillar |
| E10 | RH sill |
| E11 | LH 'A' pillar |

## Fuses in fusebox (typical)

| Fuse | Rating | Circuit protected |
|---|---|---|
| F1 | 20A | Heated rear window, central locking |
| F2 | 10A | Interior lighting, clock, radio, diagnostic socket, heater module |
| F3 | 30/10A | ABS module, diag. socket (without ABS) |
| F4 | 3A | Engine management |
| F5 | 15A | Cigar lighter |
| F6 | 10A | LH side/tail light, number plate lights, switch illumination |
| F7 | 10A | RH side/tail light |
| F8 | 10A | LH dipped beam |
| F9 | 10A | RH dipped beam |
| F10 | 10A | LH main beam |
| F11 | 10A | RH main beam |
| F12 | 30A | Heater blower |
| F13 | 15A | Light switch, instrument cluster, stop and reversing light |
| F14 | 30A | Electric windows |
| F15 | 20A | Light switch |
| F16 | 20A | Wash/wipe |
| F17 | 10A | Air conditioning, ignition, instrument cluster, heating and ventilation |
| F18 | 10A | Airbag module |
| F19 | 10A | Fuel pump |
| F20 | 15A | Engine management |
| F21 | 30/20A | Engine cooling fan or horn and hazard warning |
| F22 | 10A | Direction indicators |
| F23 | 40/30/20A | Ignition lock or ABS module or hazard warning and horn |
| F24 | 10/40A | Rear foglight or ignition lock |
| F25 | 20/30A | Hazard warning and horn or ABS |
| F26 | 10A | Radio |
| F27 | 10A | Heated oxygen sensor or tailgate release |
| F28 | - | Diode - fuel injection |
| F29 | 30/10A | Engine cooling fan or rear foglight |
| F30 | 15/3/10A | Central locking or ABS or oxygen sensor |
| F31 | - | Diode - fuel injection |
| F32 | 15A | Sunroof |
| F33 | - | Not used |
| F34 | - | Not used |
| F35 | 10A | Radio, sunroof |
| F36 | 3A | ABS |

Note:
Fuse specifications may vary from above, consult vehicle handbook.

### Fuses (before 01/97)

### Fuses (from 01/97 to 09/98)

### Fuses (from 1999)

H31420/a

Diagram 1 : Information for wiring diagrams

Diagram 2 : Starting, charging, warning lights and gauges

*Warning lights and gauges*

*Starting and charging*

* Models after September 1999

**Wire colours**

| | | | |
|---|---|---|---|
| Bk | Black | Na | Natural |
| Bn | Brown | Og | Orange |
| Bu | Blue | Rt | Red |
| Gn | Green | Sr | Silver |
| Gy | Grey | Vt | Violet |
| Ye | Yellow | Wh | White |
| LG | Light green | | |

**Key to items**

1 Battery
2 Starter motor
3 Alternator
4 Ignition switch
5 Battery fusebox
6 Main fusebox
VII = starter inhibitor relay
7 Instrument cluster
  a = instrument illumination
  b = main beam warning light
  c = airbag warning light
  d = ABS warning light
  e = low brake fluid/handbrake
      warning light
  f = alternator warning light
  g = oil pressure warning light
  h = coolant temp. warning light
  i = fuel gauge
  j = direction indicator warning light
8 Low brake fluid switch
9 Handbrake switch
10 Oil pressure switch
7 Instrument cluster (continued)

Diagram 3 : Engine management (part of) – models up to September 1999

**Key to items**

| | |
|---|---|
| 1 | Battery |
| 4 | Ignition switch |
| 5 | Battery fusebox |
| 6 | Main fusebox |
| C | = fuel injection relay |
| D | = fuel pump relay |
| 15 | Fuel injector |
| 16 | Idle speed control valve |
| 17 | Inertia switch |
| 18 | Fuel tank unit |
| 19 | Ignition coil |
| 20 | Spark plug |
| 21 | Engine management ECU |
| 22 | Canister purge solenoid |
| 23 | Vehicle speed sensor |
| 24 | Mass airflow sensor |

**Wire colours**

| | | | |
|---|---|---|---|
| **Bk** | Black | **Na** | Natural |
| **Bn** | Brown | **Og** | Orange |
| **Bu** | Blue | **Rt** | Red |
| **Gn** | Green | **Sr** | Silver |
| **Gy** | Grey | **Vt** | Violet |
| **Ye** | Yellow | **Wh** | White |
| **LG** | Light green | | |

**Diagram 4 : Engine management (continued) – models up to September 1999**

*Wire colours*

| | | | |
|---|---|---|---|
| **Bk** | Black | **Na** | Natural |
| **Bn** | Brown | **Og** | Orange |
| **Bu** | Blue | **Rt** | Red |
| **Gn** | Green | **Sr** | Silver |
| **Gy** | Grey | **Vt** | Violet |
| **Ye** | Yellow | **Wh** | White |
| **LG** | Light green | | |

*Key to items*

1 Battery
4 Ignition switch
5 Battery fusebox
6 Main fusebox
C = fuel injection relay
21 Engine management ECU
26 Cam position sensor
27 Crank position sensor
28 Heated oxygen sensor
29 Coolant temperature sensor
30 Clutch pedal switch
31 Power steering pressure switch
32 Throttle position sensor
34 Diagnostic socket
35 Air temperature sensor

Heater control module **10/F8, 15/L6**
Cooling fan relay **5/F7**
Air conditioning **15/G4**
Cooling fan relay **5/F3, 5F8**
Air conditioning **15/L5**
Air conditioning **15/B6**
ABS **6/C3**

H31423/a

**Airbag system - models up to September 1999**

\* Models after September 1999

Models after September 1999

Airbag warning light

2/H4

**Engine cooling fan (models without A/C)**

\* Models after September 1999

Engine management

**Engine cooling fan (models with A/C)**

\* Models after September 1999

**Key to items**

1 Battery
4 Ignition switch
5 Battery fusebox
6 Main fusebox
  C = fuel injection relay
  I = cooling fan relay
37 Cooling fan motor
38 Cooling fan diode
39 Cooling fan high speed relay
40 Cooling fan speed resistor
41 Airbag module
  a = safing sensor
  b = control unit
  c = crash sensor
42 Driver's airbag
43 Passenger's airbag
44 Steering wheel clock spring

**Wire colours**

| | | | |
|---|---|---|---|
| Bk Black | Na Natural |
| Bn Brown | Og Orange |
| Bu Blue | Rt Red |
| Gn Green | Sr Silver |
| Gy Grey | Vt Violet |
| Ye Yellow | Wh White |
| LG Light green | |

Engine management

Engine management

Engine management

**Diagram 5 : Engine cooling fan and airbag system**

Key to items

1 Battery
4 Ignition switch
5 Battery fusebox
5 Main fusebox
50 ABS hydraulic assembly
  a = ABS control module
  b = ABS pump
  b = TCS solenoid valve
  c = LH rear inlet valve
  d = LH rear outlet vale
  e = LH front outlet valve
  f = LH front inlet valve
  g = RH rear inlet valve
  h = RH rear outlet vale
  i = RH front inlet valve
  j = RH front outlet valve
51 LH front wheel sensor

52 LH rear wheel sensor
53 RH front wheel sensor
54 RH rear wheel sensor
55 Multifunction switch
  a = side/headlight
  a = sidelight
56 LH headlight assembly
  a = sidelight
57 RH headlight assembly
  a = sidelight
58 LH rear light assembly
  a = tail light
59 RH rear light assembly
  a = tail light
60 LH number plate light
61 RH number plate light

Wire colours

| Bk | Black | Na | Natural |
| Bn | Brown | Og | Orange |
| Bu | Blue | Rt | Red |
| Gn | Green | Sr | Silver |
| Gy | Grey | Vt | Violet |
| Ye | Yellow | Wh | White |
| LG | Light green | | |

* Models after September 1999
** Only models before January 1997

Side, tail and number plate lights

ABS system

Diagram 6 : ABS system and exterior lighting - side, tail and number plate lights

H31425/a

**Key to items**

1  Battery
4  Ignition switch
5  Battery fusebox
6  Main fusebox
   V = ignition relay
   A = dip beam relay
   B = main beam relay
55 Multifunction switch
   a = side/headlight
   b = flash/dip/main

56 LH headlight assembly
   b = main beam
   c = dip beam
   d = levelling assembly
57 RH headlight assembly
   b = main beam
   c = dip beam
   d = levelling assembly

58 LH rear light assembly
   b = reversing light
   c = stop light
59 RH rear light assembly
   c = stop light
65 High level stop light
66 Reversing light switch
67 Stop light switch

*Stop and reversing lights*

*Headlights*

**Wire colours**

| Bk | Black | Na | Natural |
|----|-------|----|---------|
| Bn | Brown | Og | Orange |
| Bu | Blue | Rt | Red |
| Gn | Green | Sr | Silver |
| Gy | Grey | Vt | Violet |
| Ye | Yellow | Wh | White |
| LG | Light green | | |

* Models after September 1999

H31426/a

*Wire colours*

| | | | |
|---|---|---|---|
| **Bk** | Black | **Na** | Natural |
| **Bn** | Brown | **Og** | Orange |
| **Bu** | Blue | **Rt** | Red |
| **Gn** | Green | **Sr** | Silver |
| **Gy** | Grey | **Vt** | Violet |
| **Ye** | Yellow | **Wh** | White |
| **LG** | Light green | | |

*Key to items*

1   Battery
4   Ignition switch
5   Battery fusebox
6   Main fusebox
55  Multifunction switch
    a = side/headlight
    c = hazard
    d = direction indicator
    e = hazard warning light
    f = indicator relay

56  LH headlight assembly
    e = direction indicator
57  RH headlight assembly
    e = direction indicator
58  LH rear light assembly
    d = direction indicator
59  RH rear light assembly
    d = direction indicator
    e = foglight
70  LH indicator side repeater
71  RH indicator side repeater

72  Heater control module
    a = foglight switch illum.
    b = heated rear window
       switch illumination
    c = rear foglight switch
    d = foglight on indicator
    e = rear foglight relay

\* Models after September 1999

*Rear foglight*

*Direction indicators and hazard warning lights*

**Diagram 8 : Exterior lighting (continued) – direction indicators, hazard warning and rear foglight**

H31427ia

**Key to items**

1  Battery
2  Ignition switch
5  Battery fusebox
6  Main fusebox
    Multifunction switch
    II  = intermittent wiper relay
    VIII = lights on buzzer
55  Multifunction switch
    a  = side/headlight
    g  = front wiper
    h  = rear wash/wipe switch
    i  = front washer
75  Tailgate contact switches
76  Front wiper motor
77  Rear wiper motor
78  Front/rear washer pump
79  Steering wheel clock springs
80  Horn switch
81  Horn
82  Interior light
83  Driver's door switch
84  Passenger's door switch

**Horn**

**Interior lighting**

**Front and rear wash/wipe**

* Models after September 1999

Wire colours
Bk  Black       Na  Natural
Bn  Brown       Og  Orange
Bu  Blue        Rt  Red
Gn  Green       Sr  Silver
Gy  Grey        Vt  Violet
Ye  Yellow      Wh  White
LG  Light green

Diagram 9 : Wash/wipe, horn and interior lighting

H31428/a

**Key to items**

1 Battery
4 Ignition switch
5 Battery fusebox
6 Main fusebox
72 Heater control module
  V = ignition relay
  VI = heated rear window relay
  f = heated screen switch
  g = heated screen indicator
75 Tailgate contact switch
90 Cigar lighter
91 Clock
92 Heated rear window
93 Heater control solenoid valve
94 Heater blower motor
95 Heater blower switch
96 Heater blower resistors
97 Radio unit
98 LH speaker
99 RH speaker

**Wire colours**

| | | | |
|---|---|---|---|
| Bk | Black | Na | Natural |
| Bn | Brown | Og | Orange |
| Bu | Blue | Rt | Red |
| Gn | Green | Sr | Silver |
| Gy | Grey | Vt | Violet |
| Ye | Yellow | Wh | White |
| LG | Light green | | |

*Heater blower*

*Audio system*

*Cigar lighter and clock*

*Heated rear window*

*Engine management*

*Interior illumination*

*Heated mirrors*

Diagram 10 : Cigar lighter, clock, heated rear window, heater blower and audio system

### Key to items

| | | | |
|---|---|---|---|
| 1 | Battery | 106 | Passenger's door lock |
| 4 | Ignition switch | 107 | Tailgate release switch * |
| 5. | Battery fusebox | 108 | Tailgate release motor * |
| 6 | Main fusebox | 109 | Driver's window switch |
| | V = ignition relay | 110 | Passenger's window switch |
| | K = tailgate release relay * | 111 | Driver's window motor |
| | 75 Tailgate contact switch | 112 | Passenger's window motor |
| | 105 Driver's door lock | | |

**Electric windows**

* Models after September 1999

**Central locking and tailgate release**

* Models after September 1999

### Wire colours

| | | | |
|---|---|---|---|
| Bk | Black | Na | Natural |
| Bn | Brown | Og | Orange |
| Bu | Blue | Rt | Red |
| Gn | Green | Sr | Silver |
| Gy | Grey | Vt | Violet |
| Ye | Yellow | Wh | White |
| LG | Light green | | |

**Diagram 11 : Central locking, tailgate release and electric windows**

H31490/a

Diagram 12 : Engine management (part of) – models from September 1999

**Wire colours**

| | | | |
|---|---|---|---|
| Bk | Black | Na | Natural |
| Bn | Brown | Og | Orange |
| Bu | Blue | Rt | Red |
| Gn | Green | Sr | Silver |
| Gy | Grey | Vt | Violet |
| Ye | Yellow | Wh | White |
| LG | Light green | | |

**Key to items**

1 Battery
4 Ignition switch
5 Battery fusebox
6 Main fusebox
    C = fuel injection relay
    D = fuel pump relay
15 Fuel injector
16 Idle speed control valve
17 Inertia switch
18 Fuel tank unit
19 Ignition coil
20 Spark plug
21 Engine management ECU
22 Canister purge solenoid
23 Vehicle speed sensor

Diagram 13 : Engine management (continued) – models from September 1999

Diagram 14 : Restraint system, electric mirrors and sunroof

Sunroof - models from September 1999

Electric mirrors - models from September 1999

Sunroof - models up to September 1999

Restraint system - models from September 1999

Heated rear window

10/B8

13/F4 Diagnostic connector

2/H4 Airbag warning light

**Wire colours**

| | | | |
|---|---|---|---|
| **Bk** | Black | **Na** | Natural |
| **Bn** | Brown | **Og** | Orange |
| **Bu** | Blue | **Rt** | Red |
| **Gn** | Green | **Sr** | Silver |
| **Gy** | Grey | **Vt** | Violet |
| **Ye** | Yellow | **Wh** | White |
| **LG** | Light green | | |

**Key to items**

1  Battery
4  Ignition switch
5  Battery fusebox
6  Main fusebox
41  Airbag module
42  Driver's airbag
43  Passenger's airbag
44  Steering wheel clock spring
115  Driver's side airbag
116  Driver's side airbag sensor
117  Passenger's side airbag
118  Passenger's side airbag sensor
119  Sunroof unit
120  Sliding roof motor
121  Sunroof switch
122  Mirror control switch
123  LH mirror assembly
124  RH mirror assembly

H32371

**Key to items**

1  Battery
4  Ignition switch
5  Battery fusebox
6  Main fusebox
   C = fuel injection relay
   V = ignition relay
   E = A/C switch relay
   I = A/C wide open throttle relay
55 Multifunction switch
   a = side/headlight
72 Heater control module
   h = A/C switch illumination
   i = recirculation switch illumination
   j = A/C switch
   k = recirculation switch
   l = A/C indicator
   m = recirculation indicator
93 Heater control solenoid valve
94 Heater blower motor
95 Heater blower switch
96 Heater blower resistors
126 Compressor clutch
127 Compressor clutch diode
128 Dual pressure switch
129 Recirculation air actuator
130 Cycling switch

*Wire colours*

Bk Black    Na Natural
Bn Brown    Og Orange
Bu Blue     Rt Red
Gn Green    Sr Silver
Gy Grey     Vt Violet
Ye Yellow   Wh White
LG Light green

**Diagram 15 : Air conditioning**

• Models after September 1999

Engine management control unit 4/J8, 13/J8
Engine management 4/J2, 13/J2
Engine management control unit 4/J5, 13/J6
Engine management control unit 4/J8,13/J8

# Notes

# Dimensions and Weights

**Note:** *All figures are approximate, and may vary according to model. Refer to manufacturer's data for exact figures.*

### Dimensions
Overall length . . . . . . . . . . . . . . . . . . . . . . . . . . . . . . . . . . . . . .	3620 mm
Overall width (excluding mirrors) . . . . . . . . . . . . . . . . . . . . . . . .	1639 mm
Overall height (unladen) . . . . . . . . . . . . . . . . . . . . . . . . . . . . . . .	1385 to 1413 mm
Wheelbase . . . . . . . . . . . . . . . . . . . . . . . . . . . . . . . . . . . . . . . . .	2448 mm

### Weights
Kerb weight:
   37 kW engine . . . . . . . . . . . . . . . . . . . . . . . . . . . . . . . . . . . . .	946 to 998 kg
   44 kW engine . . . . . . . . . . . . . . . . . . . . . . . . . . . . . . . . . . . . .	946 to 1020 kg
Maximum gross vehicle weight . . . . . . . . . . . . . . . . . . . . . . . . . .	1265 kg
Maximum towing weight . . . . . . . . . . . . . . . . . . . . . . . . . . . . . . .	Refer to your Ford dealer
Maximum trailer nose weight . . . . . . . . . . . . . . . . . . . . . . . . . . .	Refer to your Ford dealer
Maximum roof rack load . . . . . . . . . . . . . . . . . . . . . . . . . . . . . . .	75 kg

# Conversion factors

## Length (distance)

| | | | | | |
|---|---|---|---|---|---|
| Inches (in) | x 25.4 | = Millimetres (mm) | x 0.0394 | = Inches (in) |
| Feet (ft) | x 0.305 | = Metres (m) | x 3.281 | = Feet (ft) |
| Miles | x 1.609 | = Kilometres (km) | x 0.621 | = Miles |

## Volume (capacity)

| | | | | |
|---|---|---|---|---|
| Cubic inches (cu in; in³) | x 16.387 | = Cubic centimetres (cc; cm³) | x 0.061 | = Cubic inches (cu in; in³) |
| Imperial pints (Imp pt) | x 0.568 | = Litres (l) | x 1.76 | = Imperial pints (Imp pt) |
| Imperial quarts (Imp qt) | x 1.137 | = Litres (l) | x 0.88 | = Imperial quarts (Imp qt) |
| Imperial quarts (Imp qt) | x 1.201 | = US quarts (US qt) | x 0.833 | = Imperial quarts (Imp qt) |
| US quarts (US qt) | x 0.946 | = Litres (l) | x 1.057 | = US quarts (US qt) |
| Imperial gallons (Imp gal) | x 4.546 | = Litres (l) | x 0.22 | = Imperial gallons (Imp gal) |
| Imperial gallons (Imp gal) | x 1.201 | = US gallons (US gal) | x 0.833 | = Imperial gallons (Imp gal) |
| US gallons (US gal) | x 3.785 | = Litres (l) | x 0.264 | = US gallons (US gal) |

## Mass (weight)

| | | | | |
|---|---|---|---|---|
| Ounces (oz) | x 28.35 | = Grams (g) | x 0.035 | = Ounces (oz) |
| Pounds (lb) | x 0.454 | = Kilograms (kg) | x 2.205 | = Pounds (lb) |

## Force

| | | | | |
|---|---|---|---|---|
| Ounces-force (ozf; oz) | x 0.278 | = Newtons (N) | x 3.6 | = Ounces-force (ozf; oz) |
| Pounds-force (lbf; lb) | x 4.448 | = Newtons (N) | x 0.225 | = Pounds-force (lbf; lb) |
| Newtons (N) | x 0.1 | = Kilograms-force (kgf; kg) | x 9.81 | = Newtons (N) |

## Pressure

| | | | | |
|---|---|---|---|---|
| Pounds-force per square inch (psi; lbf/in²; lb/in²) | x 0.070 | = Kilograms-force per square centimetre (kgf/cm²; kg/cm²) | x 14.223 | = Pounds-force per square inch (psi; lbf/in²; lb/in²) |
| Pounds-force per square inch (psi; lbf/in²; lb/in²) | x 0.068 | = Atmospheres (atm) | x 14.696 | = Pounds-force per square inch (psi; lbf/in²; lb/in²) |
| Pounds-force per square inch (psi; lbf/in²; lb/in²) | x 0.069 | = Bars | x 14.5 | = Pounds-force per square inch (psi; lbf/in²; lb/in²) |
| Pounds-force per square inch (psi; lbf/in²; lb/in²) | x 6.895 | = Kilopascals (kPa) | x 0.145 | = Pounds-force per square inch (psi; lbf/in²; lb/in²) |
| Kilopascals (kPa) | x 0.01 | = Kilograms-force per square centimetre (kgf/cm²; kg/cm²) | x 98.1 | = Kilopascals (kPa) |
| Millibar (mbar) | x 100 | = Pascals (Pa) | x 0.01 | = Millibar (mbar) |
| Millibar (mbar) | x 0.0145 | = Pounds-force per square inch (psi; lbf/in²; lb/in²) | x 68.947 | = Millibar (mbar) |
| Millibar (mbar) | x 0.75 | = Millimetres of mercury (mmHg) | x 1.333 | = Millibar (mbar) |
| Millibar (mbar) | x 0.401 | = Inches of water (inH₂O) | x 2.491 | = Millibar (mbar) |
| Millimetres of mercury (mmHg) | x 0.535 | = Inches of water (inH₂O) | x 1.868 | = Millimetres of mercury (mmHg) |
| Inches of water (inH₂O) | x 0.036 | = Pounds-force per square inch (psi; lbf/in²; lb/in²) | x 27.68 | = Inches of water (inH₂O) |

## Torque (moment of force)

| | | | | |
|---|---|---|---|---|
| Pounds-force inches (lbf in; lb in) | x 1.152 | = Kilograms-force centimetre (kgf cm; kg cm) | x 0.868 | = Pounds-force inches (lbf in; lb in) |
| Pounds-force inches (lbf in; lb in) | x 0.113 | = Newton metres (Nm) | x 8.85 | = Pounds-force inches (lbf in; lb in) |
| Pounds-force inches (lbf in; lb in) | x 0.083 | = Pounds-force feet (lbf ft; lb ft) | x 12 | = Pounds-force inches (lbf in; lb in) |
| Pounds-force feet (lbf ft; lb ft) | x 0.138 | = Kilograms-force metres (kgf m; kg m) | x 7.233 | = Pounds-force feet (lbf ft; lb ft) |
| Pounds-force feet (lbf ft; lb ft) | x 1.356 | = Newton metres (Nm) | x 0.738 | = Pounds-force feet (lbf ft; lb ft) |
| Newton metres (Nm) | x 0.102 | = Kilograms-force metres (kgf m; kg m) | x 9.804 | = Newton metres (Nm) |

## Power

| | | | | |
|---|---|---|---|---|
| Horsepower (hp) | x 745.7 | = Watts (W) | x 0.0013 | = Horsepower (hp) |

## Velocity (speed)

| | | | | |
|---|---|---|---|---|
| Miles per hour (miles/hr; mph) | x 1.609 | = Kilometres per hour (km/hr; kph) | x 0.621 | = Miles per hour (miles/hr; mph) |

## Fuel consumption*

| | | | | |
|---|---|---|---|---|
| Miles per gallon, Imperial (mpg) | x 0.354 | = Kilometres per litre (km/l) | x 2.825 | = Miles per gallon, Imperial (mpg) |
| Miles per gallon, US (mpg) | x 0.425 | = Kilometres per litre (km/l) | x 2.352 | = Miles per gallon, US (mpg) |

## Temperature

Degrees Fahrenheit = (°C x 1.8) + 32          Degrees Celsius (Degrees Centigrade; °C) = (°F - 32) x 0.56

*It is common practice to convert from miles per gallon (mpg) to litres/100 kilometres (l/100km), where mpg x l/100 km = 282*

Spare parts are available from many sources, including maker's appointed garages, accessory shops, and motor factors. To be sure of obtaining the correct parts, it will sometimes be necessary to quote the vehicle identification number. If possible, it can also be useful to take the old parts along for positive identification. Items such as starter motors and alternators may be available under a service exchange scheme - any parts returned should be clean.

Our advice regarding spare parts is as follows.

### Officially appointed garages

This is the best source of parts which are peculiar to your car, and which are not otherwise generally available (eg, badges, interior trim, certain body panels, etc). It is also the only place at which you should buy parts if the vehicle is still under warranty.

### Accessory shops

These are very good places to buy materials and components needed for the maintenance of your car (oil, air and fuel filters, light bulbs, drivebelts, greases, brake pads, touch-up paint, etc). Components of this nature sold by a reputable shop are usually of the same standard as those used by the car manufacturer.

Besides components, these shops also sell tools and general accessories, usually have convenient opening hours, charge lower prices, and can often be found close to home. Some accessory shops have parts counters where components needed for almost any repair job can be purchased or ordered.

### Motor factors

Good factors will stock all the more important components which wear out comparatively quickly, and can sometimes supply individual components needed for the overhaul of a larger assembly (eg, brake seals and hydraulic parts, bearing shells, pistons, valves). They may also handle work such as cylinder block reboring, crankshaft regrinding, etc.

### Tyre and exhaust specialists

These outlets may be independent, or members of a local or national chain. They frequently offer competitive prices when compared with a main dealer or local garage, but it will pay to obtain several quotes before making a decision. When researching prices, also ask what "extras" may be added - for instance fitting a new valve and balancing the wheel are both commonly charged on top of the price of a new tyre.

### Other sources

Beware of parts or materials obtained from market stalls, car boot sales or similar outlets. Such items are not invariably sub-standard, but there is little chance of compensation if they do prove unsatisfactory. in the case of safety-critical components such as brake pads, there is the risk not only of financial loss, but also of an accident causing injury or death.

Second-hand components or assemblies obtained from a car breaker can be a good buy in some circumstances, but this sort of purchase is best made by the experienced DIY mechanic.

# Vehicle Identification

Modifications are a continuing and unpublicised process in vehicle manufacture, quite apart from major model changes. Spare parts manuals and lists are compiled upon a numerical basis, the individual vehicle identification numbers being essential to correct identification of the component concerned.

When ordering spare parts, always give as much information as possible. Quote the car model, year of manufacture and registration, chassis and engine numbers as appropriate.

The *Vehicle Identification Number (VIN)* plate is riveted to the bonnet lock crossmember and is visible once the bonnet has been opened. The vehicle identification (chassis) number is also stamped onto the floor of the passenger compartment, between the right-hand front seat and side sill, and also onto the top left-hand corner of the facia assembly. The number on the floor can be viewed by lifting the flap in the carpet and the number on the facia is visible through the windscreen **(see illustrations)**.

The engine number is stamped on the left-hand front face of the cylinder block.

Vehicle Identification Number plate location on the bonnet lock crossmember

VIN number stamped on the floor between the right-hand seat and side sill

VIN number on the top left-hand corner of the facia

Whenever servicing, repair or overhaul work is carried out on the car or its components, observe the following procedures and instructions. This will assist in carrying out the operation efficiently and to a professional standard of workmanship.

## Joint mating faces and gaskets

When separating components at their mating faces, never insert screwdrivers or similar implements into the joint between the faces in order to prise them apart. This can cause severe damage which results in oil leaks, coolant leaks, etc upon reassembly. Separation is usually achieved by tapping along the joint with a soft-faced hammer in order to break the seal. However, note that this method may not be suitable where dowels are used for component location.

Where a gasket is used between the mating faces of two components, a new one must be fitted on reassembly; fit it dry unless otherwise stated in the repair procedure. Make sure that the mating faces are clean and dry, with all traces of old gasket removed. When cleaning a joint face, use a tool which is unlikely to score or damage the face, and remove any burrs or nicks with an oilstone or fine file.

Make sure that tapped holes are cleaned with a pipe cleaner, and keep them free of jointing compound, if this is being used, unless specifically instructed otherwise.

Ensure that all orifices, channels or pipes are clear, and blow through them, preferably using compressed air.

## Oil seals

Oil seals can be removed by levering them out with a wide flat-bladed screwdriver or similar implement. Alternatively, a number of self-tapping screws may be screwed into the seal, and these used as a purchase for pliers or some similar device in order to pull the seal free.

Whenever an oil seal is removed from its working location, either individually or as part of an assembly, it should be renewed.

The very fine sealing lip of the seal is easily damaged, and will not seal if the surface it contacts is not completely clean and free from scratches, nicks or grooves. If the original sealing surface of the component cannot be restored, and the manufacturer has not made provision for slight relocation of the seal relative to the sealing surface, the component should be renewed.

Protect the lips of the seal from any surface which may damage them in the course of fitting. Use tape or a conical sleeve where possible. Lubricate the seal lips with oil before fitting and, on dual-lipped seals, fill the space between the lips with grease.

Unless otherwise stated, oil seals must be fitted with their sealing lips toward the lubricant to be sealed.

Use a tubular drift or block of wood of the appropriate size to install the seal and, if the seal housing is shouldered, drive the seal down to the shoulder. If the seal housing is unshouldered, the seal should be fitted with its face flush with the housing top face (unless otherwise instructed).

## Screw threads and fastenings

Seized nuts, bolts and screws are quite a common occurrence where corrosion has set in, and the use of penetrating oil or releasing fluid will often overcome this problem if the offending item is soaked for a while before attempting to release it. The use of an impact driver may also provide a means of releasing such stubborn fastening devices, when used in conjunction with the appropriate screwdriver bit or socket. If none of these methods works, it may be necessary to resort to the careful application of heat, or the use of a hacksaw or nut splitter device.

Studs are usually removed by locking two nuts together on the threaded part, and then using a spanner on the lower nut to unscrew the stud. Studs or bolts which have broken off below the surface of the component in which they are mounted can sometimes be removed using a stud extractor. Always ensure that a blind tapped hole is completely free from oil, grease, water or other fluid before installing the bolt or stud. Failure to do this could cause the housing to crack due to the hydraulic action of the bolt or stud as it is screwed in.

When tightening a castellated nut to accept a split pin, tighten the nut to the specified torque, where applicable, and then tighten further to the next split pin hole. Never slacken the nut to align the split pin hole, unless stated in the repair procedure.

When checking or retightening a nut or bolt to a specified torque setting, slacken the nut or bolt by a quarter of a turn, and then retighten to the specified setting. However, this should not be attempted where angular tightening has been used.

For some screw fastenings, notably cylinder head bolts or nuts, torque wrench settings are no longer specified for the latter stages of tightening, "angle-tightening" being called up instead. Typically, a fairly low torque wrench setting will be applied to the bolts/nuts in the correct sequence, followed by one or more stages of tightening through specified angles.

## Locknuts, locktabs and washers

Any fastening which will rotate against a component or housing during tightening should always have a washer between it and the relevant component or housing.

Spring or split washers should always be renewed when they are used to lock a critical component such as a big-end bearing retaining bolt or nut. Locktabs which are folded over to retain a nut or bolt should always be renewed.

Self-locking nuts can be re-used in non-critical areas, providing resistance can be felt when the locking portion passes over the bolt or stud thread. However, it should be noted that self-locking stiffnuts tend to lose their effectiveness after long periods of use, and should then be renewed as a matter of course.

Split pins must always be replaced with new ones of the correct size for the hole.

When thread-locking compound is found on the threads of a fastener which is to be re-used, it should be cleaned off with a wire brush and solvent, and fresh compound applied on reassembly.

## Special tools

Some repair procedures in this manual entail the use of special tools such as a press, two or three-legged pullers, spring compressors, etc. Wherever possible, suitable readily-available alternatives to the manufacturer's special tools are described, and are shown in use. In some instances, where no alternative is possible, it has been necessary to resort to the use of a manufacturer's tool, and this has been done for reasons of safety as well as the efficient completion of the repair operation. Unless you are highly-skilled and have a thorough understanding of the procedures described, never attempt to bypass the use of any special tool when the procedure described specifies its use. Not only is there a very great risk of personal injury, but expensive damage could be caused to the components involved.

## Environmental considerations

When disposing of used engine oil, brake fluid, antifreeze, etc, give due consideration to any detrimental environmental effects. Do not, for instance, pour any of the above liquids down drains into the general sewage system, or onto the ground to soak away. Many local council refuse tips provide a facility for waste oil disposal, as do some garages. If none of these facilities are available, consult your local Environmental Health Department, or the National Rivers Authority, for further advice.

With the universal tightening-up of legislation regarding the emission of environmentally-harmful substances from motor vehicles, most vehicles have tamperproof devices fitted to the main adjustment points of the fuel system. These devices are primarily designed to prevent unqualified persons from adjusting the fuel/air mixture, with the chance of a consequent increase in toxic emissions. If such devices are found during servicing or overhaul, they should, wherever possible, be renewed or refitted in accordance with the manufacturer's requirements or current legislation.

OIL CARE
FOLLOW THE CODE

OIL BANK LINE
0800 66 33 66
www.oilbankline.org.uk

*Note: It is antisocial and illegal to dump oil down the drain. To find the location of your local oil recycling bank, call this number free.*

The jack supplied with the vehicle tool kit should only be used for changing the roadwheels - see *"Wheel changing"* at the front of this manual. When carrying out any other kind of work, raise the vehicle using a hydraulic (or "trolley") jack, and always supplement the jack with axle stands positioned under the vehicle jacking points.

To raise the vehicle with a trolley jack, position the jack head either beneath the front underbody channels or beneath the rear of the sills **(see illustration)**.

To raise the vehicle with a hoist, position the hoist heads beneath the front underbody channels and rear sills **(see illustration)**.

When using axle stands as supports, position them towards the front of the underbody channels and beneath the rear axle front mountings **(see illustration)**.

The jack supplied with the vehicle locates with the jacking points on the sills (see *"Wheel changing"*). Ensure that the jack head is correctly engaged before attempting to raise the vehicle.

**Never** work under, around, or near a raised vehicle, unless it is adequately supported in at least two places with axle stands.

**Jacking points and axle stand locations**

A  Jacking points for use with a trolley jack    C  Axle stand locations
B  Jacking points for use with a hoist

# Radio/cassette unit anti-theft system - precautions

The radio/cassette unit fitted may be equipped with a built-in security code, to deter thieves. If the power source to the unit is cut, the anti-theft system will activate. Even if the power source is immediately reconnected, the radio/cassette unit will not function until the correct security code has been entered. Therefore if you do not know the correct security code for the unit, **do not** disconnect the battery negative lead, or remove the radio/cassette unit from the vehicle.

If the security code is lost or forgotten, seek the advice of your Ford dealer. On presentation of proof of ownership, a Ford dealer will be able to provide you with a new security code.

### Introduction

A selection of good tools is a fundamental requirement for anyone contemplating the maintenance and repair of a motor vehicle. For the owner who does not possess any, their purchase will prove a considerable expense, offsetting some of the savings made by doing-it-yourself. However, provided that the tools purchased meet the relevant national safety standards and are of good quality, they will last for many years and prove an extremely worthwhile investment.

To help the average owner to decide which tools are needed to carry out the various tasks detailed in this manual, we have compiled three lists of tools under the following headings: *Maintenance and minor repair*, *Repair and overhaul*, and *Special*. Newcomers to practical mechanics should start off with the *Maintenance and minor repair* tool kit, and confine themselves to the simpler jobs around the vehicle. Then, as confidence and experience grow, more difficult tasks can be undertaken, with extra tools being purchased as, and when, they are needed. In this way, a *Maintenance and minor repair* tool kit can be built up into a *Repair and overhaul* tool kit over a considerable period of time, without any major cash outlays. The experienced do-it-yourselfer will have a tool kit good enough for most repair and overhaul procedures, and will add tools from the *Special* category when it is felt that the expense is justified by the amount of use to which these tools will be put.

### Maintenance and minor repair tool kit

The tools given in this list should be considered as a minimum requirement if routine maintenance, servicing and minor repair operations are to be undertaken. We recommend the purchase of combination spanners (ring one end, open-ended the other); although more expensive than open-ended ones, they do give the advantages of both types of spanner.

- [ ] *Combination spanners:*
  *Metric - 8 to 19 mm inclusive*
- [ ] *Adjustable spanner - 35 mm jaw (approx.)*
- [ ] *Spark plug spanner (with rubber insert) - petrol models*
- [ ] *Spark plug gap adjustment tool - petrol models*
- [ ] *Set of feeler gauges*
- [ ] *Brake bleed nipple spanner*
- [ ] *Screwdrivers:*
  *Flat blade - 100 mm long x 6 mm dia*
  *Cross blade - 100 mm long x 6 mm dia*
  *Torx - various sizes (not all vehicles)*
- [ ] *Combination pliers*
- [ ] *Hacksaw (junior)*
- [ ] *Tyre pump*
- [ ] *Tyre pressure gauge*
- [ ] *Oil can*
- [ ] *Oil filter removal tool*
- [ ] *Fine emery cloth*
- [ ] *Wire brush (small)*
- [ ] *Funnel (medium size)*
- [ ] *Sump drain plug key (not all vehicles)*

### Repair and overhaul tool kit

These tools are virtually essential for anyone undertaking any major repairs to a motor vehicle, and are additional to those given in the *Maintenance and minor repair* list. Included in this list is a comprehensive set of sockets. Although these are expensive, they will be found invaluable as they are so versatile - particularly if various drives are included in the set. We recommend the half-inch square-drive type, as this can be used with most proprietary torque wrenches.

The tools in this list will sometimes need to be supplemented by tools from the *Special* list:

- [ ] *Sockets (or box spanners) to cover range in previous list (including Torx sockets)*
- [ ] *Reversible ratchet drive (for use with sockets)*
- [ ] *Extension piece, 250 mm (for use with sockets)*
- [ ] *Universal joint (for use with sockets)*
- [ ] *Flexible handle or sliding T "breaker bar" (for use with sockets)*
- [ ] *Torque wrench (for use with sockets)*
- [ ] *Self-locking grips*
- [ ] *Ball pein hammer*
- [ ] *Soft-faced mallet (plastic or rubber)*
- [ ] *Screwdrivers:*
  *Flat blade - long & sturdy, short (chubby), and narrow (electrician's) types*
  *Cross blade – long & sturdy, and short (chubby) types*
- [ ] *Pliers:*
  *Long-nosed*
  *Side cutters (electrician's)*
  *Circlip (internal and external)*
- [ ] *Cold chisel - 25 mm*
- [ ] *Scriber*
- [ ] *Scraper*
- [ ] *Centre-punch*
- [ ] *Pin punch*
- [ ] *Hacksaw*
- [ ] *Brake hose clamp*
- [ ] *Brake/clutch bleeding kit*
- [ ] *Selection of twist drills*
- [ ] *Steel rule/straight-edge*
- [ ] *Allen keys (inc. splined/Torx type)*
- [ ] *Selection of files*
- [ ] *Wire brush*
- [ ] *Axle stands*
- [ ] *Jack (strong trolley or hydraulic type)*
- [ ] *Light with extension lead*
- [ ] *Universal electrical multi-meter*

**Sockets and reversible ratchet drive**

**Brake bleeding kit**

**Torx key, socket and bit**

**Hose clamp**

**Angular-tightening gauge**

## Special tools

The tools in this list are those which are not used regularly, are expensive to buy, or which need to be used in accordance with their manufacturers' instructions. Unless relatively difficult mechanical jobs are undertaken frequently, it will not be economic to buy many of these tools. Where this is the case, you could consider clubbing together with friends (or joining a motorists' club) to make a joint purchase, or borrowing the tools against a deposit from a local garage or tool hire specialist. It is worth noting that many of the larger DIY superstores now carry a large range of special tools for hire at modest rates.

The following list contains only those tools and instruments freely available to the public, and not those special tools produced by the vehicle manufacturer specifically for its dealer network. You will find occasional references to these manufacturers' special tools in the text of this manual. Generally, an alternative method of doing the job without the vehicle manufacturers' special tool is given. However, sometimes there is no alternative to using them. Where this is the case and the relevant tool cannot be bought or borrowed, you will have to entrust the work to a dealer.

- ☐ Angular-tightening gauge
- ☐ Valve spring compressor
- ☐ Valve grinding tool
- ☐ Piston ring compressor
- ☐ Piston ring removal/installation tool
- ☐ Cylinder bore hone
- ☐ Balljoint separator
- ☐ Coil spring compressors (where applicable)
- ☐ Two/three-legged hub and bearing puller
- ☐ Impact screwdriver
- ☐ Micrometer and/or vernier calipers
- ☐ Dial gauge
- ☐ Stroboscopic timing light
- ☐ Dwell angle meter/tachometer
- ☐ Fault code reader
- ☐ Cylinder compression gauge
- ☐ Hand-operated vacuum pump and gauge
- ☐ Clutch plate alignment set
- ☐ Brake shoe steady spring cup removal tool
- ☐ Bush and bearing removal/installation set
- ☐ Stud extractors
- ☐ Tap and die set
- ☐ Lifting tackle
- ☐ Trolley jack

## Buying tools

Reputable motor accessory shops and superstores often offer excellent quality tools at discount prices, so it pays to shop around.

Remember, you don't have to buy the most expensive items on the shelf, but it is always advisable to steer clear of the very cheap tools. Beware of 'bargains' offered on market stalls or at car boot sales. There are plenty of good tools around at reasonable prices, but always aim to purchase items which meet the relevant national safety standards. If in doubt, ask the proprietor or manager of the shop for advice before making a purchase.

## Care and maintenance of tools

Having purchased a reasonable tool kit, it is necessary to keep the tools in a clean and serviceable condition. After use, always wipe off any dirt, grease and metal particles using a clean, dry cloth, before putting the tools away. Never leave them lying around after they have been used. A simple tool rack on the garage or workshop wall for items such as screwdrivers and pliers is a good idea. Store all normal spanners and sockets in a metal box. Any measuring instruments, gauges, meters, etc, must be carefully stored where they cannot be damaged or become rusty.

Take a little care when tools are used. Hammer heads inevitably become marked, and screwdrivers lose the keen edge on their blades from time to time. A little timely attention with emery cloth or a file will soon restore items like this to a good finish.

## Working facilities

Not to be forgotten when discussing tools is the workshop itself. If anything more than routine maintenance is to be carried out, a suitable working area becomes essential.

It is appreciated that many an owner-mechanic is forced by circumstances to remove an engine or similar item without the benefit of a garage or workshop. Having done this, any repairs should always be done under the cover of a roof.

Wherever possible, any dismantling should be done on a clean, flat workbench or table at a suitable working height.

Any workbench needs a vice; one with a jaw opening of 100 mm is suitable for most jobs. As mentioned previously, some clean dry storage space is also required for tools, as well as for any lubricants, cleaning fluids, touch-up paints etc, which become necessary.

Another item which may be required, and which has a much more general usage, is an electric drill with a chuck capacity of at least 8 mm. This, together with a good range of twist drills, is virtually essential for fitting accessories.

Last, but not least, always keep a supply of old newspapers and clean, lint-free rags available, and try to keep any working area as clean as possible.

**Micrometers**

**Dial test indicator ("dial gauge")**

**Strap wrench**

**Compression tester**

**Fault code reader**

This is a guide to getting your vehicle through the MOT test. Obviously it will not be possible to examine the vehicle to the same standard as the professional MOT tester. However, working through the following checks will enable you to identify any problem areas before submitting the vehicle for the test.

It has only been possible to summarise the test requirements here, based on the regulations in force at the time of printing. Test standards are becoming increasingly stringent, although there are some exemptions for older vehicles.

An assistant will be needed to help carry out some of these checks.

*The checks have been sub-divided into four categories, as follows:*

**1** Checks carried out **FROM THE DRIVER'S SEAT**

**2** Checks carried out **WITH THE VEHICLE ON THE GROUND**

**3** Checks carried out **WITH THE VEHICLE RAISED AND THE WHEELS FREE TO TURN**

**4** Checks carried out on **YOUR VEHICLE'S EXHAUST EMISSION SYSTEM**

---

**1** Checks carried out **FROM THE DRIVER'S SEAT**

## Handbrake

☐ Test the operation of the handbrake. Excessive travel (too many clicks) indicates incorrect brake or cable adjustment.
☐ Check that the handbrake cannot be released by tapping the lever sideways. Check the security of the lever mountings.

## Footbrake

☐ Depress the brake pedal and check that it does not creep down to the floor, indicating a master cylinder fault. Release the pedal, wait a few seconds, then depress it again. If the pedal travels nearly to the floor before firm resistance is felt, brake adjustment or repair is necessary. If the pedal feels spongy, there is air in the hydraulic system which must be removed by bleeding.

☐ Check that the brake pedal is secure and in good condition. Check also for signs of fluid leaks on the pedal, floor or carpets, which would indicate failed seals in the brake master cylinder.
☐ Check the servo unit (when applicable) by operating the brake pedal several times, then keeping the pedal depressed and starting the engine. As the engine starts, the pedal will move down slightly. If not, the vacuum hose or the servo itself may be faulty.

## Steering wheel and column

☐ Examine the steering wheel for fractures or looseness of the hub, spokes or rim.
☐ Move the steering wheel from side to side and then up and down. Check that the steering wheel is not loose on the column, indicating wear or a loose retaining nut. Continue moving the steering wheel as before, but also turn it slightly from left to right.
☐ Check that the steering wheel is not loose on the column, and that there is no abnormal

movement of the steering wheel, indicating wear in the column support bearings or couplings.

## Windscreen, mirrors and sunvisor

☐ The windscreen must be free of cracks or other significant damage within the driver's field of view. (Small stone chips are acceptable.) Rear view mirrors must be secure, intact, and capable of being adjusted.

☐ The driver's sunvisor must be capable of being stored in the "up" position.

## Seat belts and seats

**Note:** *The following checks are applicable to all seat belts, front and rear.*

☐ Examine the webbing of all the belts (including rear belts if fitted) for cuts, serious fraying or deterioration. Fasten and unfasten each belt to check the buckles. If applicable, check the retracting mechanism. Check the security of all seat belt mountings accessible from inside the vehicle.

☐ Seat belts with pre-tensioners, once activated, have a "flag" or similar showing on the seat belt stalk. This, in itself, is not a reason for test failure.

☐ The front seats themselves must be securely attached and the backrests must lock in the upright position.

## Doors

☐ Both front doors must be able to be opened and closed from outside and inside, and must latch securely when closed.

## 2 Checks carried out WITH THE VEHICLE ON THE GROUND

## Vehicle identification

☐ Number plates must be in good condition, secure and legible, with letters and numbers correctly spaced – spacing at (A) should be at least twice that at (B).

☐ The VIN plate and/or homologation plate must be legible.

## Electrical equipment

☐ Switch on the ignition and check the operation of the horn.

☐ Check the windscreen washers and wipers, examining the wiper blades; renew damaged or perished blades. Also check the operation of the stop-lights.

☐ Check the operation of the sidelights and number plate lights. The lenses and reflectors must be secure, clean and undamaged.

☐ Check the operation and alignment of the headlights. The headlight reflectors must not be tarnished and the lenses must be undamaged.

☐ Switch on the ignition and check the operation of the direction indicators (including the instrument panel tell-tale) and the hazard warning lights. Operation of the sidelights and stop-lights must not affect the indicators - if it does, the cause is usually a bad earth at the rear light cluster.

☐ Check the operation of the rear foglight(s), including the warning light on the instrument panel or in the switch.

☐ The ABS warning light must illuminate in accordance with the manufacturers' design. For most vehicles, the ABS warning light should illuminate when the ignition is switched on, and (if the system is operating properly) extinguish after a few seconds. Refer to the owner's handbook.

## Footbrake

☐ Examine the master cylinder, brake pipes and servo unit for leaks, loose mountings, corrosion or other damage.

☐ The fluid reservoir must be secure and the fluid level must be between the upper (**A**) and lower (**B**) markings.

☐ Inspect both front brake flexible hoses for cracks or deterioration of the rubber. Turn the steering from lock to lock, and ensure that the hoses do not contact the wheel, tyre, or any part of the steering or suspension mechanism. With the brake pedal firmly depressed, check the hoses for bulges or leaks under pressure.

## Steering and suspension

☐ Have your assistant turn the steering wheel from side to side slightly, up to the point where the steering gear just begins to transmit this movement to the roadwheels. Check for excessive free play between the steering wheel and the steering gear, indicating wear or insecurity of the steering column joints, the column-to-steering gear coupling, or the steering gear itself.

☐ Have your assistant turn the steering wheel more vigorously in each direction, so that the roadwheels just begin to turn. As this is done, examine all the steering joints, linkages, fittings and attachments. Renew any component that shows signs of wear or damage. On vehicles with power steering, check the security and condition of the steering pump, drivebelt and hoses.

☐ Check that the vehicle is standing level, and at approximately the correct ride height.

## Shock absorbers

☐ Depress each corner of the vehicle in turn, then release it. The vehicle should rise and then settle in its normal position. If the vehicle continues to rise and fall, the shock absorber is defective. A shock absorber which has seized will also cause the vehicle to fail.

## Exhaust system

☐ Start the engine. With your assistant holding a rag over the tailpipe, check the entire system for leaks. Repair or renew leaking sections.

**3** Checks carried out
**WITH THE VEHICLE RAISED AND THE WHEELS FREE TO TURN**

*Jack up the front and rear of the vehicle, and securely support it on axle stands. Position the stands clear of the suspension assemblies. Ensure that the wheels are clear of the ground and that the steering can be turned from lock to lock.*

## Steering mechanism

☐ Have your assistant turn the steering from lock to lock. Check that the steering turns smoothly, and that no part of the steering mechanism, including a wheel or tyre, fouls any brake hose or pipe or any part of the body structure.
☐ Examine the steering rack rubber gaiters for damage or insecurity of the retaining clips. If power steering is fitted, check for signs of damage or leakage of the fluid hoses, pipes or connections. Also check for excessive stiffness or binding of the steering, a missing split pin or locking device, or severe corrosion of the body structure within 30 cm of any steering component attachment point.

## Front and rear suspension and wheel bearings

☐ Starting at the front right-hand side, grasp the roadwheel at the 3 o'clock and 9 o'clock positions and rock gently but firmly. Check for free play or insecurity at the wheel bearings, suspension balljoints, or suspension mountings, pivots and attachments.
☐ Now grasp the wheel at the 12 o'clock and 6 o'clock positions and repeat the previous inspection. Spin the wheel, and check for roughness or tightness of the front wheel bearing.

☐ If excess free play is suspected at a component pivot point, this can be confirmed by using a large screwdriver or similar tool and levering between the mounting and the component attachment. This will confirm whether the wear is in the pivot bush, its retaining bolt, or in the mounting itself (the bolt holes can often become elongated).

☐ Carry out all the above checks at the other front wheel, and then at both rear wheels.

## Springs and shock absorbers

☐ Examine the suspension struts (when applicable) for serious fluid leakage, corrosion, or damage to the casing. Also check the security of the mounting points.
☐ If coil springs are fitted, check that the spring ends locate in their seats, and that the spring is not corroded, cracked or broken.
☐ If leaf springs are fitted, check that all leaves are intact, that the axle is securely attached to each spring, and that there is no deterioration of the spring eye mountings, bushes, and shackles.

☐ The same general checks apply to vehicles fitted with other suspension types, such as torsion bars, hydraulic displacer units, etc. Ensure that all mountings and attachments are secure, that there are no signs of excessive wear, corrosion or damage, and (on hydraulic types) that there are no fluid leaks or damaged pipes.
☐ Inspect the shock absorbers for signs of serious fluid leakage. Check for wear of the mounting bushes or attachments, or damage to the body of the unit.

## Driveshafts (fwd vehicles only)

☐ Rotate each front wheel in turn and inspect the constant velocity joint gaiters for splits or damage. Also check that each driveshaft is straight and undamaged.

## Braking system

☐ If possible without dismantling, check brake pad wear and disc condition. Ensure that the friction lining material has not worn excessively, (A) and that the discs are not fractured, pitted, scored or badly worn (B).

☐ Examine all the rigid brake pipes underneath the vehicle, and the flexible hose(s) at the rear. Look for corrosion, chafing or insecurity of the pipes, and for signs of bulging under pressure, chafing, splits or deterioration of the flexible hoses.
☐ Look for signs of fluid leaks at the brake calipers or on the brake backplates. Repair or renew leaking components.
☐ Slowly spin each wheel, while your assistant depresses and releases the footbrake. Ensure that each brake is operating and does not bind when the pedal is released.

☐ Examine the handbrake mechanism, checking for frayed or broken cables, excessive corrosion, or wear or insecurity of the linkage. Check that the mechanism works on each relevant wheel, and releases fully, without binding.

☐ It is not possible to test brake efficiency without special equipment, but a road test can be carried out later to check that the vehicle pulls up in a straight line.

## Fuel and exhaust systems

☐ Inspect the fuel tank (including the filler cap), fuel pipes, hoses and unions. All components must be secure and free from leaks.

☐ Examine the exhaust system over its entire length, checking for any damaged, broken or missing mountings, security of the retaining clamps and rust or corrosion.

## Wheels and tyres

☐ Examine the sidewalls and tread area of each tyre in turn. Check for cuts, tears, lumps, bulges, separation of the tread, and exposure of the ply or cord due to wear or damage. Check that the tyre bead is correctly seated on the wheel rim, that the valve is sound and properly seated, and that the wheel is not distorted or damaged.

☐ Check that the tyres are of the correct size for the vehicle, that they are of the same size

and type on each axle, and that the pressures are correct.

☐ Check the tyre tread depth. The legal minimum at the time of writing is 1.6 mm over at least three-quarters of the tread width. Abnormal tread wear may indicate incorrect front wheel alignment.

## Body corrosion

☐ Check the condition of the entire vehicle structure for signs of corrosion in load-bearing areas. (These include chassis box sections, side sills, cross-members, pillars, and all suspension, steering, braking system and seat belt mountings and anchorages.) Any corrosion which has seriously reduced the thickness of a load-bearing area is likely to cause the vehicle to fail. In this case professional repairs are likely to be needed.

☐ Damage or corrosion which causes sharp or otherwise dangerous edges to be exposed will also cause the vehicle to fail.

## 4 Checks carried out on YOUR VEHICLE'S EXHAUST EMISSION SYSTEM

## Petrol models

☐ The engine should be warmed up, and running well (ignition system in good order, air filter element clean, etc).

☐ Before testing, run the engine at around 2500 rpm for 20 seconds. Let the engine drop to idle, and watch for smoke from the exhaust. If the idle speed is too high, or if dense blue or black smoke emerges for more than 5 seconds, the vehicle will fail. Typically, blue smoke signifies oil burning (engine wear); black smoke means unburnt fuel (dirty air cleaner element, or other fuel system fault).

☐ An exhaust gas analyser for measuring carbon monoxide (CO) and hydrocarbons (HC) is now needed. If one cannot be hired or borrowed, have a local garage perform the check.

## CO emissions (mixture)

☐ The MOT tester has access to the CO limits for all vehicles. The CO level is measured at idle speed, and at 'fast idle' (2500 to 3000 rpm). The following limits are given as a general guide:

At idle speed – Less than 0.5% CO
At 'fast idle' – Less than 0.3% CO
Lambda reading – 0.97 to 1.03

☐ If the CO level is too high, this may point to poor maintenance, a fuel injection system problem, faulty lambda (oxygen) sensor or catalytic converter. Try an injector cleaning treatment, and check the vehicle's ECU for fault codes.

## HC emissions

☐ The MOT tester has access to HC limits for all vehicles. The HC level is measured at 'fast idle' (2500 to 3000 rpm). The following limits are given as a general guide:

At 'fast idle' – Less then 200 ppm

☐ Excessive HC emissions are typically caused by oil being burnt (worn engine), or by a blocked crankcase ventilation system ('breather'). If the engine oil is old and thin, an oil change may help. If the engine is running badly, check the vehicle's ECU for fault codes.

## Diesel models

☐ The only emission test for diesel engines is measuring exhaust smoke density, using a calibrated smoke meter. The test involves accelerating the engine at least 3 times to its maximum unloaded speed.

Note: On engines with a timing belt, it is VITAL that the belt is in good condition before the test is carried out.

☐ With the engine warmed up, it is first purged by running at around 2500 rpm for 20 seconds. A governor check is then carried out, by slowly accelerating the engine to its maximum speed. After this, the smoke meter is connected, and the engine is accelerated quickly to maximum speed three times. If the smoke density is less than the limits given below, the vehicle will pass:

Non-turbo vehicles: 2.5m-1
Turbocharged vehicles: 3.0m-1

☐ If excess smoke is produced, try fitting a new air cleaner element, or using an injector cleaning treatment. If the engine is running badly, where applicable, check the vehicle's ECU for fault codes. Also check the vehicle's EGR system, where applicable. At high mileages, the injectors may require professional attention.

## Engine

- ☐ Engine fails to rotate when attempting to start
- ☐ Engine rotates, but will not start
- ☐ Engine difficult to start when cold
- ☐ Engine difficult to start when hot
- ☐ Starter motor noisy or excessively-rough in engagement
- ☐ Engine starts, but stops immediately
- ☐ Engine idles erratically
- ☐ Engine misfires at idle speed
- ☐ Engine misfires throughout the driving speed range
- ☐ Engine hesitates on acceleration
- ☐ Engine stalls
- ☐ Engine lacks power
- ☐ Engine backfires
- ☐ Oil pressure warning light illuminated with engine running
- ☐ Engine runs-on after switching off
- ☐ Engine noises

## Cooling system

- ☐ Overheating
- ☐ Overcooling
- ☐ External coolant leakage
- ☐ Internal coolant leakage
- ☐ Corrosion

## Fuel and exhaust systems

- ☐ Excessive fuel consumption
- ☐ Fuel leakage and/or fuel odour
- ☐ Excessive noise or fumes from exhaust system

## Clutch

- ☐ Pedal travels to floor - no pressure or very little resistance
- ☐ Clutch fails to disengage (unable to select gears)
- ☐ Clutch slips (engine speed increases, with no increase in vehicle speed)
- ☐ Judder as clutch is engaged
- ☐ Noise when depressing or releasing clutch pedal

## Manual transmission

- ☐ Noisy in neutral with engine running
- ☐ Noisy in one particular gear
- ☐ Difficulty engaging gears
- ☐ Jumps out of gear
- ☐ Vibration
- ☐ Lubricant leaks

## Driveshafts

- ☐ Vibration when accelerating or decelerating
- ☐ Clicking or knocking noise on turns (at slow speed on full-lock)

## Braking system

- ☐ Vehicle pulls to one side under braking
- ☐ Noise (grinding or high-pitched squeal) when brakes applied
- ☐ Excessive brake pedal travel
- ☐ Brake pedal feels spongy when depressed
- ☐ Excessive brake pedal effort required to stop vehicle
- ☐ Judder felt through brake pedal or steering wheel when braking
- ☐ Brakes binding
- ☐ Rear wheels locking under normal braking

## Suspension and steering

- ☐ Vehicle pulls to one side
- ☐ Wheel wobble and vibration
- ☐ Excessive pitching and/or rolling around corners, or during braking
- ☐ Wandering or general instability
- ☐ Excessively-stiff steering
- ☐ Excessive play in steering
- ☐ Lack of power assistance
- ☐ Tyre wear excessive

## Electrical system

- ☐ Battery will not hold a charge for more than a few days
- ☐ Ignition/no-charge warning light remains illuminated with engine running
- ☐ Ignition/no-charge warning light fails to come on
- ☐ Lights inoperative
- ☐ Instrument readings inaccurate or erratic
- ☐ Horn inoperative, or unsatisfactory in operation
- ☐ Windscreen wipers inoperative, or unsatisfactory in operation
- ☐ Windscreen washers inoperative, or unsatisfactory in operation
- ☐ Electric windows inoperative, or unsatisfactory in operation
- ☐ Central locking system inoperative, or unsatisfactory in operation

# Introduction

The vehicle owner who does his or her own maintenance according to the recommended service schedules should not have to use this section of the manual very often. Modern component reliability is such that, provided those items subject to wear or deterioration are inspected or renewed at the specified intervals, sudden failure is comparatively rare. Faults do not usually just happen as a result of sudden failure, but develop over a period of time. Major mechanical failures in particular are usually preceded by characteristic symptoms over hundreds or even thousands of miles. Those components which do occasionally fail without warning are often small and easily carried in the vehicle.

With any fault-finding, the first step is to decide where to begin investigations. Sometimes this is obvious, but on other occasions, a little detective work will be necessary. The owner who makes half a dozen haphazard adjustments or replacements may be successful in curing a fault (or its symptoms), but will be none the wiser if the fault recurs, and ultimately may have spent more time and money than was necessary. A calm and logical approach will be found to be more satisfactory in the long run. Always take into account any warning signs or abnormalities that may have been noticed in the period preceding the fault - power loss, high or low gauge readings, unusual smells, etc - and remember that failure of components such as fuses or spark plugs may only be pointers to some underlying fault.

The pages which follow provide an easy-reference guide to the more common problems which may occur during the operation of the vehicle. These problems and their possible causes are grouped under headings denoting various components or systems, such as Engine, Cooling system, etc. The Chapter and/or Section which deals with the problem is also shown in brackets. Whatever the fault, certain basic principles apply. These are as follows:

*Verify the fault*. This is simply a matter of being sure that you know what the symptoms are before starting work. This is particularly important if you are investigating a fault for someone else, who may not have described it very accurately.

*Don't overlook the obvious.* For example, if the vehicle won't start, is there fuel in the tank? (Don't take anyone else's word on this particular point, and don't trust the fuel gauge either!) If an electrical fault is indicated, look for loose or broken wires before digging out the test gear.

*Cure the disease, not the symptom.* Substituting a flat battery with a fully-charged one will get you off the hard shoulder, but if the underlying cause is not attended to, the new battery will go the same way. Similarly, changing oil-fouled spark plugs for a new set will get you moving again, but remember that the reason for the fouling (if it wasn't simply an incorrect grade of plug) will have to be established and corrected.

*Don't take anything for granted.* Particularly, don't forget that a "new" component may itself be defective (especially if it's been rattling around in the boot for months), and don't leave components out of a fault diagnosis sequence just because they are new or recently-fitted. When you do finally diagnose a difficult fault, you'll probably realise that all the evidence was there from the start.

# Engine

## Engine fails to rotate when attempting to start

- [ ] Battery terminal connections loose or corroded (see "Weekly checks")
- [ ] Battery discharged or faulty (Chapter 5A)
- [ ] Broken, loose or disconnected wiring in the starting circuit (Chapter 5A)
- [ ] Defective starter solenoid or switch (Chapter 5A)
- [ ] Defective starter motor (Chapter 5A)
- [ ] Starter pinion or flywheel ring gear teeth loose or broken (Chapters 2 and 5A)
- [ ] Engine earth strap broken or disconnected (Chapter 5A)

## Engine rotates, but will not start

- [ ] Fuel cut-off switch energised (Chapter 4A).
- [ ] Battery discharged (engine rotates slowly) (Chapter 5A)
- [ ] Battery terminal connections loose or corroded (see "Weekly checks")
- [ ] Ignition components damp or damaged (Chapters 1 and 5B)
- [ ] Broken, loose or disconnected wiring in the ignition circuit (Chapters 1 and 5B)
- [ ] Worn, faulty or incorrectly-gapped spark plugs (Chapter 1)
- [ ] Fuel injection system fault (Chapter 4A)
- [ ] Major mechanical failure (eg camshaft drive) (Chapter 2A)

## Engine difficult to start when cold

- [ ] Battery discharged (Chapter 5A)
- [ ] Battery terminal connections loose or corroded (see "Weekly checks")
- [ ] Worn, faulty or incorrectly-gapped spark plugs (Chapter 1)
- [ ] Fuel injection system fault (Chapter 4A)
- [ ] Other ignition system fault (Chapters 1 and 5B)
- [ ] Low cylinder compressions (Chapter 2A)

## Engine difficult to start when hot

- [ ] Air filter element dirty or clogged (Chapter 1)
- [ ] Fuel injection system fault (Chapter 4A)
- [ ] Low cylinder compressions (Chapter 2A)

## Starter motor noisy or excessively-rough in engagement

- [ ] Starter pinion or flywheel ring gear teeth loose or broken (Chapters 2A and 5A)
- [ ] Starter motor mounting bolts loose or missing (Chapter 5A)
- [ ] Starter motor internal components worn or damaged (Chapter 5A)

## Engine starts, but stops immediately

- [ ] Loose or faulty electrical connections in the ignition circuit (Chapters 1 and 5B)
- [ ] Vacuum leak at the throttle body or inlet manifold (Chapter 4A)
- [ ] Blocked injector/fuel injection system fault (Chapter 4A)

## Engine idles erratically

- [ ] Air filter element clogged (Chapter 1)
- [ ] Vacuum leak at the throttle body, inlet manifold or associated hoses (Chapter 4A)
- [ ] Worn, faulty or incorrectly-gapped spark plugs (Chapter 1)
- [ ] Uneven or low cylinder compressions (Chapter 2A)
- [ ] Camshaft lobes worn (Chapter 2A)
- [ ] Timing chain incorrectly fitted (Chapter 2A)
- [ ] Blocked injector/fuel injection system fault (Chapter 4A)

## Engine misfires at idle speed

- [ ] Worn, faulty or incorrectly-gapped spark plugs (Chapter 1)
- [ ] Faulty spark plug HT leads (Chapter 1)
- [ ] Vacuum leak at the throttle body, inlet manifold or associated hoses (Chapter 4A)
- [ ] Blocked injector/fuel injection system fault (Chapter 4A)
- [ ] Uneven or low cylinder compressions (Chapter 2A)
- [ ] Disconnected, leaking, or perished crankcase ventilation hoses (Chapter 4B)

## Engine misfires throughout the driving speed range

- [ ] Fuel filter choked (Chapter 1)
- [ ] Fuel pump faulty, or delivery pressure low (Chapter 4A)
- [ ] Fuel tank vent blocked, or fuel pipes restricted (Chapter 4A)
- [ ] Vacuum leak at the throttle body, inlet manifold or associated hoses (Chapter 4A)
- [ ] Worn, faulty or incorrectly-gapped spark plugs (Chapter 1)
- [ ] Faulty spark plug HT leads (Chapter 1)
- [ ] Faulty ignition coil (Chapter 5B)
- [ ] Uneven or low cylinder compressions (Chapter 2A)
- [ ] Blocked injector/fuel injection system fault (Chapter 4A)

## Engine hesitates on acceleration

- [ ] Worn, faulty or incorrectly-gapped spark plugs (Chapter 1)
- [ ] Vacuum leak at the throttle body, inlet manifold or associated hoses (Chapter 4A)
- [ ] Blocked injector/fuel injection system fault (Chapter 4A)

## Engine stalls

- [ ] Vacuum leak at the throttle body, inlet manifold or associated hoses (Chapter 4A)
- [ ] Fuel filter choked (Chapter 1)
- [ ] Fuel pump faulty, or delivery pressure low (Chapter 4A)
- [ ] Fuel tank vent blocked, or fuel pipes restricted (Chapter 4A)
- [ ] Blocked injector/fuel injection system fault (Chapter 4A)

# Engine (continued)

### Engine lacks power

- ☐ Timing chain incorrectly fitted (Chapter 2A)
- ☐ Fuel filter choked (Chapter 1)
- ☐ Fuel pump faulty, or delivery pressure low (Chapter 4A)
- ☐ Uneven or low cylinder compressions (Chapter 2A)
- ☐ Worn, faulty or incorrectly-gapped spark plugs (Chapter 1)
- ☐ Vacuum leak at the throttle body, inlet manifold or associated hoses (Chapter 4A)
- ☐ Blocked injector/fuel injection system fault (Chapter 4A)
- ☐ Brakes binding (Chapters 1 and 9)
- ☐ Clutch slipping (Chapter 6)

### Engine backfires

- ☐ Timing belt incorrectly fitted (Chapter 2A)
- ☐ Vacuum leak at the throttle body, inlet manifold or associated hoses (Chapter 4A)
- ☐ Blocked injector/fuel injection system fault (Chapter 4A)

### Oil pressure warning light illuminated with engine running

- ☐ Low oil level, or incorrect oil grade (see *"Weekly checks"*)
- ☐ Faulty oil pressure sensor (Chapter 2A)
- ☐ Worn engine bearings and/or oil pump (Chapter 2B)
- ☐ High engine operating temperature (Chapter 3)
- ☐ Oil pressure relief valve defective (Chapter 2A)
- ☐ Oil pick-up strainer clogged (Chapter 2B)

### Engine runs-on after switching off

- ☐ Excessive carbon build-up in engine (Chapter 2A)
- ☐ High engine operating temperature (Chapter 3)
- ☐ Fuel injection system fault (Chapter 4A)

### Engine noises

#### Pre-ignition (pinking) or knocking during acceleration or under load

- ☐ Ignition system fault (Chapters 1 and 5B)
- ☐ Incorrect grade of spark plug (Chapter 1)
- ☐ Incorrect grade of fuel (Chapter 4A)
- ☐ Vacuum leak at the throttle body, inlet manifold or associated hoses (Chapter 4A)
- ☐ Excessive carbon build-up in engine (Chapter 2A)
- ☐ Blocked injector/fuel injection system fault (Chapter 4A)

#### Whistling or wheezing noises

- ☐ Leaking inlet manifold or throttle body gasket (Chapter 4A)
- ☐ Leaking exhaust manifold gasket or pipe-to-manifold joint (Chapter 4A)
- ☐ Leaking vacuum hose (Chapters 4A and 9)
- ☐ Blowing cylinder head gasket (Chapter 2A)

#### Tapping or rattling noises

- ☐ Worn valve gear or camshaft (Chapter 2A)
- ☐ Ancillary component fault (water pump, alternator, etc) (Chapters 3 and 5A)

#### Knocking or thumping noises

- ☐ Worn big-end bearings (regular heavy knocking, perhaps less under load) (Chapter 2B)
- ☐ Worn main bearings (rumbling and knocking, perhaps worsening under load) (Chapter 2B)
- ☐ Piston slap (most noticeable when cold) (Chapter 2B)
- ☐ Ancillary component fault (water pump, alternator, etc) (Chapters 3 and 5A)

# Cooling system

### Overheating

- ☐ Insufficient coolant in system (see *"Weekly checks"*)
- ☐ Thermostat faulty (Chapter 3)
- ☐ Radiator core blocked, or grille restricted (Chapter 3)
- ☐ Cooling fan faulty (Chapter 3)
- ☐ Inaccurate temperature gauge sender unit (Chapter 3)
- ☐ Airlock in cooling system (Chapters 1 and 3)
- ☐ Pressure cap faulty (Chapter 3)

### Overcooling

- ☐ Thermostat faulty (Chapter 3)
- ☐ Inaccurate temperature gauge sender unit (Chapter 3)
- ☐ Cooling fan faulty (Chapter 3)

### External coolant leakage

- ☐ Deteriorated or damaged hoses or hose clips (Chapter 1)
- ☐ Radiator core or heater matrix leaking (Chapter 3)
- ☐ Pressure cap faulty (Chapter 3)
- ☐ Water pump internal seal leaking (Chapter 3)
- ☐ Water pump-to-block seal leaking (Chapter 3)
- ☐ Boiling due to overheating (Chapter 3)
- ☐ Core plug leaking (Chapter 2B)

### Internal coolant leakage

- ☐ Leaking cylinder head gasket (Chapter 2A)
- ☐ Cracked cylinder head or cylinder block (Chapter 2B)

### Corrosion

- ☐ Infrequent draining and flushing (Chapter 1)
- ☐ Incorrect coolant mixture or inappropriate coolant type (see *"Weekly checks"*)

# Fuel and exhaust systems

### Excessive fuel consumption

- ☐ Air filter element dirty or clogged (Chapter 1)
- ☐ Fuel injection system fault (Chapter 4A)
- ☐ Ignition system fault (Chapters 1 and 5B)
- ☐ Tyres under-inflated (see *"Weekly checks"*)

### Fuel leakage and/or fuel odour

- ☐ Damaged or corroded fuel tank, pipes or connections (Chapter 4A)

### Excessive noise or fumes from exhaust system

- ☐ Leaking exhaust system or manifold joints (Chapters 1 and 4A)
- ☐ Leaking, corroded or damaged silencers or pipe (Chapters 1 and 4A)
- ☐ Broken mountings causing body or suspension contact (Chapter 1)

# Clutch

## Pedal travels to floor - no pressure or very little resistance

- ☐ Air in hydraulic system/faulty master or slave cylinder (Chapter 6)
- ☐ Faulty hydraulic release system (Chapter 6)
- ☐ Broken clutch release bearing or fork (Chapter 6)
- ☐ Broken diaphragm spring in clutch pressure plate (Chapter 6)

## Clutch fails to disengage (unable to select gears)

- ☐ Air in hydraulic system/faulty master or slave cylinder (Chapter 6)
- ☐ Faulty hydraulic release system (Chapter 6)
- ☐ Clutch disc sticking on gearbox input shaft splines (Chapter 6)
- ☐ Clutch disc sticking to flywheel or pressure plate (Chapter 6)
- ☐ Faulty pressure plate assembly (Chapter 6)
- ☐ Clutch release mechanism worn or incorrectly assembled (Chapter 6)

## Clutch slips (engine speed increases, with no increase in vehicle speed)

- ☐ Faulty hydraulic release system (Chapter 6)
- ☐ Clutch disc linings excessively worn (Chapter 6)
- ☐ Clutch disc linings contaminated with oil or grease (Chapter 6)
- ☐ Faulty pressure plate or weak diaphragm spring (Chapter 6)

## Judder as clutch is engaged

- ☐ Clutch disc linings contaminated with oil or grease (Chapter 6)
- ☐ Clutch disc linings excessively worn (Chapter 6)
- ☐ Faulty or distorted pressure plate or diaphragm spring (Chapter 6).
- ☐ Worn or loose engine or gearbox mountings (Chapter 2A)
- ☐ Clutch disc hub or gearbox input shaft splines worn (Chapter 6)

## Noise when depressing or releasing clutch pedal

- ☐ Worn clutch release bearing (Chapter 6)
- ☐ Worn or dry clutch pedal bushes (Chapter 6)
- ☐ Faulty pressure plate assembly (Chapter 6)
- ☐ Pressure plate diaphragm spring broken (Chapter 6)
- ☐ Broken clutch disc cushioning springs (Chapter 6)

# Manual transmission

## Noisy in neutral with engine running

- ☐ Input shaft bearings worn (noise apparent with clutch pedal released, but not when depressed) (Chapter 7)*
- ☐ Clutch release bearing worn (noise apparent with clutch pedal depressed, possibly less when released) (Chapter 6)

## Noisy in one particular gear

- ☐ Worn, damaged or chipped gear teeth (Chapter 7)*

## Difficulty engaging gears

- ☐ Clutch fault (Chapter 6)
- ☐ Worn or damaged gearchange linkage (Chapter 7)
- ☐ Worn synchroniser units (Chapter 7)*

## Jumps out of gear

- ☐ Worn or damaged gearchange linkage (Chapter 7)
- ☐ Worn synchroniser units (Chapter 7)*
- ☐ Worn selector forks (Chapter 7)*

## Vibration

- ☐ Lack of oil (Chapter 1)
- ☐ Worn bearings (Chapter 7)*

## Lubricant leaks

- ☐ Leaking differential output oil seal (Chapter 7)
- ☐ Leaking housing joint (Chapter 7)*
- ☐ Leaking input shaft oil seal (Chapter 7)*

*Although the corrective action necessary to remedy the symptoms described is beyond the scope of the home mechanic, the above information should be helpful in isolating the cause of the condition, so that the owner can communicate clearly with a professional mechanic.*

# Driveshafts

## Vibration when accelerating or decelerating

- ☐ Worn inner constant velocity joint (Chapter 8)
- ☐ Bent or distorted driveshaft (Chapter 8)

## Clicking or knocking noise on turns (at slow speed on full-lock)

- ☐ Worn outer constant velocity joint (Chapter 8)
- ☐ Lack of constant velocity joint lubricant, possibly due to damaged gaiter (Chapter 8)

# Braking system

**Note:** *Before assuming that a brake problem exists, make sure that the tyres are in good condition and correctly inflated, that the front wheel alignment is correct, and that the vehicle is not loaded with weight in an unequal manner. Apart from checking the condition of all pipe and hose connections, any faults occurring on the anti-lock braking system should be referred to a Ford dealer for diagnosis.*

### Vehicle pulls to one side under braking

☐ Worn, defective, damaged or contaminated brake pads/shoes on one side (Chapters 1 and 9)
☐ Seized or partially-seized brake caliper piston/wheel cylinder (Chapters 1 and 9)
☐ A mixture of brake pad/shoe lining materials fitted between sides (Chapters 1 and 9)
☐ Brake caliper/backplate mounting bolts loose (Chapter 9)
☐ Worn or damaged steering or suspension components (Chapters 1 and 10)

### Noise (grinding or high-pitched squeal) when brakes applied

☐ Brake pad/shoe friction lining material worn down to metal backing (Chapters 1 and 9)
☐ Excessive corrosion of brake disc/drum (may be apparent after the vehicle has been standing for some time (Chapters 1 and 9)
☐ Foreign object (stone chipping, etc) trapped between brake disc and shield (Chapters 1 and 9)

### Excessive brake pedal travel

☐ Faulty master cylinder (Chapter 9)
☐ Air in hydraulic system (Chapters 1 and 9)
☐ Faulty vacuum servo unit (Chapter 9)

### Brake pedal feels spongy when depressed

☐ Air in hydraulic system (Chapters 1 and 9)
☐ Deteriorated flexible rubber brake hoses (Chapters 1 and 9)
☐ Master cylinder mounting nuts loose (Chapter 9)
☐ Faulty master cylinder (Chapter 9)

### Excessive brake pedal effort required to stop vehicle

☐ Faulty vacuum servo unit (Chapter 9)
☐ Disconnected, damaged or insecure brake servo vacuum hose (Chapter 9)
☐ Primary or secondary hydraulic circuit failure (Chapter 9)
☐ Seized brake caliper/wheel cylinder piston (Chapter 9)
☐ Brake pads/shoes incorrectly fitted (Chapters 1 and 9)
☐ Incorrect grade of brake pads/shoes fitted (Chapters 1 and 9)
☐ Brake pad/shoe linings contaminated (Chapters 1 and 9)

### Judder felt through brake pedal or steering wheel when braking

☐ Excessive run-out or distortion of discs/drums (Chapters 1 and 9)
☐ Brake pad/shoe linings worn (Chapters 1 and 9)
☐ Brake caliper/backplate mounting bolts loose (Chapter 9)
☐ Wear in suspension or steering components or mountings (Chapters 1 and 10)

### Brakes binding

☐ Seized brake caliper/wheel cylinder piston (Chapter 9)
☐ Incorrectly-adjusted handbrake mechanism (Chapter 9)
☐ Faulty master cylinder (Chapter 9)

### Rear wheels locking under normal braking

☐ Rear brake shoe linings contaminated (Chapters 1 and 9)

# Suspension and steering

**Note:** *Before diagnosing suspension or steering faults, be sure that the trouble is not due to incorrect tyre pressures, mixtures of tyre types, or binding brakes.*

### Vehicle pulls to one side

☐ Defective tyre (see *"Weekly checks"*)
☐ Excessive wear in suspension or steering components (Chapters 1 and 10)
☐ Incorrect front wheel alignment (Chapter 10)
☐ Accident damage to steering or suspension components (Chapter 1)

### Wheel wobble and vibration

☐ Front roadwheels out of balance (vibration felt mainly through the steering wheel) (see *"Weekly checks"*)
☐ Rear roadwheels out of balance (vibration felt throughout the vehicle) (see *"Weekly checks"*)
☐ Roadwheels damaged or distorted (Chapter 10)
☐ Faulty or damaged tyre (see *"Weekly checks"*)
☐ Worn steering or suspension joints, bushes or components (Chapters 1 and 10)
☐ Wheel nuts loose (Chapter 1)

### Excessive pitching and/or rolling around corners, or during braking

☐ Defective shock absorbers (Chapters 1 and 10)
☐ Broken or weak spring and/or suspension component (Chapters 1 and 10)
☐ Worn or damaged anti-roll bar or mountings (Chapter 10)

### Wandering or general instability

☐ Incorrect front wheel alignment (Chapter 10)
☐ Worn steering or suspension joints, bushes or components (Chapters 1 and 10)
☐ Roadwheels out of balance (see *"Weekly checks"*)
☐ Faulty or damaged tyre (see *"Weekly checks"*)
☐ Wheel nuts loose (Chapter 1)
☐ Defective shock absorbers (Chapters 1 and 10)

### Excessively-stiff steering

☐ Seized steering linkage balljoint or suspension balljoint (Chapters 1 and 10)
☐ Broken auxiliary drivebelt (Chapter 1)
☐ Incorrect front wheel alignment (Chapter 10)
☐ Steering gear damaged (Chapter 10)

### Excessive play in steering

☐ Worn steering column/intermediate shaft joints (Chapter 10)
☐ Worn track rod balljoints (Chapters 1 and 10)
☐ Worn steering gear (Chapter 10)
☐ Worn steering or suspension joints, bushes or components (Chapters 1 and 10)

### Lack of power assistance

☐ Broken auxiliary drivebelt (Chapter 1)
☐ Incorrect power steering fluid level (see *"Weekly checks"*)
☐ Restriction in power steering fluid hoses (Chapter 1)
☐ Faulty power steering pump (Chapter 10)
☐ Faulty steering gear (Chapter 10)

# Suspension and steering (continued)

### Tyre wear excessive

#### Tyres worn on inside or outside edges

- [ ] Tyres under-inflated (wear on both edges) (see "Weekly checks")
- [ ] Incorrect camber or castor angles (wear on one edge only) (Chapter 10)
- [ ] Worn steering or suspension joints, bushes or components (Chapters 1 and 10)
- [ ] Excessively-hard cornering
- [ ] Accident damage

#### Tyre treads exhibit feathered edges

- [ ] Incorrect toe-setting (Chapter 10)

### Tyres worn in centre of tread

- [ ] Tyres over-inflated (see "Weekly checks")

### Tyres worn on inside and outside edges

- [ ] Tyres under-inflated (see "Weekly checks")

### Tyres worn unevenly

- [ ] Tyres/wheels out of balance (see "Weekly checks")
- [ ] Excessive wheel or tyre run-out
- [ ] Worn shock absorbers (Chapters 1 and 10)
- [ ] Faulty tyre (see "Weekly checks")

# Electrical system

**Note:** For problems associated with the starting system, refer to the faults listed under "Engine" earlier in this Section.

### Battery will not hold a charge for more than a few days

- [ ] Battery defective internally (Chapter 5A)
- [ ] Battery terminal connections loose or corroded (see "Weekly checks")
- [ ] Auxiliary drivebelt broken (Chapter 1)
- [ ] Alternator not charging at correct output (Chapter 5A)
- [ ] Alternator or voltage regulator faulty (Chapter 5A)
- [ ] Short-circuit causing continual battery drain (Chapters 5A and 12)

### Ignition/no-charge warning light remains illuminated with engine running

- [ ] Auxiliary drivebelt broken (Chapter 1)
- [ ] Internal fault in alternator or voltage regulator (Chapter 5A)
- [ ] Broken, disconnected, or loose wiring in charging circuit (Chapter 5A)

### Ignition/no-charge warning light fails to come on

- [ ] Warning light bulb blown (Chapter 12)
- [ ] Broken, disconnected, or loose wiring in warning light circuit (Chapter 12)
- [ ] Alternator faulty (Chapter 5A)

### Lights inoperative

- [ ] Bulb blown (Chapter 12)
- [ ] Corrosion of bulb or bulbholder contacts (Chapter 12)
- [ ] Blown fuse (Chapter 12)
- [ ] Faulty relay (Chapter 12)
- [ ] Broken, loose, or disconnected wiring (Chapter 12)
- [ ] Faulty switch (Chapter 12)

### Instrument readings inaccurate or erratic

#### Instrument readings increase with engine speed

- [ ] Faulty voltage regulator (Chapter 12)

#### Fuel or temperature gauges give no reading

- [ ] Faulty gauge sender unit (Chapters 3 and 4A)
- [ ] Wiring open-circuit (Chapter 12)
- [ ] Faulty gauge (Chapter 12)

#### Fuel or temperature gauges give continuous maximum reading

- [ ] Faulty gauge sender unit (Chapters 3 and 4A)
- [ ] Wiring short-circuit (Chapter 12)
- [ ] Faulty gauge (Chapter 12)

### Horn inoperative, or unsatisfactory in operation

#### Horn operates all the time

- [ ] Horn push either earthed or stuck down (Chapter 12)
- [ ] Horn cable-to-horn push earthed (Chapter 12)

#### Horn fails to operate

- [ ] Blown fuse (Chapter 12)
- [ ] Cable or cable connections loose, broken or disconnected (Chapter 12)
- [ ] Faulty horn (Chapter 12)

#### Horn emits intermittent or unsatisfactory sound

- [ ] Cable connections loose (Chapter 12)
- [ ] Horn mountings loose (Chapter 12)
- [ ] Faulty horn (Chapter 12)

### Windscreen wipers inoperative, or unsatisfactory in operation

#### Wipers fail to operate, or operate very slowly

- [ ] Wiper blades stuck to screen, or linkage seized or binding (Chapter 12)
- [ ] Blown fuse (Chapter 12)
- [ ] Cable or cable connections loose, broken or disconnected (Chapter 12)
- [ ] Faulty relay (Chapter 12)
- [ ] Faulty wiper motor (Chapter 12)

#### Wiper blades sweep over too large or too small an area of the glass

- [ ] Wiper arms incorrectly positioned on spindles (Chapter 12)
- [ ] Excessive wear of wiper linkage (Chapter 12)
- [ ] Wiper motor or linkage mountings loose or insecure (Chapter 12)

#### Wiper blades fail to clean the glass effectively

- [ ] Wiper blade rubbers worn or perished (see "Weekly checks")
- [ ] Wiper arm tension springs broken, or arm pivots seized (Chapter 12)
- [ ] Insufficient windscreen washer additive to adequately remove road film (see "Weekly checks")

### Windscreen washers inoperative, or unsatisfactory in operation

#### One or more washer jets inoperative

- [ ] Blocked washer jet (Chapter 12)
- [ ] Disconnected, kinked or restricted fluid hose (Chapter 12)
- [ ] Insufficient fluid in washer reservoir (see "Weekly checks")

# Electrical system (continued)

## Washer pump fails to operate

☐ Broken or disconnected wiring or connections (Chapter 12)
☐ Blown fuse (Chapter 12)
☐ Faulty washer switch (Chapter 12)
☐ Faulty washer pump (Chapter 12)

## Washer pump runs for some time before fluid is emitted from jets

☐ Faulty one-way valve in fluid supply hose (Chapter 12)

## *Electric windows inoperative, or unsatisfactory in operation*

### Window glass will only move in one direction

☐ Faulty switch (Chapter 12)

### Window glass slow to move

☐ Regulator seized or damaged, or in need of lubrication (Chapter 11)
☐ Door internal components or trim fouling regulator (Chapter 11)
☐ Faulty motor (Chapter 11)

### Window glass fails to move

☐ Blown fuse (Chapter 12)
☐ Faulty relay (Chapter 12)
☐ Broken or disconnected wiring or connections (Chapter 12)
☐ Faulty motor (Chapter 11)

## *Central locking system inoperative, or unsatisfactory in operation*

### Complete system failure

☐ Blown fuse (Chapter 12)
☐ Faulty relay (Chapter 12)
☐ Broken or disconnected wiring or connections (Chapter 12)
☐ Faulty motor (Chapter 11)

### Latch locks but will not unlock, or unlocks but will not lock

☐ Broken or disconnected latch operating rods or levers (Chapter 11)
☐ Faulty relay (Chapter 12)
☐ Faulty motor (Chapter 11)

### One solenoid/motor fails to operate

☐ Broken or disconnected wiring or connections (Chapter 12)
☐ Faulty operating assembly (Chapter 11)
☐ Broken, binding or disconnected latch operating rods or levers (Chapter 11)
☐ Fault in door latch (Chapter 11)

## A

**ABS (Anti-lock brake system)** A system, usually electronically controlled, that senses incipient wheel lockup during braking and relieves hydraulic pressure at wheels that are about to skid.

**Air bag** An inflatable bag hidden in the steering wheel (driver's side) or the dash or glovebox (passenger side). In a head-on collision, the bags inflate, preventing the driver and front passenger from being thrown forward into the steering wheel or windscreen.

**Air cleaner** A metal or plastic housing, containing a filter element, which removes dust and dirt from the air being drawn into the engine.

**Air filter element** The actual filter in an air cleaner system, usually manufactured from pleated paper and requiring renewal at regular intervals.

*Air filter*

**Allen key** A hexagonal wrench which fits into a recessed hexagonal hole.

**Alligator clip** A long-nosed spring-loaded metal clip with meshing teeth. Used to make temporary electrical connections.

**Alternator** A component in the electrical system which converts mechanical energy from a drivebelt into electrical energy to charge the battery and to operate the starting system, ignition system and electrical accessories.

**Ampere (amp)** A unit of measurement for the flow of electric current. One amp is the amount of current produced by one volt acting through a resistance of one ohm.

**Anaerobic sealer** A substance used to prevent bolts and screws from loosening. Anaerobic means that it does not require oxygen for activation. The Loctite brand is widely used.

**Antifreeze** A substance (usually ethylene glycol) mixed with water, and added to a vehicle's cooling system, to prevent freezing of the coolant in winter. Antifreeze also contains chemicals to inhibit corrosion and the formation of rust and other deposits that would tend to clog the radiator and coolant passages and reduce cooling efficiency.

**Anti-seize compound** A coating that reduces the risk of seizing on fasteners that are subjected to high temperatures, such as exhaust manifold bolts and nuts.

**Asbestos** A natural fibrous mineral with great heat resistance, commonly used in the composition of brake friction materials.

Asbestos is a health hazard and the dust created by brake systems should never be inhaled or ingested.

**Axle** A shaft on which a wheel revolves, or which revolves with a wheel. Also, a solid beam that connects the two wheels at one end of the vehicle. An axle which also transmits power to the wheels is known as a live axle.

**Axleshaft** A single rotating shaft, on either side of the differential, which delivers power from the final drive assembly to the drive wheels. Also called a driveshaft or a halfshaft.

## B

**Ball bearing** An anti-friction bearing consisting of a hardened inner and outer race with hardened steel balls between two races.

**Bearing** The curved surface on a shaft or in a bore, or the part assembled into either, that permits relative motion between them with minimum wear and friction.

*Bearing*

**Big-end bearing** The bearing in the end of the connecting rod that's attached to the crankshaft.

**Bleed nipple** A valve on a brake wheel cylinder, caliper or other hydraulic component that is opened to purge the hydraulic system of air. Also called a bleed screw.

**Brake bleeding** Procedure for removing air from lines of a hydraulic brake system.

*Brake bleeding*

**Brake disc** The component of a disc brake that rotates with the wheels.

**Brake drum** The component of a drum brake that rotates with the wheels.

**Brake linings** The friction material which contacts the brake disc or drum to retard the vehicle's speed. The linings are bonded or riveted to the brake pads or shoes.

**Brake pads** The replaceable friction pads that pinch the brake disc when the brakes are applied. Brake pads consist of a friction material bonded or riveted to a rigid backing plate.

**Brake shoe** The crescent-shaped carrier to which the brake linings are mounted and which forces the lining against the rotating drum during braking.

**Braking systems** For more information on braking systems, consult the *Haynes Automotive Brake Manual*.

**Breaker bar** A long socket wrench handle providing greater leverage.

**Bulkhead** The insulated partition between the engine and the passenger compartment.

## C

**Caliper** The non-rotating part of a disc-brake assembly that straddles the disc and carries the brake pads. The caliper also contains the hydraulic components that cause the pads to pinch the disc when the brakes are applied. A caliper is also a measuring tool that can be set to measure inside or outside dimensions of an object.

**Camshaft** A rotating shaft on which a series of cam lobes operate the valve mechanisms. The camshaft may be driven by gears, by sprockets and chain or by sprockets and a belt.

**Canister** A container in an evaporative emission control system; contains activated charcoal granules to trap vapours from the fuel system.

*Canister*

**Carburettor** A device which mixes fuel with air in the proper proportions to provide a desired power output from a spark ignition internal combustion engine.

**Castellated** Resembling the parapets along the top of a castle wall. For example, a castellated balljoint stud nut.

**Castor** In wheel alignment, the backward or forward tilt of the steering axis. Castor is positive when the steering axis is inclined rearward at the top.

**Catalytic converter** A silencer-like device in the exhaust system which converts certain pollutants in the exhaust gases into less harmful substances.

*Catalytic converter*

**Circlip** A ring-shaped clip used to prevent endwise movement of cylindrical parts and shafts. An internal circlip is installed in a groove in a housing; an external circlip fits into a groove on the outside of a cylindrical piece such as a shaft.

**Clearance** The amount of space between two parts. For example, between a piston and a cylinder, between a bearing and a journal, etc.

**Coil spring** A spiral of elastic steel found in various sizes throughout a vehicle, for example as a springing medium in the suspension and in the valve train.

**Compression** Reduction in volume, and increase in pressure and temperature, of a gas, caused by squeezing it into a smaller space.

**Compression ratio** The relationship between cylinder volume when the piston is at top dead centre and cylinder volume when the piston is at bottom dead centre.

**Constant velocity (CV) joint** A type of universal joint that cancels out vibrations caused by driving power being transmitted through an angle.

**Core plug** A disc or cup-shaped metal device inserted in a hole in a casting through which core was removed when the casting was formed. Also known as a freeze plug or expansion plug.

**Crankcase** The lower part of the engine block in which the crankshaft rotates.

**Crankshaft** The main rotating member, or shaft, running the length of the crankcase, with offset "throws" to which the connecting rods are attached.

*Crankshaft assembly*

**Crocodile clip** See Alligator clip

## D

**Diagnostic code** Code numbers obtained by accessing the diagnostic mode of an engine management computer. This code can be used to determine the area in the system where a malfunction may be located.

**Disc brake** A brake design incorporating a rotating disc onto which brake pads are squeezed. The resulting friction converts the energy of a moving vehicle into heat.

**Double-overhead cam (DOHC)** An engine that uses two overhead camshafts, usually one for the intake valves and one for the exhaust valves.

**Drivebelt(s)** The belt(s) used to drive accessories such as the alternator, water pump, power steering pump, air conditioning compressor, etc. off the crankshaft pulley.

*Accessory drivebelts*

**Driveshaft** Any shaft used to transmit motion. Commonly used when referring to the axleshafts on a front wheel drive vehicle.

**Drum brake** A type of brake using a drum-shaped metal cylinder attached to the inner surface of the wheel. When the brake pedal is pressed, curved brake shoes with friction linings press against the inside of the drum to slow or stop the vehicle.

## E

**EGR valve** A valve used to introduce exhaust gases into the intake air stream.

**Electronic control unit (ECU)** A computer which controls (for instance) ignition and fuel injection systems, or an anti-lock braking system. For more information refer to the *Haynes Automotive Electrical and Electronic Systems Manual.*

**Electronic Fuel Injection (EFI)** A computer controlled fuel system that distributes fuel through an injector located in each intake port of the engine.

**Emergency brake** A braking system, independent of the main hydraulic system, that can be used to slow or stop the vehicle if the primary brakes fail, or to hold the vehicle stationary even though the brake pedal isn't depressed. It usually consists of a hand lever that actuates either front or rear brakes mechanically through a series of cables and linkages. Also known as a handbrake or parking brake.

**Endfloat** The amount of lengthwise movement between two parts. As applied to a crankshaft, the distance that the crankshaft can move forward and back in the cylinder block.

**Engine management system (EMS)** A computer controlled system which manages the fuel injection and the ignition systems in an integrated fashion.

**Exhaust manifold** A part with several passages through which exhaust gases leave the engine combustion chambers and enter the exhaust pipe.

## F

**Fan clutch** A viscous (fluid) drive coupling device which permits variable engine fan speeds in relation to engine speeds.

**Feeler blade** A thin strip or blade of hardened steel, ground to an exact thickness, used to check or measure clearances between parts.

*Feeler blade*

**Firing order** The order in which the engine cylinders fire, or deliver their power strokes, beginning with the number one cylinder.

**Flywheel** A heavy spinning wheel in which energy is absorbed and stored by means of momentum. On cars, the flywheel is attached to the crankshaft to smooth out firing impulses.

**Free play** The amount of travel before any action takes place. The "looseness" in a linkage, or an assembly of parts, between the initial application of force and actual movement. For example, the distance the brake pedal moves before the pistons in the master cylinder are actuated.

**Fuse** An electrical device which protects a circuit against accidental overload. The typical fuse contains a soft piece of metal which is calibrated to melt at a predetermined current flow (expressed as amps) and break the circuit.

**Fusible link** A circuit protection device consisting of a conductor surrounded by heat-resistant insulation. The conductor is smaller than the wire it protects, so it acts as the weakest link in the circuit. Unlike a blown fuse, a failed fusible link must frequently be cut from the wire for replacement.

## G

**Gap** The distance the spark must travel in jumping from the centre electrode to the side electrode in a spark plug. Also refers to the spacing between the points in a contact breaker assembly in a conventional points-type ignition, or to the distance between the reluctor or rotor and the pickup coil in an electronic ignition.

*Adjusting spark plug gap*

**Gasket** Any thin, soft material - usually cork, cardboard, asbestos or soft metal - installed between two metal surfaces to ensure a good seal. For instance, the cylinder head gasket seals the joint between the block and the cylinder head.

*Gasket*

**Gauge** An instrument panel display used to monitor engine conditions. A gauge with a movable pointer on a dial or a fixed scale is an analogue gauge. A gauge with a numerical readout is called a digital gauge.

## H

**Halfshaft** A rotating shaft that transmits power from the final drive unit to a drive wheel, usually when referring to a live rear axle.

**Harmonic balancer** A device designed to reduce torsion or twisting vibration in the crankshaft. May be incorporated in the crankshaft pulley. Also known as a vibration damper.

**Hone** An abrasive tool for correcting small irregularities or differences in diameter in an engine cylinder, brake cylinder, etc.

**Hydraulic tappet** A tappet that utilises hydraulic pressure from the engine's lubrication system to maintain zero clearance (constant contact with both camshaft and valve stem). Automatically adjusts to variation in valve stem length. Hydraulic tappets also reduce valve noise.

## I

**Ignition timing** The moment at which the spark plug fires, usually expressed in the number of crankshaft degrees before the piston reaches the top of its stroke.

**Inlet manifold** A tube or housing with passages through which flows the air-fuel mixture (carburettor vehicles and vehicles with throttle body injection) or air only (port fuel-injected vehicles) to the port openings in the cylinder head.

## J

**Jump start** Starting the engine of a vehicle with a discharged or weak battery by attaching jump leads from the weak battery to a charged or helper battery.

## L

**Load Sensing Proportioning Valve (LSPV)** A brake hydraulic system control valve that works like a proportioning valve, but also takes into consideration the amount of weight carried by the rear axle.

**Locknut** A nut used to lock an adjustment nut, or other threaded component, in place. For example, a locknut is employed to keep the adjusting nut on the rocker arm in position.

**Lockwasher** A form of washer designed to prevent an attaching nut from working loose.

## M

**MacPherson strut** A type of front suspension system devised by Earle MacPherson at Ford of England. In its original form, a simple lateral link with the anti-roll bar creates the lower control arm. A long strut - an integral coil spring and shock absorber - is mounted between the body and the steering knuckle. Many modern so-called MacPherson strut systems use a conventional lower A-arm and don't rely on the anti-roll bar for location.

**Multimeter** An electrical test instrument with the capability to measure voltage, current and resistance.

## N

**NOx** Oxides of Nitrogen. A common toxic pollutant emitted by petrol and diesel engines at higher temperatures.

## O

**Ohm** The unit of electrical resistance. One volt applied to a resistance of one ohm will produce a current of one amp.

**Ohmmeter** An instrument for measuring electrical resistance.

**O-ring** A type of sealing ring made of a special rubber-like material; in use, the O-ring is compressed into a groove to provide the sealing action.

**Overhead cam (ohc) engine** An engine with the camshaft(s) located on top of the cylinder head(s).

**Overhead valve (ohv) engine** An engine with the valves located in the cylinder head, but with the camshaft located in the engine block.

**Oxygen sensor** A device installed in the engine exhaust manifold, which senses the oxygen content in the exhaust and converts this information into an electric current. Also called a Lambda sensor.

## P

**Phillips screw** A type of screw head having a cross instead of a slot for a corresponding type of screwdriver.

**Plastigage** A thin strip of plastic thread, available in different sizes, used for measuring clearances. For example, a strip of Plastigage is laid across a bearing journal. The parts are assembled and dismantled; the width of the crushed strip indicates the clearance between journal and bearing.

*Plastigage*

**Propeller shaft** The long hollow tube with universal joints at both ends that carries power from the transmission to the differential on front-engined rear wheel drive vehicles.

**Proportioning valve** A hydraulic control valve which limits the amount of pressure to the rear brakes during panic stops to prevent wheel lock-up.

## R

**Rack-and-pinion steering** A steering system with a pinion gear on the end of the steering shaft that mates with a rack (think of a geared wheel opened up and laid flat). When the steering wheel is turned, the pinion turns, moving the rack to the left or right. This movement is transmitted through the track rods to the steering arms at the wheels.

**Radiator** A liquid-to-air heat transfer device designed to reduce the temperature of the coolant in an internal combustion engine cooling system.

**Refrigerant** Any substance used as a heat transfer agent in an air-conditioning system. R-12 has been the principle refrigerant for many years; recently, however, manufacturers have begun using R-134a, a non-CFC substance that is considered less harmful to the ozone in the upper atmosphere.

**Rocker arm** A lever arm that rocks on a shaft or pivots on a stud. In an overhead valve engine, the rocker arm converts the upward movement of the pushrod into a downward movement to open a valve.

**Rotor** In a distributor, the rotating device inside the cap that connects the centre electrode and the outer terminals as it turns, distributing the high voltage from the coil secondary winding to the proper spark plug. Also, that part of an alternator which rotates inside the stator. Also, the rotating assembly of a turbocharger, including the compressor wheel, shaft and turbine wheel.

**Runout** The amount of wobble (in-and-out movement) of a gear or wheel as it's rotated. The amount a shaft rotates "out-of-true." The out-of-round condition of a rotating part.

# S

**Sealant** A liquid or paste used to prevent leakage at a joint. Sometimes used in conjunction with a gasket.

**Sealed beam lamp** An older headlight design which integrates the reflector, lens and filaments into a hermetically-sealed one-piece unit. When a filament burns out or the lens cracks, the entire unit is simply replaced.

**Serpentine drivebelt** A single, long, wide accessory drivebelt that's used on some newer vehicles to drive all the accessories, instead of a series of smaller, shorter belts. Serpentine drivebelts are usually tensioned by an automatic tensioner.

*Serpentine drivebelt*

**Shim** Thin spacer, commonly used to adjust the clearance or relative positions between two parts. For example, shims inserted into or under bucket tappets control valve clearances. Clearance is adjusted by changing the thickness of the shim.

**Slide hammer** A special puller that screws into or hooks onto a component such as a shaft or bearing; a heavy sliding handle on the shaft bottoms against the end of the shaft to knock the component free.

**Sprocket** A tooth or projection on the periphery of a wheel, shaped to engage with a chain or drivebelt. Commonly used to refer to the sprocket wheel itself.

**Starter inhibitor switch** On vehicles with an automatic transmission, a switch that prevents starting if the vehicle is not in Neutral or Park.

**Strut** See MacPherson strut.

# T

**Tappet** A cylindrical component which transmits motion from the cam to the valve stem, either directly or via a pushrod and rocker arm. Also called a cam follower.

**Thermostat** A heat-controlled valve that regulates the flow of coolant between the cylinder block and the radiator, so maintaining optimum engine operating temperature. A thermostat is also used in some air cleaners in which the temperature is regulated.

**Thrust bearing** The bearing in the clutch assembly that is moved in to the release levers by clutch pedal action to disengage the clutch. Also referred to as a release bearing.

**Timing belt** A toothed belt which drives the camshaft. Serious engine damage may result if it breaks in service.

**Timing chain** A chain which drives the camshaft.

**Toe-in** The amount the front wheels are closer together at the front than at the rear. On rear wheel drive vehicles, a slight amount of toe-in is usually specified to keep the front wheels running parallel on the road by offsetting other forces that tend to spread the wheels apart.

**Toe-out** The amount the front wheels are closer together at the rear than at the front. On front wheel drive vehicles, a slight amount of toe-out is usually specified.

**Tools** For full information on choosing and using tools, refer to the *Haynes Automotive Tools Manual*.

**Tracer** A stripe of a second colour applied to a wire insulator to distinguish that wire from another one with the same colour insulator.

**Tune-up** A process of accurate and careful adjustments and parts replacement to obtain the best possible engine performance.

**Turbocharger** A centrifugal device, driven by exhaust gases, that pressurises the intake air. Normally used to increase the power output from a given engine displacement, but can also be used primarily to reduce exhaust emissions (as on VW's "Umwelt" Diesel engine).

# U

**Universal joint or U-joint** A double-pivoted connection for transmitting power from a driving to a driven shaft through an angle. A U-joint consists of two Y-shaped yokes and a cross-shaped member called the spider.

# V

**Valve** A device through which the flow of liquid, gas, vacuum, or loose material in bulk may be started, stopped, or regulated by a movable part that opens, shuts, or partially obstructs one or more ports or passageways. A valve is also the movable part of such a device.

**Valve clearance** The clearance between the valve tip (the end of the valve stem) and the rocker arm or tappet. The valve clearance is measured when the valve is closed.

**Vernier caliper** A precision measuring instrument that measures inside and outside dimensions. Not quite as accurate as a micrometer, but more convenient.

**Viscosity** The thickness of a liquid or its resistance to flow.

**Volt** A unit for expressing electrical "pressure" in a circuit. One volt that will produce a current of one ampere through a resistance of one ohm.

# W

**Welding** Various processes used to join metal items by heating the areas to be joined to a molten state and fusing them together. For more information refer to the *Haynes Automotive Welding Manual*.

**Wiring diagram** A drawing portraying the components and wires in a vehicle's electrical system, using standardised symbols. For more information refer to the *Haynes Automotive Electrical and Electronic Systems Manual*.

**Note:** *References throughout this index are in the form* **"Chapter number"•"page number"**

# Haynes Manuals – The Complete **UK Car** List

| Title | Book No. |
|---|---|
| **ALFA ROMEO** Alfasud/Sprint (74 - 88) up to F * | 0292 |
| Alfa Romeo Alfetta (73 - 87) up to E * | 0531 |
| **AUDI** 80, 90 & Coupe Petrol (79 - Nov 88) up to F | 0605 |
| Audi 80, 90 & Coupe Petrol (Oct 86 - 90) D to H | 1491 |
| Audi 100 & 200 Petrol (Oct 82 - 90) up to H | 0907 |
| Audi 100 & A6 Petrol & Diesel (May 91 - May 97) H to P | 3504 |
| Audi A3 Petrol & Diesel (96 - May 03) P to 03 | 4253 |
| Audi A4 Petrol & Diesel (95 - 00) M to X | 3575 |
| Audi A4 Petrol & Diesel (01 - 04) X to 54 | 4609 |
| **AUSTIN** A35 & A40 (56 - 67) up to F * | 0118 |
| Austin/MG/Rover Maestro 1.3 & 1.6 Petrol (83 - 95) up to M | 0922 |
| Austin/MG Metro (80 - May 90) up to G | 0718 |
| Austin/Rover Montego 1.3 & 1.6 Petrol (84 - 94) A to L | 1066 |
| Austin/MG/Rover Montego 2.0 Petrol (84 - 95) A to M | 1067 |
| Mini (59 - 69) up to H * | 0527 |
| Mini (69 - 01) up to X | 0646 |
| Austin/Rover 2.0 litre Diesel Engine (86 - 93) C to L | 1857 |
| Austin Healey 100/6 & 3000 (56 - 68) up to G * | 0049 |
| **BEDFORD** CF Petrol (69 - 87) up to E | 0163 |
| Bedford/Vauxhall Rascal & Suzuki Supercarry (86 - Oct 94) C to M | 3015 |
| **BMW** 316, 320 & 320i (4-cyl) (75 - Feb 83) up to Y * | 0276 |
| BMW 320, 320i, 323i & 325i (6-cyl) (Oct 77 - Sept 87) up to E | 0815 |
| BMW 3- & 5-Series Petrol (81 - 91) up to J | 1948 |
| BMW 3-Series Petrol (Apr 91 - 99) H to V | 3210 |
| BMW 3-Series Petrol (Sept 98 - 03) S to 53 | 4067 |
| BMW 520i & 525e (Oct 81 - June 88) up to E | 1560 |
| BMW 525, 528 & 528i (73 - Sept 81) up to X * | 0632 |
| BMW 5-Series 6-cyl Petrol (April 96 - Aug 03) N to 03 | 4151 |
| BMW 1500, 1502, 1600, 1602, 2000 & 2002 (59 - 77) up to S * | 0240 |
| **CHRYSLER** PT Cruiser Petrol (00 - 03) W to 53 | 4058 |
| **CITROËN** 2CV, Ami & Dyane (67 - 90) up to H | 0196 |
| Citroën AX Petrol & Diesel (87 - 97) D to P | 3014 |
| Citroën Berlingo & Peugeot Partner Petrol & Diesel (96 - 05) P to 55 | 4281 |
| Citroën BX Petrol (83 - 94) A to L | 0908 |
| Citroën C15 Van Petrol & Diesel (89 - Oct 98) F to S | 3509 |
| Citroën C3 Petrol & Diesel (02 - 05) 51 to 05 | 4197 |
| Citroën CX Petrol (75 - 88) up to F | 0528 |
| Citroën Saxo Petrol & Diesel (96 - 04) N to 54 | 3506 |
| Citroën Visa Petrol (79 - 88) up to F | 0620 |
| Citroën Xantia Petrol & Diesel (93 - 01) K to Y | 3082 |
| Citroën XM Petrol & Diesel (89 - 00) G to X | 3451 |
| Citroën Xsara Petrol & Diesel (97 - Sept 00) R to W | 3751 |
| Citroën Xsara Picasso Petrol & Diesel (00 - 02) W to 52 | 3944 |
| Citroën ZX Diesel (91 - 98) J to S | 1922 |
| Citroën ZX Petrol (91 - 98) H to S | 1881 |
| Citroën 1.7 & 1.9 litre Diesel Engine (84 - 96) A to N | 1379 |
| **FIAT** 126 (73 - 87) up to E * | 0305 |
| Fiat 500 (57 - 73) up to M * | 0090 |
| Fiat Bravo & Brava Petrol (95 - 00) N to W | 3572 |
| Fiat Cinquecento (93 - 98) K to R | 3501 |
| Fiat Panda (81 - 95) up to M | 0793 |
| Fiat Punto Petrol & Diesel (94 - Oct 99) L to V | 3251 |
| Fiat Punto Petrol (Oct 99 - July 03) V to 03 | 4066 |
| Fiat Regata Petrol (84 - 88) A to F | 1167 |
| Fiat Tipo Petrol (88 - 91) E to J | 1625 |
| Fiat Uno Petrol (83 - 95) up to M | 0923 |
| Fiat X1/9 (74 - 89) up to G * | 0273 |
| **FORD** Anglia (59 - 68) up to G * | 0001 |
| Ford Capri II (& III) 1.6 & 2.0 (74 - 87) up to E * | 0283 |
| Ford Capri II (& III) 2.8 & 3.0 V6 (74 - 87) up to E | 1309 |

| Title | Book No. |
|---|---|
| Ford Cortina Mk I & Corsair 1500 ('62 - '66) up to D* | 0214 |
| Ford Cortina Mk III 1300 & 1600 (70 - 76) up to P * | 0070 |
| Ford Escort Mk I 1100 & 1300 (68 - 74) up to N * | 0171 |
| Ford Escort Mk I Mexico, RS 1600 & RS 2000 (70 - 74) up to N * | 0139 |
| Ford Escort Mk II Mexico, RS 1800 & RS 2000 (75 - 80) up to W * | 0735 |
| Ford Escort (75 - Aug 80) up to V * | 0280 |
| Ford Escort Petrol (Sept 80 - Sept 90) up to H | 0686 |
| Ford Escort & Orion Petrol (Sept 90 - 00) H to X | 1737 |
| Ford Escort & Orion Diesel (Sept 90 - 00) H to X | 4081 |
| Ford Fiesta (76 - Aug 83) up to Y | 0334 |
| Ford Fiesta Petrol (Aug 83 - Feb 89) A to F | 1030 |
| Ford Fiesta Petrol (Feb 89 - Oct 95) F to N | 1595 |
| Ford Fiesta Petrol & Diesel (Oct 95 - Mar 02) N to 02 | 3397 |
| Ford Fiesta Petrol & Diesel (Apr 02 - 05) 02 to 54 | 4170 |
| Ford Focus Petrol & Diesel (98 - 01) S to Y | 3759 |
| Ford Focus Petrol & Diesel (Oct 01 - 05) 51 to 05 | 4167 |
| Ford Galaxy Petrol & Diesel (95 - Aug 00) M to W | 3984 |
| Ford Granada Petrol (Sept 77 - Feb 85) up to B * | 0481 |
| Ford Granada & Scorpio Petrol (Mar 85 - 94) B to M | 1245 |
| Ford Ka (96 - 02) P to 52 | 3570 |
| Ford Mondeo Petrol (93 - Sept 00) K to X | 1923 |
| Ford Mondeo Petrol & Diesel (Oct 00 - Jul 03) X to 03 | 3990 |
| Ford Mondeo Petrol & Diesel (July 03 - 07) 03 to 56 | 4619 |
| Ford Mondeo Diesel (93 - 96) L to N | 3465 |
| Ford Orion Petrol (83 - Sept 90) up to H | 1009 |
| Ford Sierra 4-cyl Petrol (82 - 93) up to K | 0903 |
| Ford Sierra V6 Petrol (82 - 91) up to J | 0904 |
| Ford Transit Petrol (Mk 2) (78 - Jan 86) up to C | 0719 |
| Ford Transit Petrol (Mk 3) (Feb 86 - 89) C to G | 1468 |
| Ford Transit Diesel (Feb 86 - 99) C to T | 3019 |
| Ford 1.6 & 1.8 litre Diesel Engine (84 - 96) A to N | 1172 |
| Ford 2.1, 2.3 & 2.5 litre Diesel Engine (77 - 90) up to H | 1606 |
| **FREIGHT ROVER** Sherpa Petrol (74 - 87) up to E | 0463 |
| **HILLMAN** Avenger (70 - 82) up to Y | 0037 |
| Hillman Imp (63 - 76) up to R * | 0022 |
| **HONDA** Civic (Feb 84 - Oct 87) A to E | 1226 |
| Honda Civic (Nov 91 - 96) J to N | 3199 |
| Honda Civic Petrol (Mar 95 - 00) M to X | 4050 |
| Honda Civic Petrol & Diesel (01 - 05) X to 55 | 4611 |
| Honda Jazz (01 - Feb 08) 51 - 57 | 4735 |
| **HYUNDAI** Pony (85 - 94) C to M | 3398 |
| **JAGUAR** E Type (61 - 72) up to L * | 0140 |
| Jaguar MkI & II, 240 & 340 (55 - 69) up to H * | 0098 |
| Jaguar XJ6, XJ & Sovereign; Daimler Sovereign (68 - Oct 86) up to D | 0242 |
| Jaguar XJ6 & Sovereign (Oct 86 - Sept 94) D to M | 3261 |
| Jaguar XJ12, XJS & Sovereign; Daimler Double Six (72 - 88) up to F | 0478 |
| **JEEP** Cherokee Petrol (93 - 96) K to N | 1943 |
| **LADA** 1200, 1300, 1500 & 1600 (74 - 91) up to J | 0413 |
| Lada Samara (87 - 91) D to J | 1610 |
| **LAND ROVER** 90, 110 & Defender Diesel (83 - 07) up to 56 | 3017 |
| Land Rover Discovery Petrol & Diesel (89 - 98) G to S | 3016 |
| Land Rover Discovery Diesel (Nov 98 - Jul 04) S to 04 | 4606 |
| Land Rover Freelander Petrol & Diesel (97 - Sept 03) R to 53 | 3929 |
| Land Rover Freelander Petrol & Diesel (Oct 03 - Oct 06) 53 to 56 | 4623 |
| Land Rover Series IIA & III Diesel (58 - 85) up to C | 0529 |
| Land Rover Series II, IIA & III 4-cyl Petrol (58 - 85) up to C | 0314 |

| Title | Book No. |
|---|---|
| **MAZDA** 323 (Mar 81 - Oct 89) up to G | 1608 |
| Mazda 323 (Oct 89 - 98) G to R | 3455 |
| Mazda 626 (May 83 - Sept 87) up to E | 0929 |
| Mazda B1600, B1800 & B2000 Pick-up Petrol (72 - 88) up to F | 0267 |
| Mazda RX-7 (79 - 85) up to C * | 0460 |
| **MERCEDES-BENZ** 190, 190E & 190D Petrol & Diesel (83 - 93) A to L | 3450 |
| Mercedes-Benz 200D, 240D, 240TD, 300D & 300TD 123 Series Diesel (Oct 76 - 85) | 1114 |
| Mercedes-Benz 250 & 280 (68 - 72) up to L * | 0346 |
| Mercedes-Benz 250 & 280 123 Series Petrol (Oct 76 - 84) up to B * | 0677 |
| Mercedes-Benz 124 Series Petrol & Diesel (85 - Aug 93) C to K | 3253 |
| Mercedes-Benz C-Class Petrol & Diesel (93 - Aug 00) L to W | 3511 |
| **MGA** (55 - 62) * | 0475 |
| MGB (62 - 80) up to W | 0111 |
| MG Midget & Austin-Healey Sprite (58 - 80) up to W * | 0265 |
| **MINI** Petrol (July 01 - 05) Y to 05 | 4273 |
| **MITSUBISHI** Shogun & L200 Pick-Ups Petrol (83 - 94) up to M | 1944 |
| **MORRIS** Ital 1.3 (80 - 84) up to B | 0705 |
| Morris Minor 1000 (56 - 71) up to K | 0024 |
| **NISSAN** Almera Petrol (95 - Feb 00) N to V | 4053 |
| Nissan Almera & Tino Petrol (Feb 00 - 07) V to 56 | 4612 |
| Nissan Bluebird (May 84 - Mar 86) A to C | 1223 |
| Nissan Bluebird Petrol (Mar 86 - 90) C to H | 1473 |
| Nissan Cherry (Sept 82 - 86) up to D | 1031 |
| Nissan Micra (83 - Jan 93) up to K | 0931 |
| Nissan Micra (93 - 02) K to 52 | 3254 |
| Nissan Primera Petrol (90 - Aug 99) H to T | 1851 |
| Nissan Stanza (82 - 86) up to D | 0824 |
| Nissan Sunny Petrol (May 82 - Oct 86) up to D | 0895 |
| Nissan Sunny Petrol (Oct 86 - Mar 91) D to H | 1378 |
| Nissan Sunny Petrol (Apr 91 - 95) H to N | 3219 |
| **OPEL** Ascona & Manta (B Series) (Sept 75 - 88) up to F * | 0316 |
| Opel Ascona Petrol (81 - 88) | 3215 |
| Opel Astra Petrol (Oct 91 - Feb 98) | 3156 |
| Opel Corsa Petrol (83 - Mar 93) | 3160 |
| Opel Corsa Petrol (Mar 93 - 97) | 3159 |
| Opel Kadett Petrol (Nov 79 - Oct 84) up to B | 0634 |
| Opel Kadett Petrol (Oct 84 - Oct 91) | 3196 |
| Opel Omega & Senator Petrol (Nov 86 - 94) | 3157 |
| Opel Rekord Petrol (Feb 78 - Oct 86) up to D | 0543 |
| Opel Vectra Petrol (Oct 88 - Oct 95) | 3158 |
| **PEUGEOT** 106 Petrol & Diesel (91 - 04) J to 53 | 1882 |
| Peugeot 205 Petrol (83 - 97) A to P | 0932 |
| Peugeot 206 Petrol & Diesel (98 - 01) S to X | 3757 |
| Peugeot 206 Petrol & Diesel (02 - 06) 51 to 06 | 4613 |
| Peugeot 306 Petrol & Diesel (93 - 02) K to 02 | 3073 |
| Peugeot 307 Petrol & Diesel (01 - 04) Y to 54 | 4147 |
| Peugeot 309 Petrol (86 - 93) C to K | 1266 |
| Peugeot 405 Petrol (88 - 97) E to P | 1559 |
| Peugeot 405 Diesel (88 - 97) E to P | 3198 |
| Peugeot 406 Petrol & Diesel (96 - Mar 99) N to T | 3394 |
| Peugeot 406 Petrol & Diesel (Mar 99 - 02) T to 52 | 3982 |
| Peugeot 505 Petrol (79 - 89) up to G | 0762 |
| Peugeot 1.7/1.8 & 1.9 litre Diesel Engine (82 - 96) up to N | 0950 |
| Peugeot 2.0, 2.1, 2.3 & 2.5 litre Diesel Engines (74 - 90) up to H | 1607 |
| **PORSCHE** 911 (65 - 85) up to C | 0264 |

| Title | Book No. |
|---|---|
| Porsche 924 & 924 Turbo (76 - 85) up to C | 0397 |
| **PROTON** (89 - 97) F to P | 3255 |
| **RANGE ROVER** V8 Petrol (70 - Oct 92) up to K | 0606 |
| **RELIANT** Robin & Kitten (73 - 83) up to A * | 0436 |
| **RENAULT** 4 (61 - 86) up to D * | 0072 |
| Renault 5 Petrol (Feb 85 - 96) B to N | 1219 |
| Renault 9 & 11 Petrol (82 - 89) up to F | 0822 |
| Renault 18 Petrol (79 - 86) up to D | 0598 |
| Renault 19 Petrol (89 - 96) F to N | 1646 |
| Renault 19 Diesel (89 - 96) F to N | 1946 |
| Renault 21 Petrol (86 - 94) C to M | 1397 |
| Renault 25 Petrol & Diesel (84 - 92) B to K | 1228 |
| Renault Clio Petrol (91 - May 98) H to R | 1853 |
| Renault Clio Diesel (91 - June 96) H to N | 3031 |
| Renault Clio Petrol & Diesel (May 98 - May 01) R to Y | 3906 |
| Renault Clio Petrol & Diesel (June '01 - '05) Y to 55 | 4168 |
| Renault Espace Petrol & Diesel (85 - 96) C to N | 3197 |
| Renault Laguna Petrol & Diesel (94 - 00) L to W | 3252 |
| Renault Laguna Petrol & Diesel (Feb 01 - Feb 05) X to 54 | 4283 |
| Renault Mégane & Scénic Petrol & Diesel (96 - 99) N to T | 3395 |
| Renault Mégane & Scénic Petrol & Diesel (Apr 99 - 02) T to 52 | 3916 |
| Renault Megane Petrol & Diesel (Oct 02 - 05) 52 to 55 | 4284 |
| Renault Scenic Petrol & Diesel (Sept 03 - 06) 53 to 06 | 4297 |
| **ROVER** 213 & 216 (84 - 89) A to G | 1116 |
| Rover 214 & 414 Petrol (89 - 96) G to N | 1689 |
| Rover 216 & 416 Petrol (89 - 96) G to N | 1830 |
| Rover 211, 214, 216, 218 & 220 Petrol & Diesel (Dec 95 - 99) N to V | 3399 |
| Rover 25 & MG ZR Petrol & Diesel (Oct 99 - 04) V to 54 | 4145 |
| Rover 414, 416 & 420 Petrol & Diesel (May 95 - 98) M to R | 3453 |
| Rover 45 / MG ZS Petrol & Diesel (99 - 05) V to 55 | 4384 |
| Rover 618, 620 & 623 Petrol (93 - 97) K to P | 3257 |
| Rover 75 / MG ZT Petrol & Diesel (99 - 06) S to 06 | 4292 |
| Rover 820, 825 & 827 Petrol (86 - 95) D to N | 1380 |
| Rover 3500 (76 - 87) up to E * | 0365 |
| Rover Metro, 111 & 114 Petrol (May 90 - 98) G to S | 1711 |
| **SAAB** 95 & 96 (66 - 76) up to R * | 0198 |
| Saab 90, 99 & 900 (79 - Oct 93) up to L | 0765 |
| Saab 900 (Oct 93 - 98) L to R | 3512 |
| Saab 9000 (4-cyl) (85 - 98) C to S | 1686 |
| Saab 9-3 Petrol & Diesel (98 - Aug 02) R to 02 | 4614 |
| Saab 9-5 4-cyl Petrol (97 - 04) R to 54 | 4156 |
| **SEAT** Ibiza & Cordoba Petrol & Diesel (Oct 93 - Oct 99) L to V | 3571 |
| Seat Ibiza & Malaga Petrol (85 - 92) B to K | 1609 |
| **SKODA** Estelle (77 - 89) up to G | 0604 |
| Skoda Fabia Petrol & Diesel (00 - 06) W to 06 | 4376 |
| Skoda Favorit (89 - 96) F to N | 1801 |
| Skoda Felicia Petrol & Diesel (95 - 01) M to X | 3505 |
| Skoda Octavia Petrol & Diesel (98 - Apr 04) R to 04 | 4285 |
| **SUBARU** 1600 & 1800 (Nov 79 - 90) up to H * | 0995 |
| **SUNBEAM** Alpine, Rapier & H120 (67 - 74) up to N * | 0051 |
| **SUZUKI** SJ Series, Samurai & Vitara (4-cyl) Petrol (82 - 97) up to P | 1942 |
| Suzuki Supercarry & Bedford/Vauxhall Rascal (86 - Oct 94) C to M | 3015 |
| **TALBOT** Alpine, Solara, Minx & Rapier (75 - 86) up to D | 0337 |

| Title | Book No. |
|---|---|
| Talbot Horizon Petrol (78 - 86) up to D | 0473 |
| Talbot Samba (82 - 86) up to D | 0823 |
| **TOYOTA** Avensis Petrol (98 - Jan 03) R to 52 | 4264 |
| Toyota Carina E Petrol (May 92 - 97) J to P | 3256 |
| Toyota Corolla (80 - 85) up to C | 0683 |
| Toyota Corolla (Sept 83 - Sept 87) A to E | 1024 |
| Toyota Corolla (Sept 87 - Aug 92) E to K | 1683 |
| Toyota Corolla Petrol (Aug 92 - 97) K to P | 3259 |
| Toyota Corolla Petrol (July 97 - Feb 02) P to 51 | 4286 |
| Toyota Hi-Ace & Hi-Lux Petrol (69 - Oct 83) up to A | 0304 |
| Toyota Yaris Petrol (99 - 05) T to 05 | 4265 |
| **TRIUMPH** GT6 & Vitesse (62 - 74 ) up to N * | 0112 |
| Triumph Herald (59 - 71) up to K * | 0010 |
| Triumph Spitfire (62 - 81) up to X | 0113 |
| Triumph Stag (70 - 78) up to T * | 0441 |
| Triumph TR2, TR3, TR3A, TR4 & TR4A (52 - 67) up to F * | 0028 |
| Triumph TR5 & 6 (67 - 75) up to P * | 0031 |
| Triumph TR7 (75 - 82) up to Y * | 0322 |
| **VAUXHALL** Astra Petrol (80 - Oct 84) up to B | 0635 |
| Vauxhall Astra & Belmont Petrol (Oct 84 - Oct 91) B to J | 1136 |
| Vauxhall Astra Petrol (Oct 91 - Feb 98) J to R | 1832 |
| Vauxhall/Opel Astra & Zafira Petrol (Feb 98 - Apr 04) R to 04 | 3758 |
| Vauxhall/Opel Astra & Zafira Diesel (Feb 98 - Apr 04) R to 04 | 3797 |
| Vauxhall/Opel Astra Petrol (04 - 07) 04 - 07 | 4732 |
| Vauxhall/Opel Astra Diesel (04 - 07) 04 - 07 | 4733 |
| Vauxhall/Opel Calibra (90 - 98) G to S | 3502 |
| Vauxhall Carlton Petrol (Oct 78 - Oct 86) up to D | 0480 |
| Vauxhall Carlton & Senator Petrol (Nov 86 - 94) D to L | 1469 |
| Vauxhall Cavalier Petrol (81 - Oct 88) up to F | 0812 |
| Vauxhall Cavalier Petrol (Oct 88 - 95) F to N | 1570 |
| Vauxhall Chevette (75 - 84) up to B | 0285 |
| Vauxhall/Opel Corsa Diesel (Mar 93 - Oct 00) K to X | 4087 |
| Vauxhall Corsa Petrol (Mar 93 - 97) K to R | 1985 |
| Vauxhall/Opel Corsa Petrol (Apr 97 - Oct 00) P to X | 3921 |
| Vauxhall/Opel Corsa Petrol & Diesel (Oct 00 - Sept 03) X to 53 | 4079 |
| Vauxhall/Opel Corsa Petrol & Diesel (Oct 03 - Aug 06) 53 to 06 | 4617 |
| Vauxhall/Opel Frontera Petrol & Diesel (91 - Sept 98) J to S | 3454 |
| Vauxhall Nova Petrol (83 - 93) up to K | 0909 |
| Vauxhall/Opel Omega Petrol (94 - 99) L to T | 3510 |
| Vauxhall/Opel Vectra Petrol & Diesel (95 - Feb 99) N to S | 3396 |
| Vauxhall/Opel Vectra Petrol & Diesel (Mar 99 - May 02) T to 02 | 3930 |
| Vauxhall/Opel Vectra Petrol & Diesel (June 02 - Sept 05) 02 to 55 | 4618 |
| Vauxhall/Opel 1.5, 1.6 & 1.7 litre Diesel Engine (82 - 96) up to N | 1222 |
| **VW** 411 & 412 (68 - 75) up to P * | 0091 |
| VW Beetle 1200 (54 - 77) up to S | 0036 |
| VW Beetle 1300 & 1500 (65 - 75) up to P | 0039 |
| VW 1302 & 1302S (70 - 72) up to L * | 0110 |
| VW Beetle 1303, 1303S & GT (72 - 75) up to P | 0159 |
| VW Beetle Petrol & Diesel (Apr 99 - 01) T to 51 | 3798 |
| VW Golf & Jetta Mk 1 Petrol 1.1 & 1.3 (74 - 84) up to A | 0716 |
| VW Golf, Jetta & Scirocco Mk 1 Petrol 1.5, 1.6 & 1.8 (74 - 84) up to A | 0726 |

| Title | Book No. |
|---|---|
| VW Golf & Jetta Mk 1 Diesel (78 - 84) up to A | 0451 |
| VW Golf & Jetta Mk 2 Petrol (Mar 84 - Feb 92) A to J | 1081 |
| VW Golf & Vento Petrol & Diesel (Feb 92 - Mar 98) J to R | 3097 |
| VW Golf & Bora Petrol & Diesel (April 98 - 00) R to X | 3727 |
| VW Golf & Bora 4-cyl Petrol & Diesel (01 - 03) X to 53 | 4169 |
| VW Golf & Jetta Petrol & Diesel (04 - 07) 53 to 07 | 4610 |
| VW LT Petrol Vans & Light Trucks (76 - 87) up to E | 0637 |
| VW Passat & Santana Petrol (Sept 81 - May 88) up to E | 0814 |
| VW Passat 4-cyl Petrol & Diesel (May 88 - 96) E to P | 3498 |
| VW Passat 4-cyl Petrol & Diesel (Dec 96 - Nov 00) P to X | 3917 |
| VW Passat Petrol & Diesel (Dec 00 - May 05) X to 05 | 4279 |
| VW Polo & Derby (76 - Jan 82) up to X | 0335 |
| VW Polo (82 - Oct 90) up to H | 0813 |
| VW Polo Petrol (Nov 90 - Aug 94) H to L | 3245 |
| VW Polo Hatchback Petrol & Diesel (94 - 99) M to S | 3500 |
| VW Polo Hatchback Petrol (00 - Jan 02) V to 51 | 4150 |
| VW Polo Petrol & Diesel (02 - May 05) 51 to 05 | 4608 |
| VW Scirocco (82 - 90) up to H * | 1224 |
| VW Transporter 1600 (68 - 79) up to V | 0082 |
| VW Transporter 1700, 1800 & 2000 (72 - 79) up to V * | 0226 |
| VW Transporter (air-cooled) Petrol (79 - 82) up to Y * | 0638 |
| VW Transporter (water-cooled) Petrol (82 - 90) up to H | 3452 |
| VW Type 3 (63 - 73) up to M * | 0084 |
| **VOLVO** 120 & 130 Series (& P1800) (61 - 73) up to M * | 0203 |
| Volvo 142, 144 & 145 (66 - 74) up to N * | 0129 |
| Volvo 240 Series Petrol (74 - 93) up to K | 0270 |
| Volvo 262, 264 & 260/265 (75 - 85) up to C * | 0400 |
| Volvo 340, 343, 345 & 360 (76 - 91) up to J | 0715 |
| Volvo 440, 460 & 480 Petrol (87 - 97) D to P | 1691 |
| Volvo 740 & 760 Petrol (82 - 91) up to J | 1258 |
| Volvo 850 Petrol (92 - 96) J to P | 3260 |
| Volvo 940 petrol (90 - 98) H to R | 3249 |
| Volvo S40 & V40 Petrol (96 - Mar 04) N to 04 | 3569 |
| Volvo S40 & V50 Petrol & Diesel (Mar 04 - Jun 07) 04 to 07 | 4731 |
| Volvo S70, V70 & C70 Petrol (96 - 99) P to V | 3573 |
| Volvo V70 / S80 Petrol & Diesel (98 - 05) S to 55 | 4263 |

### AUTOMOTIVE TECHBOOKS
| | |
|---|---|
| Automotive Electrical and Electronic Systems Manual | 3049 |
| Automotive Gearbox Overhaul Manual | 3473 |
| Automotive Service Summaries Manual | 3475 |
| Automotive Timing Belts Manual – Austin/Rover | 3549 |
| Automotive Timing Belts Manual – Ford | 3474 |
| Automotive Timing Belts Manual – Peugeot/Citroën | 3568 |
| Automotive Timing Belts Manual – Vauxhall/Opel | 3577 |

### DIY MANUAL SERIES
| | |
|---|---|
| The Haynes Air Conditioning Manual | 4192 |
| The Haynes Car Electrical Systems Manual | 4251 |
| The Haynes Manual on Bodywork | 4198 |
| The Haynes Manual on Brakes | 4178 |
| The Haynes Manual on Carburettors | 4177 |
| The Haynes Manual on Diesel Engines | 4174 |
| The Haynes Manual on Engine Management | 4199 |
| The Haynes Manual on Fault Codes | 4175 |
| The Haynes Manual on Practical Electrical Systems | 4267 |
| The Haynes Manual on Small Engines | 4250 |
| The Haynes Manual on Welding | 4176 |

\* Classic reprint

CL23.12/07

# Preserving Our Motoring Heritage

<
*The Model J Duesenberg Derham Tourster. Only eight of these magnificent cars were ever built – this is the only example to be found outside the United States of America*

Almost every car you've ever loved, loathed or desired is gathered under one roof at the Haynes Motor Museum. Over 300 immaculately presented cars and motorbikes represent every aspect of our motoring heritage, from elegant reminders of bygone days, such as the superb Model J Duesenberg to curiosities like the bug-eyed BMW Isetta. There are also many old friends and flames. Perhaps you remember the 1959 Ford Popular that you did your courting in? The magnificent 'Red Collection' is a spectacle of classic sports cars including AC, Alfa Romeo, Austin Healey, Ferrari, Lamborghini, Maserati, MG, Riley, Porsche and Triumph.

## *A Perfect Day Out*

Each and every vehicle at the Haynes Motor Museum has played its part in the history and culture of Motoring. Today, they make a wonderful spectacle and a great day out for all the family. Bring the kids, bring Mum and Dad, but above all bring your camera to capture those golden memories for ever. You will also find an impressive array of motoring memorabilia, a comfortable 70 seat video cinema and one of the most extensive transport book shops in Britain. The Pit Stop Cafe serves everything from a cup of tea to wholesome, home-made meals or, if you prefer, you can enjoy the large picnic area nestled in the beautiful rural surroundings of Somerset.

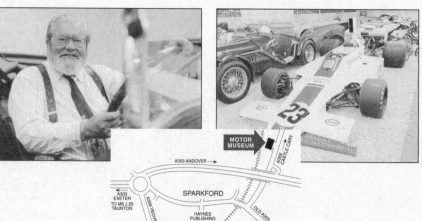

>
*John Haynes O.B.E., Founder and Chairman of the museum at the wheel of a Haynes Light 12.*

<
*Graham Hill's Lola Cosworth Formula 1 car next to a 1934 Riley Sports.*

The Museum is situated on the A359 Yeovil to Frome road at Sparkford, just off the A303 in Somerset. It is about 40 miles south of Bristol, and 25 minutes drive from the M5 intersection at Taunton.
Open 9.30am - 5.30pm (10.00am - 4.00pm Winter) 7 days a week, *except Christmas Day, Boxing Day and New Years Day*
Special rates available for schools, coach parties and outings  Charitable Trust No. 292048